France
in the
Middle Ages
987–1460

A History of France will, in five volumes, provide an account of 1,000 years of French history. The authors are among the most distinguished French historians, and the reception given to the first three volumes when they appeared in France in 1987 and 1988 suggests that this will be the standard history of France for many years to come.

Already published

France in the Middle Ages 987–1460
Georges Duby

The Royal French State 1460–1610
Emmanuel Le Roy Ladurie

Revolutionary France 1770–1880
François Furet

The French Republic 1879–1992
Maurice Agulhon

Forthcoming

The Ancien Régime 1610–1774
Emmanuel Le Roy Ladurie

France
in the
Middle Ages
987–1460

From Hugh Capet to
Joan of Arc

GEORGES DUBY

Translated by
Juliet Vale

Blackwell
Publishing

English translation © 1991, 1993 by Blackwell Publishers Ltd
a Blackwell Publishing company
First published in France as Le Moyen Age 987–1460
© 1987 by Hachette, Paris

350 Main Street, Malden, MA 02148-5018, USA
108 Cowley Road, Oxford OX4 1JF, UK
550 Swanston Street, Carlton South, Melbourne, Victoria 3053, Australia
Kurfürstendamm 57, 10707 Berlin, Germany

First published in English 1991 by Blackwell Publishers Ltd
First published in USA 1991
Reprinted 1992
First published in paperback 1993
Reprinted 1994, 1996 (twice), 1997, 1998, 1999, 2000 (twice), 2002

Library of Congress Cataloging-in-Publication Data

Duby, Georges
  [Moyen Age 987–1460, English]
  France in the Middle Ages 987–1460; from Hugh Capet to Joan of Arc/
Georges Duby: translated by Juliet Vale.
      p.   cm.—(A History of France)
  Translation of: Le Moyen Age 987–1460.
  Includes bibliographical references and index.
  ISBN 0–631–18945–9 (pbk)
  1. France—Civilization. 2. France—History—Medieval Period, 987–1515.
3. France—Church history—Middle Ages, 987–1515.
4. Hugh Capet, King of France, ca. 938–996. 5. Joan, of Arc, Saint, 1412–1431.
  I. Title. II. Series.
  DC33.2.D7513   1991   91–7753
  944'.02—dc20   CIP

A catalogue record for this title is available from the British Library.

Set in 10.5 on 13pt Plantin
by Best-set Typesetter Ltd, Hong Kong
Printed and bound in the United Kingdom
by Athenaeum Press Ltd, Gateshead, Tyne & Wear

For further information on
Blackwell Publishing, visit our website:
http://www.blackwellpublishing.com

Contents

Translator's Note

For the English-language edition of this book I have revised the bibliography and added a limited number of footnotes, generally with a view to widening the perspective on a particular point. Technical terms have been tacitly expanded or explained in the text wherever possible.

I am grateful to the British Library, London, and the Ashmolean Library, the Bodleian Library and the Library of the Taylorian Institute, Oxford, for their unfailing help. For advice on specific points I am indebted to Philip Bartholomew, Dr Hélène La Rue and Dr M. G. A. Vale, who also read a draft of the translation. It is a pleasure to acknowledge in addition the practical support of my parents.

Foreword

The *Hachette History of France* which Emmanuel Le Roy Ladurie, François Furet, Maurice Agulhon and I have undertaken will concentrate primarily upon political history. However, there are already many excellent and detailed books about the thousand-year or more span that we call 'the Middle Ages' in the area covered by present-day France. I do not see my role as providing yet another such volume. In fact, I have written a rather different kind of book, based on different assumptions, which I must now explain to my readers.

My task was to provide the first volume in a composite history of France. How should it start? In his *L'Identité de la France* Fernand Braudel's investigation of origins led him back into the depths of prehistory, but I decided to confine myself to the relatively limited period of the Middle Ages, to which I have devoted many years of research. My investigation therefore starts relatively late, in the tenth century, since I have little specialist knowledge of the previous period. It also stops at an early date, in the middle of the thirteenth century, because my own detailed research has not covered the later period. This period has been the subject of meticulous study by Bernard Guenée, Francis Rapp, Jacques Le Goff and their pupils: any detailed consideration here would simply be a case of repeating their conclusions in a less effective form. Nevertheless, members of a team have certain responsibilities towards each other, and although I had considerable freedom over my starting-point, the end of my narrative had to bear some relation to the subsequent volume. As a result, this book consists of two very unequal parts. The first is a detailed analysis; the second, much shorter, is a free and relatively cursory narrative bridging this volume with the next. I have restricted myself to a fairly bald outline of events after the early part of the reign of Louis IX (1226–70), stressing what seem to me to be the cardinal features as far as the history of power is concerned.

This is not a summary of French history, nor is it a history of French civilization. My aim has been to document the way in which the State gradually emerged from the feudal system. Of course, political evolution did not take place in a vacuum. I have therefore paid particular attention to the context – and particularly the intellectual climate – in which these changes took place and which they, in turn, also influenced. Monetary circulation, cathedral-building and the flowering of courtly love all find a place, for example; but these phenomena are always discussed in relation to my main theme: the gradual evolution of power-relationships.

Finally, I must also draw attention to two particular approaches that I have adopted. Firstly, I have considered some events in great detail, where contemporary accounts illuminate underlying socio-political structures, as well as the particular combination of factors operating at that moment. Secondly, I have tried to stay as close as possible to contemporary sources. My aim has been to present the medieval world through the eyes of contemporaries and, as far as possible, to experience their own perception of their place within it.

I have already stressed that this is a history of change, more especially of a period when changes gathered speed. In the ninth century the vast area corresponding to modern France was still sparsely populated; its inhabitants were poorly equipped and remained remarkably uncouth. Christianity had by no means eradicated pagan practices, even close to the cities founded by the Romans. Nevertheless, in the course of several generations, population levels in rural areas slowly increased. At the same time, monasteries and cathedrals were prompted to draw on the rich heritage of the Carolingian Renaissance. Scholars read classical texts and commentaries that had been saved from destruction, and dreamt of recasting society in a new mould, more favourable to God. This great leap forward dragged these lands out of their relatively uncivilized state, and also makes it easier for the historian to identify political power and the context in which it functioned.[1]

For the fact of the matter is that, initially, writing was rare and written sources seldom reliable. Power was exercised mainly by spoken word and gesture. Sources are therefore intermittent, like rays of light occasionally piercing the darkness. Furthermore, these texts are characterized by a rigid vocabulary that was slow to reflect change. A number of words – all of them Latin – were employed, whose sense changed gradually over the

---

[1] For a different perspective, see E. James, *The Origins of France. From Clovis to the Capetians, 500–1000* (Basingstoke/London, 1982) – tr.

years and acquired different meanings in different places. What do terms such as *potestas* or *bannum* really mean in a cartulary? Would they have the same meaning if the document had been written elsewhere? Scholarly scribal fondness for classical, rhetorical terms in preference to the express-ions of everyday speech complicated the situation further. All these prac-tices tended to obscure what was actually happening. The picture of political power that reaches the historian from these sources is strictly the preserve of the princes of the Church and a handful of scholars defending their prerogatives against the claims of secular lords. Their evidence was written in the thick of these disputes and – consciously or unconsciously – presents a distorted picture.

Now that the limitations of the sources have been outlined, I can make some preliminary remarks about the political history of the period around the year 1000. Two major features are clearly identifiable: all secular power at that date was essentially domestic; it barely impinged on ecclesiastical power. There are two other less important aspects: power was only exer-cised by men, and a large number always managed to elude it.

Every political structure was seen in terms of a household – witness the vocabulary employed. Almost every word used in connection with execu-tive power has a domestic origin. Words such as *salle*, *chambre* and *hôtel*, still found in the political and judicial vocabulary of modern French, refer specifically to the lord's house.[2]

Contemporary scholars viewed inequality as providential, an integral part of the created world: at every level of society, this was invariably experienced within a family context, from the prince in his palace to the serf bound to the soil. A husband's rights over his wife extended from the chamber to the marriage-bed, of course. In the hall – the public and ceremonial room – the son had to submit to his father and young men to their elders. Within the house, some had precedence, while it was the lot of others to follow; the same order was observed outside if the household processed elsewhere.

In this culture the most forceful expressions in what we would call the 'political' sphere were related to manual gestures: seizing, releasing, hold-ing. The son was 'in the hand' of his father, the wife 'in the hand' of her husband. The expression implied protection and support, assuming an essentially paternal relationship to the individual in question. A man who placed his hands between those of another in the ceremony of homage accepted a filial position, and acknowledged that henceforth he would respect the other and come to his aid. However, this obligation also conferred the right to be consulted by his superior about all decisions.

---

[2] Cf. the two 'chambers' of the Houses of Parliament in English usage – tr.

These actions can all be paralleled in a familial context: the solidarity they secured was responsible for the perceived honourability of service, as well as its profit. The word *servicium* (service) was a forceful expression, derived from the Latin *servus*, associated with slavery. Its origins lay deep within the family. Every family naturally tended to become larger, and the head of every family wanted to grow richer, so that he could give more gifts and increase the numbers of men and women whom he could support in his household – whether they were his own children or had placed themselves in his hands by the ceremony of commendation, or non-noble homage (*commendise*). 'Eating the lord's bread' as part of his household, they served him, and thus his power grew. Power was always extended by means of a generative or an adoptive model.

Since all power was firmly bound to a domestic context, it became hereditary, even when associated with public office. No house should be allowed to die out; it was, by definition, a self-perpetuating unit. The son revered his father during his lifetime, but he would one day take his place, holding in his own hand the power relinquished by the father; he would then wield the same power over his widowed mother, his brothers and his own children. It was universally accepted that power was transmitted by consanguinity, or blood ties, for it was by blood that the virtues and charisma necessary for the exercise of power were also transmitted, as well as the rights of both father and mother. All claims to power thus had a genealogical basis.

This fact was held to excuse the sin of copulation in the eyes of God and his priests. It was only a minor transgression, in so far as it ensured the transmission of power and thus sustained the divine order. This was such a powerful prototype that it was even projected into an ecclesiastical context. In the so-called *gestes episcopales* (bishops' lives), which recounted the great deeds of the bishops of a particular diocese, the succession of prelates is presented as if it were a real genealogy and the cathedral, or mother-church (*mater ecclesia*), as a true mother, from whose womb sprang a whole series of bishops to wield spiritual power.

At the beginning of the eleventh century, the count of the Normans instructed Dudo, canon of St Quentin and a sound Frankish writer, to compose a history of the principality of Normandy. (His account is the oldest surviving work of this kind.) The writer decided to structure his work genealogically: there were four sections, each corresponding to a Norman ruler – Hasting, Rollo, William and Richard – and showing the sequence of descent from one to the other (although Rollo was not in fact the son of Hasting). This was because, even in the context of such a vast province as Normandy, people could conceive of power only in terms of an inheritance, handed down through a family from one generation to the next. So it was that at this period there was a family setting for all the events which we would call 'political'. Marriage alliances and inheritance were thus issues of prime strategic importance. Intense juridical debate focused on questions such as whose right it was to give women in marriage, as well as which one of a number of descendants was entitled to assume the power held by their ancestor.

It had long been accepted that the roots of power were ultimately divine: with the progress of Christianity, it came increasingly to be believed that power emanated from the God worshipped in churches and served by the clergy. The 'mirrors of princes' (exemplary moral treatises written by Carolingian bishops for the instruction of secular rulers) discuss marriage, because these prelates understandably wanted to introduce an element of sacrality into the profane institution which determined the transmission of political power. The bitterest political conflicts in eleventh-century France were fought for the control of marriage. Could it be left to the heads of families, or should it become the responsibility of the Church? The clergy finally won the day. Henceforth everything relating to marriage, including the transfer of power through inheritance, was under the administrative and judicial control of the Church – a fact that was to have incalculable consequences for Western Christendom.

Admittedly, it was not until the reign of Louis IX that priests formally joined the hands of the two parties in the porch of the Church. In 1200 the groom's father was still the principal player in the marriage ceremony; it was his responsibility to ask for God's blessing upon the couple. In other words, the divine grace indispensable for the transmission of political power was conveyed by the head of the house and the priests' role was confined to blessing the marriage-bed.

The fact that the clergy appeared at the heart of the family can be explained by the previous total absence there of anyone invested with sacramental power. Once a seigneurial estate was rich enough to support them, there was a bevy of clerks and the lord sat with them and joined in their liturgies, no matter how defiled he might be with martial and sexual excesses. Every man had a spiritual function if he exercised some form of earthly power – even if it was no more than that of a husband whose wife had kneeled before him on their wedding day and now called him 'master'. He was responsible not only for the bodily welfare, but also for the spiritual well-being of all members of his family, the living and the dead. If he sinned, his transgression fell upon them; but his good works produced divine favour on their account. It was therefore incumbent upon him to lead a good life and give part of what he had in offerings for the good of his soul. The sacrificial act, like the oath, lay at the heart of every political structure. It was the master's duty to instruct his family by words and example. His ultimate wish was to have the strength to exhort his sons and nephews for the last time as he lay dying.

Those who held public office were also responsible for leading all their subjects towards salvation. God had entrusted a section of his people to them. He had even placed in the lord's hands the non-Christians living there, for whom he was also responsible. Very considerable pressure could be legitimately exerted upon these non-Christians, for it was the ruler's duty to force non-believers to accept the Christian faith. It was the duty of all who held public office to assist those who preached the gospel, combatted pagan practices, and curbed unorthodoxy. He should put confirmed heretics to death, to prevent them from corrupting the rest of the community. His supreme duty, however, was to establish peace and justice among his subjects and – as far as was possible on earth – to draw imperfect human society closer to the perfection of the angels.

Peace and justice were believed to be reflections (or rather, refractions) of the heavenly household onto the earth below. As a result of this fundamental assumption, public power inevitably acquired a sacred character. If a power-relation did not proceed naturally from consanguinity, marriage alliance or the artificial parenthood resulting from commendation, it was based upon a sacramental act, the swearing of an oath (*sacramentum*). An oath was a sworn agreement, given by a religious gesture (placing the hand upon a sacred object, Bible, cross or reliquary) and a religious formula, 'So God me help'. By this means the sacred was woven into the fabric of political relations. To break the connecting thread was to call down the wrath of God as surely as a refusal to be meshed into the whole. It was because heretics refused to take the oath that heresy at once acquired a political character.

Use of physical force was legitimate only in carrying out the duties of an 'office' which – like the priesthood – was characterized by justice and peace. 'Justice and peace are the bedrock of your office,' the king of France was informed in 1023. The sword, emblem of public office, was only unsheathed when it was carried in front of the office-holder or if he wielded it himself. Scenes from the Bayeux Tapestry, for instance, show William the Conqueror holding a naked sword when he sits in judgement. It was a simple sign of power, displayed when the ruler was attempting to establish peace through negotiations, with reference to previous experience and the body of accumulated lore on the subject. If agreement could not be reached, the ruler (whose duty it was to establish peace) turned to divine judgement and presided over a judicial ordeal, a judicial duel or perhaps trial by fire or water. By these means they believed the truth would be revealed before the entire community as they gathered round the sword raised in justice. The sword could also become a repressive weapon, if the ruler failed to protect the weak, who were incapable of self-defence or vengeance. Whenever he drew his sword, the sword-bearer had to remember that he was the agent of divine justice, bound to observe God's laws. Piety was therefore incumbent upon him, and he was the subordinate of the priests who determined the appropriate forms of devotion.

The sacred character of power meant that priests had enormous influence. Firstly, they had a monopoly of written culture. They wrote incomprehensible hieroglyphics on parchment, used words no one else understood and read books which they said contained models for the basis of all lawful action. As secular law codes were eroded and customary law became clouded with uncertainties, it was the priests who worked throughout the eleventh century to assemble collections of divinely inspired laws. For they were lords of spiritual justice (superior to temporal justice), in whose name miscreants were outlawed from the Christian community and divine grace. This was called excommunication. The guilty parties were excluded for a specified period, during which they did penance. During this time they had no power over men or women and had to lay down their swords. They were denied the support of their families and forced to wander, travelling the roads as pilgrims. Last of all, the sacred quality of power meant that priests kept a watchful eye upon the way princes were performing their duties – anathematizing wicked rulers, singing the praises of good ones, and officiating at coronations. It was still relatively easy to become a saint in the eleventh century. Anyone who had held high office – even if he had done no more than fulfil his appointed task – had a good chance of canonization. In about 1030 a monk called Helgaud, of the monastery of Fleury-sur-Loire, wrote a biography of the king of France. He saw only one stain on the king's life – the carnal sin of marriage within the forbidden degrees. He attempted to demonstrate the way in which this transgression had been purified by a series of penitential acts. The simplest actions acquire liturgical significance in his narrative. Its subject, King Robert II – later known as 'Robert the Pious' – was God's lieutenant on earth. It was fitting that he should be judged a saint.

Power was domestic and sacred; it was also always held by men, because it was believed that divine power could be delegated only to men. Contemporaries believed that as a result of their physical constitution women were not only frailer, but also closer to the fleshly aspects of life and were therefore justifiably subordinate to men. A few women undoubtedly had power over other members of their own sex and over very young children in the privacy of their own homes. Consanguinity gave others an inherited right to public office, which made them extremely valuable. The men who had possession of these women also held the power which resided in them. There was therefore fierce competition for heiresses, who were a major factor in all political intrigues of the period, precisely because public authority could be wielded only by a man. It was unthinkable that women should celebrate mass, simply because they were women: women were, by definition, excluded from the priesthood. It was equally unthinkable that they should carry a sword: women could not, by definition, participate in the processes of justice and of peace.

My final observation is that in practice it proved impossible to exert total power. There were still vast areas of wilderness and tracts of uncultivated land, where there was no 'domestic' organization on the household pattern. Neither written law nor custom had any force there. Twelfth-century romances employ the image of the forest, at once dangerous and liberating for these areas. In fact, the forest was by no means empty. It was not difficult to find means of subsistence. Nothing was easier than escape from orthodox society.

Until the thirteenth century, there was a continual increase in the number of people living a marginal existence beyond the rule of law. In fact, their numbers were so large that one may legitimately query the use of the term 'marginal' for these voluntary exiles. In reality they, too, generally existed as a group. But whereas the society they had rejected was organized according to a divinely ordained vertical hierarchy, these people grouped themselves in horizontal structures. These were also based on a familial model, but used the paradigm of brotherly equality rather than that of paternal authority. The band was the dominant unit in these vast expanses. The sacred still had a role in funeral rites, a combination of Christian oaths, pagan drinking bouts and collective drunkenness. First among the groups of 'friends' who lived in this way were the ubiquitous brigands. Many of them had joined the Norse and Islamic invasion forces in the tenth century. Chroniclers of the year 1000 describe them as '*juvenes* (youths)'; in other words, they were young men without any definite place in the basic social framework founded on marriage. Two centuries later they were even referred to as 'children' or 'shepherd boys'. Then we must add all those who had escaped from society to lead a life closer to God. Many of them lived in stable, quasi-monastic communities, but refused all forms of subordination, convinced that they could thus form a better and more perfect order, closer to that which reigned in heaven. Many others sought spiritual perfection in the multitude of splinter groups that occupied the twilight area between heresy and orthodoxy. Last of all, we should perhaps ask whether the widely feared magic power attributed to women (all women according to some male authorities) meant that they did not also belong to these areas, where male power was impotent.

List of Illustrations

List of Plates
(*abbreviated*)

Facing pages 100–101

Plate 1   William duke of Normandy sits in judgement.
Plate 2   Romanesque reliefs of signs of the zodiac (Leo and Aries).
Plate 3   Jewelled reliquary figure of St Foy.
Plate 4   Cylindrical tower built by Philip Augustus.
Plate 5   Abbey church of St Denis, Paris: the nave looking east.
Plate 6   Cathedral of Notre-Dame, Paris: St Anne portal tympanum.
Plate 7   Stone altarpiece for the church of Avenas-en-Beaujolais.
Plate 8   Melchisedeck administering the sacrament to Abraham.
Plate 9   Chartres cathedral: Royal Portal, west front tympana.

Kings of France
1 *The Carolingians*

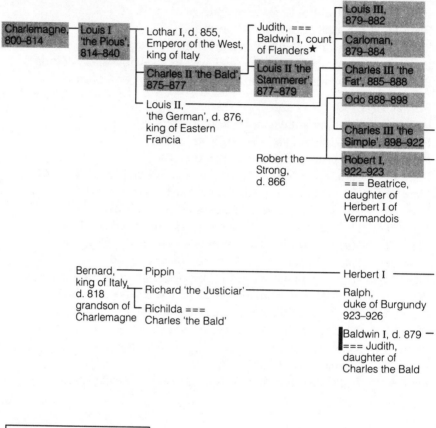

			Louis III, 879–882
Charlemagne, 800–814	Louis I 'the Pious', 814–840	Lothar I, d. 855, Emperor of the West, king of Italy	
		Judith, === Baldwin I, count of Flanders★	Carloman, 879–884
		Charles II 'the Bald', 875–877	Charles III 'the Fat', 885–888
		Louis II 'the Stammerer', 877–879	Odo 888–898
		Louis II, 'the German', d. 876, king of Eastern Francia	
			Charles III 'the Simple', 898–922
		Robert the Strong, d. 866	Robert I, 922–923 === Beatrice, daughter of Herbert I of Vermandois

Bernard, — Pippin ——————————————— Herbert I ——————
king of Italy,
d. 818 ┬─ Richard 'the Justiciar' ——————— Ralph,
grandson of │ duke of Burgundy
Charlemagne └─ Richilda === 923–926
 Charles 'the Bald'

Baldwin I, d. 879 —
=== Judith,
daughter of
Charles the Bald

Rollo, d. *c.*932 ——

▌Flanders	★ Flanders
⸗Blois	‡ Blois
▌Anjou	✳ Anjou
⸬Normandy	■ Normandy
Aquitaine	⊙ Aquitaine

Note on tables of the kings of France

These tables should be read horizontally from left to right. They trace the lines of descent of different lineages; a vertical reading gives some indication of approximate contemporaries from different families. (Individuals may appear more than once as a result of intermarriage.)

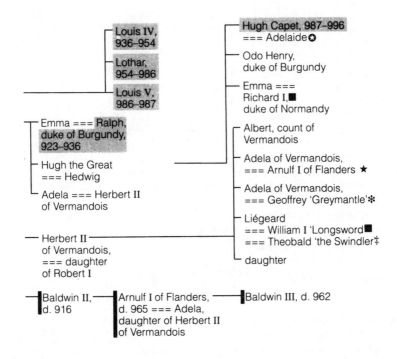

Louis IV, 936–954

Lothar, 954–986

Louis V, 986–987

Emma === Ralph, duke of Burgundy, 923–936

Hugh the Great === Hedwig

Adela === Herbert II of Vermandois

Herbert II of Vermandois, === daughter of Robert I

Hugh Capet, 987–996 === Adelaide ✪

Odo Henry, duke of Burgundy

Emma === Richard I, ■ duke of Normandy

Albert, count of Vermandois

Adela of Vermandois, === Arnulf I of Flanders ★

Adela of Vermandois, === Geoffrey 'Greymantle' ✳

Liégeard === William I 'Longsword ■ === Theobald 'the Swindler'‡

daughter

Baldwin II, d. 916

Arnulf I of Flanders, d. 965 === Adela, daughter of Herbert II of Vermandois

Baldwin III, d. 962

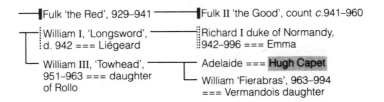

Fulk 'the Red', 929–941

Fulk II 'the Good', count c.941–960

William I, 'Longsword', d. 942 === Liégeard

Richard I duke of Normandy, 942–996 === Emma

William III, 'Towhead', 951–963 === daughter of Rollo

Adelaide === Hugh Capet

William 'Fierabras', 963–994 === Vermandois daughter

Kings of France
2 *The Capetians*

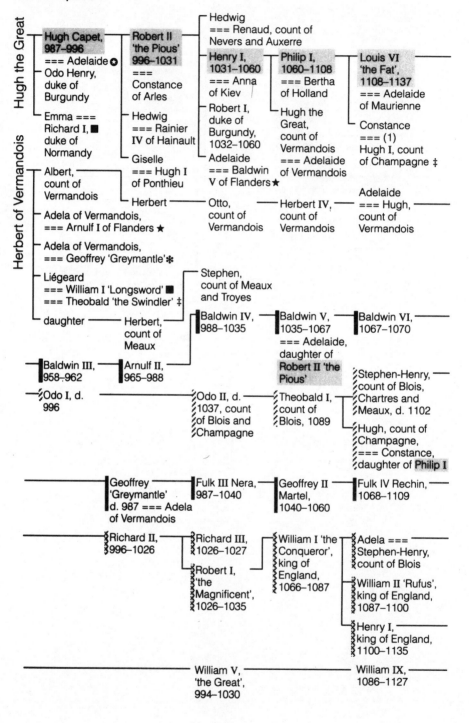

Hugh the Great

Hugh Capet, 987–996
=== Adelaide ✪
Odo Henry, duke of Burgundy
Emma === Richard I, ■ duke of Normandy

Robert II 'the Pious' 996–1031
=== Constance of Arles
Hedwig === Rainier IV of Hainault
Giselle === Hugh I of Ponthieu
Herbert

Hedwig === Renaud, count of Nevers and Auxerre

Henry I, 1031–1060
=== Anna of Kiev
Robert I, duke of Burgundy, 1032–1060
Adelaide === Baldwin V of Flanders ★

Philip I, 1060–1108
=== Bertha of Holland
Hugh the Great, count of Vermandois === Adelaide of Vermandois

Louis VI 'the Fat', 1108–1137
=== Adelaide of Maurienne
Constance === (1) Hugh I, count of Champagne ‡

Otto, count of Vermandois

Herbert IV, count of Vermandois

Adelaide === Hugh, count of Vermandois

Herbert of Vermandois

Albert, count of Vermandois
Adela of Vermandois, === Arnulf I of Flanders ★
Adela of Vermandois, === Geoffrey 'Greymantle' ✱
Liégeard === William I 'Longsword' ■ === Theobald 'the Swindler' ‡
daughter

Herbert, count of Meaux

Stephen, count of Meaux and Troyes

Baldwin IV, 988–1035

Baldwin V, 1035–1067
=== Adelaide, daughter of **Robert II 'the Pious'**

Baldwin VI, 1067–1070

Stephen-Henry, count of Blois, Chartres and Meaux, d. 1102

Hugh, count of Champagne, === Constance, daughter of **Philip I**

Baldwin III, 958–962

Arnulf II, 965–988

Odo I, d. 996

Odo II, d. 1037, count of Blois and Champagne

Theobald I, count of Blois, 1089

Geoffrey 'Greymantle' d. 987 === Adela of Vermandois

Fulk III Nera, 987–1040

Geoffrey II Martel, 1040–1060

Fulk IV Rechin, 1068–1109

Richard II, 996–1026

Richard III, 1026–1027
Robert I, 'the Magnificent', 1026–1035

William I 'the Conqueror', king of England, 1066–1087

Adela === Stephen-Henry, count of Blois
William II 'Rufus', king of England, 1087–1100
Henry I, king of England, 1100–1135

William V, 'the Great', 994–1030

William IX, 1086–1127

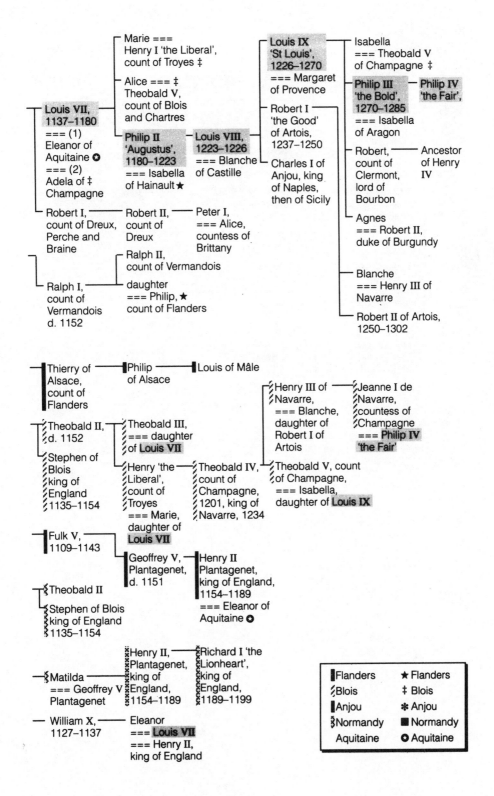

Marie ===
Henry I 'the Liberal',
count of Troyes ‡

Alice === ‡
Theobald V,
count of Blois
and Chartres

Louis VII,
1137–1180
=== (1)
Eleanor of
Aquitaine ◐
=== (2)
Adela of ‡
Champagne

Philip II
'Augustus',
1180–1223
=== Isabella
of Hainault ★

Louis VIII,
1223–1226
=== Blanche
of Castille

Louis IX
'St Louis',
1226–1270
=== Margaret
of Provence

Robert I
'the Good'
of Artois,
1237–1250

Charles I of
Anjou, king
of Naples,
then of Sicily

Isabella
=== Theobald V
of Champagne ‡

Philip III
'the Bold',
1270–1285
=== Isabella
of Aragon

Philip IV
'the Fair',

Robert,
count of
Clermont,
lord of
Bourbon

Ancestor
of Henry
IV

Agnes
=== Robert II,
duke of Burgundy

Robert I,
count of Dreux,
Perche and
Braine

Robert II,
count of
Dreux

Peter I,
=== Alice,
countess of
Brittany

Ralph II,
count of Vermandois

Blanche
=== Henry III of
Navarre

Robert II of Artois,
1250–1302

Ralph I,
count of
Vermandois
d. 1152

daughter
=== Philip, ★
count of Flanders

Thierry of
Alsace,
count of
Flanders

Philip
of Alsace

Louis of Mâle

Henry III of
Navarre,
=== Blanche,
daughter of
Robert I of
Artois

Jeanne I de
Navarre,
countess of
Champagne
=== Philip IV
'the Fair'

Theobald II,
d. 1152

Theobald III,
=== daughter
of Louis VII

Stephen of
Blois
king of
England
1135–1154

Henry 'the
Liberal',
count of
Troyes
=== Marie,
daughter of
Louis VII

Theobald IV,
count of
Champagne,
1201, king of
Navarre, 1234

Theobald V, count
of Champagne,
=== Isabella,
daughter of Louis IX

Fulk V,
1109–1143

Geoffrey V,
Plantagenet,
d. 1151

Henry II
Plantagenet,
king of England,
1154–1189
=== Eleanor of
Aquitaine ◐

Theobald II

Stephen of Blois
king of England
1135–1154

Matilda
=== Geoffrey V
Plantagenet

Henry II,
Plantagenet,
king of
England,
1154–1189

Richard I 'the
Lionheart',
king of
England,
1189–1199

William X,
1127–1137

Eleanor
=== Louis VII
=== Henry II,
king of England

▮Flanders	★ Flanders
⁑Blois	‡ Blois
▮Anjou	✳ Anjou
⁑Normandy	▪ Normandy
Aquitaine	◐ Aquitaine

Kings of France
3 *The Valois*

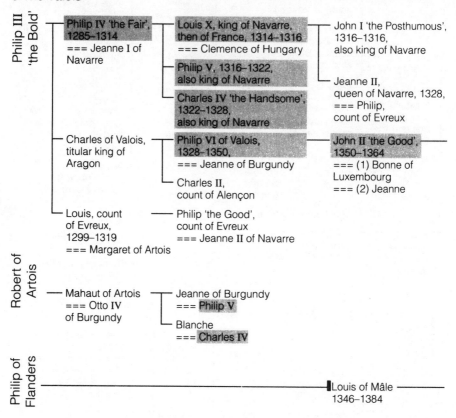

Philip III 'the Bold'

Philip IV 'the Fair', 1285–1314
=== Jeanne I of Navarre

Louis X, king of Navarre, then of France, 1314–1316
=== Clemence of Hungary

John I 'the Posthumous', 1316–1316, also king of Navarre

Philip V, 1316–1322, also king of Navarre

Charles IV 'the Handsome', 1322–1328, also king of Navarre

Jeanne II, queen of Navarre, 1328, === Philip, count of Evreux

Charles of Valois, titular king of Aragon

Philip VI of Valois, 1328–1350, === Jeanne of Burgundy

John II 'the Good', 1350–1364
=== (1) Bonne of Luxembourg
=== (2) Jeanne

Charles II, count of Alençon

Louis, count of Evreux, 1299–1319
=== Margaret of Artois

Philip 'the Good', count of Evreux
=== Jeanne II of Navarre

Robert of Artois

Mahaut of Artois
=== Otto IV of Burgundy

Jeanne of Burgundy
=== Philip V

Blanche
=== Charles IV

Philip of Flanders

Louis of Mâle 1346–1384

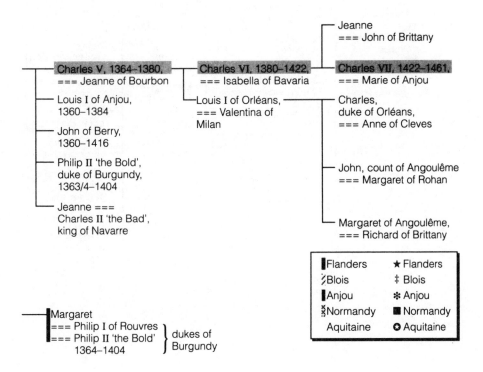

Jeanne
=== John of Brittany

Charles V, 1364–1380,
=== Jeanne of Bourbon

Charles VI, 1380–1422,
=== Isabella of Bavaria

Charles VII, 1422–1461,
=== Marie of Anjou

Louis I of Anjou,
1360–1384

Louis I of Orléans,
=== Valentina of
Milan

Charles,
duke of Orléans,
=== Anne of Cleves

John of Berry,
1360–1416

Philip II 'the Bold',
duke of Burgundy,
1363/4–1404

John, count of Angoulême
=== Margaret of Rohan

Jeanne ===
Charles II 'the Bad',
king of Navarre

Margaret of Angoulême,
=== Richard of Brittany

▌Flanders	★ Flanders		
⸜Blois	‡ Blois		
▌Anjou	✳ Anjou		
⸬Normandy	■ Normandy		
Aquitaine	✪ Aquitaine		

Margaret
=== Philip I of Rouvres
=== Philip II 'the Bold'
1364–1404
} dukes of
Burgundy

4 *The first Capetians*

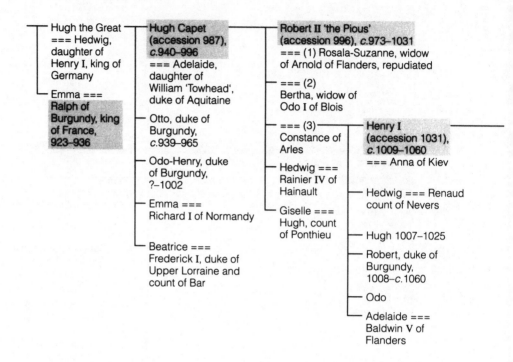

Hugh the Great === Hedwig, daughter of Henry I, king of Germany

Emma === Ralph of Burgundy, king of France, 923–936

Hugh Capet (accession 987), c.940–996 === Adelaide, daughter of William 'Towhead', duke of Aquitaine

Otto, duke of Burgundy, c.939–965

Odo-Henry, duke of Burgundy, ?–1002

Emma === Richard I of Normandy

Beatrice === Frederick I, duke of Upper Lorraine and count of Bar

Robert II 'the Pious' (accession 996), c.973–1031 === (1) Rosala-Suzanne, widow of Arnold of Flanders, repudiated

=== (2) Bertha, widow of Odo I of Blois

=== (3) Constance of Arles

Hedwig === Rainier IV of Hainault

Giselle === Hugh, count of Ponthieu

Henry I (accession 1031), c.1009–1060 === Anna of Kiev

Hedwig === Renaud count of Nevers

Hugh 1007–1025

Robert, duke of Burgundy, 1008–c.1060

Odo

Adelaide === Baldwin V of Flanders

Philip I (accession 1060), 1053–1108
=== (1) Bertha of Holland
=== (2) Bertrada of Montfort

— Hugh the Great,
count of Vermandois

Louis VI 'the Fat' (accession 1108), c.1080–1137
=== (1) Lucienne
of Rochefort
=== (2) Adelaide
of Maurienne

— Constance
=== (1) Hugh I,
count of Champagne
=== (2) Bohemond I,
prince of Antioch

— Philip of Mantes
d. c.1129

— Florus

— Cecilia
=== (1) Tancred of Antioch
=== (2) Pons of Tripoli

Louis VII (accession 1137), c.1130–1180
=== (1) Eleanor of Aquitaine
=== (2) Constance of Castile
=== (3) Adela of Champagne

— Isabella (illegitimate)

— Philip 1115–1131

— Henry,
archbishop of Rheims,
c.1122–1175

— Robert I,
count of Dreux and
Braine, 1137–1184

— Hugh (died young)

— Constance
=== (1) Eustace IV of Blois,
count of Boulogne
=== (2) Raymond V of
Toulouse

— Philip,
bishop-elect of Paris,
c.1133–1161

— Peter I of Courtenay,
c.1126–1182

Philip II 'Augustus' (accession 1190), 1165–1223

— Alice,
c.1170–pre-1225
=== William II,
count of Ponthieu

— Alice,
1151–c.1195
=== Theobald V,
count of Blois and
Chartres

— Marie ===
Henry I 'the Liberal',
count of Troyes

5 *The House of Anjou*

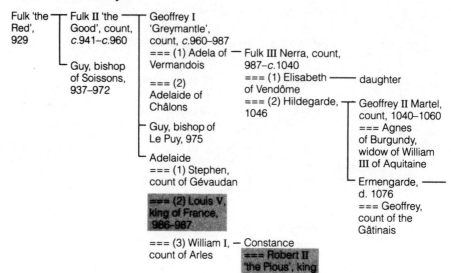

Fulk 'the Red', 929 —┬— Fulk II 'the Good', count, c.941–c.960 —┬— Geoffrey I 'Greymantle', count, c.960–987
=== (1) Adela of Vermandois
=== (2) Adelaide of Châlons

— Fulk III Nerra, count, 987–c.1040
=== (1) Elisabeth of Vendôme —— daughter
=== (2) Hildegarde, 1046 —┬— Geoffrey II Martel, count, 1040–1060
=== Agnes of Burgundy, widow of William III of Aquitaine
└— Ermengarde, d. 1076 ——
=== Geoffrey, count of the Gâtinais

— Guy, bishop of Soissons, 937–972

— Guy, bishop of Le Puy, 975

— Adelaide
=== (1) Stephen, count of Gévaudan
=== (2) Louis V, king of France, 986–987
=== (3) William I, count of Arles — Constance
=== Robert II 'the Pious', king of France

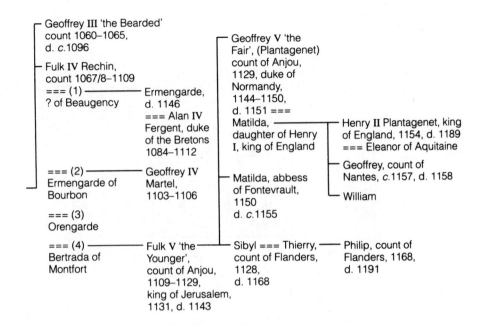

Geoffrey III 'the Bearded'
count 1060–1065,
d. c.1096

Fulk IV Rechin,
count 1067/8–1109
=== (1) ————— Ermengarde,
? of Beaugency   d. 1146
                     === Alan IV
                     Fergent, duke
                     of the Bretons
                     1084–1112

=== (2) ————— Geoffrey IV
Ermengarde of   Martel,
Bourbon   1103–1106

=== (3)
Orengarde

=== (4) ————— Fulk V 'the ——— Sibyl === Thierry, ——— Philip, count of
Bertrada of   Younger',   count of Flanders,   Flanders, 1168,
Montfort   count of Anjou, 1128,   d. 1191
                1109–1129,   d. 1168
                king of Jerusalem,
                1131, d. 1143

Geoffrey V 'the
Fair', (Plantagenet)
count of Anjou,
1129, duke of
Normandy,
1144–1150,
d. 1151 ===
Matilda, ——————— Henry II Plantagenet, king
daughter of Henry   of England, 1154, d. 1189
I, king of England === Eleanor of Aquitaine

                    Geoffrey, count of
Matilda, abbess   Nantes, c.1157, d. 1158
of Fontevrault,
1150   William
d. c.1155

6 *The Dukes of Normandy*

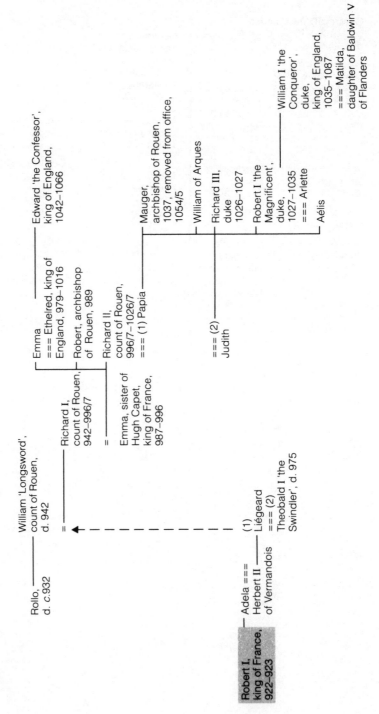

PART I

The Inheritance

I shall begin this study by attempting to place in context the salient features of the political system whose development I hope to trace, using the evidence of an excellent monastic chronicler of the 1040s, Ralph Glaber. His first name proclaims him a man of noble birth and he was clearly well educated and perceptive. As a Cluniac monk, he had contacts over a wide area; for the monastery of Cluny had dependent houses throughout most of Christendom. Ralph's most detailed evidence comes from his native Burgundy, for he lived between Auxerre and Cluny, travelling between the two monasteries. His purpose was to narrate recent events, seeking to understand their place in the divine plan governing the history of men. His work is complex, with a sophisticated structure, but I shall isolate just three characteristics to guide my own inquiries.

For Ralph did not write the history of a principality, like the earlier Dudo of St Quentin, nor the life of a king as another monk, Helgaud of Fleury, had done. His theme was the destiny of all the people of God, set within the framework that seemed most appropriate to him, that of the Holy Roman Empire restored by Charlemagne in 800. In his eyes, political stability rested on the twin pillars of the kings of the eastern and western Franks, Henry and Robert. Finally, Ralph believed that the human race had just emerged from some kind of ordeal and he linked the period of disorder and tumult that had just passed directly to the anniversary of Christ's death in the year 1000. These disturbances had been inflicted by divine wrath, and they had cleansed the Christian people of their sins. Now that a sound relationship with the Almighty was once more happily established, the people had resumed their progress towards the perfection of the promised land, whose gates would open at the end of time. The overall concept is one of progress, but preceded by a painful and inevitable period of political change.

1

The Empire

In the eyes of Ralph Glaber, Christendom was expanding. His contemporaries could have seen the earth, the 'terrestrial orb', in a hanging presented by Charles the Bald to the abbey of St Denis, as well as on a more recent *mappa mundi* (map of the world) given by the wife of Hugh Capet. Christendom only occupied a small part; its mission was therefore expansion. If this growth were to be achieved, then Christendom had to remain bound by the unifying political framework of the Christian Empire, which was the source of its strength. The area covered by present-day France formed part of this Empire. After years of turbulence, it at last stood firm. It was under threat from evil forces, however, and had constantly to be repaired. There was one dominant theme: since the temporal world was moving continually towards decay, progress was always to be found in renovation, rather than innovation. In 1023 the kings of the Franks (with the agreement of the bishop of Rome, that is, the Pope), decided to participate in one of these periodic reforms, seeing themselves as the guides to whom God had entrusted his people. Expansion and thus, by implication, maintenance of the cohesion of the body politic (*res publica*) were in fact entrusted to two separate powers, secular and ecclesiastical.

There were therefore two ways of promoting divine order upon earth and serving God; and there were two bodies (ecclesiastical and secular) by which this could be done, just as there were two laws, one human and one divine. Subject to divine law, which fostered asceticism and celibacy, the ecclesiastical arm was less impure. It consequently occupied the highest place in the political hierarchy. It was also influenced more strongly by ancient Rome, whose legacy had passed virtually exclusively to the Church, whether in education, music, architecture or sculpture. The institutions of the Church had been formed in the mould of the institutions of ancient Rome, and such aspects of the imperial political system as had survived were almost all to be found in the Church.

Ecclesiastical power was rooted in the cities, the indestructible remnants of classical towns, which were numerous and less ruinous in the south of France. In each of these there was a bishop, successor to the magistrate of classical Rome. All around him effective public power was given outward expression through the disciplined forms of classical architecture in the city walls, the great triumphal arches and the grid plan of its streets. In the heart of the town, the symbols of civic power were concentrated in the bishop's palace and several churches. Excavations at Aix-en-Provence have revealed a remarkable degree of continuity. The imperial court of justice on the north side of the forum provided foundations for the eleventh-century cathedral, while the early medieval bishop's palace occupied exactly the same site as a great house dating from the second century B.C. In other words, all the town's energies were focused on episcopal power and absorbed by it.

The cathedral and its associated structures had been rebuilt by conscientious Carolingian bishops in most of the towns of Gaul. But now building recommenced, stimulated by economic expansion. Let us take the case of Archbishop Adalbero of Rheims, as related by the chronicler Richer of Rheims:

After his accession in 969, he demolished the arches which occupied almost a quarter of the length of the church from the entrance; he decorated the high altar with a gold cross and built translucent walls on either side, for the whole church was to be bathed in light. For the greater honour of the church he had elaborately worked crowns hung up; it was lit with decorated windows [stained glass was already an indispensable form of ornament, transforming the sun's rays]; the whole building resounded to the notes of the bells he had had cast.

Châlons, Sens, Beauvais, Senlis, Troyes, Verdun, Metz, Orléans and Chartres were all similarly rebuilt in the early eleventh century. Narrative sources of the period praise the bishops above all for their work as builders. The buildings were for the glory of God, but they also expressed episcopal prestige and affirmed the bishop's power in the face of his secular rivals.

Bishops were keen to build; they also believed that they had a duty to build and to give expression to the ruling power to which their own high birth had called them. For the bishops were drawn from the highest echelons of the nobility. Destined for high office by the name he had received, a future bishop was brought up in a monastery or attached to the chapel of one of the most powerful secular princes, then among the priestly households attached to each cathedral. After he had been anointed with chrism at his consecration, he was believed to be imbued with spiritual wisdom and able to perceive divine mysteries. Henceforth he was the source of all sacrality in the city and within the limits of the surrounding area of which it was the centre. It was his task to administer the major forms of penance, calling down the wrath of God upon the hardened sinner.

The bishop alone was the shepherd of his flock, but he was assisted by a whole host of clergy, to whom he was as a father, for they were created by him through the sacrament of ordination and it was his duty to educate them. A school was consequently set up near the cathedral, the seat of scholarly culture, which was altogether foreign to the people of the town and a powerful weapon in the struggle for power. The bishop sent some of these priests out into the countryside. It was his duty to control them, make pastoral visits to them and call them periodically to his palace. It was also his responsibility to ensure that they preached the gospel and administered the sacraments and benediction as they should. In north-eastern France a diocesan system of formal supervision was already in operation at the beginning of the eleventh century. Sworn informers in each parish had the job of tracking down murder, incest and unorthodox beliefs and reporting them to the bishop's officers. As a result of the inevitable intermingling of the religious and the secular such informers enjoyed great influence. Under the pretext of eradicating sin, the bishop claimed supreme control over every area of society and every aspect of behaviour.

Even so, he encountered considerable resistance. This was partly because the aristocracy propounded a set of moral values that was different from the bishop's: they held widely differing attitudes on questions of marriage and vengeance, for example. The continued survival of very ancient rites caused further problems. Although priests tried to stop them, the people still believed firmly in the need for ritual dances, spells and potions as supplementary means of propitiating the supernatural. Finally, there were heretics, men and women who professed themselves Christian, but denied the mediation of the sacraments, Church or priest.

Each bishop kept the peace within his diocese. Married to the Church, he was surrounded by his own household clerks and served by a college of canons. However, they often resented the bishop's position and made strenuous efforts to develop their own power-base. The upper reaches of the Roman administrative system had survived in a much less complete form. In each metropolitan see (once the capital of a Roman province), the archbishop still preserved some authority over his suffragans, if only because they were consecrated at his hands. Rheims, Tours, Sens, Bourges, Lyon, Besançon, Arles, Auch, Bordeaux, Narbonne and even Aix (whose importance grew enormously in the eleventh century) were thus focal points on the political map. The formal title of 'primate' (disputed between Lyon, Sens and Rheims) was a question of mere vanity. The very existence of such a title, however, is itself evidence of the survival of a concept of Gaul. For a description of what was understood by 'Gaul', we have only to turn to a historical work composed by Richer, a monk of St Rémy at Rheims. It was called *The struggles of the Gauls* and reflects the political events of tenth-century France.

There was a special place for those who served God shut away from the world in numerous monasteries, of which the majority dated from the Carolingian period, when they had been built on the sites of the classical graveyards that surrounded every city. These men (monastic houses for women were very rare) lived apart from the rest of society in family groups under the authority of their father, the abbot. Almost all of them were laymen and they had committed themselves to fight day and night against the forces of evil. (This commitment reflects something of the militaristic character of the rule of St Benedict, which was followed in virtually every monastery.) On the outposts of God's kingdom, they were in a state of permanent alert, and fought evil by reciting the liturgical offices and by mortification of the flesh. They had no pastoral function whatsoever. A few monks were priests, but they said mass within the monastic community. All ties with the rest of the world had been broken.

The reform of the Benedictine monasteries that had been under way for some decades bore fruit at the beginning of the eleventh century. The monks undoubtedly lived a purer life than any other members of the clergy: their celibacy made them the closest of all men to the condition of the angels. This convinced them of their superiority to the rest of mankind. When Abbot Abbo of Fleury-sur-Loire wrote a political treatise for the king of the Franks, he placed monks at the summit of the earthly hierarchy. It was their closeness to things celestial that made monks seem most fitted to call down divine mercies, especially upon the dead.

One consequence of monastic reform was to concentrate power primarily in the larger of these reformed monasteries. The monks there had power over men's souls, or spiritual power; for it was universally believed that health, success, salvation and divine favour depended on the prayer of the monks and the miraculous power of the holy relics entrusted to them. The monks also had material power: the great majority of transfers of land and jurisdiction mentioned in contemporary documents record their passage as alms or as a pious gift – most frequently a bequest – from laymen into the hands of abbots and priors.[1] Their wealth made the monasteries centres of

---

[1] See Barbara Rosenwein, *To be the Neighbour of St Peter: the Social Meaning of Cluny's Property (Ithaca, N.Y., 1989)* – tr.

learning and artistic activity. The most vigorous and boldest of these endeavours aimed to improve the quality of their worship. Expenditure was greater here than elsewhere, and this, too, was an affirmation of monastic power.

The monks found episcopal control increasingly irksome as their own power increased. Their abbots tried desperately to escape from the shackles of the diocese and they looked to the Papacy for exemption; for papal claims to universal domination relied on monastic support. Their claims to independence seriously undermined the spiritual side of the hierarchical political system, which was the legacy of ancient Rome. The most dangerous challenge to diocesan power came from monasticism triumphant. As men made themselves ready for the Second Coming of Christ, the idea of a transfer of sovereignty to those who were best prepared for this event – the monks – gained ground. Contemporaries believed that God had placed them above other men so that they could guide the rest of mankind towards the divine light. Naturally there was rivalry between different monastic houses. The monastery of Fleury-sur-Loire claimed supremacy because the monks possessed the supposed relics of St Benedict, founder of western monasticism. However, a network of influential monastic congregations was the real key to their influence. Alliances based on quasi-familial bonds began to be established, with fraternal links between distant monasteries and filial ties between the mother-house and dependent priories. By this means powerful monasteries such as St Victor at Marseilles or Cluny were able to extend their spheres of influence as, tentacle-like, these associations stretched further away from the mother-house. It began to look very much like empire-building.

I suspect that memories of the Roman Empire were more vivid at this date at Cluny than anywhere else in France. The monastery was dedicated to the Roman saints Peter and Paul; it was bound to Rome through a symbolic payment every five years for papal protection and also by the exemption from episcopal jurisdiction granted by the Pope to all Cluniac priories, as well as the mother-house. Backed by the Papacy and increasingly influential, Cluny saw itself as the antechamber to Paradise; but in about 1025, Adalbero, bishop of Laon, bluntly accused the monastery of sheer imperialism.

When Ralph Glaber wrote his chronicle, divine grace was once more manifest upon the earth. Half the world remained sunk in error, however – the south and the east, as viewed from Jerusalem and Calvary. Ralph clarifies the situation with reference to the crucifixion: Christ on the cross had looked to the west, while his right arm (the one he would raise in benediction) was stretched northwards. But his back was turned to the east and the left arm, used in censure, pointed to the south. This explained the extension of Christianity northwards and westwards, with the recent conversion of the Normans and the Hungarians.

Describing this situation, Ralph reveals that, for him, the people of God were like a group of families. Since their conversion, the Normans were like 'a single family', linked as if by marriage to the Franks and Burgundians, who had been Christian longer. Their duke was like the father of a family and his success in establishing an exemplary peace in the duchy could be attributed to his own physical strength (for he was stronger in arms than other men) and his exceptional liberality – the virtue which frees a man through the combination of generosity and considered judgement in all things.

This interpretation reveals clearly the role within the single, unifying empire of an indispensable power, quite distinct from that wielded by the men of prayer. It was quite evident that in some cases psalmody, exhortation and anathema alone were insufficient to put an end to all evils, and that a second, armed militia was required that would be prepared to use force, repression and coercion to establish Christian justice throughout the world.

D. Iogna-Prat has examined the writings of Ralph and other Cluniac monks and found them strongly influenced by Carolingian Neoplatonism, which saw three forces governing human society: the spirit, the intellect and the senses. The monks' celibacy placed them in the highest sphere, the spiritual, where they reigned with Christ and shared his sovereignty. Retirement from the world (the guarantee of their celibacy) was an essential prerequisite for this superiority, but it meant that they could not execute justice themselves or correct the great mass of the common people who inhabited the sensual world. The monks could not leave their task, or what Dudo of St Quentin called the 'theoretical' path, but they should provide a source of inspiration for the men whose course lay along the 'practical' path. These were the men of the middle or intellectual sphere, whose duty was to lead and who were accordingly endowed with the virtues of strength and liberality. The monks were responsible for preaching to these men, encouraging them to refrain from sexual excesses and undue violence. Thus at the beginning of the tenth century Odo, abbot of Cluny, wrote a biography of Gerald of Aurillac – chaste, liberal, moderate in arms – as an example for other princes. At the beginning of the eleventh century Cluny extended these claims to responsibility for the education of bishops, who had to be equipped for a life of action in the 'intellectual' sphere, more earth-bound than the monastic life and therefore subordinate to it. The ultimate aim was the reform of the secular Church from within.

According to this scheme of things, 'spiritual' power was superior to intellectual, which was itself divided between two groups, priests and warriors. Of these, the warriors were inferior to the priests, because they were further from the spiritual realm and because the circumstances of their lives inevitably involved them more with the sensual. Ralph called them the two 'sacred' orders, because they both descended from what late antiquity called the '*sacrum palatium*', or imperial palace.

The Empire's function was to govern the temporal sphere. Here there was also a hierarchical, bipartite division. 'The best guarantee of peace is for no prince to dare to claim the imperial sceptre and proclaim himself Emperor, without the Pope first judging him by the probity of his life fit for public office and then crowning him,' declared Ralph Glaber, and proceeded to describe the coronation of Henry II as Emperor in 1014. As Henry approached Rome, Pope Benedict VIII went ahead of him as a master of a house receiving a distinguished visitor should do, surrounded by both his lay and ecclesiastical servants. In full view of the people of Rome he gave the Emperor-elect a gift, a gesture demonstrating his superiority over the recipient.

The new Emperor received the imperial insignia at the hands of the Pope, among them a golden orb studded with two bands of jewels and surmounted by a cross. Taking in his hands this object, which represented 'the mass of the world', Henry became the supreme ruler on earth (*princeps*); but he reigned only under the banner of the cross and endowed with the multiple virtues represented by the jewels. Then the new Emperor himself interpreted the meaning of the ceremony: 'By this gift you wish to demonstrate the subordinate nature of imperial power.' The spiritual power was to give moral instruction to the temporal. Henry added: 'No one is worthy to hold this object unless he treads worldly pomp underfoot and follows the cross of our Lord.' The Emperor then made a conscious act of self-denial and had the imperial orb taken to Cluny, as a symbolic demonstration of the submission of the intellect to the spirit.

Charged with reigning over the entire world, the Emperor had to establish his own household, or 'sacred palace', which should ideally be a seed-bed for all the many men who would help him maintain justice everywhere. He should welcome, nourish and educate in his household the young men brought to him by their families. They were inevitably of noble birth, for strength and liberality – essential characteristics in the Emperor's auxiliaries – were genetically determined. In theory, the imperial palace was a double school. The Emperor's chapel produced future bishops and clergy, while the imperial guard produced military leaders whose duty was to humble the proud, protect the weak against tyrannical rulers, and either annihilate the infidels or bring them by conversion into the great family of the Church, as in the case of the Norsemen and the Hungarians. 'Princely (that is, temporal) power' was delegated to them by the Emperor. He made them 'princes' (*principes*) like himself, with the title of 'duke', in the regions occupied by different peoples into which Christendom was divided, known as kingdoms. Within these areas, their task was to organize, in their turn, the two orders of temporal power, and establish those whom they had themselves brought up in the cities, where one group was given a lettered education, the other instructed in arms and the secular affairs which would be their responsibility as counts. These successive delegations of authority resulted in a two-tiered structure – at one level was the kingdom and below that the cities and the surrounding area (*pays*), for which the city was the focus. There were close ties between those who ruled at these different levels – affection of the superior for his inferiors, reciprocated by respect on their part. It is very likely that a bond of this kind developed during a long, formative period in the ruler's household. It certainly continued to secure the loyalty of young men (*juvenes*) to the *senior*, or head, of the household in which they had grown up, the man from whom they held public office, or an '*honor*', as it is called in contemporary Latin documents. This 'honour', or public office, gave them the right to command and to be called 'lord' (*dominus*) by those whom they ruled.

German historians, notably Hagen Keller working on Italian and K. F. Werner on French material, have found evidence in the temporal and secular sphere of the survival of the administrative system established in the Christian Empire of late antiquity. Titles, terminology and conceptualization all lend strength to their view that these officials were viewed as a secular *militia*, whose duty was to serve the *res publica*, or public authority. There was a series of ranks, culminating in those who were immediately subordinate to counts and bishops. They were distinguished by the sword-belt, a symbol in this context of the 'princely power' of which they held a small share. These men had a part to play in public affairs by virtue of the swords they carried . They constituted the third and lowest level of the body politic. In the mid-tenth century the word *miles* (knight) is first used to describe these men. The earliest occurrences are to be found in documents produced in bishoprics which had remained centres of learning. The term *miles* reflects the fact that these warriors were part of the 'militia', or hierarchical body of powerful men who were responsible for leading, defending and correcting the 'defenceless people'.

This does not imply that the people had no weapons of their own, but that the common people did not carry a sword, the distinguishing mark of

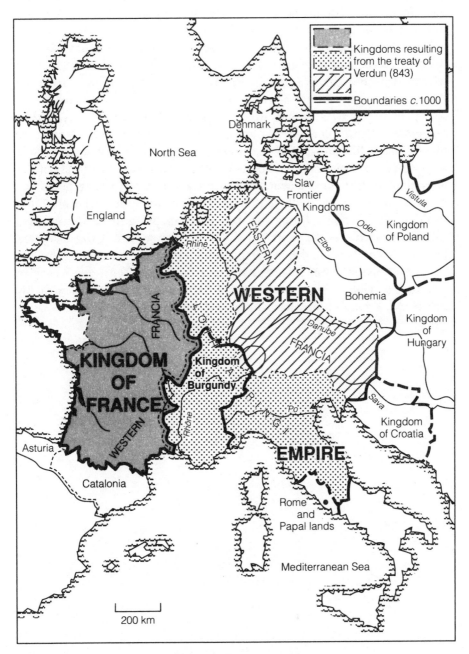

Legend:

Kingdoms resulting from the treaty of Verdun (843)

Boundaries c.1000

Denmark

North Sea

Slav
Frontier
Kingdoms

Vistula

England

Rhine

EASTERN

Oder

Elbe

Kingdom
of Poland

WESTERN

Bohemia

FRANCIA

Danube

FRANCIA

Kingdom
of
Hungary

KINGDOM
OF
FRANCE

Kingdom
of
Burgundy

LORRAINE

Sava

Rhône

Po

WESTERN

Rhône

Kingdom
of Croatia

Asturia

EMPIRE

Catalonia

Rome
and
Papal lands

Mediterranean Sea

200 km

Figure 1   Europe c. 1000.

a knight. For they were subjects, generally referred to as 'the poor' throughout the Carolingian period. The weak point (which threatened to corrupt the entire system) was the fact that individuals were always tempted to abuse legitimate power for personal profit. This was why the spiritual power had to keep a watch on the temporal and instruct those who held it. For this reason, divine providence intended warriors to be subordinate to the clergy. This was the view expressed by Gerard, archbishop of Cambrai, in about 1025. 'Admittedly', he wrote, 'their office exonerates them, if the sin was unintentional,' but that did not expunge the sin itself; 'the prayers of the devout men whom the knights protect must atone for their transgressions.' In other words, the two facets of the body politic were complementary, and there was a reciprocity of service between them: one body prayed for the souls of the other, who protected them. It was therefore fitting that the priest should gird on the knight's sword. For God was the source of all earthly power, and it was delegated by him down through the hierarchy from Emperor to knights. But the exercise of divine power was naturally entrusted to those whose lives were delicated to God – his servants, ruled by his law and members of his household. First and foremost of these, of course, was the Pope.

2

The Frankish People

The vast Empire of Western Christendom was inhabited by 'diverse nations of peoples', as Regino of Prüm wrote at the beginning of the tenth century, 'differentiated from each other by race, customs, language and laws'. Gaul was just one part of this Empire, and contemporary writers were well aware of internal divisions there. Within Gaul, Flodoard of Rheims distinguished 'the Franks, the Burgundians, the Aquitanians, the Bretons, the Normans, the men of Flanders, those from the land of the Goths and of the "march" of Spain'. Ralph Glaber, a Burgundian, found the manners of the Aquitanians deplorable, whereas he felt considerable affinity with the Franks. In any case, he had no doubt that the Frankish people were pre-eminent in the Empire.

There was gradual acceptance of the idea of a gradual shift (*translatio*) of political focus westwards from the East – a notion whose origins are to be found in the cosmology of the crucifixion discussed in the previous chapter. In contemporary eyes, this explained the successive transfer of power from the Greeks to the Romans and then to the Franks. The idea was strengthened by memories of the alliance made between the leader of the Franks and the Pope in the eighth century, which led to the formal restoration of the Empire with the coronation of Charlemagne in 800. There was also the more distant memory of Clovis's pact with the Catholic Church, as a result of which he and his people saw themselves as especially chosen by God. In their eyes the pact had been an important factor in his victories over pagan and heretic barbarians. There was a firmly rooted conviction that the Franks had established the Church in Gaul. The prologue of the *Lex Salica* (Salic Law), which had been retranscribed in the eighth century, praised them because they had taken care of 'the bodies of the holy martyrs burnt by the Romans, tortured by them, or thrown to wild animals', digging up their remains and preserving them in fine gold and jewelled reliquaries. Most of the scholarly historical writers at this date came from the lands of the Franks and they were convinced that this chosen people had freed the inhabitants of Gaul from the yoke of Roman oppression. This assertion was based upon the books which they found in cathedral and monastic libraries, especially the *History of the Franks* written by Gregory of Tours in the late sixth century. His account of the baptism of Clovis is particularly relevant, and an eighth-century continuation provided the Franks with Trojan ancestors. The Empire remained essentially Roman, but it was viewed as a necessary framework within which the Franks could maintain justice and peace, in accordance with divine will. The Franks were seen to have fulfilled this destiny, for now the Empire (*imperium*) was ruled by their kings. In the words of Abbot Abbo of Fleury to Hugh Capet and his son and associate in office, the future Robert II: their power was 'royal, that is to say imperial'.

In 1023 this same Robert ('the Pious') had a formal meeting with another king of the Franks, Henry, king of Eastern Francia. They decided to work together for universal peace. Their meeting took place close to the river Meuse, which divided their lands. For the land settled by the Franks when their migration westward was complete (covering part of Gaul and Germania) had been divided into three inheritances by a treaty made at Verdun in 843. Three of the sons of Louis the Pious had then each received an equal portion of the Empire: Robert now held the westernmost portion, or West Francia. Its eastern borders were largely defined by the course of four rivers, the Scheldt, the Meuse, the Sâone and the Rhône. South of the Pyrenees it also included Catalonia, the 'march' (or frontier province) on the Spanish border.

By the time Ralph Glaber was writing, the remaining territory of the former Carolingian Empire was concentrated in the hands of the Ottonian king of Germany, who claimed the title of Emperor. His rule was acknowledged in Lorraine (the Frankish part of Gaul), but hardly at all in the ecclesiastical provinces of Besançon, Vienne and Arles. The fact that these areas had formerly been kingdoms was now no more than a distant memory. In practical terms they had no king, and this was to have important consequences for the future development of the French State. Monarchy was strong in the north, however, on the one hand, in Germany and along the Rhine; on the other, in France, along the rivers Loire and Seine.

For in contemporary minds 'Francia' was the land held by Robert, or Western Francia. This was where the long wanderings of the Franks had come to an end; this was the base for their future conquests. This had been Clovis's kingdom; he had converted to Christianity at Rheims, and received the consular insignia from the Emperor at Tours in 508. St Martin had been the object of Clovis's especial devotion, and he had declared him patron saint of the Franks. He lived in Paris after his great victories and was buried there; he had summoned all the bishops of Gaul to Orléans in 511. Moreover, the memory of Charlemagne was also strongest in this area, preserved by the great monasteries there. They prayed for his soul, and forged false charters in his name to support a variety of claims. Manuscripts of Einhard's biography of the Emperor were to be found in monastic libraries.

Gradually Charlemagne came to be seen as king of the Franks. By the year 1000, Frankish identity was firmly established in the west, while in the east there was a process of dissociation for which Heinrich Fichtenau coined the term 'defrancization'. By this date the kingdom of East Francia was assumed to be that of the Teutons. The expression '*regnum Teutonicorum*' (the kingdom of the Teutons) became increasingly widespread there, emphasizing an identity distinct from the '*regnum Francorum*' (the kingdom of the Franks) in the west. For Frankish historians, this part of Gaul had become synonymous with France.

At the monastery of Fleury-sur-Loire (close to Orléans and in the heartland of Francia), Aimon of Fleury wrote a new history of the Frankish people for King Robert. He added the legend of the holy ampulla to that of their Trojan origins. He had found this story in the *Life of St Rémy* written by Hincmar of Rheims in 878. Hincmar expanded Gregory of Tours' account of the baptism of Clovis by St Rémy, seeing them as a second Constantine and Sylvester. He relates how 'a dove whiter than snow' was seen to descend from the sky carrying oil in an ampulla. According to Aimon of Fleury, this was miraculous oil which renewed itself constantly, because it was used for the coronation of kings.

Kingship was a barbarian institution. The Romans had given the title '*rex*' (king) to leaders of peoples who had, more or less willingly, been absorbed within the Empire. These kings were responsible for governing the individual nations, judging men according to local customs, leading them into battle and checking their excesses. Since he acknowledged ethnic autonomy, the Emperor was careful to invest these kings with the insignia of their office and a formal title, ensuring that they, too, had a place within the systematic hierarchy of the *res publica*, or Roman State. However, the title 'king' was also to be found in the Bible, not least in the two Books of Kings in the Old Testament. This provided the model of kingship for the churchmen who believed it was their duty to control kings. In their eyes, the king of the Franks should not be merely a second Constantine, but also a second David and a second Solomon. Indeed, he should try and surpass them, taking especial care to avoid the uxoriousness and adultery of David and Solomon. For this was the sin that seemed to them to threaten kings above all others. Robert II did not avoid it; nor would his grandson, Philip. The bishops were particularly vigilant on this point, since any deviation from sexual norms gave them an opportunity of demonstrating their authority over the crowned king.

The Frankish kings were constantly surrounded by the episcopate. The organization of Lothar's funeral procession in 986 reflects this. The bishops and their priests were the first to precede the bier, reflecting the established hierarchy, and in the midst of them were carried the immutable symbols of royalty, the crown and other insignia.

The king became king by a ceremony very similar to the consecration of a bishop. Since the time of Hincmar of Rheims, at the end of the ninth century, the same rites had been observed. In response to the archbishop, the aspirant king pronounced in front of clergy and people the words not of an oath, but a promise – just as a bishop did. He addressed the bishops first: 'I promise to protect your canonical privileges, laws and justice, and those of your churches. As far as it lies in my power, and with God's help, I will guarantee by law the protection of each bishop and his churches, as a king should.' Then he turned to the people: 'I promise three things in the name of Christ to the Christian people who are entrusted to me. First of all, every Christian will keep the faith, in true peace; secondly, I will oppose all rapaciousness and iniquity; thirdly, I will dispense justice with equity and mercy.' Then the archbishop, as God's representative, 'elected' the king and the people applauded his decision. Unction followed: the holy ampulla had been brought in solemn procession from the monastery of St Rémy, where it was kept. It was because St Rémy was at Rheims that the kings of the Franks were crowned there. Although Hugh Capet was crowned at Noyon and his son, Robert II, at Orléans, by the end of the century there was universal agreement that coronation was the prerogative of the archbishop of Rheims. The miraculous oil was then mixed with the chrism with which the king was anointed. As a new coronation ordinance of 1270 put it, 'Alone of all earthly kings, the king of France has the glorious privilege of being anointed with holy oil sent from heaven.' The psalm 'They have anointed Solomon' was sung during the ceremony of unction. This was followed by the presentation of the royal insignia, the sceptre (the equivalent of the bishop's crozier) and the ring (the equivalent of that which bound the bishop to the people of his diocese).[1]

This was the collegiality of king and bishops proclaimed by Louis VII in

[1] Ring and sceptre were of course common attributes of medieval kingship throughout Europe – tr.

1143: 'Kings and bishops alone are consecrated by the unction of the chrism. By this unction they are set above all others and put at the head of the people of God, so that they can lead them.' For consecration did not only bestow on the king the *intellectus* which – according to Cluniac precepts – was required by all rulers; it also filled him with *sapientia* (wisdom), 'by means of which', Adalbero of Laon told King Robert, 'you can distinguish those things which are celestial and immutable, and know the heavenly Jerusalem'. The king was the only layman in his kingdom to whom this vision was granted, who was able to discern the heavenly order, which provided a model for the justice he should dispense in his earthly kingdom. Consecration gave the king a place in the priestly or sacerdotal hierarchy or, as Adalbero put it, 'He was accorded the status of a man of prayer.' This placed him above the order of warriors. By virtue of his consecration, he possessed powers over the warriors responsible for protecting churches: he was at the same time their superior and father, for 'noble families are descended from the blood of kings'. The king was the source of all nobility and the miracles he performed provided further evidence of his superiority. In his *Life* of King Robert, Helgaud of Fleury describes the king restoring sight to the blind simply by sprinkling water on them.

Nevertheless, as part of the college of bishops, the king of the Franks also came under episcopal control. Adalbero again supplies evidence: 'All mankind must submit to the heavenly kingdom (represented on earth by the Church, ruled by divine law); no prince is exempt.' Even the king, exercising princely power, was subject to this. One part of the king's person might be the bishop's equal, the other was indubitably his subordinate.

The alliance between king and bishops was an uneasy one, but it proved to be a trump card and the most valuable remnant of the Carolingian political inheritance and the system whereby in each city the sovereign's delegate, the bishop, would keep watch on the count. Unlike their Teutonic counterparts in Eastern Francia, the kings of Western Francia were not tempted to develop this system in the tenth century and cede comital rights to the bishops in their cities.[2] This practice appeared only briefly in Western Francia, during the reign of Otto I, Emperor-king of Germany, in the second half of the tenth century. He filled the cathedrals with household clerks and granted comital powers to the archbishop of Rheims and his suffragans at Laon, Châlons, Beauvais and Noyon and to the

---

[2] The area ruled by the kings of the West Franks contracted in the tenth century (see below, pp. 24–5) and the inhabitants increasingly thought of themselves as 'Franks' and their land as 'Francia' – tr.

bishop of Langres. These prelates did not relinquish these rights and their successors became the six ecclesiastical peers of the French crown. But there was no further appropriation of lay powers by the episcopate. As a result, the investiture contest of the twelfth century had a less devastating effect on Francia than the German Empire.

According to Adalbero of Laon, one of the king's tasks was to maintain the stability of the *res publica* and restore a 'sound peace' after the tribulations which Satan had unleashed upon the earth to coincide with the millennium. To this end, the king summoned his bishops in council, to obtain from them the 'aid' and 'counsel' that he would afterwards ask of those of his warriors who held an 'honour', or public office, from him. For they all, ecclesiastical and secular alike, had this duty to the king. Royal power was based upon their 'fidelity'. This is clear in the writings of Abbo of Fleury, where one of the chapters is entitled 'Fidelity owed to the king'. The Frankish king's power extended over a vast area, but was only effective if the 'great lords of the kingdom' paid the king 'the reverence to which he was entitled'. The king's position was unique: he had no temporal overlord, and treated the Emperor (king of Eastern Francia) as an equal, despite his claims to universal, imperial power. Adalbero would undoubtedly have agreed with Ralph Glaber that 'There are two pre-eminent rulers; one a king, the other an Emperor.' But he was quick to add that Robert's predecessors 'had each been king and Emperor simultaneously', recalling that there had been times when the Emperor had fled before the king of West Francia. His final observation was that the king was the only person not to receive an *emolumentum* (or tangible reward) for his services, because his office was held from God alone. Kingship was the keystone of the entire political system.

Robert II was king of Western Francia at the millennium. He had been duly elected and consecrated king in 987, just a few months after his father. According to the words of the coronation ceremony, he had been chosen for the qualities which he had inherited from his illustrious forebears. All the histories of the Frankish people written at this period affirm the concept of a royal race, insisting on dynastic continuity from Pharamond, a legendary descendant of King Priam of Troy. No scholar doubted that the charismatic qualities of kingship were inherited. The practical application of this theory was sometimes problematical, however. Should the kingdom be shared among brothers, for example? This had been done in 843, but there had been no subsequent division of Western Francia, the part given to Charles the Bald. King Lothar decided that one of his two sons should be a bishop and had the other crowned in his own lifetime, firmaly believing in the indivisibility of kingly office. The great lordships (or 'honours') held directly from the king were similarly indivisible: the Norman dukes, for example, produced numerous sons, but only one of them came forward as duke to receive oaths of fidelity from his most powerful subjects. Several times in the course of the tenth century, however, the French king died leaving a descendant who, although of age, was incapable of ruling adequately. When Louis IV died in 954, his son Lothar was only twelve years old and his rights were protected by his maternal uncles, the Emperor Otto I and Bruno, archbishop of Cologne. According to Richer, they advised their sister Gerberga, Louis IV's widow, to request 'aid and counsel' from Hugh, then 'duke of the Gauls' and vice-regent of Francia. The latter summoned all the bishops, as well as the territorial princes who ruled Burgundy, Aquitaine and even Gothia. The child was consecrated with the 'unanimous approval of the great lords of the different nations' at St Rémy, beside the royal tombs. In this case, minority was the only problem. The situation was more complicated in 987 when Louis V died only a year after his father, Lothar. He had no sons, and his paternal uncle, Charles, might have been chosen, had it not been for his marriage to a woman of less noble birth. An assembly of the lords of the kingdom at Senlis, presided over by the archbishop of Rheims, rejected Charles's claims on these grounds, and chose instead Hugh, known as 'Capet', who possessed all the necessary moral and physical qualities. Hugh was duly elected and consecrated.

Charles and his supporters vainly accused Hugh Capet of usurpation. Contemporary chroniclers, such as Aimon of Fleury and Richer of Rheims, believed the transfer of the crown to the member of another family to be legitimate in these circumstances: since Hugh was equipped with the most important virtues of the Carolingian kings, he could be expected to exercise Carolingian kingship better than his rival. The Capetian supporter Odoranus of Sens even alleged that Louis V had left the kingdom to Hugh. In fact, at the time of a dispute at Sens between the bishop and Robert II (*c*.1015–*c*.1030), a history of the Franks was composed referring to Charles as Louis V's brother (rather than his uncle) and calling Hugh Capet a usurper. This assertion was repeated (notably by Hugh of Fleury) and it was generally accepted by the end of the twelfth century. Nevertheless, in the context of previous accessions, that of Hugh Capet seemed (to perspicacious contemporaries) merely another episode in the series of political intrigues manipulated by the Ottonian Empire.

For in fact Hugh was not merely chosen for his character and political acumen. Adalbero reassured Hugh's son Robert: 'You are king and Emperor by virtue of your ancestors' long line of descent.' Hugh Capet's father, Hugh the Great, had been the son of one king of the Franks

(Robert I) and the nephew of another (Odo). Admittedly, he had not succeeded to a kingdom. When his brother-in-law King Ralph died in 936, Hugh the Great had played a major role in securing the succession of Louis IV, thereby re-establishing the Carolingian dynasty. At this point he assumed the title 'duke of the Franks' (*dux Francorum*), or 'duke of the Gauls', as Richer has it. Hugh the Great had inherited the rights to episcopal and comital appointments in Neustria (north-western France). He was the overlord of counts with lands along the Seine and around Paris, as well as being lay abbot of St Martin at Tours. This was the largest collegiate church in France, with 200 canons praying around the relics of the saint who had been responsible for the conversion of Gaul, patron of the Franks. The most important of these relics was St Martin's cloak, or *chape*, which gave Hugh the Great's son (the future king) his sobriquet 'Capet'. Hugh the Great also held the important monasteries of St Denis and St Germain-des-Prés. In practice, it was he who ruled the lands of Clovis. The Norman leaders acknowledged his supremacy. Moreover, Louis IV made this powerful relation 'the second after himself in all his kingdoms', a kind of super-prince; for he was the king's lieutenant in both Francia and all the old Carolingian imperial lands claimed by the king. According to Flodoard, Louis IV granted him Burgundy and Aquitaine as well.

In the course of the tenth century, the descendants of Robert the Strong, marquis of Neustria, gradually established themselves as a powerful dynasty within the Carolingian administrative system. Hugh the Great, head of this house, made marriage alliances for his children as if he were a king; he sent his liegeman the archbishop of Orléans on an embassy to the Pope, just as a king would. Hugh Capet's son Robert was brought up like a king's son in the cathedral school at Rheims, the best in the land and close to the holy ampulla of the kings of France. Like all princely houses, that of Capet experienced succession crises. When Hugh the Great died in 956, his three sons were all minors; the same maternal uncles (the Emperor Otto and Archbishop Bruno) who had been guardians of Louis IV's children two years before now protected these three orphaned nephews. The standard inheritance customs of the upper nobility operated: the recently acquired duchy of Burgundy passed to a younger brother, while Hugh Capet (the oldest) received the duchy of Francia, the patrimony of his Robertian ancestors. With the support of his Ottonian relatives and the archbishop of Rheims, he was able to stand up to Lothar and his allies and maintain his supremacy in Gaul. His succession to the throne seemed entirely natural; there was no need to make great play of his (rather remote) Carolingian connections. Already duke of the Franks, Hugh now became their king and, with the crown, accepted responsibility for the various subordinate kingdoms, corresponding to the different 'peoples' in West Francia – Burgundians, Normans, Flemings, Aquitanians and Goths. The *regnum* of Francia itself disappeared; or rather, it merged with the larger unit which encompassed all these other kingdoms, although there was no change in the nature of royal power, chancery practice or insignia. Hugh Capet merely added a more general duty to his local one, and carried out these obligations, just as he had those of a territorial prince. He had no anxieties about the kingdom on his death, confident that it would pass to one of his sons.

The election and consecration of his oldest son Robert on 30 December 987, just six months after his own coronation, should not be interpreted as a sign of insecurity. Lothar had done precisely the same eight years earlier. The count of Barcelona had asked for Hugh Capet's help against a Muslim invasion, and Hugh might well march south; it was therefore imperative that a substitute should be ready, imbued through unction with the necessary virtues. There is nothing to suggest that this was disputed, for by birth and the blood of his royal father and great-grandfather (after whom he was named), Robert was destined to become leader of the Frankish people in his turn.

3

The Principalities

As we saw in the previous chapter, the land which Robert II held directly from God contained several kingdoms. Each comprised a separate 'nation', and was the *patrie*, or native land, of the people who lived there. Each was ruled by a territorial prince, who was the sovereign's substitute and enjoyed the same prerogatives as he did. Like the sovereign, he was lord of 'fisc' and 'forest'; he, too, had rights of lodging and control of fortifications. From time to time each territorial prince would meet neighbouring princes in the thickly wooded frontier lands on either side of the borders between their principalities, just as the king of the Franks and the king of the Germans met on their borders. These were friendly encounters, with an exchange of gifts, hunting and the martial exercises which were the forerunners of the tournament. These subordinate kingdoms were successors to the great Carolingian military commands (or 'marches') of the second half of the ninth century.

In order to establish control over these conquered peoples, the Carolingians had tried to ensure that lands everywhere were peopled by Franks: all public offices ('honours') were entrusted to them and, additionally, members of the royal household (*vassi dominici*) were settled in every territory. Even so, the proportion of Franks holding positions of authority was very uneven across the kingdom as a whole. In its broad outline this could be roughly divided into two areas with sharply contrasting cultures lying either side of a zone running across Gaul from east to west, from Tournus along the Saône to a point south of the Loire estuary. Most of the northern part had been ruled by the Franks for centuries. It had been much more difficult for them to establish supremacy in the south; progress had been fitful in these provinces, where a much greater degree of romanization had produced quite different social structures. The south was a different world.

The history of France is dominated by this bipartite division, and I propose to digress with a brief description of each of the great territorial principalities, beginning with the north.

The Bretons had settled in the Armorican peninsula as a result of the great migrations of the early Middle Ages. The Franks had never succeeded in defeating them and at the beginning of the eleventh century still regarded them as savages, with no place in the established order of things. Contemporary scholars believed that they were characterized above all by a lack of sexual conformity, and the Bretons were held to be bigamous. In reality, Brittany as a political entity was larger than the territory settled originally, because the Breton kings had stood firm in the face of Carolingian aggression and succeeded in capturing the Frankish counties of Nantes and Rennes. Although the Breton rulers had ceased to style themselves kings some while before and their bishops were suffragans of Tours, Brittany was effectively autonomous, and as such the Frankish kings regarded it as a threat. More recently it had been settled by people from the north, the Normans; and four other principalities came into being as a result of their arrival on the scene.

First of all there was the region granted to Hugh Capet's ancestors (which was later to become the duchy of Francia), adjoining the lands settled by the Norsemen in the valleys of the Loire and the Seine. The Frankish kings had granted Richard, count of Autun, a marquisate (or authority over the other counts of the region) in return for organizing defences to withstand Norse invasions and securing a decisive victory over them at the very end of the ninth century. He was granted the title 'duke of the Burgundians'. The dukes of Francia succeeded in absorbing this duchy into their own lands by means of marriage alliances. As his uncle's heir, Robert II of France inherited the duchy, but there was considerable resistance to his succession. Burgundy retained its independence, however; for it passed to Robert II's son Robert, who defined his own powers clearly in a document of 1053: 'Since the death of my father, king of the Franks, I have exercised ducal power in the kingdom of the Burgundians.' The house of Burgundy was closely related to the kings of France throughout the Middle Ages and, as a result, the duchy was bound more closely than any other to the crown. We shall observe the importance of this family tie in the distribution and evolution of political power in Burgundy.

Blood ties also dictated the destiny of Flanders, the second 'march' carved out against Norse pirates: one of the daughters of Charles the Bald was abducted by the marquis of Flanders. This union was eventually recognized and thus a dynasty of Carolingian stock was founded. By the year 1000 his descendants ruled uncontested on both sides of the linguistic boundary, over a people with very singular customs. The count of Flanders was the only one in this area and had no other title.

The fourth principality was Normandy, and here the Norse invaders had managed to invade and settle. By an early tenth-century treaty made at St Clair-sur-Epte, the Frankish king granted comital powers over all the occupied territory to the Viking chief (who had now converted to Christianity), together with the ecclesiastical province of Rouen. This demonstrates clearly the way in which new political structures were meshed into what remained of the old order after the ravages of the Viking invasions, for Roman walls still defined the city received by Rollo. As in Flanders, he was the only count in the region. In the second half of the tenth century the dukes of Normandy performed the rite of homage to the duke of Francia, and became his men. They were careful to maintain their independence, however: Rollo's grandson, Richard I, styled himself 'marquis of the Normans' and referred to his 'kingdom'; he assumed the title of 'duke' when the duchy of Francia was absorbed once more into the kingdom of the Franks. In 1015 his son Richard II styled himself duke and patrician, asserting his right to control the Church and appoint counts inferior to him. The duchy of Normandy encroached upon Breton territory, but its inhabitants gradually adopted Frankish culture and practices. Dudo of St Quentin's task was to describe this process of integration. Paganism, brutality and sexual unorthodoxy were left behind. He describes Rollo's beneficent rule after his conversion, his vigorous exploitation of the land and law-giving; William, so completely christianized that he wanted to become a monk; and finally Richard, brought up at the court of the Frankish kings, cultured and endowed with every virtue.

As the Normans gradually adopted Frankish culture, they were themselves thought of as Franks. The text beneath one of the scenes in the Bayeux Tapestry reads: 'Here the English and the Franks fell in battle.' It was the Franks who conquered England in 1066. A few years later Guibert of Nogent expressed a similar view, referring to Bohémond, the Norman ruler of Sicily: Bohémond was a Frank, because he came from Normandy, 'which is part of Francia'. However, if it was part of Francia, it was also a distinct part, with a separate identity. Dudo emphasizes the Normans' Danish antecedents, but he also added a legendary genealogy, whereby – like the Franks – they were descended from the Trojans.

There were thus five pre-eminent noble families in the north of France, one of which wore the crown. All those territorial princes – first the Burgundians, then in the Frankish domain and in Flanders, Normandy and Brittany – were keen supporters of monastic reform and especially of the Cluniacs. There were also counts pure and simple, more recent arrivals on the political scene. At the end of the tenth century they had acquired a quasi-vice-regal status in the districts for which they were responsible, evading the control of their theoretical superiors, the marquises. The counts of Boulogne achieved this kind of independence on the borders of Flanders and the Vermandois, and the counts of Nevers and Mâcon on the margins of southern Burgundy. In Francia, contact with Normandy and Brittany meant that, in the very areas where Robertian power had its roots, military deputies rose to become counts at exactly the period when the duke of Francia's influence also greatly increased. His own power-base was gradually pushed back towards Orléans by the counts of Le Mans, Angers and Blois. Hugh Capet managed to retain the abbey of St Martin at Tours, but – as at Chartres and Châteaudun – the town of Tours was controlled by the count of Blois. The latter was the protector of the abbey of Marmoutier in the Touraine (a Cluniac dependency since 984); he claimed the title of 'count palatine' (believing that this made him second only to the king in the royal household) and also seized the counties of Troyes and Meaux. King Robert's major political aim was to check the growing power of the count of Blois and he plotted against him throughout his reign, playing him off against the count of Anjou. At the beginning of the eleventh century the counts of Anjou and Blois claimed the status of territorial princes, referring to their *auctoritas* (authority) just as if they were marquises, employing the same formulae and pursuing an identical policy of marriage alliances. Like them, they looked to important monasteries for support to justify their assumption of the title 'venerable', used by the great princes of the Church. Nevertheless, their powers were always more restricted than those of the dukes, especially in relation to the episcopate. They never acquired control of the secular clergy and the rights they did obtain over episcopal lordships were contested and returned to episcopal hands sooner than elsewhere.

When the Franks left the Loire valley and travelled south, it was a very different story. They soon came across men and women who dressed differently, had different table manners and did not even speak the same language. A twelfth-century text rather like a guidebook for pilgrims travelling to Compostella warned them that it would be difficult to understand the people they met and to make themselves understood: it would not be too bad in Poitou; in Saintonge the language would seem very rural, deteriorating further around Bordeaux; in Gascony the forms of speech employed could only be described as 'barbarous', while the Basques 'bay like hounds', and communication would be quite impossible.

If they were disconcerted by the language, northerners found devotional practices positively shocking. Bernard, canon of Angers and director of the cathedral school there, was horrified by the veneration of the statues of saints 'in the Auvergne, Rodez and Toulouse'. He had no doubt at all that the practice was a survival of pagan idol worship and that the people were really invoking the Roman gods Jupiter, Mars, Venus and Diana. Bernard was not far wrong. Disturbing sculptures, such as the jewelled reliquary figure of St Foy at Conques, are clearly distant descendants of the statues of ancient Rome. For in the south, Rome remained a living presence.

The Franks hardly ever went to southern France except on pilgrimage, when most were simply passing through on their way to Spain, praying at famous churches all along the route to Compostella. Others made more specific journeys: Robert II, for example, made a great penitential round of famous shrines in the last weeks of his life, leaving Bourges to venerate relics at Souvigny, Brioude, St Gilles, Toulouse and Conques. The Franks had pillaged these same lands only a short while before. During the decades of Carolingian expansion the south had been endlessly ravaged by marauding bands from eastern Gaul. Some of their leaders had married women from the south, founding dynasties that quickly achieved cultural integration. The task of the king of the Franks was to check these incursions and to secure inevitably fragile agreements between the leaders of these bands and the local nobility. Here, too, the reign of Charles the Bald had been a period of equilibrium and short-lived peace. It was at this date that the king's friends were first appointed to public office, and 'marches' were created and entrusted to counts with exceptional powers.

Independence was the next stage of political evolution, from the early tenth century onwards. Only the northern part of the huge diocese of Bourges remained formally annexed to Francia; all the rest of the south of France lay outside Frankish control. Northern influence was still reflected in aspects of the political system – in words such as *hominium* (homage) and *feodum* (fief) and undoubtedly in other usages as well, although these are much more difficult for the historian to identify. In fact, the meaning of words and gestures of northern origin changed to fit existing practices in the south; a shared vocabulary concealed profound differences. In the first place, the men' who held political power were quite different from their northern counterparts: many were of Frankish descent, but there were also many southerners, and they all laid claim to pre-Frankish antecedents. Research by A. Debord has shown how this veneration of ancestors is reflected in Aquitaine on numerous sarcophagi and in Gallo-Roman funerary inscriptions. Ancient graves were a vital element in the collective memory, along with lives of the saints and accounts of their miracles. As a result, noble families sought their ancestors in the local saints of the late Roman period and – since most of these saints came from senatorial families – they traced their dynasties right back to Gallo-Roman patrician families. As in the north, all forms of power were transmitted by blood, but its dynastic origins were viewed in a completely different light. The mechanisms of power were also entirely different; for Roman law operated in the south, based upon written contract and *convenientia* – agreements made between free men within the bounds of the law. Such agreements formed the basis of peace and princely authority.

Again, as in the north, political geography was a combination of ethnic identity and the surviving remnants of the Carolingian administrative system. First of all there were the Basques, with a long tradition of independence, whose language and leaders made them quite as foreign as the Bretons. Gascony was their principality, a region that had been converted to Christianity much more recently than Brittany. Cultural integration with the Franks here proceeded as much by territorial expansion (especially towards Bordeaux) as by marriage alliances between local rulers and Frankish comital families.

The memory of the Goths and their ancient kingdom of Gothia was preserved above all in the great cities of Toulouse and Narbonne. Even so, throughout the south of France the collective consciousness was imbued with the memory of ancient Rome, the mainspring of the region's cultural life; and the Romans were still the dominant race. Revealing evidence of this is to be found in the beautiful reliefs of the signs of the zodiac, now embedded in the walls of the church of St Sernin at Toulouse. These were carved at the end of the eleventh or beginning of the twelfth century, and the man who commissioned them had a magnificent inscription carved, relating these images to the Roman Emperor. The survival of classical structures meant that public authority was rooted much more firmly in the cities than was the case in northern France. In the south counts or viscounts lived in the cities, not far away from the bishop. The two neighbouring powers, ecclesiastical and secular, were so closely associated that it was sometimes difficult to distinguish between their different areas of responsibility. The two offices were sometimes held by the same individual, frequently by members of the same family: in the early eleventh century it was a common practice for one brother to hold the *episcopatus*, the other the *comitatus*.

As in the north, territorial princes with powers over the counts were responsible for keeping the peace in areas that included several cities. Much of the Carolingian administrative system survived at this level. All those who held these higher offices were of Frankish origin; they viewed the land they ruled – and for which they claimed the title of marquis – as having very much the same status as the frontier kingdoms ('marches') established in the ninth century. The marquis of Provence (whose lands lay outside the Frankish kingdom) and the count of Barcelona (who ruled the Spanish march) faced a direct threat from Islam. They led counter-offensives, one of which reached Cordova, the other extended from Arles to the Alps in one direction and to the Mediterranean in the other. As a result, the Saracens were driven out of the mountainous and coastal regions, and the land all along the Rhône valley was reconquered and distributed to supporters.

Successful marriage alliances in particular had been responsible for the absorption of all other comital powers by the three comital dynasties of Arles, Barcelona and Toulouse. They exercised what E. Magnou has described as 'quasi-royal' power over a vast area. Raymond, count of Toulouse and marquis of Gothia, held lands stretching from the Agenais to Mount Ventoux and the Narbonnais. These principalities were all strengthened by universal acceptance of written law and by oaths of fidelity guaranteed by written agreements. Although they had been carved out a century before, these counties showed no sign of disintegration.

Last of all there was Aquitaine, which the Carolingians had conquered with the utmost difficulty; it had remained a true kingdom within their Empire. There had long been a king of Aquitaine, son of the king of the Franks; then – on the northern model – the kingdom was given to a duke in the early tenth century. He tried to increase his power by obtaining oaths of personal fidelity and acts of homage from the counts in his territory. In Neustria Charles the Simple had attempted to strengthen Rollo's bonds of personal loyalty by this means at the same period; a little later Hugh the Great did the same with Richard of Normandy. Writing twenty years after the event, Abbot Odo of Cluny described how William, duke of the Aquitanians, had told the count of Aurillac to abandon the *militia regia* (service performed directly to the king) and pay homage to himself, as duke. This sheds some light on the process by which political institutions previously in a state of decline were reinvigorated. It also illuminates the intentions of the territorial princes, who wanted to place themselves between the king and the counts who were his vassals, ensuring that their immediate loyalty was to themselves. These were domestic and personal ties of friendship, if not of love, for William is represented as appealing to Gerald of Aurillac 'for the sake of love'. Gerald in fact resisted ducal pressure; but other counts succumbed and the policy was generally successful. Subsequent dukes in their palace at Poitiers were virtually kings in the eyes of the local nobility. They were in effect kings in all but coronation, and the epithets applied to them use royal and imperial vocabulary, reflecting their elevated status: 'most holy duke', 'most serene prince'. Then there was William V ('the Great'), duke of Aquitaine at the millennium. His biographers describe him behaving like a king – reading at night, guided by the advice of bishops ('his' bishops, says Fulbert of Chartres). Like the duke of Normandy and the counts of Anjou and Barcelona, he went on long pilgrimages to Rome and Compostella, to secure divine favour for his people. He also tracked down precious relics, securing the head of St John the Baptist for St Jean-d'Angély. He was a protector of the abbey of St Martial at Limoges, where the saint had his tomb. For Adhémar of Chabannes, St Martial was the 'prince' and 'father of Aquitaine', while the synod affirming the saint's importance at William the Great's behest called him 'blessed apostle' and 'premier missionary of the Christian faith in the various regions of Gaul'. Like St Stephen, whose relics were preserved at the cathedral of Limoges, he was one of the earliest missionaries and predecessor of the early martyr St Martin, subsequently venerated at Tours. He also established the first dioceses in France – notably that of Paris, where he sent his first disciple, Denis. The primacy of Martial over the other patron saints of France is clear, and the duke of Aquitaine exploited this to the full, declaring himself the successor of the 'prince' Martial, bathing in the reflected glory of the 'apostle' and thereby investing his own office with sacrality.

In the secular world his power was less secure. There were continual problems with the count of Angoulême, another enthusiastic pilgrim, who had travelled as far as Jerusalem. He was the protector of the renowned St Cybard, and the monks of St Martial welcomed him with great ceremony when he passed through Limoges on his return from the Holy Land, as did 'all the lords of Poitou and Saintonge, as well as the region of Angoulême', when he approached the city on his return from Jerusalem. Monasticism posed a much more serious threat: more specifically, the Cluniac monasticism that had originated in the abbey of Cluny founded by William the Great's forebear, William IV the Pious, duke of Aquitaine. There was a particularly large number of dependent priories in these southern regions with their tangible reminders of the classical past and rulers who frequently made the journey to Rome. It was no coincidence that an abbot of Cluny should have written the *Life* of Gerald, count of Aurillac, another famous pilgrim to Rome, who had resisted pressure from the duke of Aquitaine and retained comital independence for the greater glory of God. The monks were the true rivals to ducal power in Aquitaine.

The king of the Franks certainly posed no threat. He had not so much as been seen there for a long while. The count of Barcelona waited for Hugh Capet in vain. Robert the Pious did visit Aquitaine, it is true; but he went as a visitor, laden with presents – a heavy gold dish and precious textiles – in the hope of seeing the skull of St John the Baptist. Other great lords were also present, among them Odo of Blois and the duke of the Vascones, and Adhémar of Chabannes emphasizes the precedence accorded Robert at the head of the procession. As far as William of Aquitaine was concerned, however, Robert was no more than a distinguished visitor, to be treated with all due respect. It is interesting that Robert II avoided the 'kingdom' of St Martial in his final pilgrimage south of the Loire, travelling through quieter areas instead – the Bourbonnais, the Auvergne and the Cevennes of south-eastern France.

This was to be the direction of future Capetian expansion. Territorial aggrandizement in other directions was blocked by powerful rulers. None of them could equal the king's authority: only Robert and his son and associate, Henry, bore the title 'rex'. There were many kingdoms in Gaul, but only one king, the king of the Franks, who owed his incontestable pre-eminence to the unction of his coronation.

4

Disturbances

I now come to the most clearly identifiable of the three characteristics which I isolated in the work of Ralph Glaber. Upheavals were part of normal life, but they seemed to him to have become much more disruptive as the millennium approached. (This observation was responsible for much of the subsequent popularity of the work, which was the basis for the romantic myth of the terrors of the millennium.) In fact, Ralph's observations from his Cluniac priory were clear-sighted. The course of Europe's slow and gradual progress across several generations had been obscured by the cruel impact of external events, especially large-scale invasions; but during the period when Ralph was writing, this progress gathered speed, triggering dramatic upheavals. These disturbances were relatively short-lived, however. 'In the year 1000 after the passion of Our Lord . . . the heavy rains and storms abated, obedient to God's loving mercy . . . the earth was covered with luxuriant vegetation and abundance of fruits.' There was undoubtedly a crisis: western civilization was shaken by the aftermath of a sudden leap of progress.

For the monk Ralph all the events he recorded were manifestations of God's favour or of his anger. Some relate to what we would term economic conditions and I shall not dwell on these. One was seen as part of the 'scourges of penitence' – a serious but relatively short-lived famine (1030–3), the result of an abrupt change in climate and exceptionally high amounts of spring rainfall in a society with very little control over levels of production, stocks or transport. This undoubtedly indicates a sudden rise in population, which it effectively curtailed. Other sources also support a sharp demographic increase. Men and women were all directly dependent on the soil for their sustenance. Prolonged periods of bad weather heralded food shortages, but when favourable conditions returned for a sufficient length of time, the peasants had a surplus, even after they had met the demands of their masters – the warrior classes and the clergy. These favourable circumstances prompted a rise in population: recent examination of skeletons in excavated cemeteries indicates that they were healthy and undoubtedly fecund people.

Two other phenomena are closely related to this rise in population. On the one hand, far many more people now travelled, by no means all of them necessarily male or rich. On the other, there was a great increase in the quantity of precious metals in circulation, either as a result of mining or released from cathedral treasuries. Ralph had seen people 'remove church decorations to sell them for the profit of the poor'. This is an indication that there was by no means universal poverty; unscrupulous merchants clearly existed, a fact that presupposes vigorous trade (with its concomitant markets, fairs and coinage) stimulated by the release of bullion. The silver and gold that had been hoarded while trade was moribund began to circulate once more. At another point Ralph refers to Orléans, the most important city in the royal domain. It lay in ruins. This was clearly the trough of the depression. Then the noble and learned bishop decided to take action and rebuild the cathedral from top to bottom. While work was in progress, workmen found hidden treasure. It was brought to the bishop, who gave it to 'those in charge of the building works, ordering that all of it should be put towards the rebuilding'. It was believed that this gesture – the denial of worldly riches and their direction to God's purposes – would lead God to look mercifully upon the land, sending rain when it was needed and security on the roads. It was not just the cathedral that was rebuilt: 'on the orders of the bishop', all the churches in the city were to be 'made more beautiful than any had been before'. Everywhere it was as if the world woke up and shook itself, putting on the 'white robe of new churches'. There were new opportunities for work, for the building required more labourers from the villages; money circulated to equip the teams of workers and pay their wages. Communications between town and villages were re-opened to mutual advantage, but the town especially profited. On the same page the observant Ralph Glaber noted that 'new houses soon appeared in the city itself'.

Contemporaries were surprised at the degree of change, which they correctly linked to the end of the barbarian invasions. They did not realize that the shock of these invasions (especially those of the Norsemen) was responsible for the final collapse of structures that were already decayed and ineffectual. The administration of great estates comes particularly to mind in this context. These contemporaries forgot that one effect of the pillaging had been to put Church treasure into circulation, and that in the intervals between raids they had themselves been prepared to trade their booty, stimulating commerce immeasurably.

A slight improvement in climate must also figure in any analysis of this economic expansion; but what was really crucial was that the whole system of production began to operate more quickly. This was the result of the interaction of a number of factors. Population was undoubtedly one of the most powerful, but impossible to quantify at this date. It is clear that population was rising by the year 1000 and that it continued to increase for 250 years, so that by *c*.1250 populations had grown threefold. There are no accurate trade figures before the late thirteenth century, however, and it is impossible to analyse the interaction of all the different influences.

I no longer believe that technical improvements played a great part; in my earliest work I overestimated their importance. They are also difficult to trace: only the development of mills is well documented before the twelfth century. P. Dockès struck at the heart of the matter when he asked: 'What were the benefits to the peasant of having his corn ground in a mill?' Grinding corn had been women's work, so that even if the new method saved time, it did not release labour that could be directed towards the production of cereal crops. The development of mills seems to have been linked rather to improved seigneurial taxation. Nevertheless, there quite clearly was a rise in peasant production between the Carolingian period and the twelfth century, the two periods for which we have detailed evidence of agrarian activities. Stewards of great twelfth-century estates paid much more attention to draught animals, evidently aware of the value of plough teams. There is an undeniable connection between this practice and the higher yields recorded everywhere, as well as with the greater size of peasant holdings and, ultimately, population growth. Meanwhile, we can do little more than conjecture.

Let us therefore enter the realm of conjecture. I am inclined to believe that a change in attitude towards the family unit, with much greater stress laid on the couple, also had a positive impact. I must stress once more that this is pure hypothesis. For a long while the heads of noble houses had gradually allowed their household servants to live in their own households and bring up their own children. Once they were judged adults, these children went on to serve the master in their turn, providing him with a new and growing work-force with virtually no effort on his part. In this way – and re-enforced by Christianity – a reproductive ethic developed, which viewed contraception, abortion and infanticide as grave crimes. I believe this was further strengthened by a new attitude to marriage, manifested first among the peasant classes, that placed great emphasis on procreation and the care of young children.

Economic growth seems to have been rapid everywhere. Nevertheless, it was most marked in southern Gaul, in those regions which had been less devastated by the disasters of the early Middle Ages, where trade was less

stagnant and where the population may have been – and this is only a
tentative suggestion – somewhat higher. The change here was consequently
less marked than in the north, where depredations had been much greater,
but where the natural environment was much more favourable to agricultural progress. The north developed more quickly, drawing level with
the south and then overtaking it. We should also note that increased
monetary circulation affected the edges of Gaulish territory first. In the
north-west the Normans had captured huge quantities of coin in the course
of their raids, and these activities by no means ceased with the Franciza-
tion of Normandy. The transfer of booty to Normandy after the conquest
of England by Duke William (King William I of England) in 1066 had an
enormous impact on the continental economy; but ultimately the trade that
it revived on both sides of the Channel was more important. The receipts
of a customs post near Cherbourg increased fourteenfold between 1049 and
1093. The southern frontier abutted lands whose currencies were more
highly developed – this was, in Alexander Murray's memorable phrase,
'the Far West', the source of fantastic wealth. Beyond lay Islamic Spain;
farther still, southern Italy – lands rich in stupendous booty. (P. Bonnassie
has calculated the volume of gold in circulation in Barcelona in 1000.)
Shortly afterwards the Normans returned home laden with spoils from
Campania. Later still, in the 1060s, the abbey of Cluny levied a form of
tribute in gold (the *cense*) from the kings of Castile, which enabled them to
build a third abbey church on a magnificent scale, before the second had
been completed.

This brings us to military factors stimulating growth. According to
Ralph Glaber, the people cried 'Peace, peace, peace' with their arms raised
to heaven; but the chronicler's response was to point to the prosperity
around them. For prosperity was the daughter of war. Larger populations
automatically increased seigneurial incomes, and the warrior class enjoyed
improved weapons. They built new castles, wore stronger breastplates,
and rode fierier steeds. Investment of this kind also brought twofold
advantages. First of all it produced a better disciplined ruling class, well
disposed to production and trade, but also ready for pillaging expeditions
outside their own territories. Secondly, it encouraged the production of
oats, a crop that had to be grown in an intensive three-field system of crop
rotation. Finally, these activities provided employment and stimulated
monetary circulation through the wages paid for work on fortifications and
to metal-workers.

Ralph Glaber also noted another series of symptoms. For him the hidden
relics discovered almost everywhere in this fertile land were seeds of
prosperity and evidence of divine favour; conversely, disasters were viewed
as manifestations of evil permitted by God to bring mankind to repentance.

This perspective inevitably tended to obscure changes in contemporary power-relations.

Disturbances of this kind first affected the upper echelons of the Church, the highest and most vulnerable part of the socio-political pyramid. The form of corruption known as simony (trade in ecclesiastical office) was rife. Simony was a form of greed (*cupiditas*, the desire to possess what is tainted), and it suppressed the sacrificial love (*caritas*) which was supposed to characterize the clergy. In the hope of obtaining ecclesiastical preferment, clerks gave money to princes, who were only exercising their legitimate rights to ecclesiastical appointment. This form of corruption is a further index of economic expansion. Nevertheless, it would be wrong to think of this as some kind of auction of ecclesiastical positions. It was simply that money had infiltrated the gift-giving which lay at the heart of social relations. The princes did not aim to choose the best candidate, but the one whom they 'loved' the most, because they had received the most attractive gifts from him or, more commonly, because he was a close relation; to a large extent simony was synonymous with nepotism. This was sufficient to strengthen the reformers' conviction that the sacred was being subordinated to temporal powers.

Ralph Glaber also refers to the rebellious attitude of young men (*juvenes*) towards older men whom they should have respected. This was evident in the 1020s. In Catalan sources, for example, there is a sudden spate of sons ridiculing their fathers and brothers fighting, as if the entire social structure was seized with convulsions. I believe this new form of unrest stemmed from changes in kinship patterns in the social group immediately below the territorial princes. Dynasties were now beginning to found lineages closely associated with indivisible hereditary public office. There were changes in inheritance practices, with the eldest son benefitting at the expense of his younger brothers, who found it increasingly difficult to marry. These changes inevitably brought frustration and with it bitterness, hatred and violence.

At the same time, heresy appeared everywhere, in Artois, Champagne and Aquitaine. This, too, seems to have been closely linked to economic expansion. Heresy flourished because of the growing importance of the schools, where churchmen studied the Scriptures. The majority of the heretics of this period were intellectuals and – according to Ralph Glaber – the best of them; they came from the royal chapel at Orléans, part of the household of King Robert.[1] Heresy was another product of general

---

[1] For a different view, see R.I. Moore, *The Origins of European Dissent* (2nd edn, Oxford, 1985) – tr.

progress. It was also a reaction to the much higher levels of personal wealth
and the social dislocation that ensued. Heretics called on men to turn their
backs on the material world and to come closer to the spiritual by abstain-
ing from everything related to man's carnal impulses: they should not
make love, shed blood, eat meat or handle money. Moreover, these forms
of heresy proclaimed a new, egalitarian society, a return to mankind's
original condition in anticipation of the end of the world. The heretics
believed that all God's children would have to till the earth for their
sustenance, as they waited for the Second Coming in the fellowship of paradise regained. Heresy thus challenged all forms of power. It attacked the
clergy – priests were redundant and rebuilding and decorating churches
was the highest form of vanity. It attacked the warrior class – they, too,
were superfluous, and it was a sin to carry weapons or build castles. It
attacked the rich – for all money corrupted and lordship was synonymous
with injustice. Finally, it attacked the power of men over women –
marriage was evil and so was procreation, since it promoted carnal sin. It is
obvious that heresy was directed against all the social changes of which it
was itself the product. Society's reaction was to declare this longing for
purity evil, and to condemn to the stake as agents of the devil all those who
propounded these Utopian ideals. Heresy was feared with some justification; for those whom the new changes had in some way injured – perhaps
through the strengthening of lineages or a deeper sense of inequality – were
drawn into these proliferating sects. In the 1030s heresy seemed to offer
passive resistance to change.

The sources for this period were not written to reveal social trends: the
fact that they do so is an indication of the degree of unrest. I will consider
three different episodes. Twenty-four years after the event, William of
Jumièges described the uprising of the peasants in Normandy on the
accession of Duke Richard II (1026). He described it as a sworn conspiracy
(*conjuration*) against peace in the land (*paix de la patrie*). The use of these
words automatically designated the rebels as perverse and in revolt against
the natural order of things, because the conspiracy was based on an
agreement between equals, sealed by oath – itself a subversive practice
because an oath was sacred – and because it aimed to break the peace,
which was the divinely appointed order of things. The rebellion started in
a large number of conventicles (*conventiculae* – a common term for heretical
sects and used quite deliberately here). The peasants wanted to live as
they pleased, without superior control; they also insisted that they should
not be taxed for access to forests and rivers. Theirs was essentially a protest against new forms of taxation. Delegates held a general assembly in
the centre of the principality, whereupon the young duke instructed his
maternal uncle to suppress the revolt and put an end to their assembly.

The participants were captured and sent back to their villages mutilated and useless, with their hands and feet cut off. This was effective and the Norman peasants 'returned to their ploughs' and fulfilled their true social function, working for the benefit of others.

The second episode took place in the Berry region and is recounted by a monk of Fleury forty years later, in 1038. The archbishop of Bourges had the misguided notion of mobilizing all adult freemen against secular lords who were exercising unprecedented power – in this case it was the lords who were deemed peace-breakers. The people took up their arms with great enthusiasm, but God was on the side of the powerful; despite the archbishop's blessing, the peasants were totally defeated, no more than little bundles skewered on their opponents' lances.

My third example comes from the city of Le Mans, where in 1069 there was a rising against the bishop and his cathedral chapter, who ruled the city and were levying new taxes. Here, too, there was a sworn conspiracy. This time it was not only peasants who were involved, but also warriors and women of noble birth, as well as those of no repute. The rioters made the mistake of attacking a fortress held by a public authority and compounded the crime by doing so on a Sunday, in defiance of civil and religious prohibitions. Divine judgement followed, and they were duly defeated and punished. Heretics were burnt at the stake and peasants impaled or mutilated, because of their resistance to new forms of government which they found intolerable. How did this situation come about?

Fear of pagan invasion receded at the end of the tenth century: the Vikings no longer had permanent settlements on the marshes near the Atlantic coast, while the Saracens had been driven from the shores of Provence and the passes over the Alps were safe once more. The warriors then turned their attention inward, and used their weapons against the common people, whom they regarded as more affluent than they had once been.

Scribal vocabulary at this date reflects the survival of very ancient settlement patterns which circumscribed peasant communities. The area controlled by each city was subdivided into a number of units, variously termed *ager, vicaria* or *centena*, where freemen would meet periodically to settle disputes and discuss local issues. Three times a year the count presided over these assemblies as the king's representative; during the intervening periods he was represented by a *vicaire*. The 'conventicles' of the Norman uprising were undoubtedly these local assemblies. They comprised peasants from different villages, and the term *villa* employed to describe them recalls the great estates of antiquity, which served as reference points and, possibly, centres for the collection of taxes. The area covered by the *villa* almost always comprised several distinct houses (*casa*) and 'courts' (*curtis, cortilis*). These were enclosed pieces of land where each family sheltered separately at night, brought their animals for safe keeping, and stored food surpluses and utensils. These were the basic units of administrative organization. Fixed settlements of this kind were often called *'manses'* (from the Latin verb *manere*, meaning 'to live') and they offered rulers a means of control over their subjects.

There were very considerable differences between these households. Some were much richer than others, and the ancient system of slavery had by no means disappeared. Inhabitants were still classed as free – *francs* as they were termed in the Mâconnais (although this was part of Burgundy, rather than Francia) – and unfree. The vocabulary of servitude was still employed because, through the accident of birth, some individuals were the property of another. Within each household, however, a different form of private and domestic power operated, with the submission of women to men, young to old, servants to their master. In fact, a considerable part of the population was employed in domestic service. Excavations at Charavines in the Dauphiné (on the edge of lakes and wasteland, both important food sources) have revealed traces of large wooden-framed wattle and daub buildings, surrounded by a palisade. Humble domestic implements used by servants were found there, as well as weapons and trinkets belonging to their masters. Inevitably, large households like these also exercised some kind of more or less private power over smaller ones. The situation was very fluid, because the population was always changing. Inventories drawn up to guarantee the rights of landholders frequently refer to empty *manses*, whose occupants had left for an indefinite period to look for new land (*ad requirendum*). The same documents also reveal considerable variations in the degree of control exercised over the inhabitants.

Strict control was still maintained over some households. This was the case where the heads of great estates had established slavery in the past and the descendants of the original slaves were serfs. These peasants were bound to obedience and to unlimited work for their master – with the women spinning, and weaving at home, the men periodically joining teams of forced labour. The master recruited his permanent domestic staff from these households; he also had a right to take any of their possessions, particularly on the death of a father or mother; he also determined the marriage of their daughters. In practice these serf households were merely annexes to the households of their masters. At the other extreme – and especially in thinly populated areas – there were communities of 'free' farmers and shepherds, bound to each other only by proximity, re-enforced by marriage alliances. By far the majority of peasant households were set firmly within a long-established network of dependence, in which their subordinate position was expressed by the periodic delivery of offerings to the lord. Of minimal value to the recipient, they were an indispensable expression of allegiance. At all the great festivals (Christmas, Easter, Martinmas and the feast of St John the Baptist in midsummer) the dependent peasants went in a great procession to their lord's house, each carrying one or two coins and perhaps a piece of bacon or a measure of wine; in return, the lord provided a great feast, at which most of what they had brought was duly consumed. The lord presided, expressing through the lavish provision of food and drink his authority over the peasants and his right to settle their quarrels. The crucial aspect of this ceremony was the visible reverence done to the lord. Thus an interlocking system was developed in rural society parallel to that of the very highest echelons, whereby the great magnates were integrated into the kingdom of Francia, subordinate to the king. Within the system, there were any number of variants – from extensive manors where the lord rode a fine horse and carried shining arms to a mean hut, where a couple of serfs struggled to prevent their children from starving or freezing to death.

When the monk Ralph Glaber referred to social diversity, he emphasized the importance of the middle strata, sandwiching the *moyens*, or *mediocres* (people of middling degree), between the great and rich and the very lowly. The evidence suggests that at the very beginning of the eleventh century it was this section of society that produced the sworn associations of rebels which provoked revolt in Normandy and Maine. (There were similar revolts in Provence against the *vicomte* of Marseilles and the lord of La Javie.) For at exactly this time the gradations and nuances of the old social system were being replaced by a much more polarized bipartite division, where one class had the right to rule over and exploit the other. The lords were raised up and given the right to carry swords; the workers and the 'poor' were denied this right and suppressed. The gulf between them was total and the *mediocres* who had previously occupied the social middle ground were completely bypassed. A few managed to join the ranks of those who benefitted from this change; most of them sank lower, where they were confused with the unfree classes. This brutal change was the product of two separate but convergent movements whose effects coalesced. One of these movements came from below, and placed new limits on village society; the other came from above, and fragmented the area within which public power had previously been exercised.

PART II

Lordship

5

The Village

The paucity of source material makes it virtually impossible even to glimpse the effect of this change in social structure upon the countryside and peasant society. Population increase had the greatest impact and demographic pressure coincided with much more widespread consumption of bread, which became the staple foodstuff after 1100. More land was consequently devoted to the production of cereal crops, with fields ploughed, sown and harvested. This inevitably reduced the area of un-cultivated land available for gathering wild foods, as well as for pasture. In their turn, the previously migrant peasant population became progressively settled. The peasants put down roots in areas where the land had already been assiduously cultivated and improved by permanent settlers. There are numerous instances of this process. One of the Cluny cartularies, for example, refers to a man and a woman who had previously led an itinerant existence in different areas but had decided to settle in a village on the banks of the Saône around the year 1000; they married and produced a veritable peasant dynasty, some of whom spread out onto the uncultivated land nearby. The document adds that when they first settled, the two migrants had to submit to the authority of the 'lords of the area'. The history of land use was thus intimately bound up with the history of power. The lords encouraged permanent settlement, because they could then control the population more effectively.

For the past fifteen or so years, French historians working on settlement have been greatly influenced by two models, which were developed for different regions of Europe. The first is based on material from northern Europe, especially Germany. This supports the view that a very primitive form of rural housing – light, quickly constructed and fragile, of no value in comparison with the land itself – survived for a long while. This model therefore suggests that the population did not become permanently settled until the eleventh century. The second theory has been more influential and is soundly based on Pierre Toubert's research on the Latium of central Italy. He described the process of *incastellamento* whereby family units regrouped in the course of the tenth and eleventh centuries. Whereas previously they had been scattered at random across the plain, now – generally under pressure from the local lord – they settled in permanent colonies perched on hilltops, like the region's fortresses, each forming the nucleus of a new social structure. Robert Fossier combined both these theories in his account of rural settlement. In his view, Toubert's evidence represents a single, localized instance of a much more widespread phenomenon, which can also be documented from France at the same period. He identified this period as 990–1060, coinciding exactly with all the changes which struck Ralph Glaber so forcibly. According to Fossier, this marked the 'birth of the village'. Randomly scattered huts were now constructed in one place, sometimes surrounded with a wall or palisade and often given their own juridical status. Although they might be rebuilt several times in response to the changing needs of the family group and different agricultural methods, the settlements themselves were not moved, because the houses were made from more durable materials. Once a village had come into being in this way, it became the nucleus of the surrounding countryside, as the land was progressively organized and allocated for fields, pasture and vineyards or left uncultivated as a resource for the entire community. This process of coalescence invariably had a focal point, such as the castle or, more commonly, the parish church and its cemetery, or *atrium*. Since time immemorial the dead had been buried in groups, but they had always been placed well away from the living community. At some juncture between the early Middle Ages and the twelfth century this practice changed, and the cemetery came to be sited next to the church; the dead were not allowed inside the building itself, but pressed close up against its walls. It is possible that the dead may have been grouped near the parish church before there was a permanent village settlement. In that case it is possible that the parish (a completely new form of social structure binding the living and the dead closely together in anticipation of the resurrection) was the primary social catalyst for the shift to permanent settlement.

There is very little evidence for the history of the French village before the fourteenth century. Documentation is sparse and inexact, while place-names are invariably confusing. There have been remarkable strides in archaeology, however, and excavated material is a more reliable source. Unfortunately, excavations are expensive and cover a limited area, while the scope of the subject demands wide-ranging treatment. Since it is extremely difficult to examine densely populated areas, the parts of France which have been most thoroughly investigated are remote regions, like Charavines, where there are very few inhabitants today. Moreover, it is impossible to date these archaeological remains with much precision or to place the evidence for new, rebuilt or deserted settlements within a chronological framework. As a result, it is extremely difficult to make satisfactory comparisons between archaeological evidence and documentary material. Despite these qualifications, I doubt whether French settlement patterns were so very fluid before the development of the nucleated village. Peasant huts were admittedly extremely flimsy in some regions. Against this we must set texts dating from the eighth century (or possibly even the seventh for parts of northern Gaul) which refer to *cour* (court), *courtil* (garden) or *manse* (peasant tenement): for it was the outer palisade and the area it enclosed, not the relatively transient buildings themselves, which had legal status. Indeed, this status was unchanged even when the land was deserted for a while. Within such enclosures the land was cultivated intensively for vegetable crops. Human settlement, with its concomitant animals and poultry, had greatly enriched the soil, so that the yield was very much higher than that of the tilled fields. I believe that for a long while portions of a much larger area continued to be used intermittently for pasture. Enclosed fields, on the other hand, became permanent much sooner, not simply because they were near human habitation – for vineyards were also necessarily enclosed, without any such link – but because the very stability made this land the obvious choice for harvesting cereals, the most valuable and indispensable of all crops.

The concept of a specific period of concentrated settlement is helpful, but settlement undoubtedly progressed at different speeds and took various forms in the very diverse regions of France. You have only to look at the countryside today – our best source by far – to see the truth of this. The development of rural communities in Normandy and Lorraine, for example, was clearly very different from that of Provence, where there are still traces of great classical estates like those of the Latium. The word *castrum* gradually appeared here between the mid-eleventh and the mid-twelfth centuries, referring to the clusters of houses huddling closely together which replaced the previous settlement. The motivation for settlement was also different in each region. I shall illustrate this from the Mâconnais, the region of France that I have studied in greatest detail.

Today this area – stretching from the estates of the great abbey of Cluny into the hills of the Mâconnais itself – is sprinkled with tiny villages and hamlets, most of them built on the site of an earlier Roman *villa*. Antiquity and permanence are the most striking features of the settlement pattern here. Nevertheless, evidence from a range of sources shows that there was in fact a process of deliberate selection of settlement sites between the tenth and the twelfth centuries. Before the Second World War there were 25 villages, 61 hamlets and 283 farmsteads in the present district (*canton*) of Cluny. Documentary evidence is exceptionally rich for this area at an early date: 161 place-names are recorded *c*.1000, 77 of these do not recur. Some were replaced by other names, but many designate a site that was deserted at a later date. There was therefore an overall trend towards a more nucleated settlement pattern. In fact, a site was rarely completely deserted: one or two families usually stayed and worked the land, benefitting from the advantages of the location. Since there were no radical changes in farming practices dictating changes in ownership and occupation in the Mâconnais at this period, these changes undoubtedly took place in response to seigneurial pressure. This is well documented in local sources.

Let us consider the depopulation of the *villa Serciacum* first. There were at least a dozen *courtils* (usually meaning garden plots) there in the mid-eleventh century; we do not know whether they were adjacent or widely scattered. In 1080 the treasurer at Cluny (the monk responsible for the abbey's finances) paid a high price for the rights of all the occupants of this land, no fewer than eighteen lords and forty peasant families. When the peasants left their homes, their place was taken by a single monastic grange, directly exploited by the monastery. It is still known by the name it was given then, La Grange-Sercie.

In other places the reverse process occurred, and houses were concentrated in one place. Settlements grew up around fortresses during the eleventh century, for example. They provided 'overflow' accommodation for the warriors' servants and craftsmen. Whenever a colony of such artisans was established outside the castle itself, a number of peasant families came to join it, and in this way a village was formed. A similar development occurred at Cluny itself, with the development of a *bourg* (small town) outside the monastery gates at the same period. Double settlements of this kind also sprang up where a castle was built on the site of a Roman *villa*; thus today, villages like Berzé-la-Ville and Berzé-le-Châtel are some distance from their counterparts built at Bâgé-la-Ville and Bâgé-le-Châtel.

Elsewhere the cemetery provided the focal point: the sacred atrium around the church was extended to the living as well as the dead, offering them security within its confines. Within this area all violence was prohibited and taxes could not be levied by force. In villages such as Mazille in the Mâconnais, the church remained isolated within the cemetery, and the serfs built their houses close to the manor. At Pierreclos, on the other hand, neighbouring hamlets were deserted in favour of the cemetery when (after protracted negotiation) the local lord gave a written assurance that it would not be violated. Finally, at a much later date (the end of the twelfth century), Cortevaix, Salornay and Prissé attracted settlers because the lords offered *franchises* (fiscal concessions) in a deliberate attempt to attract new settlers.

Close analysis thus demonstrates that the process of settlement was long, slow and complex. By the reign of Louis IX the hill villages of the Mâconnais already occupied their final sites; but in the bocage of neighbouring Bresse, settlement had hardly begun, and isolated farms were still scattered across the landscape of woodland and pasture. There is clear evidence of nucleated village settlement well before the tenth century in districts that had been densely populated in the Roman period. To the north of the Paris basin, for example, intensive archaeological excavation has revealed permanent settlement that was established as early as the eighth or even the seventh century. The *villae* mentioned in contemporary estate surveys were already fully fledged villages with a graveyard at their centre, as at Le Thillay (near Gonesse). Aerial photography has demonstrated continuity of settlement at Le Plessis-Gassot, where a loose pattern in the Carolingian period gave way to a close-knit settlement centred on church and manor-house. Here, construction in the eleventh century of a defensive mound (or motte) in the corner of the site apparently provided the stimulus for regrouping. Concentrated settlements were undoubtedly encouraged by local lords responsible for keeping the peace in rural areas. However, it is still important to distinguish between ecclesiastical and secular power in this context.

All the evidence points to the parish as the normal (and earliest) social unit in the countryside, routinely described in Italian documents as 'the peasant community'. I think it likely that the parish network related first to the graveyards, and this is why they are to be found in the centre of the parish. It was imperative that the dead should rest in peace and unharmed. The Anglo-Norman poet Wace, who wrote a history of the dukes of Normandy (*Le Roman de Rou*), tells an anecdote about Duke Richard I's encounter in a remote chapel with an irate ghost, who explicitly commanded him to leave the dead unprotected. In Wace's account the incident is placed at the end of the tenth century; but archaeological evidence demonstrates that in reality the juxtaposition of the living and the dead dates from a much earlier period. Robert Fossier cites a decision of the council of Trebur in 895, but this was surely long after cemeteries had been moved close to the church where the community was baptized. My own belief is that this happened when – at some point in the seventh or eighth centuries – the practice of burial with grave goods ceased. If the graveyard could be closely supervised by the priest, there was a better chance of eliminating superstitious pagan practices, to which women were especially attached. They had been condemned by Bishop Burchard of Wörms at the beginning of the eleventh century, while Regino of Prüm had tried to eradicate them a hundred years before. These traditions proved extremely persistent, however. The clergy were still struggling with essentially pre-Christian rituals in the thirteenth century, powerless to put an end to ritual dances in the churchyard – the ancient place of sanctuary – or to the extraordinary processions led there by village boys on particular dates.

Documents from the Auvergne and the Mâconnais show that in the Carolingian period the Church was already organizing the living into parish units (or 'flocks', the original meaning of the word *parochia* (parish)). A well-defined parish structure provided an administrative framework in Lorraine from the beginning of the tenth century. In the turbulent period described by Ralph Glaber a century later, the parish unit was undoubtedly strengthened everywhere by the need to rebut heresy and purify the Church. This period saw the rebuilding of rural parish churches; in areas such as the Mâconnais or Saintonge, where they were not rebuilt in any subsequent upsurge of piety, almost all the parish churches date from this period. It was at precisely this juncture that the momentous decision was taken to declare both church and the plot on which it stood an area of rigorously enforced peace. The boundaries of the cemetery were clearly marked with crosses, and it became a place of sanctuary, where peasants from neighbouring hamlets sought refuge in times of war. Churches built after this date – a large number were constructed in the Charente in the last quarter of the eleventh century, for example – also played a part in peasant settlement.

The most important activity of secular rulers at this period was their policy of directing agricultural expansion towards previously uncultivated lands. Between the late eleventh and the thirteenth centuries – the timing varied from region to region – lords with regalian powers over wasteland (or, in practice, their officials) found that woodlands and marshes could produce high yields once they were populated with new and taxable subjects. They set out to attract settlers who would clear the land, promising them less exacting dues than those levied on the inhabitants of longer-established settlements. Once a settlement charter had been granted, plans of all the building plots were drawn up. There are a substantial number of French towns and villages founded at this period called 'Villeneuve'. They fall into two main types, one with the houses grouped together, the other with plots either side of a long village street. After the thirteenth century, clearing was less highly organized, but at its zenith it had been responsible for the creation of new villages.

Seigneurial intervention also became more marked in traditional settlements throughout France after the year 1000, with lords building defensive walls around settlements or founding a fair or a market there, both very profitable sources of revenue. Sometimes a completely new village was created; but more frequently an old site grew at the expense of its neighbours, whose population dwindled and sometimes disappeared completely. This trend became more marked in the mid-eleventh century, when the first *castelnaus* were founded in the south-west. As their name suggests, these were primarily defensive settlements. The *bourgs* appeared in about 1060 in Poitou and Normandy, and became much more numerous a century later, when there was a great increase in commercial activity. For although they had military associations and were often built close to a castle originally, the weekly market was their most important single feature.

The pattern and density of village settlement was thus determined by political considerations. It was also carried out under seigneurial control – the cemeteries themselves, after all, fell under the aegis of God, the supreme lord. The eleventh century saw an attempt to separate spiritual from temporal concerns, and the council of Rheims (1049) decreed that the altar – focus of all that was most sacred – should be placed in the chancel, separate from the rest of the church building; the church itself was to be entrusted to the care of a patron, who was also to choose the priest. The priest clearly had enormous influence over the village population, since he had charge of the sanctuary light, banners and all their magic emblems, and it was he who absolved the dead and held out the promise of salvation to the living. It was largely through the mediation of the priest that the lord had any contact with the poor. As for the *bourgs*, they were often no more than an appendage to the castle. Nevertheless, as a very general rule, the village was built at some distance from the lord's own residence. When fortified manors (*maisons fortes*) began to be built at the end of the twelfth century, they appeared on the edge of the lord's lands. This physical separation into two polarized camps was to have significant consequences for the subsequent distribution of power.

It is important not to consider these tendencies in isolation from the vigorous movement within peasant communities towards an existence and identity independent of their local lord. Smiths, saddlers and other craftsmen in the towns developing at monastery or castle gate were all employed by the local lords; once the peasantry began to receive money payments, they also provided the artisans with employment. The money payments themselves were of course one result of increased commercial activity in the town and its market. Rural households started to produce goods for sale, and some were more successful than others. This resulted in a considerable gulf between the richest and the poorest peasants by the end of the eleventh century; the gap between them widened considerably in the twelfth century, tending to split village communities in two. Counter-balancing this trend were the factors which promoted village unity, imposed by the availability of land and by increasingly organized land use. In regions such as Lorraine, where the village unit was very clearly defined, or in Burgundy, where settlement outside the allocated area was forbidden, accepted limits were gradually established; as a result, communal exploitation of the land for foodstuffs was actively promoted. Finally, all these bonds formed a network centred on the parish church and in opposition to the local lord.

For it was here, in the heart of the parish, that the dead were buried together, babies were baptized in the same font and the men of the village gathered round the priest. (It is likely that women were forbidden – on the grounds of uncleanness – to enter the church far more frequently than has usually been supposed.) The sanctuary light burned for each member of the village community, and they all walked in procession on appointed days to secure rain for their crops. Of course, there were also enclaves within the parish; the lord's devotions were observed in his private chapel, where his own chaplain officiated. This is further evidence of the way in which the lords of the manor tried to keep themselves apart from the common people. The villagers, however, were bound together by the shared rites of the Christian year, and were more aware of the ties between them than of the differences between villeins and free men, those who owned oxen and those who did not. The parish church was the only substantial building in the village, and it was here that food stocks were brought in time of danger. When Normandy was racked by civil war at the beginning of the twelfth century, church towers were stuffed full of chests, sacks and storage jars. There is evidence from the year 1000 for the survival of very ancient practices of mutual support, and here we can see the origins of what were to become parish confraternities. Church authorities were worried about them, and a council at Lisieux (1034) banned *religiones* (village feasts), which were feared to be the seed-beds of revolt. However, the Church's opposition to these *frairies* (brotherhoods) was finally overcome in the twelfth century, when they were charged with responsibility for church upkeep and the distribution of alms.

All these bonds contributed to peasant solidarity and enabled the villagers to offer more effective opposition. They had considerable justification for their antagonism towards the lord, for he had enormous influence over their lives. It was he who collected their tithes, for whom the church was a source of revenue, like his mills and his bakehouses. As the largest landholder by far, the lord controlled the farming year, deciding the date of the harvest and other key events and exercising his right to cream off the village's manpower at the most propitious moment. Waterways, pasture land, clearings and woodland were all owned and closely controlled by him: he was quite within his rights, if he decided to ban the villagers' grazing animals from one part of the woodland, or let his pigs have most of the acorn crop. He was the sworn enemy of all poachers, and levied taxes on every aspect of the villagers' lives. The lord owned the castle where they sought refuge in troubled times and the barns where their harvest was stored, and he guaranteed parish security. However, he made the village pay dearly for his protection, ruthlessly upholding law and order with the imposition of harsh sentences, confiscation and heavy fines. Finally, they feared and resented the lord's agents, intermediaries who were part of the village and yet set apart from it. They were usually from the lowest levels of village society, drawn from villein families descended from slaves, whose dependence on the lord was a guarantee of their loyalty. These agents were bent on improving their own position, and did not hesitate to exploit all the highly lucrative coercive powers delegated to them. Whether they were the lord's forester, his *prévôt*, or the parish priest, these men undoubtedly grew rich; if they were married, their position descended from father to son in petty dynasties. In some ways they were a peasant aristocracy. Their function, or '*ministerium*', as it was described in contemporary documents, was the most effective means of social advancement in the village and the only way to break down the new administrative barriers which had trapped the common people since the eleventh century. By 1100 the nobility were demonstrably concerned about the relatively elevated status which their arrogant subordinates had acquired. By this date it was difficult to tell them apart from the warriors with whom they associated, since they also rode about armed and on horseback.

It was imperative for the villagers to find a means of settling their own disputes if they were to stand up for themselves and keep a matter from coming before the lord's court. They met annually to decide the level of contribution to be paid by each household for the lord's protection, and in this rough and ready manner seigneurial taxation in fact strengthened village unity. They made a corporate defence of 'good' customs, and the lord was careful not to infringe them. Periodically, they recited a list of their rights and obligations before the *prévôt*, tending always to gloss over the obligations and stress their rights. There was the same tendency when they were convened as a jury and had to expound ancient, established legal practice. The subjects' power lay precisely in the fact that they were the custodians of local custom, and their influence was sufficient to impose these practices on their lord. In the eyes of God, the system certainly made clear-cut distinctions between those who commanded and those whose place was to obey, but in practice the lord's authority was continually balked by customary usage – in effect, the power of the local community, since they were the accepted experts in this field. Constant dialogue was consequently indispensable to local government, for which the parish provided a natural framework. Since it was by virtue of living in the parish that the inhabitants were liable to exploitation by the lord, the parish thus also inevitably provided the framework for some exploitation of the peasant population.

We can see, therefore, that there was undoubtedly a continual process of settlement, whereby a predominantly scattered population became concentrated in villages, which might be built on a more or less distinctly nucleated, non-nucleated or herringbone pattern. It was through the village structure that the common people (or 'the plebeians', as they were described by contemporary writers who were particularly impressed with their own superior birth) had a role in the ordering of their communities. In most regions there was an essentially stable framework of village settlement by the beginning of the eleventh century, when the Church attempted to make the 'poor' the backbone of a peaceful society. In 1038 Archbishop Aimon of Bourges tried to ensure law and order by having every grown man swear to keep the peace: the peasantry marched in protest against their wicked lords under the banners they carried at religious festivals, led by their own priests. Already at this date the parish system formed the basic unit of peasant society. When, a century later, Louis VI attempted to check the power of the *tyrans* (over-mighty subject) in much the same manner as Archbishop Aimon, he made full use of the parish system. The king's apologist, Abbot Suger of St Denis, describes how a village priest and his flock broke down the walls of the castle of Le Puiset. In Normandy, Orderic Vitalis stressed the importance of the parish, saying that the French king was known as the '*père des communes*' (father of the communes), because he valued them so highly. Later, when the bishops of southern France were attempting to maintain law and order, they too instructed their officials (the '*juges de la paix*') to receive oaths of mutual aid, parish by parish.

Traces of the network established at this period can still be found in the French administrative system. Originally, each division corresponded to an area of distinct customary usage. As writing became more widespread, lords and subjects co-operated in the gradual transformation of the body of oral custom into a written code, in order to put an end to interminable testimonies, as well as securing the people's rights and liberties against encroachment by their masters. In this way contentious areas were at least clearly identified. The transition to a more closely defined written code was clearly a liberating experience, reflected in the associated vocabulary, where words like *franchise, commune* and *liberté* have retained their emotive connotations. With agricultural expansion, the reorganization of seigneurial administration and the Christian revival which was the result of improved pastoral care, peasant communities gradually became more influential. This process continued into the reign of Louis IX. By that date it was gradually becoming accepted practice to identify a peasant by the name of his parish, and the lordship was also increasingly confused with the village and subsumed within it. Within this framework the French landscape was already established in the contrasting forms it still exhibits today.

Wace, writing in about 1170, emphasized the difference between peasants who lived in an enclosed bocage landscape (where fields were surrounded by hedges, assarting was confined almost exclusively to infertile areas, and settlements were much more independent of each other) and the inhabitants of much more open countryside, where large villages were spread over a wide area. But the romances read aloud in seigneurial courts present a more profound contrast between two differing worlds. In one the land is ordered, subordinate to the world of men and the framework imposed by the clergy, nobility and their administrators – tax-collectors, substantial tenant farmers and semi-independent tradespeople such as millers and smiths. Church, castle, servants: here, once more, are three orders of society. Moreover, this period witnessed a re-emergence of the concept of the complementary functions of the three estates, which had first been expressed 150 years before by the bishops of Laon and Cambrai, when they hoped to tighten their agents' control over the peasantry during the period when the imposition of lordship on the countryside had just been completed. The other world was that of the 'forest', free and uncontrolled. During the twelfth century, demand from both towns and the more affluent sections of society for the products of uncultivated land (wood, charcoal, iron, glass, wool and mutton) had begun to make the owners of wasteland conscious of the need to protect it from encroaching clearance. What remained of forest, heath and marshland was the ideal backdrop for adventure. Here dragons, fairies and all sorts of strange beings might still be encountered. They were the setting for the various trials which preceded the rites of passage into adulthood, and here ancient superstitions still lurked. These wastelands were by no means entirely deserted, for they were frequented by hermit and charcoal-burner, as well as by the knight errant – almost unreal representatives of the same tripartite division of society, but here unchecked and beyond the law. It is no coincidence that it was in this 'other world' that John of Marmoutier (in his posthumous eulogy of Geoffrey Plantagenet, count of Anjou, written *c*.1180) set an encounter between his hero and a wild man of the woods, who terrified him, but came to his aid as well. Guiding the count of Anjou safely through the dense woodland in which he was lost, the wild man instructed him in just government as they travelled. In the narrative he exhorts the count to hold fast to his legitimate rights and to withstand all the efforts of his officers (whether knights, clergy or *prévôts*) to persuade him to go beyond them, so that he might alleviate the sufferings of the rural poor.

6

The Castle

The movement which led to village settlement in the countryside is difficult to trace. It is much easier to follow the other principal tendency of the period, because the process by which the system of lordship was developed and established was a much quicker one. Moreover, since it affected the apex of the social pyramid, it was also very much better documented. Contemporary Latin texts use words such as *dominatio*, *dominium* or simply *potestas* (power) when they refer to lordship – terms which were all taken from royal and imperial forms of government, where power was delegated by king or Emperor to their vassals. Chancery scribes described this as 'principal', or primary, power; and in practice it lay in the hands of the territorial princes. In the ninth and tenth centuries the title *Dominus* was used for God; it was otherwise only applied to the king and his closest associates, the counts, and the bishops. Each of these words specified a form of power that was essentially different from the private power wielded by a great landholder over the tenants who farmed parts of his domain, or that of the head of a family over his relatives and the members of his household, both bond and free men. (The latter were dependent upon him for protection, and gave him gifts periodically in exchange.) Power (*potestas*) and dominion (*dominatio*) were chiefly reserved to rulers, who were responsible for peace and justice. After the year 1000, however, this power became fragmented and passed into the hands of a much larger number of individuals, while the area over which it was exercised was simultaneously reduced.

This fragmentation was the result of a long process whereby political structures adapted to the difficulties of effective long-distance government. The political framework which it replaced had been based on the functioning of key elements – town, transport, coinage – which had deteriorated dramatically in the very early Middle Ages. The situation improved with

Frankish military expansion in the eighth century, but there were no administrative changes to meet a totally different social structure. Commercial paralysis, combined with improvements in agriculture, meant that this was now essentially a peasant society. Authority could only be exerted over a limited area, encompassing some ten to twenty parishes, a mere fraction of the region for which the count was originally responsible. Within this framework there was continuous tension between the public office of peace and justice and the practical control exerted by rich individuals over their dependents within their own lands. From a very early date, public authorities had employed such men as intermediaries to govern the lower strata of society. Eventually, it was admitted that they in fact held the powers implied by *potestas*. I said earlier that this was a rapid development; it would be more accurate to say that the vocabulary of documentary sources was transformed at remarkable speed. It would be easy to interpret this as some kind of revolution, when it was in fact only the revelation of long-established practices previously masked by traditional scribal formulae. They were finally abandoned as scribes came to realize how little they corresponded to contemporary social reality. When the time was ripe, the formulaic shell fell away of its own accord. In every region of France which has been the subject of detailed research, the impression is of a sudden break and 'radical change', to quote P. Bonnassie. The critical point occurred in the 1020s, and new divisions of power were established in the three or four decades that followed.

By contrast with private patronage, lordship operated right across a specific territory, in the same way as royal or comital power. Contemporaries sometimes used the term *vicaria* (vicariate) for it, which had sometimes previously described groups of vills, whose free inhabitants had a shared judicial role. New terms were also developed: *mandamentum* stressed the legitimate delegation of the lord's authority; *salvamentum*, or *castellania* (castellany), emphasized his protective role. The first reference to *castellania* in the Charente is found *c.*1060; it clearly alludes to the *castrum*, or castle, which lay at the heart of this new social unit. Their distinctive towers were a landmark in the countryside, echoing the walls of the city which enshrined regalian powers, distant descendants of the classical State. The castle was an ambivalent symbol: it was both the seat of justice and the base of a potentially oppressive power, a sign of the lord's duty to protect his people and also of his right to command and, if necessary, punish them.

Archaeology has revealed that there were fortifications all over France from a very early date. Whether they were on top of rocky peaks or surrounded by water at the bottom of a valley, these raised defensive sites enclosed an area large enough to offer shelter to an entire local population, together with their animals and provisions. Many such walled sites served the same function at the end of the ninth century as they had in the very early Middle Ages. Nevertheless, the system of fortification established at the very beginning of the feudal period was totally different from this primitive arrangement. In the first place, there were far more fortified sites and castles. Numerous fortresses were built upon the remains of Roman cities, incorporating whatever remained of the gates, baths and amphitheatres. In the countryside large numbers of sites that had been fortified at an earlier date were abandoned in favour of new locations. There was no overall plan for this new development; indeed, they were often built close together. At Saignon (near Apt), for example, and at Amboise, three castles were built within a hundred metres of each other in the late eleventh century, each with its own distinct jurisdiction. Another characteristic of these new fortifications was the way in which their defensive functions had contracted and were now concentrated almost exclusively upon the keep, or *donjon* – the French word is derived (like 'danger') from *dominium*, expressing seigneurial power. The three-storey keep was built of wood, or in stone in southern France (and very occasionally in the north), and usually covered a very limited area. It was not a residential building; that was constructed some distance away and incorporated the hall (*salle*), where seigneurial justice was publicly exercised. The keep's function was military and – possibly more importantly – symbolic. It also acted as a storehouse for valuables. One of the castellans of Amboise, for example, slept elsewhere with his men, but hid his wife (who had just given birth to an heir) for safe keeping in the middle floor, accessible only by a movable ladder. Above were the look-outs surveying the surrounding countryside and the lord's banner, emblem of his power. If the keep was not sited on a rocky outcrop, it was built on top of a mound of earth some dozen metres high, with a surface area covering some twelve square metres. This was the 'motte', surrounded by the moat, which had been dug out to provide the necessary earth for this mound. It towered over a 'bailey', or lower courtyard, surrounded by less formidable defences which enclosed living quarters and domestic offices. This was the popular image of a stronghold, and it is the picture of both Norman castles and towns presented by the embroiderers (probably English) of the Bayeux Tapestry around 1090.

The painstaking work of archaeologists in the area around Angoulême and in Normandy, Provence, Champagne and Bresse has demonstrated that some mottes were built on the sites of residences formerly occupied by public officials. These studies have also revealed a number of incomplete building projects, dating especially from the 1060s and 1070s. Excavation has provided confirmation of the remarkable density of these mottes: there is evidence for at least thirteen mottes in the tiny Norman *canton* (district) of the Cinglais (which today comprises a mere forty-eight *communes*), besides documentary proof of a further three castles. A. Debord found evidence of 150 mottes in the Charente region. Here, too, this was a far larger number than that recorded in the written sources. It is most unlikely that they could all have had a major peace-keeping function in the surrounding area. The majority were little more than annexes to seigneurial castles, which were the centres of real power

It is rare for excavations to provide specific evidence of date, which must be sought in documentary sources. Nevertheless, these references are often difficult to interpret: if a castle is mentioned, it undoubtedly existed at that point, but this is no guide to the date at which it was built. Nevertheless, attempts have been made to establish a chronology of castle-building, within these limitations. Some fifteen mottes are cited in Anjou before the year 1000 and a dozen in the Charente, where one of the most

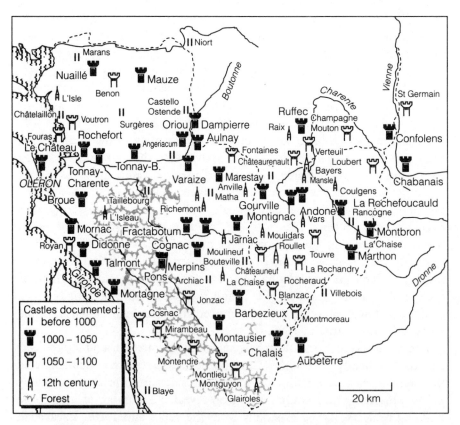

Figure 2   Castles in the Charente in the eleventh and twelfth centuries

detailed surveys has been carried out. All were centres of comital or episcopal authority. But scribal practice may be responsible for these isolated references: it is possible that in the period before the old terminology was abandoned, fortifications devoid of public function were simply not mentioned. References to castles increase rapidly in the first half of the eleventh century. A further ten are recorded in Anjou, another thirty-six in the Charente, and of these a third appear to have been held by individuals who did not exercise any authority delegated from their overlord. References to previously undocumented mottes in Lorraine and Anjou are highest in the period 1050–75; however, this was also the period which saw a great increase in the number of documents produced. According to Debord, the majority of these castles were built by great landholders to support the exercise of power which was 'neither a continuation of old patterns of patronage, nor a substitute for the weakened regalian duty to preserve peace and uphold justice (the *ban*)'. In other words, there was no continuity with previous practices. It is likely that there was widespread and uncontrolled castle-building during the period which saw the fusion of public and private justice. The Norman document *Constitutiones et justitiae*, drawn up in 1091, supports this view. It put in writing the principles established by William the Conqueror forty years earlier, when he reasserted his rights and attempted to control castle-building, because this threatened his own authority. The problem continued, for the text of 1091 spells out that, 'in Normandy the digging of ditches with the aid of a ladder is prohibited, as is the construction of more than a single palisade; there must not be a circular walkway around it, nor angles created along its course; the fortification of a rocky outcrop or island is forbidden in all circumstances.' Relatively low walls might be built around existing baileys, but there were to be no new mottes or castles. This is clear evidence that castles continued to be built in the mid-eleventh century, and that territorial princes were forced to exert considerable pressure in order to contain this tendency.

The keep was a power-base. Its commander sometimes ruled in the name of a superior, a king or count. He was always known by the office entrusted to him, as 'castellan' or *castellanus*. In the majority of cases, however, he had no effective overlord. He was the master – a fact reflected in the title of *dominus* he assumed (*sire* or 'lord' in the vernacular), which had been previously reserved for king or prelate. And indeed, he exercised full regalian powers. However the castle was held, it was the castellan's responsibility to uphold justice – for no one doubted that rulers had been entrusted with the sword of justice, so that peace could be maintained on earth. He flew the banner round which the warriors gathered once he had uttered the castle's war-cry. For this was a public office and, as such, indivisible. When the lord was dying, or if he became senile and could no longer carry out his functions, he passed on the exercise of his authority to one of his sons (usually the eldest), or – if there were no sons – to a brother or nephew; the least favoured successor was his eldest daughter's husband, but this was sometimes the only option. His successor was formally acknowledged as lord in the castle hall by everybody present. This was also an opportunity to address them all and remind them of their obligations. The description of this ritual in the *History of the Lords of Amboise* of the mid-twelfth century is to all intents and purposes identical to that of the tenth-century account by Dudo of St Quentin of the ceremonies of the Norman freebooters when they realized that they were failing, or left on pilgrimage.

This 'master' was the indisputable leader and head of a body of men. 'Head of a house' is the description in one charter from the Mâconnais of 1100. Beneath him was his *maisnie* or *manade* (household), which fell into two distinct parts: there were the servants responsible for looking after horses and equipment and then the warriors. Like their lord, who was sometimes known as the *'maître du château'* (literally, 'master of the castle'), his warriors were also defined by their relationship to the castle, and known as the *'guerriers du château'* (warriors of the castle) – the expression habitually employed by scribes in charters and chronicles of the period. The lord was regarded very much as the 'father' of this group. The strong influence of the familial model is reflected in the fact that the lord had to ask his warriors for advice before he arranged the marriage of a son or a daughter, and their agreement to any succession was imperative.

Sometimes (notably when the lordship passed to a son-in-law) their agreement paid no more than lip-service to the old lord's wishes, and the successor was viewed by some of the garrison as a hostile intruder. When a new lord died in strange circumstances, suspicions were directed first towards his wife, soon after to the warriors of the castle garrison. Younger brothers, nephews, cousins and, above all, bastards might all be found within their ranks, each of them a potential heir. For the 'family' of knights at the castle was also a clan. The group's cohesiveness did not stem from this, however, but depended above all upon concepts of friendship and loyalty to foster a sense of group identity and comradeship, the corner-stones of corporate action. This is reflected in their sobriquets – 'the fat', 'the poorly shod' or 'the red-headed', which were eventually passed from father to son. Finally, just as in a monastery the monks held – jointly with their 'father' abbot – the possessions and rights which belonged to the saints whose relics were venerated there, in the same way the lord's warriors were co-possessors of seigneurial authority, and the lord could not act without their advice. They also helped the lord to assert that authority.

Bonnassie is correct in seeing the periodic tours of the locality by mounted warriors from the castle as a means of intimidating the peasantry and ensuring their greater docility. It was the fact that they were on horseback that distinguished these raids by the lord's men from those of the common soldiers, whom they in turn controlled and terrorized. They were totally loyal in adversity, emboldened by the knowledge that if a castle fell into enemy hands, it was not unusual for the permanent garrison to be blinded or have their right hands cut off if they were not all killed outright.

Life for these warriors was brutal and fiercely competitive; they slept together as a body in the castle hall (like monks in their dorter) after the tables for their communal meal had been removed, and their feelings towards their fellow-warriors were probably often ambivalent, veering sharply from love to hatred. Their numbers were increased by other knights who did periods of service there because they owed allegiance to the castellan. These others lived on their own lands, which were usually situated within the castellany, sometimes farther afield. This is how the castle guard was organized at Vendôme in about 1025: in April and May (months which saw the most intense military activity, represented in the calendar scenes carved above the porches of great churches by a soldier cantering through leafy trees) the count himself formed the guard with his 'chamber knights' – the group I have just described; for seven other months of the year, however, the castle was guarded by a different class of warriors. In this case the same Latin word, *miles* (soldier), is used to describe them, but here it refers to the individual, rather than the group. Scribes who were careful about social distinctions qualified the forename with *miles*, while the surname (which became increasingly common in the early eleventh century) referred to the land they held. These men were socially superior to the others: contemporary writers describe two categories of mounted warriors, and the *milites gregarii*, who spent their life together as members of their lord's entourage, were definitely inferior to those who were equally bound to perform military service and castle guard, but did so freely as a privilege of their birth.

Exceptionally rich sources from the abbey of Cluny indicate that in the early eleventh century knights in this area, who had an individual title and had been girded with a sword-belt (symbol of their function), came from families which had once provided the Carolingian kings of France with counts and bishops. With the introduction of castellan lordship, however, their noble descent and ancestral lands naturally placed them above the rest of the population. They did not all come from families who had the right to raise mottes of their own, which is why they performed military service in the neighbouring castle, the assembly point for the entire locality in any emergency. When the royal army advanced towards the Mâconnais

to quell the brigands that were terrorizing the area in the mid-twelfth
century, small groups assembled separately in different castles. When the
lord raised his banner, they helped him in attack or defence. They came
to the castle to perform an agreed period of military service (the contemporary term was *stage*) within its walls. At Vendôme, for example,
seven landholders in succession spent a month with the count during the
quiet period of the year, when there was unlikely to be much military
activity, enjoying his hospitality within the narrow confines of the castle.
While they performed their castle guard, these knights lived at their lord's
expense and enjoyed his largesse. Specific revenues were also assigned to
them from the profits of the castellany. The sum was unlikely to be very
large, but at this period the symbolic worth of a gift was as important as its
monetary value. It was a sign of the bond between lord and knight, called
'*fevum*' in contemporary documents.

Some of the count's own warriors joined this group as the lord arranged
marriages for them one by one and endowed them with land. They retained closer links with the castle: twenty-five of the fifty-five knights who
performed castle guard at Picquigny (in Picardy) in the late twelfth century
had lands nearby, and owed longer periods of service. It seems very
probable that they were the descendants of household knights who had
been retained in precisely this way. The military elite of the region was
thus not confined entirely to the old nobility; it did tend to close ranks,
however. By virtue of their service, its members effectively escaped the
other obligations and dues imposed by the castellan. Every dependent
member (male and female) of their household also benefitted from this
exemption. Their individual houses were surrounded by small-scale earth-
works and often flanked by the parish church; each one was an enclave
within castellan jurisdiction, where it was both the lord's right and his duty
to maintain law and order. Within the little world of his own dependents,
the subordinate lord exercised the same kind of power as the castellan
himself over a much larger region. Thus, benefitting from such extensive
authority and exempt from seigneurial taxation (although sharing in its
profits through the many different gifts they received from the lord), these
warriors formed a class in the true sense of the word, exploiting the
peasants, the worker class. The nobility was not a completely closed
section of society, but the fact that it was hereditary made it exceptionally
stable.

In the few regions of northern France for which there is adequate
historical evidence, there seems to have been little increase in the number
of noble families during the eleventh and twelfth centuries; if anything,
there was a tendency towards contraction. I believe this was because the
nobility adopted the family model of the territorial princes, which had

evolved to sustain the exercise of their public authority. We have already seen how, in the tenth century, the power of the territorial princes was indivisible: a single male inherited it, entire and complete, from his predecessor, father or brother. Strict matrimonial policies ensured that disputes were generally avoided. The head of the family endeavoured to find husbands for all his daughters, so that new alliances might be formed through the close ties that later developed between the children of these unions and their maternal uncles. Great care was taken, however, to ensure that wives were not found for all the sons. Unless an opportunity arose for providing a younger son with land and resources to establish his own household, only one of the sons was married. These precautions ensured that there was a continuous line of descent in royal and princely houses. When public authority became fragmented, the same customs were applied within each castellany in order to preserve it in its entirety. Then it was gradually transferred through the knights who performed castle guard and held fiefs, and so on down through the social pyramid. When Canon Lambert of Wattrelos recorded his genealogy in the *Annales Cameracenses* in the mid-twelfth century, he believed the founder of his house to have been a great-great-uncle who had been a knight in an episcopal household; he had been given a domain of his own by his lord a century before.

The net result of these practices was to limit male marriage and introduce a very considerable disruptive element into aristocratic society. Most adult male sexual activity was inevitably illicit, and the number of bastard offspring consequently increased, although in fact they were not the prime cause of unrest. The majority were destined for a career in arms, and were probably better integrated within the family group than their legitimate brothers, since their total exclusion from the inheritance meant that they were allowed to stay in the family home. Legitimate sons and nephews, however, were generally sent to another noble household at the end of their childhood. Just as early medieval kings brought up the sons of their vassals, so the territorial princes made the sons of castellans welcome at their courts, and the castellans in turn took in and trained the sons of local knights. This practice both fostered and simultaneously mitigated disorder. Once they were old enough to bear arms, these younger sons did not return to their father's household, but stayed with their adoptive father, serving him ably in the hope that one day they would be rewarded with the supreme prize of wife and lands. The lord himself was glad to have these *juvenes* (young men) with him, for they were the mainstay of his power and prestige. But their very presence justifiably made him more aggressive, and it was for this reason that they were a destabilizing factor. These volatile and over-mighty warrior bands, always eager for fighting or plundering expeditions, posed a considerable threat to the peace which it was their leaders' duty to preserve. The political system which had been established during the crisis described by Ralph Glaber concealed a warrior element that was extremely difficult to control. It did at least have the advantage of checking the growth of unruly bands of peasants, since access to knighthood was strictly controlled by birth.

In the eyes of the scribes of eleventh-century charters, the structure of lay society was extremely simple. It had two components: one consisted of the warriors and retainers of the prince, for whom the Latin word *miles* was employed (rendered in the vernacular as *chevalier*, or 'knight'); the other of the peasants who worked the land, the *rustici*. The latter were completely controlled by the lord, whatever their status – whether they were natives of the place (*manants*), new arrivals (*hôtes*) obliged to make some kind of formal submission to the lord about which very little is known, or visitors (*aubains*), who came under the lord's protection whilst they were in his lands. They were also referred to simply as 'the poor', in recognition of their vulnerable position and inability to defend themselves. The castellan's duty towards them was twofold. In the first place, he was responsible for their safety, especially that of travellers, who had to be protected from unscrupulous inhabitants. If they were the victims of crime, he had to ensure retribution on their behalf, punishing murder, theft, rape, arson and adultery. These were capital crimes, committed against the community, and this vengeance therefore took the form of public justice. The injured party did not have to lodge a formal plea for the culprit to be brought to justice and punished by exposure, flagellation, mutilation or hanging. This was high justice and no one – not even the dependent nobility – was exempt from it.

In exchange for the security he gave them, the lord made demands on the peasantry. Like the king, his first requirement was for assistance so that he could carry out his role. Able-bodied inhabitants were expected to follow the lord's mounted troops on foot. Theoretically they were unarmed, but in practice they carried any weapon but a sword – and the nobles' fear of popular uprising is testimony to their efficacy. Above all, they were expected to make a contribution to public defence through manual work, especially forced labour. It was the peasantry who dug out ditches and raised the motte, cut stakes for palisades and built them. It has been calculated that fifty men had to work for forty days in order to build a small fortress, but sometimes the work had to be done much more quickly: according to the *Chronicle* of the counts of Angoulême, 700 labourers – the entire male population of an area in the count's jurisdiction – completed a castle in just three days. Knights were little use against an enemy castle, and miners were drawn from the village population; it was they who breached the castle walls and helped Louis VI to bring low the proudest of his rebellious vassals. In this instance their work was seen as sacred, furthering the divine cause upon earth. But other sources suggest that their role in battle was generally far less elevated. Every chronicler attributes base deeds to the peasantry, contrasting them with the higher moral code of the knights. If the historian of the lords of Amboise is to be believed, the unfortunate decapitation during a skirmish of an enemy castellan (a relative of their own lord, moreover) was the responsibility of peasants mobilized to accompany the knights. Finally, they had also to do a regular period of duty on the castle keep: at Vendôme it was the peasants' responsibility during June, July and August. One possible reason for the building of so many castles may have been the desire to concentrate conscripted soldiers in a number of selected sites; they probably also hoped to divert some of the profits of peasant commerce towards the castle.

Most important of all, however, were the various dues paid by the ordinary peasant to the lord. Two words were mainly employed to describe them: *exactio*, or levy (without any of the negative connotations of the modern word 'exaction') and *consuetudo*, meaning custom. The latter became common about the year 1000. In surviving written sources it is found especially in royal charters confirming ecclesiastical privileges, most frequently in relation to church liberties. These documents secured the abolition of specific and allegedly excessive dues from men over whom ecclesiastical lords claimed to have jurisdiction. These dues were described as evil customs, or 'new' – which came to the same thing. It would be wrong to assume that they really were unjust. The only reason why bishops, monks or canons demanded the suppression of levies collected by someone else was in order that they should be paid to them instead. For frequently they also owned castles, manned by bands of knights, and offered the same protection to the peasantry of the surrounding area as a secular lord. They were consequently entitled to make the same demands – sometimes heavier – and they certainly collected what was owed to them more efficiently, because ecclesiastical lordships were managed on a more rational basis.

If some customs were described as bad, others were by implication good. Indeed, the very word 'custom' implies the consent of the men who paid them and who preserved the memory of just practices. They were just because they appeared to offer specific advantages. The level of seigneurial taxation was determined by the constantly shifting balance between the desire of the lords for profit and the resistance of the peasantry to their demands, combined with the skill with which they replied to the lord's inquiries. The concept of oppressive lordship is thoroughly unhelpful, and it is important to remember that in return for the contributions which they made, the peasants received advantages comparable to those which we expect from the modern State.

Finally, it is important to remember that the tithe system was not created complete, but evolved gradually from the system which had supported the State long before. When the officials of the late Roman Empire had to travel on public business, they had a right to free lodging and hospitality for themselves and their retinue. The eleventh- and twelfth-century right of free lodging (which saw a lord move into his tenants' houses in town or countryside) was rooted in ancient tradition. This was why it was accepted, despite its devastating effect upon the community. It is possible that for some while this was the only contribution expected from the inhabitants of a district in return for the maintenance of law and order. The late Roman period also saw people who used roads, bridges and rivers paying those whose duty it was (on behalf of the State) to maintain the peace necessary for trade and to guarantee fair measures. Road tolls (*péages*) inevitably succeeded the taxes levied on goods transported by water (*tonlieux*).

What was new was the transfer of executive power to the hands of subordinate officials of much lower rank, the *prévôts* whom the castellans expected to collect their dues. The increasing greed of everyone associated with public administration was also unprecedented. For the lords themselves, lordship meant business, but even more so for their agents. As peasant communities became more prosperous, so the lord's dues also grew. They ensured that their right to tithe (or to take a proportion of the peasants' surplus) and levy tolls became accepted custom. This was the price of security, and it was one which tended to rise all the time. However, the fact that the peasants were forced to make collective payments meant that they were better placed to resist pressure for increases from the lord and his agents. The lord's duty to protect the community and avenge any wronged member through the prosecution of justice was not open to question, however, and it had been the practice since time immemorial for a judge to levy fines on offenders or confiscate goods for capital crimes, as a contribution towards the restoration of public order.

The level of seigneurial taxation inevitably tended to rise, precisely because it was based upon custom and established practice. There was, in fact, an increase over a period of time, but at a rate which was indisputably less than that of the rise in the peasant population or the profits upon which it was calculated. A smaller proportion of peasant surplus seems to have gone to the lord in the twelfth century than in the year 1000. The system certainly had a powerful influence upon social and economic development in France. It forced the peasants to work the soil as profitably as possible in order to meet the lord's demands, simultaneously reducing their free time and ensuring the circulation of any surpluses. The circulation of liquid capital increased rapidly during this period. Piety was the most important force behind this trend, motivating donations to churches in the hope of salvation, but the second factor was the lord's authority to levy fines and confiscate goods. This might swell the sums the lord shared among his followers, or it might – especially among knights of a lower rank – simply be squandered. It also tended to iron out distinctions between the peasantry. This was partly because seigneurial dues were levied indiscriminately upon free and villein households alike, which tended to eliminate the distinctions between them: the old words for 'slave' all gradually became obsolete in the course of the eleventh century. In this context the entire village community was treated alike; and in the earlier period, levels were sufficiently high for discrepancies in peasant wealth to be reassimilated. Finally, these exactions created a huge gulf between those who had to pay them and the fighting men and churchmen who were exempt on account of the services they rendered to society in their different ways. In other words, seigneurial taxation divided society into two separate camps. On one side, solidarity developed from resistance; on the other, there was the arrogance of privilege and contempt for those outside it.

The territory protected by a castle was called a '*détroit*' (or district) in contemporary documents, a word derived from the Latin *distringere*, meaning to coerce. Order had to be established by force within this area, and it was uncompromising towards the common people. The man who commanded the castle was *dominus*, or master: he was set over the peasants who lived in the surrounding area and over any who travelled through this territory. In the spoken vernacular he was referred to as '*sire*', a word derived from Latin *senior*, meaning the oldest. This expression was a very precise definition of the other form of power exercised by the lord, that of a fighting lord over his warriors.

The warriors were also bound by a system of constraint, but one which they had entered of their own free will. It was their duty to love the lord under whose banner they fought, just as young men loved the father of a family. Their relationship was to be like the bond between nephew and maternal uncle, so strong in earlier Germanic societies, or between Roland and Charlemagne, or Tristan and King Mark. This was the natural condition of blood-relations, a fact that made lineage and marriage alliances exceptionally important in this society. The knights of a castellany were not all interrelated, however, and the requisite loyalty and devotion were instilled in part by symbolic gestures of adoption. The knight-aspirant was required to kneel and place both his hands between those of his future lord. In addition to this fundamental sign of the abdication of self-interest (which the lord demanded from the most humble dependent), there was also the kiss of peace, which was a positive gesture of mutual alliance exchanged between lord and man standing side by side as equals. This was the ceremony of homage, a ritual which bound the two men to mutual love, counsel and aid. Then there was an oath, by which the young knight swore allegiance, or fealty, to the older (his lord), promising that he would be obedient and loyal.

Contractual obligations of this kind, which were freely undertaken, were based upon an ethic instilled at court by the lord himself and the priests of his household. This ethic had previously been embodied in a purely oral tradition; in the twelfth century it was also expressed in written literary forms, communicated through heroes for whom loyalty was the cardinal virtue. The authors of these didactic works took the concept of friendship found in Cicero and Seneca and applied it to the duty of vassal to lord, where self-sacrifice for another might indeed be required. The knightly class, with their swords and horses, were dependent upon the peasantry for material support, but this was the ethos which upheld public order. Where this code was insufficiently powerful, the turbulent elements within such a rapacious and militarily based society soon became out of hand, for their quick tempers soon led to feuds and resentment. The lord had to settle endless disputes between the highest-ranking knights outside his household, who claimed the prerogative rights of nobility. Nobility obliged them to practice specific virtues, as their ancestors before them, subordinate to none. In the poem he addressed to King Robert of France, Adalbero of Laon stated: 'It is the nobility's privilege to be free from subordination to any other power, with the exception of crimes that are referred to royal justice.' In other words they did not enjoy unqualified immunity from prosecution. But who would check nobles who overstepped the law when – as in the eleventh century – the king himself was weak?

Seigneurial justice was extended to knights of the region who had done homage to the lord. This was done with a certain amount of tact and flexibility, however. Sometimes the lord might turn to the essentially superstitious practice of the ordeal in order to put an end to feuding, organizing single combats which seem to have been little more than regulated vendettas. These were controlled brawls between two single opponents, conducted publicly within an enclosed space, a context in which the search for right took on all the allure of competitive sport. Alternatively, the lord might act as formal arbitrator, listening to arguments from supporters of both parties, hoping to achieve a compromise which might be sealed with the ritual kiss of peace. In practice, his authority was made effective through hospitality. Knights were less quarrelsome in groups – hence the undertaking given by those of them who did not reside at the castle permanently to spend a fixed period there each year when requested by their lord, and to lodge their sons with him during their adolescence. In this more structured environment the warriors were more disciplined and easily controlled: their life was spent in a tightly knit group, sharing every aspect of their daily life on campaign and eating together in their lord's castle in times of peace. Here the supremely important virtue of largesse had a crucial role to play. The lord's generosity ensured the loyalty of his vassals and guaranteed peace, for it was his duty to share out the profits of seigneurial justice. It was the price the lord had to pay for their service. The only check on the knights living within this confined space stemmed from this reciprocity. They expected the lord to use some of the profits of justice and seigneurial taxation to provide them with entertainment, feasts, wives, lodging and, eventually, a fief. In exchange they gave him aid and council. It was this mutual obligation which to some extent checked the most extreme outbursts of violence within the group of warriors attached to each castle.

What preserved their group identity more than anything else, however, was their enthusiasm for combat and the sheer enjoyment of raiding expeditions together. This of course was a powerful impulse towards disorder in each lordship. The hordes of carefree warriors who from time to time poured out of the castle in a ravaging swarm were an inevitable cause of unrest. Monastic chroniclers went so far as to pun on the Latin words *militia* and *malitia*, identifying evil with the soldiery from the castle. To put an end to this did not require tighter control of the individual knight – he was already integrated within a highly structured group existence at the castle. Rather, it was the modes of combat themselves and the premium placed upon raiding expeditions and aggression as a means of securing group identity that had to be tackled. This was the greatest single problem resulting from the fragmentation of political and judicial power. Throughout France the lords from whom these castellanies were theoretically held strove to solve this major problem.

I think it is appropriate to analyse a specific example at this juncture, using a text which was recopied by a monk of St Cybard of Angoulême in the middle of the eleventh century. It is of especial interest because the author uses a form of Latin particularly close to the contemporary vernacular, so that for once these events are recorded in expressions close to those actually employed by churchmen of the period. The scribe was a cleric, but employed in a secular and domestic capacity as a household clerk: his aim was to record events as clearly as possible, so that they could be understood by as many people as possible, and this is what makes his narrative refreshingly unsophisticated. That is not to say that it is characterized by transparent honesty; there are passages where the truth is indubitably suppressed. Nevertheless, it is immensely revealing about the way in which medieval man saw these events.

The writer's subject is the long-standing quarrel between the castellan, Hugh, lord of Lusignan, and William, referred to in this narrative as the count of the 'Aquitanians', or the count of Poitiers. At the time of writing these two had become reconciled, and Hugh had once more paid homage to the ageing count and his eldest son. (The two are linked, as the French Robert II and his son were at this date: in both cases the older man hoped to secure a trouble-free succession for his son by their association at the end of his life.) Hugh ordered the document to be drawn up, and it is inevitably biased towards his point of view; it was to be a record of the agreement that had just been reached between himself and William of Poitiers, but was doubtless also intended to provide adequate pretext for any future dispute and to incorporate bargaining points for any subsequent negotiations. Written documents carried increasing weight in this part of France. Ritual undoubtedly still played a vital role, and public utterances in front of a large assembly were the most binding aspect of any agreement; but an accompanying document (suitably covered with text in everyday Latin, rather than that of scholars or churchmen) was becoming standard practice. This particular text can be dated from internal evidence to the 1020s.

Its subject is the relations between the most prestigious of the French territorial princes and the lord of a castle near Poitiers, the principality's most important town. At this period other sources refer to the count as William 'the Great'. His apologists endow him with an aura of glory and success. Adhémar of Chabannes, for example, claimed that he 'subordinated the entire region of Aquitaine to his lordship', that the count of Anjou performed homage to him, while he also won the favour of the French king and the friendship of the Emperor. On a visit to Rome the Pope supposedly addressed him by the imperial title of 'Augustus', and 'he would have been taken for a king rather than a duke at any public ceremony'. In our text William does not cut such a grand figure. He breaks his word, lies and maintains his position by deceit and trickery. In reality his power was not so very great; nor did he fulfil the obligations of his office, for Aquitaine was racked by bloody quarrels. The writer paints a grim picture of mutilation, arson, pillage and incessant feuding.

The primary cause of these disputes was the fragmentation into separate components of the old political system which had provided a foundation for the peace which it was the territorial princes' duty to uphold. Three terms described these component parts: 'fisc', referred to the prince's public authority; 'honour', the function of *vicomtes* and castellans; and finally 'castle' – and here the reality underpinning the other two terms is revealed. For castles were the stakes in the deadly game played out in Aquitaine. The text reveals clearly what contemporaries understood by *castrum* (castle): it was a coherent whole, consisting of the defensive build-ings and the knights who garrisoned them, together with their legitimate rights (*rectitudines*) over the subject peasantry in the surrounding country-side. The combined value of these assets was considerable: the report of an estimated 50,000 *sous*' worth of damage resulting from a single attack on the castle of Confolens alone was exaggerated, but makes the general point. A castle, with all its associated wealth, was exceptionally vulnerable. It was particularly susceptible to arson, although sometimes the keep (possibly built in stone) or some other central building survived. At Confolens, for example, the 'old castle' survived relatively intact, but the surrounding wooden palisades and bailey were completely destroyed. The knights within were equally at risk. Our source describes how Hugh captured a castle without destroying it and proceeded to have the entire garrison thrown from the top of the keep, thereby purging the entire area of his enemies. The *vicomte* of Thouars captured and burnt a castle: in this case the defeated knights escaped with their lives, but their right hands were amputated, ensuring that they would never fight again. No doubt this was an act of uncontrolled rage; certainly, it was not the canniest thing to do, and when Hugh of Lusignan took revenge and captured forty-three of the *vicomte*'s knights, he ransomed them for the substantial sum of 40,000 *sous*, which virtually offset the costs of the expedition. In themselves the castle buildings were worth little more than a cottage of one of the peasant tenants: they could be quickly demolished and almost as speedily rebuilt and equipped. In fact the victor often started rebuilding while the ruins of the old castle were still smouldering. He did not always complete the work, and this may be one explanation for the large number of mottes revealed by excavation. In any case the fiscs and 'honours', which had upheld the old political system and were still believed to give authority to the new, changed hands continually. It was a violent and cruel way of life: who in fact controlled it?

Here it may be helpful to return to our first impression, that the lack of any real power was the real cause of the count of Aquitaine's treachery, although for much of the time it might appear that this demi-king called the tune throughout the region. Hostilities were frequently interrupted, in fact. Significantly, the most common expression in this long narrative is '*finem facere*' (bring to an end). It is used particularly in relation to raids and *chevauchées*. In the ensuing lull the opposing sides were brought together for negotiations, in an attempt to bring their dispute to an amicable and peaceful end. The ancient word *placitum* is frequently used in this context, with overtones of the ninth century, when all the great lords of the Empire were summoned to hear Charlemagne pass formal judgement. It is true that from time to time Count William made a formal progress to the borders of his lands to hold court there. This would be the setting for discussions with neighbouring princes – at Blaye, for instance, with Sancho, duke of Gascony; or on his northern frontier with Count Fulk of Anjou. These meetings held in the 'marches' (or boundary lands) were intended to be friendly and peaceful. William was also a great peacemaker within the duchy as count of Poitiers. When there was conflict within a lordship, he first imposed a thirty-day truce (such as that which halted conflict between Hugh of Lusignan and Bernard of La Marche after three days of fighting); then, at some point during the following two weeks, he personally joined the right hands of the two opponents in a ceremony of formal reunion (known as the '*fin*'), curiously similar to the plighting of troth before marriage.

The *fin* was generally an agreement between the two reconciled parties. The word *conventum* is also very common, meaning an agreement based upon mutual trust. These good intentions were backed by guarantees. The bishop of Angoulême bore witness to the first formal agreement between Count William and Hugh of Lusignan: 'He saw, he listened and he kissed the count's hand' – a gesture all the more significant because this was the hand that held the sword of justice. There is a clear sequence of three principal actions: hearing, seeing and commitment to the agreement, promising aid to the injured party. The agreement was further underwritten by formal pledges, a practice known as *otage*. If the dispute centred upon a castle, this might take the form of the knights who garrisoned it; or it might be land, such as their fief. Whatever the nature of the hostages offered by the two sides, the territorial prince laid sole claim to them, as custodian of peace in the region.

Of course the count was not in a position to regulate all such agreement. Warriors often reached independent agreement. There were also any number of ineffective *fins*, as well as assemblies which ended in total failure, with the protagonists going their separate ways still unreconciled. Nevertheless, the count could break any agreements which had been concluded without him and to his disadvantage. What is most striking is the way in which the territorial prince remained personally responsible for the maintenance of peace within his lands. This gave rise to a great flurry of punitive expeditions and displays of force. The prince was far from being in control of this situation, but neither did he follow passively in its wake.

Equally, the count had first claim to all fortified sites. The authority to dispose of them as he wished and to reap the advantages of this largesse was in many ways the bedrock of his power. Other benefits that accrued to him through the exercise of princely authority, such as the widows and orphans of former followers, were also judiciously distributed amongst his followers. Castles and the vicecomital powers that were now identified with them were only granted conditionally; anyone who wanted to construct a new building on the site of an old one had, at least theoretically, to obtain his consent first. His power overrode inheritance customs: it was by 'grace' of the territorial prince that a nephew succeeded to his uncle's rights – the count claiming a part of the succession in the course of the transaction. William made considerable use of his right of reversion to ensure that no one individual held sizeable clusters of castles. Division and dispersal was his policy wherever possible, and supplicants were often given no more than a portion of seigneurial rights. It is by no means clear that the rights of a son to his father's inheritance were automatically acknowledged. Certainly Hugh of Lusignan seems to have been deprived of some portions of his patrimony. There were disadvantages to this policy; it bred resentment and bitterness, with men motivated above all by greed. Castles were the source of endless disagreements; the lord chosen by the prince and holding the castellany in commendation from him might be opposed by those who recalled that the fortress had once been held by a distant cousin, or by the influential garrison: they might form an alliance against him and substitute one of their own number as lord. The authority of the territorial prince had its roots in long-established political practice, but it was by no means uncontested and William could only make full use of it by resorting to devious means. He was forced to strengthen his position by recourse to the customs regulating private agreements, with increasing emphasis upon personal dependence. This was the essential prerequisite for the evolution of a different political system, which we call 'feudalism'.

The document which is our source was drawn up because Hugh had just made formal acknowledgement of his status as the liegeman (*homo*) of the count of Aquitaine. It is interesting that this is not the word employed by the scribe, however, to describe the warriors attached to the castle. Here he uses *vassalus* (vassal) instead. In other words, he perceived that the relationship between prince and castellan (or other castle-holding lord) was essentially different from that between the castellan and his knights.[1]

---

[1] For a slightly different analysis, see '*Conventum inter Guillelmum Aquitanorum comes et Hugonem Chiliarchum*', ed. J. Martindale, *English Historical Review*, 84(1969), pp. 528–48–tr.

Despite the biased nature of this account, emphasizing as it does all the
humiliating aspects of the Lusignan position with a view to excusing his
revolt and, if need be, also condoning future contumacy – despite all this,
it is clear that the tie between lord and man was regarded as exceptionally
strong. This power lay in its appeal to concepts of love and personal
friendship. The liegeman was, by definition, his overlord's good and
trusted friend. (The word *fidelis* – meaning a man who keeps his word – is
sometimes also used.) This reciprocal bond created obligations on both
sides; our text naturally enough stresses the overlord's commitment to
mutual trustworthiness. If he made a promise, it was 'as a lord should
make promises to his liegeman'; if he gave an undertaking, it was 'as a
lord should keep faith with his liegeman'. Despite the garbled Latin, a
quality far stronger than mere fidelity is communicated, and a much
more demanding bond than mere friendship between two individuals is
portrayed, particularly exacting in its commitment to mutual aid. This was
not a mutual obligation between equals, however. The lord's 'good faith'
was met by total self-sacrifice on the part of his liegeman, who now
effectively belonged to his overlord. 'You are mine' (or, more accurately,
'exist through me' – the Latin is *'ex me'*, with distinct overtones of
paternity and procreation); 'You are my man and your duty is to do my
will', Count William tells Hugh at one point, and indeed this is what Hugh
himself asserts throughout. If we are to believe his own words, Hugh was
quite ready to be his lord's loyal servant, despite his keen sense of betrayal
and bitterness: 'I put my whole trust in you'; 'I have been your servant.'

In particular, Hugh had to accept his liege lord's command to perform
homage to other lords, against his own wishes and inclination. Indeed, at
one point in the narrative, Count William tells him, 'You are my liegeman,
and if I were to command you to do homage to a peasant, it would be your
duty to obey.' In reality, Hugh of Lusignan appears to have had to accept
three other lords: the count of Anjou, the bishop of Poitiers and the count
of La Marche. To the two latter he paid the form of homage known as
'commendation', so that he might hold part of the rights to a castle from
them. The initiative for these double, triple and even quadruple agreements seems to have come from the count of Aquitaine. The count had to
persuade his liegeman to transfer the love he had for himself to another.
This was only achieved with considerable difficulty: in one case Hugh held
out against his lord's wishes for a year. Counts and bishops were of the
same rank as himself, and undoubtedly constituted a threat to his authority. William seems to have used the lord of Lusignan very much as a
pawn on the chessboard of regional politics, putting him in a position of
dependence with these various rivals so that he might perhaps eventually
secure another castle – rather as a father made marriage alliances with a

view to increasing his influence within another dynasty. Finally, these 'commendations' were just as binding upon Hugh as his act of homage to William. 'You are my man, and in my jurisdiction,' the count of Anjou reminds him, as he forbids Hugh to seize something to which he has no right. In these cases homage was performed for material advantage.

In fact every knight expected a concrete reward from his lord in return for his service, whether it took the form of a wife or the grant of an 'honour' or lordship. Service was pointless without the lord's largesse. The count of Poitiers controlled many castles, but in practice he was forced to give them to his knights in return for their homage. If he promised and did not deliver, the castle would be taken from him by force. For the lord's worst enemies were the knights who had waited too long for his generosity and, believing themselves deceived (or, as they would have put it, betrayed), finally turned against him. This was what happened in the case of Hugh of Lusignan, who relates how he came 'to mistrust the count because of the deviousness he had so often encountered'. The count, he alleged, had endlessly broken the bond of trust that a lord owed his liegeman, because he would not give him castles or parts of castles. This was the specific cause of Hugh's frustration. William had not supported him when the knights of Civray surrendered the castle there (to which he laid claim) to the count of La Marche; 'the lord whom he had accepted on the advice of the count of Poitiers had deprived him of his authority (fisc).' If this secondary bond was broken, then it was the duty of the liege lord to look after his vassal's interest and recover whatever was due to him. In practice he could only hope to reconcile the two parties; in this case, peace was very soon broken, as the lord of Lusignan attacked a motte held by Bernard of La Marche, burnt it and proceeded to ask William for permission to build another castle there. This particular castle was in fact held from the count of Anjou. William took a cautious line and ordered Hugh to desist. There were lengthy discussions; promises were made; but ultimately Hugh defied his lord: 'You have spoken many fine words to me, my lord, but you have betrayed me. . . . Do not attempt to harm my interests, because if you do, I will not be your liegeman any more and I will no longer serve you.' Hugh finally gave in and withdrew his garrison from the castle. But he also saw this as a liberating gesture, arguing that if his lord had refused to come to his aid, the oath of fealty he had sworn was no longer valid. In Hugh's hands, the 'fief' of the castle which he had seized gave material support to his defiance, and expressed his freedom from further obligations towards the count of Aquitaine.

Almost immediately, however, Hugh sought to re-establish the bond with his lord and re-enter his service, and I believe this to be highly significant. It demonstrates the clear ascendancy of the territorial princes.

It was abnormal for a knight to be without a liege lord. Within the context of the territorial principality, as in the French kingdom as a whole, there was a general conviction that a man who had charge of a castle (itself a public building) had, by definition, to have some kind of dependent relationship with the individual responsible for public peace throughout the region. Nevertheless, the lord of Lusignan demanded an additional reward to secure his services. The count was in a strong position and refused him: 'If the whole world were at my disposal, I would not give you more than tuppence.' The gauntlet had been thrown down and relations were formally severed in a ceremony at the count's castle at Poitiers, where Hugh demanded what he believed were his rights from his lord with no success whatsoever. Everybody present listened (for this was a time for words rather than gestures), as Hugh publicly 'defied the count'. This formal defiance was consistently and explicitly qualified, 'with the exception of the city [of Poitiers] and the person of the count'. For Hugh was not rebelling against the count in his position of public authority, with which he had no quarrel; and his loyalty as a 'citizen' of the city of Poitiers prevented him from committing any bodily harm to the count as the official responsible for maintaining public peace. Only the personal bond of love and friendship between the two men had been severed. Hostility took the place of service, but it was hostility in a private context, reflected in the term used to describe it, *werra* (*guerre*, or war). 'In the name of private war', William had seized everything that Hugh's vassals held from him by public authority. Hugh retaliated by capturing a poorly guarded fortress so that he was in a strong position to negotiate. Talks succeeded fighting; it was a formally conducted dispute, like so many others, but this time the count was one of the protagonists. Negotiations centred upon the nature of the indispensable gift – the castle.

Hugh wanted everything: the 'honour' his father had held; the same share in the castle he had just seized as his ancestors had once enjoyed; the other castle which he had captured and destroyed, but which he was meant to hold from the count of Anjou; and last of all, his uncle's 'honour', bestowed upon him by the count, but of which he was no doubt subsequently deprived. The count refused all these demands with the exception of his uncle's lordship. The course of the exchanges that followed are highly illuminating. Hugh said, 'I fear you will harm me, as you have on countless other occasions.' William replied, 'You can place every trust in me, for I will give you trustworthy pledges (*fiances*).' Whereupon Hugh objected, 'You are my lord and I should be able to trust you completely without recourse to pledges. I place myself at your mercy and God's.' Eventually, Hugh adopted the role of the prodigal son and asked only that 'by the holy cross upon which Christ hung', the count would agree not to impose anything which would do him harm. The final terms of the agreement were these: 'The count and his son place their trust whole-heartedly in Hugh; they receive him as their liegeman in full faith and trust; they have granted Hugh all his demands; he has sworn allegiance to them and they have also granted him the "honour" of his uncle, as it was held one year before his death.' Here the text stops, and it is by no means unambiguous. Four salient features emerge, however.

Castles were first and foremost the fundamental basis of social order, but they were also an integral part of the 'city' (the most obvious relic of the late Roman State) and the loyalty owed by the castellans to their territorial prince was similar in many ways to the loyalty owed to the State at other periods. They held office in return for the grant of a lordship and enjoyed the rights and resources of their castellanies.

Satellite lords of the territorial princes, on the other hand, were called 'vassals'; they participated in seigneurial power and profits through the fief which they held from the prince. The vocabulary employed stresses the personal nature of the bonds of dependence woven round each castle.

There were problems when the count (who had inherited the power of the territorial princes) had to reckon with the machinations of bishops and neighbouring counts, who were always ready to encroach upon his lands. He had to be able to rely above all upon his liegemen, who quarrelled over the possession of castles and whose intense rivalry sometimes erupted into violence because of secondary agreements based upon temporary guaran-tees. The count had to control these short-term arrangements in his role as guardian of public order. His aim was to have all such agreements formally concluded in the courts which he held from time to time and to ensure that they were then maintained. This was more easily said than done, and in practice the dispute invariably flared up again.

The territorial prince made use of the personal bond to counterbalance these shortcomings, aiming to rally those who held honours round himself, just as these lords provided a focus for the knights of the castle. At the same time he was fully aware that this non-tenurial relationship was an entirely different kind of bond, where loyalty to the public authority was re-enforced by a personal tie. When the territorial prince 'received' a particular castellan into his allegiance, and the castellan pledged his loyalty in turn, the lesser noble henceforth depended on the prince as a son on his father. But the gift of allegiance required gifts in return from the prince. Everything depended upon *credentia*, or trust, for the liegeman trusted not only in his lord, but also in his lord's generosity; his loyalty was under-pinned by the expectation of largesse. In practice, this was an insatiable desire that the prince could never satisfy, since there were no rules and no set definitions of either service or its price. Consequently a territorial prince was always open to accusations of breaking his word and entangled in promises which he could not possibly keep. Falsehoods were endemic at this level of society. Of course the prince could simply refuse to accede to the demands made upon him. Almost none of the very considerable demands made by Hugh were granted. For the time being he was prepared to accept this situation, but he reserved the right to obtain more from the count in the future, and the written account which he had drawn up would then serve as the basis for any future accusation of treachery.

Affective relations thus tended to take the place of the administrative structures which had formerly upheld public order. They did not have the same rigour and consistency. Indeed, they were less formally organized than relations between the castellan and the knights of his castle. If public authority was to be re-established, it was essential for relations with the territorial prince to be formally codified. This is why, at precisely this time, William the Great of Aquitaine turned for assistance and clarification to Fulbert of Chartres, the greatest legal expert of the period. He was, naturally, also a bishop, and there were two reasons for the consultation. In the first place, because the bond between liegeman and liege lord was based upon an oath, which was sacred. Secondly, the Church was governed by a written law, which was rapidly approaching its final form. It has been demonstrated that this was in fact based upon the works of Cicero, rather than canon law.

What were the obligations of the liegeman towards his lord? He was not to harm him or his interests in any way. Fulbert of Chartres used six Ciceronian terms to define this area of loyalty. In the first place there was the person of his lord; then there were the private affairs of his household and the castles which the lord held directly and which offered the knight the security of public protection. This was what Hugh of Lusignan specifically promised to continue to respect after he had broken the personal tie with William; he would still honour his obligations to public authority. The lord's justice, matters in which his honour was at stake, his possessions and any undertakings that he might plan were also inviolable. In other words, loyalty was synonymous with sworn security, and there are close parallels with features of the late Roman political system, which had survived until the early eleventh century. Nevertheless, Fulbert also added some positive aspects. If a vassal held land from his lord, he had not only to refrain from harming his lord, but had to aid him as well, so that this reward should be truly earned. In the six areas we have mentioned he was bound to give his lord assistance and counsel (this was in effect a definition of 'service'), assuming – and this was the point which was so important to Hugh – that the lord discharged his reciprocal obligation. If he did not, he was said to have 'broken his word'. In this case the lord was guilty; however, the vassal who did not carry out his duties toward his lord was more so, for he was perfidious and foresworn. The lord had merely made a promise, whereas his vassal had sworn a solemn oath. If he was convicted of perjury, he could be punished by canon law, as the earthly manifestation of 'divine law'.

The bishop of Chartres was, of course, keenly aware of the interest of the Church: for the Church claimed jurisdiction over cases of perjury, as over marriage disputes and conflicts between temporal powers. He proposed substituting an institution formally sanctioned by a legal code for the unsatisfactory and unreliable combination of familial duty and sworn oath. But this proposal radically changed all the component parts of the system he envisaged. Emphasis was now placed on an element which had hardly featured in Hugh's account of his dispute, the 'benefice', or, more precisely, the provision of land which created the obligation to serve and love his lord. It was no longer a question of a promised gift, but a concrete possession transferred in reality, where the knight now actually lived. This was something very different from a fief, which implied no more than a share in the profits of authority. This reversal revealed feudalism in its clearest form, where investiture with a piece of land and sworn homage and fealty were indissolubly linked; this change meant that the fief was now of cardinal importance.

This was the ideal model drawn for Count William by the lawyer–bishop. It represented a shift from imprecise expectations to specific, positive obligations. Before it was implemented, however, there was a long period of *ad hoc* experimentation. Most importantly of all, the territorial princes had to provide lands to accompany the 'honours' once held by the ancestors of their present vassals, before they could receive service from them.

The evidence of this Poitevin document facilitates a better understanding of the way in which French territorial princes exercised power at this period. Castle-holding was crucial everywhere. In some areas they remained primarily in the hands of the territorial prince. This was the case in the county of Flanders, a region that remained relatively undeveloped and where the Carolingian system had continued. A castellan held each castle from the count of Flanders, who from time to time took up residence close by. In the absence of the count, the castellan presided over judicial assemblies, assisted by free men who were called '*échevins*', as they had been in the Carolingian period. The count was accompanied by all the region's warriors, organized within a single unit, whenever he travelled round his lands. Subordinate counts (such as the count of Guînes) recognized the superiority of the count of Flanders.

There was a similar situation in Normandy. Dudo of St Quentin had celebrated the structure instituted by Rollo, which still prevailed. Rollo had instituted the '*ban*'. According to Dudo, the *ban* was a form of interdict. This was the term for the sanction applied by bishops to those who broke the peace within their diocese; the individual responsible for instigating disorder in a secular context was similarly placed beyond customary law and banned from human society. This was an effective measure, but it led to an increase in pillaging. The duke wanted positive proof, and ordered that ploughs should be left unguarded in the open to demonstrate the firm foundations of peace within his duchy. In the duke's vast lands the *vicomtes* were completely loyal to him, just as the castellans were the faithful servants of the count in Flanders. As for the great lords, they were bound to the duke by 'the oath of loyalty and the ceremony of homage'. Nevertheless, these regulations were threatened by disagreements among the duke's relatives, although the tie of friendship should have bound them most closely to the duke. In the first place there were too many of them, because of the polygamy of their Viking ancestors. Jealous of the duke's succession to the entire dukedom, brothers, uncles and cousins intrigued constantly in the hope of supplanting him or at least seizing some of his lands. Ducal power thus sustained periodic crises. The most serious of these erupted in the first half of the eleventh century. Like most of his predecessors, Duke William was illegitimate; now that the Church had condemned 'Danish concubinage', he was publicly called 'bastard', so that his right to the dukedom might be called into question. In reality, casting aspersions upon his legitimacy was just a convenient pretext for questioning his right to the dukedom. He stood up to them, using the exceptionally strongly fortified castle of Caen as his base. The king of France was glad to have an opportunity to demonstrate his power and influence, and supported him against these relatives, as did William's own genuine clientage, 'new men' employed in his service. William reasserted control over the *vicomtes*, re-established the public peace and used his largesse to secure the services of warriors who, in return, were bound to serve him, properly equipped with a hauberk. To make absolutely sure of his power, William also set off to conquer England, an enterprise that occupied the energies of young warriors not only from Normandy, but from all the regions along the Channel coast. As God's warrior in a holy war, the papal banner flew over his troops and they were accompanied by holy relics. His victory at the battle of Hastings was complete: Harold, his adversary, was killed and William, duke of Normandy, became king of

England. All his loyal supporters were given lands in England, a valuable source of revenue, which he used to build two magnificent abbeys (a monastery and a nunnery) at Caen, partly as thank-offerings for divine mercies and partly to atone for the incest with which stricter clerics reproached him. Moreover, he returned from England with demonstrable sources of lavish rewards with which to secure the loyalty of the Norman nobles. On his death the succession was once more disputed between his sons. The youngest was ultimately successful, and he had the old regulations specifically forbidding the building of private castles read aloud in a general assembly of the nobility, demonstrating yet again that control of castles was of prime importance.

The Angevin principality also had an extremely strong base, for the count built stone castles and led his warriors on profitable expeditions against the Bretons, the Normans, the Franks and the Goths. The counts of Arles and Barcelona and the duke of Gascony pursued a similar policy, leading their knights outside the principality to pillage and preserving tight control within it. When danger threatened and the enemy was on the borders, their own power was strengthened. They could then justifiably attack their neighbours and provide themselves with ample booty with which to reward their followers. The territorial princes who captured castles on the exposed flanks of the French kingdom were conquerors, or 'liberators', of the surrounding countryside.

The territorial princes whose lands were less exposed, such as the duke of Aquitaine, undoubtedly enjoyed enormous prestige. They were related to the Holy Roman Emperor and undertook long pilgrimages with great pomp and ceremony. They collected other princes round them for magnificent ceremonies associated with the discovery or translation of wonderful relics; they summoned bishops to councils and spent huge sums on building churches. However, they were content to maintain a military role that was confined to peace-keeping and emulated the outward appearance of a Charles the Bald or an Otto III. It is possible that they were themselves deluded by the magnificence of these ceremonies – not without reason – and forgot that their first priority was to underpin their power on the ground, castle by castle. In fact, their power crumbled as castles became increasingly independent and (as A. Debord has pointed out) threatened the jurisdiction of prince and subordinate counts. There was progressive erosion of the *ban*, well demonstrated in the southern part of the duchy of Burgundy. In the early eleventh century all ties of allegiance between the count of Mâcon (who was a member of the important lineage of the dukes of Burgundy) and the dukes had been broken. But at the same period the lords of castles in the Mâconnais ceased regular attendance at the courts of the count, whose decisions were consequently ineffectual.

Fifty years later the count controlled no more than a skeletal outline of
the old peace-keeping framework: the citadel of the city (which was its
foundation) and the old roads – all that remained of the Roman system –
with a few tolls and the odd castle here and there. The lords of the most
important castles dispensed justice themselves, settling quarrels between
their knights, while their officers presided over disputes among lower
sections of society to their own profit. On the southern border of the
county of Mâcon, the lord of Beaujeu had succeeded in carving out a small
principality for himself; it was a unified lordship and for this reason was
destined for a brilliant future, despite its size.

A similar dislocation can be observed in the kingdom of France. Although Robert the Pious settled the question of worldwide peace with the
Emperor, in his own ancestral lands he allowed the power of local lords to
grow unchecked, even allowing some of them to assume the title of count.
These men were admittedly loyal to him; indeed, in the latter half of the
eleventh century they formed the largest and most stable element of the
royal entourage, together with the king's relatives and the higher officials
of his household. In their own lands, however, they exploited every
possible regalian right, just as if these were inherited patrimonies.

Despite this dilution of power, however, the idea – communicated in
formulae and titles – remained that this was essentially public power and,
although transmitted by count or duke, its ultimate source was seen to be
God and his consecrated representative on earth, the king. The king saw
the territorial princes as his faithful liegemen, and this was how they saw
themselves, even if (like William of Normandy) they also possessed a
kingdom of their own beyond the borders of France. However, they all
had their own interpretation of the loyalty owed to the king, as is effectively demonstrated by two documents from the same period as Fulbert of
Chartres' letter and the account of the agreement reached between Hugh of
Lusignan and the duke of Aquitaine.

Dudo of St Quentin was quite as erudite as Fulbert, but as a loyal ducal
servant he communicated the opinions of his master. He expressed the
view of the Norman court at Rouen about the bond between Duke Richard
and the king of the Franks. Originally there had been a gift, but one which
carried no obligations: by the terms of the treaty of St Clair-sur-Epte in
911, the king 'gave' Rollo this 'kingdom' to be held 'as an allod in
perpetuity'. An allod was an inheritance which was not subject to any
overlord, although Dudo certainly makes no attempt to conceal the fact
that Rollo also paid homage to the king of France. However, his account is
very insistent on one point, asserting that the Norman noble refused to

bow down as the ceremony required: he remained standing upright, a free man, and took no oath. For their part, the king of France and his great nobles supposedly swore to support him with their 'life, limbs and honour' – words familiar from Fulbert of Chartres as part of the oath made by the vassal to his lord. The clear intention here was to invert the relationship, with the Franks owing all, the Normans nothing. As for Rollo's grandson, Richard I, if we are to believe Dudo, he governed Normandy 'like a king, subject to no one but God, and servant of neither king nor duke' (a clear reference to Hugh the Great, duke of the Franks, father of Hugh Capet). Normandy was emphatically not a fief.

Even Dudo of St Quentin (a Norman writer in ducal employ) admitted the personal bond which in fact bound Richard II of Normandy to King Robert II of France at the time he was writing. For him this tie was the extension of an alliance freely made in the previous century, its only obligation being to keep the peace. He invents a conversation to define these limits. Hugh the Great tells the intermediary who will take his message to Richard I: 'It is not a Frankish custom [one of Dudo's great themes is the integration of Normandy within Francia] for a prince or a duke to hold a lordship without forming a bond – voluntarily or by coercion – between himself and the Emperor, king or duke. If he does not take this step of his own accord, he risks being forced to do so.'

At the beginning of the eleventh century it was generally accepted that, since territorial principalities were part of the kingdom of the Franks, the princes therefore had a tie of some kind to the king. The intermediary replied that Richard had wanted to serve the king, but had been deceived: 'It would be better if he could serve you'. So the matter was duly settled. Richard of Normandy agreed to provide military aid for the king of France, to serve him and play a fitting part in the organization of the public peace under the authority of the king of West Francia, of which Normandy was part. Duke Richard I therefore placed his hands in homage between those of Hugh, who naturally responded with a gift. This was not Normandy, however, but his daughter in marriage: homage thus sealed a family alliance. Such an alliance carried with it merely the obligation of doing nothing to jeopardize the compact between the two houses. The present duke did homage to the king of France, as successor to the duke of Francia, but the ceremony was only performed as if to his equal, on the 'marches' (or frontiers) of his lands.

Our next text introduces a less high-ranking territorial prince without claims to a 'kingdom' of his own: the count of Blois, whom the French king was preparing to deprive of all his honours, on the grounds of disloyalty. The count protested in a letter, apparently drafted by Fulbert of Chartres. As old structures broke down, Fulbert's legal mind sought to clarify the legal position. It was true, he said, that the count had broken his personal bond, but then King Robert had not fulfilled his obligations. Moreover, the title to a county was not a gift that he could withdraw, even if the count proved a disloyal servant. Without question, the king could justifiably deprive a count of his title if his behaviour was 'tyrannical' in the full sense of the term. However, this was not the case. It was important to maintain a distinction between honour and fief, between the exercise of public office and the personal loyalty of a vassal.

This letter dates from 1023, from the period which J.-F. Lemarignier has identified as a crucial turning-point. Before this date the royal court – like the great Carolingian assemblies and following the precepts laid down by Abbo of Fleury thirty years before – had been composed of three-quarters of the great magnates of the kingdom – archbishops, bishops, abbots and territorial princes and counts. After this date the proportion dropped to one-third and stayed at this level. The princes were all present at the king's coronation and this gave them the impression that they actually made him king. But they were no longer a familiar sight in the royal household and the king was a remote focus for their respect. The king was no longer a source of profit; he was of no practical value to them. Was he in fact capable of fulfilling his role in society and keeping the peace in God's name? Did God himself now rule through new institutions, founded some fifty years previously?

When Ralph Glaber completed his work shortly before the mid-eleventh century, he had witnessed a progressive decline in the disruptive effect of the warrior class upon society. In his opinion this alteration came about because of a change of heart, as a result of which they were prepared to agree to replace the numerous and defective individual contracts with the large-scale sworn leagues necessary for the permanent establishment of peace. According to his narrative, 'It was first of all in Aquitaine that bishops, abbots and other ecclesiastics began to gather the entire population in assemblies to which they brought the bodies of various saints and innumerable reliquaries full of relics.' The initiative came from the south of the kingdom, where the king was never seen and the influence of Cluniac monasticism was widespread. The first councils were held as the millennium approached at Le Puy, Narbonne and Charroux, convened by these ecclesiastical leaders. However, the territorial princes were closely associated with the bishops in this endeavour.

At the heart of these assemblies were the relics of the saints, to whom the responsibility for maintaining public peace was henceforth entrusted. Ultimately, men had faith in their power. Everyone knew how the saints defended their own possessions, as well as the lordships of the monasteries that tended their mortal remains. At Conques, St Foy was positively ill-tempered and vindictive: knights who were rash enough to steal the monastery's wine or sheep were struck down with apoplexy, flux or hemiplegia; while St Benedict was said to unleash black hounds of madness against all those who harmed the monastery where his remains lay. The broader responsibilities that had once fallen to the weakened secular powers were now entrusted to greater and lesser miracle-working saints, in order to restore peace and social harmony.

'Since then', continued Ralph Glaber, 'the prelates and all the local secular lords announced that councils for the re-establishment of peace and the institution of the Christian faith were to be held, first in the province of Arles, then in that of Lyon, followed by the rest of Burgundy to the farthermost borders of the Frankish kingdom.' Since public justice was now pre-eminently a divine responsibility, it naturally operated within the framework of ecclesiastical administration, the province and the diocese, and consequently of the Western Empire. These councils were often held at the confluence of several ecclesiastical provinces or sometimes at the boundaries of secular kingdoms, such as that which took place at Anse, between Mâcon and Lyon, or at Verdun-sur-le-Doubs. Since the restoration of peace represented a return to the unfallen state of the Garden of Eden, these moves were inseparable from more general questions of faith. Formal rejection of force of arms took place within a context of general penitence. 'At the councils everyone agreed to sanctify the week by renouncing wine on Fridays and meat on Saturdays.' Among the edicts promulgated at the Council of Anse in 994, several emphasized the inviolability of the sabbath: there was to be no trade then, and 'only things to be consumed the same day were to be purchased'. The Burgundian peace-keeping assemblies envisaged renewal of these peace-keeping agreements every seven years, precisely because seven years was the period of purification stipulated for murderers in penitential manuals: during this period they were to lay down their arms, fast and abstain from carnal relations. By such means, God's people were locked into a system of collective penitence.

Ralph Glaber also refers to 'records divided into chapters'. 'The sacred agreements made with almighty God' were thus recorded in writing, just as the wording of the oaths made by each party were recorded at the *convenientiae* (councils) of southern France. In fact everyone present at the councils took an oath comparable to that which the Carolingian kings had demanded from their subjects; similar, too, to the vows made by Cluniac monks in the presence of all the members of their house, of which a written record was also made. These peace-making and penitential assemblies had a distinctly monastic character, in fact. An 'inviolable peace' was sworn, implying renunciation of all feuds. 'The holy places of every church' were established as recognized areas of asylum, except for those who had violated the council's agreements, who could be 'snatched from the very altar' to ensure their punishment. All ecclesiastics, on the other hand, were afforded especial protection.

That is all that Ralph Glaber tells us on this subject, and the significance of these new institutions has to be assessed from other texts. It is clear that – at least to begin with – some of these were forged in the interests of the Church, with a view to protecting their lands from domination by secular lords and from their exactions and 'wicked practices'. There are two key words in these texts, 'castle' and 'plunder'. The building of castles near monasteries was strictly prohibited, as was the construction of strongholds (*potestates*) or jurisdictions; moreover, the seizing of 'plunder' from the monastery was strictly prohibited, and such documents make it clear that the term refers to horses and cattle. Finally, the ban refers explicitly to lay authorities, to the officials of secular justice and holders of military power, more specifically to those responsible for the administration of public justice and the levying of exactions. The aim was above all to contain the power stemming from the castles and to protect the possessions of God and his saints, which were henceforth to be held only from ecclesiastical authorities.

These claims were initially supported by the territorial princes, for the great monasteries which were home to the relics of famous saints provided the strongest defence against the threat of growing seigneurial power. This was why William the Great of Aquitaine was among the promoters of the peace of God and why Robert II presided over peace-keeping assemblies in Burgundy (which then formed part of his lands). The duke of Normandy and the count of Flanders similarly presided over the assemblies held in their 'kingdoms', although they did not relinquish their own tight control over castles and castle-building. They viewed these peace-making institutions from a different perspective, looking to them for control of the warrior class, the section of society responsible for violence and disorder.

The prohibitions were directed specifically against knights (*caballarii*, *milites*), criticizing their 'pride' and excesses; some texts singled out the lower-ranking knights for particular criticism. In a council of 1031 Bishop Jourdain of Limoges pronounced a series of solemn anathemas on these men and their weapons; and from this group, above all, the organizers of general assemblies required oaths that they would respect the new regulations which had been devised to contain the threat they posed to society.

In the valleys of the Rhône and the Saône and (after 1020) in the Frankish kingdom, a knight (*cavalier*) had to swear: 'I will not attack the Church, her lands or her stores; I will not attack priests or monks or their escorts, should they be unarmed themselves.' In the course of private war (waged under the banner of a minor lord to avenge murder or an insult), which continued unabated – it never occurred to anyone to ban this form of aggression – he was not allowed to capture cattle for ransom, 'nor peasant men or women, nor merchants'. The knight agreed to refrain from whipping and robbing the peasantry. He also swore not to cut down vines, ransack mills, nor to take the most valuable animals (mules, horses, mares and broken colts) from the fields between Lent and All Saints Day (1 November). He swore not to burn houses, unless an enemy was hidden there, or unless they were adjacent to a castle – a clear indication of the way in which the *bourg* had an explicitly military role. Nevertheless, there was a clear distinction between private war and public war led by the king and bishops, figures whose consecration gave them responsibility for the peace of God. They were entitled to requisition supplies for their armies from mills and religious houses, but all forms of pillage were strictly forbidden them.

The knight's oath kept him from robbery, except in two cases: 'If I am building a castle, or besieging it [this was in stark contrast to the area surrounding a church, where peace held sway; violence was endemic in the area around a castle]; and also in the land of my allod or fief, which falls under my protection.' Lordship was not undermined by these new peace-keeping institutions. On the contrary, the code which they embodied gave it a legal foundation. In his own lands, where peace-keeping was his responsibility, the knight retained the right to seize whatever he wanted. The peace-keeping regulations outlined the framework within which the common people could be exploited: barriers were constructed around ecclesiastical lordships, and the conditions established in secular lordships effectively granted the lord the right of extortion over the inhabitants and travellers who enjoyed his protection.

Furthermore, the knight agreed not to aid any criminal who had offended against public justice, regardless of the bonds of blood, friendship or vassalage that might exist between them. The support of these natural affiliations was to be denied this criminal, just as he had no right to sanctuary. The knight promised especial aid to noble women, widows and nuns travelling alone, as well as wine merchants. Such arrangements clearly underline contemporary class distinctions, with completely different treatment for a knight's lady and a peasant woman; they are also evidence of the considerable threat of abduction that hung over heiresses, who were considered fair prey. Finally, they are proof of the unprecedented forms of activity stimulated by trade, and this traffic provided an important impetus for seigneurial taxation, which was being established at this time.

The wording of the oath also illustrates clearly the relationship between knight and peasant. 'I will give a peasant who has harmed another peasant or a knight two weeks' respite, but after that I am entitled to capture him; however, I will not take more of his goods than is permitted under customary law.' This is an indication of peasant criminality, but it also reveals the repressive forms of justice that weighed heavily upon the peasantry, demonstrating clearly that it was the knight's duty to punish them and that he was entitled to make heavy inroads into the possessions of the 'poor'. But here seigneurial power was clearly influenced by moral concerns: the lord was bound by customary law; any informal reconciliations (perhaps brought about 'by the intervention of neighbours', as the custumal of the *bourg* of Cluny was to put it a little later) made during the period of delay pre-empted punitive action on the lord's part.

'I will not attack or rob a knight riding unarmed during Lent.' In other words, any man on horseback who did not belong to one of his own groupings was presumed to be an enemy, and every encounter between knights who were not known to each other began with a joust, just as in twelfth-century romance. Gradually the idea developed of a period during which all forms of military aggression were forbidden, even between knights who would be expected to fight to the death. During periods of penitential observance, a general truce was instituted. One such operated in northern France between 1023 and 1025. (This corrects Ralph Glaber, who places the appearance of a new type of agreement in 1040 and 'first of all in Aquitaine'.) The final element that completed this peace-keeping apparatus, Glaber tells us, was a complete ban – on pain of excommunication – 'on absolutely everyone, from Tuesday evening until dawn on the following Monday, to take anything whatsoever from anyone by force, either to exact vengeance or even to seize a pledge guaranteeing the terms of an agreement'.

The movement for the 'peace and truce of God' thus succeeded in circumscribing military violence, while also providing an outlet for these energies within the same framework. This success led to the development of a social theory which was the foundation of all ideas about the division of power in France until the Revolution of 1789. According to this hypothesis there had always been three divinely ordained categories of men, of which one prayed, another fought and the last group laboured with their hands. Political stability was based on the mutual exchange of services supplied by each man according to his function. This idealized image also legitimated an open rift at the heart of secular society: military action was confined to a small number of individuals authorized to live off the manual labour of others; seigneurial taxation could be seen as an extension of divine will. On the other hand, however, this hypothesis completed the system of prohibitions placed upon the warfaring classes by assigning them positive duties, emphasizing that their material advantages were only justified by the service they rendered to the rest of society.

Combined with Fulbert of Chartres' views on the obligations of feudal lords, this image of a perfect society carried within it the germ of a chivalric ideology based on the progressive sacralization of initiation rites, a trend parallelled by developments in the marriage ceremony. At the end of his training and education, a young knight was formally presented with his arms in a ceremony by which he was also fully admitted into the company of adult warriors. The priests naturally claimed it as their prerogative to place the sword – symbol of the knight's military function – on the altar and belt it on the new knight, just as they belted on a new king's sword after his consecration. They attained this objective, and are documented in this role in the late twelfth century, when the knighting ceremony also imposed obligations upon the aspirant comparable to those which preceded the king's oath at his coronation: it was the knight's duty to protect churches, widows and orphans, as well as to extend Christendom by crusade. While the peace-keeping institutions were demonstrating their efficacy in the eleventh century, the concept of a holy war was grafted onto the theoretical tripartite division of society.

When the first assemblies for peace were held in northern France, this idea was articulated by bishops who opposed them. The bishops opposed other clerics as well, resentful of their influence at the royal court, and were also undermined by theories of monasticism which saw monks as superior to the secular clergy and the entire diocesan structure. In the view of these bishops, it was extremely risky to assemble entire populations as sworn groups of equals, for they were afraid that there would be a re-emergence of the guilds which the ninth-century bishops had worked so hard to destroy. Finally, men such as Gerard of Cambrai and Adalbero of Laon, who had great respect for Carolingian traditions, even though they promulgated the truce of God in their dioceses, feared that the system of the peace of God did not place adequate checks on royal power.

The system in fact respected royal prerogatives. In France, Burgundy and even in Flanders, where the count must be considered under the same heading, the consecrated king was called upon to lead punitive expeditions against warriors who abused their military role. The peace of God had been instituted at a time when the monarchy was demonstrably weak, but, when the king was once more in a position 'to chastize the crimes of powerful men', the same peace-keeping institutions served as the basis for the restoration of the monarchical State. By its precepts lay rulers were un-doubtedly reduced to a purely subordinate role: this is very clear in Aquitaine, where the duke had relied on peace-keeping institutions, but lost control of them after 1025; his power was henceforth eclipsed by ecclesiastical lords. The primary effect of the establishment of the peace and truce of God was to strengthen the bishops, giving them new and powerful weapons. Adhémar of Chabannes tells us that 'Knightly pillage and devastation of the poor roused the bishop of Limoges to introduce a new practice; mass and divine service of all kinds were suspended in churches and monasteries, to deprive the people of all forms of worship, as if they were pagans. He called this punishment excommunication.' This sanction was controlled by the prelates. 'Christian justice' was now to be added to the judicial powers they exercised over the secular clergy and monasteries. This justified their jurisdiction over and punishment of the laity who offended against the peace of God. Bishops thus became increasingly involved in contemporary politics and their own political importance increased; it also stimulated the more extreme forms of greed, aggravating – in the eyes of its critics – the existing defects of the secular clergy. The need for reform was all the greater.

7

The Church

The 1020s and 1030s saw the development of two contradictory trends. The fragmentation of political power and its contraction within narrower limits was virtually complete. Population increase and the development of trade, on the other hand, were encouraging a new tendency towards the reconstruction of much larger political units. This was first apparent in the institution which had changed least, the Church. Since contemporaries still viewed history as progressively corrupt, reform was seen as a return to the past and the restoration of a better age.

The impetus came from the academic study of the political terminology of ancient Rome. Referring to the classical concept of *libertas* (freedom), scholars formulated the idea that the Church and her worldly possessions should not be subordinated to any temporal power. Drawing a distinction between *auctoritas* and *potestas*, they maintained that while power could be exercised by secular rulers, they were subject to ecclesiastical authority. The institutions of the peace of God and the theoretical tripartite division of society developed from these principles. But reform also implied renewal of the Church, whose incorruptibility gave it a place superior to all other earthly powers. Further reform was necessary, as well as correction of the notion that monasticism was superior to episcopacy.

Until the twelfth century, monasteries were undoubtedly the most powerful institutions in France. The basis of their power was twofold. In the first place there were the saints, for the most efficacious were associated with monasteries rather than cathedrals. This was very clear at Paris in 1128–9: ergotic poisoning was rife and the preachers thundered on, declaring this plague to be an expression of divine anger at the pernicious concern of many men for their personal appearance, with their unmanly long hair and long pointed shoes like those worn by women. The sick visited Notre-Dame in vain for a cure: for the epidemic to recede, the reliquary of St Geneviève had to be transported over the hill into the city. Such miracles were well publicized, and this in turn focused popular piety increasingly upon relics, directing the alms of the faithful to the monks who preserved them and brought them out of the crypt for display at appropriate moments. The stream of offerings to great monastic houses well endowed with famous relics grew throughout the first seven decades of the eleventh century, flooding them with lands, serfs, immunity, exemption and customary rights and privileges.

The saints were more generous with their favours, however, when their servants were free from sin. The health and prosperity of the surrounding region thus depended on the sanctity of the monastic communities that had grown up around the tombs of the saints. The abbeys that had suffered from the infidel raids of the tenth century were therefore the first to be reformed. The territorial princes, great and small (many of whom were also lay abbots) were aware of their duty, and also realized that their own prestige would be greatly enhanced. Accordingly, they played a leading part in the movement for reform. The body of St Victor was preserved in an ancient monastery at Marseilles, a possession of the *vicomtes*. This monastery was rebuilt after the Saracen raids, and in 1005 the *vicomte* decided to give it full 'liberty'. He charged the bishop (his brother, successor to their uncle) to obtain papal consent and pronounce the formulae freeing the abbey and its possessions from all secular intervention in its affairs. By this means the stability necessary for reform was also secured.

Immunity and exemption thus preceded moral reform, and administrative reform followed. Devout monks appointed by territorial princes to oversee reform went from one monastery to another, installing a few monks about whom they had no doubts in the houses they had visited, to act as the leaven of good observance. The individual responsible for the reform of a monastery was very much the community's father-figure, and his memory was often venerated after his death; sometimes he agreed to stay on as their abbot, represented in his absence by one of the monks, the prior – in this way a monastic family was established. At the same time, looser ties of brotherhood were formed through formal unions with other communities of monks and canons (whose obits would also be duly celebrated at Cluny), strengthening their sense of identity. Contemporary theologians attributed the huge monastic populations throughout the length and breadth of Latin Christendom (in other words, the Western Empire) to the work of *caritas* (Christian love). In the first half of the eleventh century, reformed (or Cluniac) monasticism was the strongest and most solidly based body in those regions which later became the kingdom of France; this vigour was undoubtedly responsible for the suppression of heresy.

Monastic communities aimed to free themselves from episcopal control, substituting for the bishop the patronage of the Pope within the framework of the Western Empire. In 1005 the Pope approved the stipulation of the bishop of Marseilles that 'no bishop . . . should dare to take any possession whatsoever away from the monastery'. The abbot of Fleury received the same papal privilege at this date; in 1025 all Cluniac houses were granted these exemptions. Monastic reform made holes in the fabric of the diocese and dislocated it, just as castellan independence had dislocated the *comté*. Papal prestige was increased, stimulating interest in Rome's classical past and triggering a veritable renaissance.

The best-regulated, most numerous and most powerful monks were members of the numerous Cluniac foundations (dependencies of the re-formed Benedictine house at Cluny) and they dreamt of leading this renaissance. Convinced of their supreme mission to lead others towards divine perfection, they viewed bishops as mere auxiliaries, to be summoned from a diocese beyond their own territorial boundaries to distribute benediction and unction when required and to ordain particular monks. For the Cluniac order was beginning to appropriate priestly functions: monks had previously been no more than penitent laymen; they hoped now to become priests as well. The order did not intend to send these priests out to the people: on the contrary, they exploited the ever-growing number of parish churches given to them just as any secular lord, installing a class of subordinate clergy to carry out parochial duties which were too mundane for the monks to consider performing. The monks kept their heads firmly in the clouds. If they could enter holy orders, then the eucharist could be celebrated in their sumptuous, exclusive abbey churches 'without ceasing from break of day until the hour of rest', and with such magnificence that they would seem 'more like angels than mere men'. Such angelic affinity naturally placed them above all other priests, not least bishops.

They also achieved supremacy over the territorial princes. The Cluniacs persuaded these rulers that they and their ancestors should be associated with Cluny in personal confraternity, similar to the unions of monastic houses. The monks' end was achieved by the quality of the prayers sung in the abbey of the mother-church and the numerous dependent priories: Cluny had few miraculous relics. The monks themselves had left the secular world, but they were still connected to it through the towns (*bourgs*) which burgeoned outside the gates of the most important monasteries and by the huge areas within their own walls set aside for the reception of visitors, rich and poor. The order's high reputation in the secular world was rooted in the liturgy. Cluniac reform of the Rule of St Benedict strove always to elaborate divine service. Monastic aspirations to the condition of the angels impelled them to make divine praise increasingly magnificent (so that the dazzling joys of paradise might be prefigured in the splendours of earthly worship) and to bring to paradise all Christians, the living and – above all – the dead. Cluniac zeal was concentrated above all on funeral ceremonies at this date, and their efforts were rewarded; for the Emperor, kings and territorial princes were all won over, together with their dead relatives. The Cluniac order (*ordo cluniacensis*) established under the patronage of the Roman martyrs SS Peter and Paul developed its own framework between 1020 and 1090. Odilo and Hugh were the first abbots, each with an abbacy that lasted some fifty years. The order was in effect a monarchy based on the model of the family: political thought knew no other form at this period. The political aspirations of the Cluniacs found its clearest expression in their building programme, which swallowed up all the surplus revenue which the order received for its devotions, above all the offices of the dead. This was directed first by Odilo, who instituted the rebuilding of the great abbey church at Cluny on a classical Roman plan, ordering Roman columns to be transported overland from the south of France, where they were still plentiful. Then it was the turn of Abbot Hugh, who decided to pull down his predecessor's scarcely completed edifice and build another new, much larger and much lighter church. The new church (whose choir was consecrated by the Pope in 1095) was bigger than those built round the tombs of SS Peter and Paul in Rome; the nave was exceptionally long and stretched ahead like a long road leading to heaven. Above the west door were sculptures like those found upon the ruins of classical temples at Arles or Narbonne. Monastic power thus also stimulated a renaissance in sculpture. It is difficult for us to register its extraordinary impact upon contemporaries. Statues no longer hid in shadowy vaulting, like the disturbing statue of St Foy at Conques; instead they stood open to the elements for all to see, just as the sculptures of classical Rome.

Cluny saw itself as a second Rome and aspired to take the place of failing secular kingdoms; Adalbero of Laon is quite clear on this point in 1025. The Cluniacs benefitted from the new prestige of the Papacy, and the order was also called upon to arbitrate in quarrels between Pope and Emperor, preaching clemency at the meeting of Gregory VII and Henry IV at Canossa in 1076. Moreover, the grand prior of Cluny himself became Pope in 1088, taking the name of Urban II. However, the episcopate – whose roots also lay in the imperial past – remained an obstacle to fulfilling this dream of omnipotence. The bishops had by no means left the earth for celestial spheres. They remained in their traditional place, firmly rooted in the temporal world, blood-relations of the higher nobility and institutionally bound to the French monarchy. The monks maintained that these factors linked the bishops too closely with temporal concerns and – not without justification – denounced them as simoniacs. There was, however, the incontrovertible fact that the Cluniac's first and indispensable ally, the Pope (although he had previously been a monk) was a bishop. It was the Pope himself, as bishop of Rome, who set in hand reform of the episcopate in the mid-eleventh century.

According to the moralists, there was a pressing need for reform of the clergy, above all of their attitudes to sexual relations and to money. In the eleventh century virtually all the clergy were married. Admittedly, bishops did not marry, but their chastity was open to question. They were supposed to set an example of continence and impose it on their diocesan clergy. The reformers urged the imperative of chastity, arguing that the people as a whole were affected, since the priests handled the sacraments and what was most holy passed through their hands; if they had been defiled by physical relations with a woman, nothing holy could be transmitted to them. According to the tripartite division of society, those who exercised the highest (religious) function should lead a pure life, which should certainly not feature concubinage, even if it was not celibate (like a monk's) or particularly chaste. Reform and the restoration of what was assumed to be the divine order of things in effect established a gulf in human society almost as deep as that which divided male and female, and one which was also sexually referential. Reform once set in hand instituted a kind of dualism at the heart of the social and cultural life of the West, with a strict segregation of priests (who were forbidden to marry) from the laity, who were encouraged to do so.

In the eyes of the reformers, it was also scandalous that once the priestly office was isolated from carnal relations, it was still conferred by the impure hands of temporal rulers, duty-bound to sexual intercourse to ensure reproduction and the continuance of their lineage. It was therefore essential to remove their rights to episcopal appointment, since the bishop was the spiritual father of his diocesan clergy. This second requirement had direct political implications. Reform which aimed to make the Church a veritable State, endowed with *auctoritas* and *libertas*, and thus superior to all other States and completely autonomous, also implied internal appointment to all ecclesiastical positions. At that time, following Carolingian practice, princes appointed to bishoprics, and the most effective selected their own relatives. At his accession, William the Conqueror's uncle was archbishop of Rouen, the bishops of Lisieux and Avranches were cousins, and his brother would become bishop of Bayeux. William was the Pope's faithful ally. *Episcopatus* (episcopal power and the temporal endowment required for its exercise) was virtually always an integral part of a family's patrimony, as in the case of Marseilles. Admittedly, there was no question

of money if the head of a house appointed one of his sons or nephews to a
bishopric. However, since all the men of a family held the possessions
of the bishopric indivisibly between them, it was legitimate to talk of
commerce and simony. There was a clearer case of simony if someone from
another family was appointed to the mother-church, with powers of justice
extended by the institutions of the peace of God, as well as the garrisoned
castles and powerful lordships dependent on the see, either inside the city
or beyond its walls. Granting such a conspicuous slice of power seemed
very like a 'benefice', with nothing to distinguish it from the grant of
secular lordship. The episcopal recipient thus felt himself obliged to 'love'
and serve the lord from whom he held this favour. This was established
practice. Now that money circulated freely, he also offered his patron
money. Thus the growth of trade meant that what had been essentially a
formal expression of friendship was now interpreted as a commercial
transaction. To demonstrate this more clearly, I shall once more discuss a
specific example. Like all our sources, it is exceptional, because sustained
evidence from this period is extremely rare. Normal practice is illuminated
by episodes which deviate from it, however. In this case the action takes
place in the archbishopric of Narbonne.

Narbonne had been an immense Roman city, and most of its classical
buildings were still standing in the eleventh century. A large church had
been built around the tomb of the local saint, Paul, served by an autonomous collegiate foundation. It had its own lordship, its *bourg* inhabited by
servants of the church and the many people who made their living from the
large numbers of pilgrims. The archbishop had his throne in the cathedral,
where he dispensed justice. A century or more earlier, the city's fortunes
had been restored by its proximity to the sea and the border with Muslim
Spain. It also profited from the salt trade, since the Domitian Way passed
through the city. (With wine, salt was the only bulk commodity in which
there was substantial long-distance trade at this period.) In the ninth
century Charles the Bald had granted half the tolls levied by the lord of
the region on tonnage, shipping and the salt-marshes to the archbishop.
The prelates also exploited what was unquestionably the largest Jewish
community in France, collecting very substantial sums from able craftsmen, first-rate scholars and clever, wealthy merchants, who were all
anxious to buy themselves a little security. These prerogatives brought a
constantly growing return. Since the beginning of the century, three other
settlements had grown up near the cathedral, one significantly called
villeneuve. Each of them continued to expand within its own limits. Each
collection of simple dwellings was surrounded with ditches and knights
were garrisoned on the old Roman city walls. This was all part of the
archiepiscopal lordship, but the archbishop did not possess sole rights: my

source comes from his main rival, the *vicomte*. Like Hugh of Lusignan, he had a record made by one of his household clerics in order to defend his rights in the ecclesiastical court, where the judges demanded written proof. The *vicomte's* grievances against the archbishop were set out before the great council of 1059 presided over by Raimbaud of Reillane, archbishop of Arles and also a prince of the Church. He too lived surrounded by tangible expressions of imperial Rome, profited from the salt trade and was lord over secular knights, just like his colleague in Narbonne.

I, Berengar, *vicomte* of the city of Narbonne make a formal and public indictment against my metropolitan (the archbishop of Narbonne), your brother in Christ, before this holy assembly of God's vicars on earth, legates of the sovereign Roman pontiff, the earthly representative of St Peter, prince of the apostles, and of archbishops and bishops acting in his name and abbots . . . expert in questions of the faith, so that this complaint may be read, heard, judged and settled.

Rome was thus represented in Arles, in more tangible form than distant memories of the legions, through her own reforming bishop, who intended to start his programme of reform in the south of France, either in person or by his special envoys, the papal legates. Six years earlier, one such legate, the monk Hildebrand (later to become Gregory VII) had been the motivating force behind a comparable council at Embrun, where the archbishop had been convicted of simony and deposed. Reform was well and truly under way. For a lay prince in conflict with a prelate to appeal to an archiepiscopal synod dominated by the Papacy, without any other secular lord, in itself demonstrates clearly the transfer of *imperium* (supreme authority) to the leaders of the Church. The theory and institutions of the peace of God had triumphed, and ecclesiastical reform designed to extend these principles inevitably relegated secular princes to a subordinate position.

In his attack Berengar began by describing what the *archiepiscopatus* (archbishopric) had once been like: a particularly beautiful part of southern France – 'one of the finest'. Interestingly, he refers to Charlemagne, whose memory was still green in the area covered by classical Septimania and the former kingdom of the Goths. The description makes a judicious assessment of the basis of archiepiscopal power: fine domain lands and, above all, castles. This was the cathedral's foundation. Once it had been beautifully furnished, 'full of books, decorated with retables and gold crosses, shining with gold crowns and jewels'. It had dazzled the beholder, as befitted the prefiguration of heavenly Jerusalem. Finally, the good prelates had carried out their duties impeccably: castles and lands were not handed over to lay lords, but administered directly by priests; a college of canons sang the offices of the Church at the appointed hours. The present archbishop, however, had allowed this fine and effective instrument to fall into decay, and this was the basis of Berengar's complaint. As a responsible ruler, he wanted to ensure that the sacred was fittingly represented within his city.

Surely, the dispassionate observer will ask, the *vicomte* must have provided money for the appointment of this incompetent archbishop? In fact, the *vicomte* was not in the least worried by the purchase of the see. At the time, he had supported it, and he had indeed been primarily responsible for the sale forty years before. When the previous archbishop died in 1019, the count of Cerdagne had sought the appointment for one of his sons, the ten-year-old Guifred. (We should not over-react to his youth, for he was only four years short of majority, and in contemporary eyes his age at least had the virtue of guaranteeing chastity.) Negotiations were set in motion with the men who had an interest in the archbishopric, because they held command within the city of Narbonne – jointly the count of Rouergue (marquis of Gothia) and the *vicomte* of Narbonne. The purchaser could pay a high price, for Cerdagne was a frontier lordship, and at this date the petty Muslim kings in Spain paid the Franks tribute in gold and silver. The count himself was exceptionally devout, a relative of Oliva, abbot of Ripoll and bishop of Vich, one of the most fervent proponents of reform. The count had founded the monastery of St Martin-du-Canigou, to which he retired for the last fifteen years of his life. He wanted to secure an ecclesiastical appointment for one of his children, so that this son might pray for the souls of his relatives. For this he offered 100,000 *sous*, in all good faith. Berengar was also very young; he was already associated with his father in the government of the lordship, but without a deciding voice. His father and mother refused the count's offer: the archbishopric had been in their family for several generations. In 977 Berengar's grandfather had settled his succession by declaring that one of his sons should become *vicomte*, the other archbishop. (This was the prelate whose death had precipitated the crisis.) At Narbonne, as in many other cities, the offices of archbishop and *vicomte* (*archiepiscopatus* and *vicecomitatus*) were held indivisibly by the whole family. In this way order was guaranteed. It was disrupted because the old *vicomte* and his wife had finally succumbed not merely to pressure from the count of Rouergue, but also from their son. For Berengar had married the daughter of the count of Besalù, brother of the count of Cerdagne. Guifred was thus his younger cousin by marriage. For him the sale was a means of ousting his father. This was a time when families were torn apart by the inter-generational conflict that followed the establishment of a lineage-based society. Berengar admitted that he had threatened to kill his father to make him change his mind.

Guifred was consecrated archbishop, but only after he had sworn not to harm the person, possessions or honour of the *vicomtes*. At first he carried out his duties well. His enemy gave two examples of the archbishop's virtue at this period. Guifred had sought out and found in Spain the relics of the cathedral's patron saints, the martyrs Just and Pasteur, which he had acquired and brought back to the cathedral, thus increasing its sanctity, to the benefit of the whole town. By all accounts this operation had been undertaken in the context of the military expeditions in Spain which had begun to drive back Islam; the young archbishop seems to have had a taste for war. Guifred had also held councils to extend the peace of God: one of these (held in 1043) forbade priests to carry weapons. The archbishop solemnly vowed not to carry arms himself, nor to lead any further expeditions, threatening to anathematize any of his clergy who continued to fight. In a more recent assembly (held in 1054) he had explicitly extended the peace of God to merchants, laying down a period of truce from Wednesday evening until Monday morning and condemning all· violence between Christians: 'The Christian who kills a fellow-Christian sheds the blood of Christ.' Warriors were henceforth only to fight in 'just' wars against the infidel, on crusade. The indictment against Guifred thus presents him at the forefront of ecclesiastical reform. It was undoubtedly this that lay at the root of his conflict with the *vicomte*.

Applying the principles of reform, the archbishop had tried to withdraw ecclesiastical possessions from secular control. To this end he had built new castles and garrisoned them with his own knights, whom he rewarded generously to ensure their personal loyalty and a more spirited defence of the 'liberty of the Church'. Berengar felt his authority flouted when he saw the fortifications of a rival power at the very gates of his own castle. He accused the archbishop of squandering the cathedral's patrimony on his knights. Fighting was the inevitable outcome: 'the knights of the two castles' clashed and a whole series of brawls and reprisals ensued. One day, Berengar said, some knights left the archbishop's castle and killed one of his knights and their action was defended by the archbishop, who refused to bring them to justice. Or at least, not in the way that Berengar would have wished. On another occasion two of his knights at St Sauveur d'Aniane had been captured by Guifred's knights. There could be no doubt of the archbishop's rapacity; he was no more than godfather to a gang of waged pillagers.

Then there was the question of simony. The archbishop had bought the bishopric of Urgel for his brother for 100,000 *sous*. Again, Berengar was not shocked by the purchase itself, but he had two criticisms. In this instance, he said, Guifred was wrong to have done homage by placing his hands between those of the countess of Urgel, who was responsible for the *comté* during her son's minority. According to the *vicomte*, the entire nobility of the region were sickened by this action. (It is not clear what aspect they found so repellent – the spectacle of an archbishop performing homage or the fact that it involved contact with a woman.) To raise money for this purchase, Guifred then had the gold- and silver-leaf scraped from altar tables, reliquaries and crosses; vases were melted down by usurious Jewish metal-workers. It was a fine example of ecclesiastical asset-stripping. Books had also been sold. He had pillaged the fabric of Narbonne cathedral and diminished the splendour of worship there. Berengar thus made his accusation as the church's titular patron and the potential inheritor of its allegedly depleted wealth.

At this point the text describes the lengthy conflict between the two protagonists, a period of hostilities punctuated by truces. One of these short-lived agreements, concluded through the arbitration of the suffragan bishops, succeeded in dividing equally the profits of 'Christian justice' (that is, fines paid for violation of the peace of God). The *vicomte* gave up his share – no less that 10,000 *sous* – for the upkeep of the cathedral. This level of income is some indication of the stakes for which the two rivals were playing; it also demonstrates that capital invested in episcopal office yielded a good return. Finally, the fact that the *vicomte* had to surrender his share of these profits of justice represented a victory for the archbishop, whose jurisdiction over the peace of God throughout the city had been acknowledged. But these fragile settlements did not last long. It looks as if the *vicomte* succeeded in turning the canons of the cathedral, led by the archdeacon, against his rival over the offerings made to the shrine of SS Just and Pasteur. Berengar proposed a form of mediation: the parties should plead their case before the archbishop of Arles, and he would give pledges up to 10,000 *sous*; meanwhile no one was to touch the offerings. The archbishop's response was formal secession: clad in the *pallium*, the splendid vestment which symbolized his office, he left the city, taking the disputed relics with him. Guifred made a country church his archiepiscopal seat, with the service-books, crosses and great crucifix from Narbonne cathedral, and he constituted a new chapter of good, reformed priests.

This was disastrous for Narbonne: according to the *vicomte*, 'the nobles and all the people of the region used to come and visit the city and the cathedral, where penitents offered gifts and contributions for the work of the Church; Guifred turned them away.' Moreover, he used the income from such offerings to pay his knights. The city had a serious grievance. Further negotiations followed, with an exchange of pledges and oaths. The archbishop allegedly swore to return, but then broke his oath and refused to budge. Finally, as a last resort, Berengar adopted a cunning but risky plan, employing a woman from Narbonne related to both himself and the archbishop. As Guifred's cousin, she begged him to change his mind.

1 William, duke of Normandy sits in judgement with drawn sword. Bayeux Tapestry, c. 1085. (Tapisserie de Bayeux et avec autorisation spéciale de la Ville de Bayeux)

2 Romanesque reliefs of two of the signs of the zodiac (Leo and Aries), now embedded in a wall of the church of St Sernin, Toulouse (late 11th or early 12th century). (Reproduced by kind permission of Mairie de Toulouse)

3 Jewelled reliquary figure of St Foy, showing the saint seated in majesty. Conques abbey (9th–10th century). (Reproduced by kind permission of Photographie Giraudon, Paris)

4 Cylindrical tower built by Philip Augustus at Villeneuve-sur-Yonne (early 13th century). (Reproduced by kind permission of Roger-Viollet, Paris)

5 Abbey church of St Denis, Paris: the nave looking east to the mid-twelfth-century choir, showing the interior flooded with light. (Reproduced by kind permission of The Ancient Art and Architecture Collection: © Ronald Sheridan)

6 Cathedral of Notre-Dame, Paris: tympanum of the portal of St Anne, showing the benefactor Louis VII with the model of a church in his hands (third quarter of the 12th century). (Reproduced by kind permission of The Ancient Art and Architecture Collection: © Ronald Sheridan)

7 Stone altarpiece carved for the church of Avenas-en-Beaujolais, showing Christ in glory with the apostles (12th century). (Reproduced by kind permission of The Ancient Art and Architecture Collection: © Ronald Sheridan)

8 Enamel plaque showing Melchisedeck, king and priest, administering the
sacrament to Abraham (second half of 12th century). Paris, Musée du Louvre.
(Reproduced by kind permission of Photographie Giraudon, Paris)

9 Chartres cathedral: triple tympana of the Royal Portal, west front (mid-12th
century). (Reproduced by kind permission of La Crypte, Éditions Houvet, Chartres)

10 Cathedral of Notre-Dame, Paris: eastward view from the nave to the choir (1180–1220). (Reproduced by kind permission of Photographie Giraudon, Paris)

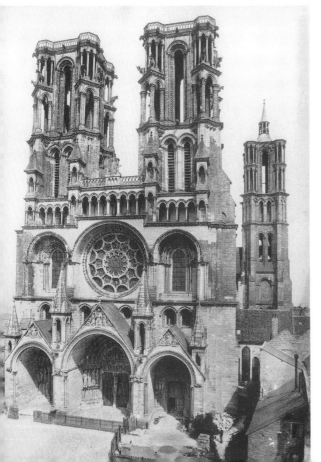

11 West front of Laon cathedral (begun c. 1170). (Reproduced by kind permission of Roger-Viollet, Paris)

12 Cathedral of Clermont-Ferrand, showing the spread of northern Gothic forms into the Central Massif (mid to late 13th century). (Reproduced by kind permission of Roger-Viollet, Paris)

13 Abbey of St Denis, Paris: the great bronze west doors, surmounted by God in majesty (second quarter of the 12th century). (Reproduced by kind permission of The Ancient Art and Architecture Collection: © Ronald Sheridan)

14 Cathedral of Notre-Dame, Paris: façade with the Gallery of the Kings (1190–
1220). (Reproduced by kind permission of Alinari-Giraudon, Paris)

15 Senlis cathedral: west portal with coronation of the Virgin (late 12th century).
(Reproduced by kind permission of The Ancient Art and Architecture Collection:
© Ronald Sheridan)

When this failed, she stole the relics from their temporary sanctuary – supposedly without the knowledge of her husband, for this was all but sacrilege. (The *vicomte* sought to minimize this transgression by claiming that they were not even being kept on consecrated ground.) Nevertheless, it was a capital crime, meriting very severe punishment under the code of the peace of God. The archbishop immediately responded by anathematizing Berengar and his wife and children, despite all their efforts to escape such a terrible blow, throwing themselves at his feet in the court. According to our source, the archbishop 'excommunicated all the land'. The area affected was in fact the *cité* of Narbonne, where there were no longer baptisms, funerals, masses or benedictions. The *vicomte*'s subjects were deprived of all sacred rites in the hope that they would pressurize the *vicomte* to submit. As a compromise, he suggested arbitration before the judges responsible for the peace of God. There was no question of further negotiation under the auspices of the relatives or friends of the two protagonists. The issue would be debated within the hierarchical framework of ecclesiastical jurisdiction.

This framework was the legacy of the administrative structure of imperial Rome, but it also prefigured that of the future State. This is the significance of ecclesiastical reform and the movement for the peace of God in the history of public authority in France. Sentence would be passed by an assembly of the bishops of the province, presided over by the neighbouring archbishop, rather than their own, since he was a party to the case. Berengar swore in advance to pay damages up to 10,000 *sous*. (Is this reference to another 10,000 *sous*, with 100,000 *sous* just a short while before, an exaggeration? Were scribes simply incapable of handling large numbers at this period? Or were vast quantities of coin already in circulation, sustained by the breakup of Church treasuries and the dealings of Jewish financiers, who traded in precious metals in Islamic Spain?) A council was therefore duly assembled at Arles in the presence of papal envoys. Berengar presented his case, emphasizing Guifred's simony, but making no accusations on the subject. His complaint was not that the archbishop had handed over money for an episcopal appointment, but that 'he had sold everything connected with the Church in order to raise the money for such purchases. . . . If you do not believe me, ask the bishops of Lodève and Elne, who owe their dioceses to him.' Berengar also accused the archbishop of accepting money for the consecration of churches. Everyone knew that the archbishop of Embrun had been deposed on just this count, and Guifred himself was excommunicated by the Pope in 1055 or 1057: we do not know why, possibly for simony, but more probably for his acquiescence in the count of Barcelona's questionable marriage.

This dispute centred on temporal power and its profits, but spiritual power was also involved. The archbishop pronounced his anathema and the *vicomte* condemned episcopal transgressions, confident of a hearing from reforming clerics, with their eyes on the Pope and his delegates. For the monks of Cluny were not alone in their dreams of renewed imperialism. The secular clergy also had visions of a new empire controlled by priests, with their own hierarchy and the papal throne at its summit. For priests to govern the rest of society, their own lives had to be un-impeachable, and lax bishops deposed. Accordingly, the reformers listened to what the *vicomte* of Narbonne had to say. He threatened that '[if I do not obtain justice] I will ignore Guifred's excommunication, I will not observe any truce whatsoever in my lands and I will never again appeal to papal judgement.' But the legates were unruffled. Berengar's deposit-ion would enable them to check a powerful prelate and force him to acknowledge papal supremacy, for fear of being deposed and being re-placed by a more docile cleric. As for the *vicomte*, their hold over him was still greater. This was not because he had contracted a bigamous or incestuous marriage, as was the case with the count of Barcelona or, at a later date, the king of France. Rather, it was through the normal operation of the recently established mechanisms of the peace of God. If Berengar broke that peace, he was legitimately excluded from the community, his lands were placed under interdict and he would be plagued by his own wretched household.

We do not know what sentence was passed by the council of Arles, only that Guifred was not removed from office, and that seven years later he made a formal agreement with Berengar's son, now also associated with his ageing father. This was not the result of ecclesiastical initiative, but that of Raymond of St-Gilles, count of Toulouse, now also count of Rouergue and marquis of Gothia. His intervention, from 1066 onwards, heralds the resurgence of lay power. The terms of this agreement divided the territory of the entire city strictly into two, including the highly profitable Jewish quarter. It was renewed and extended in 1112, when further clauses stipulated how the salt-marshes, houses and fortifications were to be shared and laid down the division of justice, allotting the *vicomte* jurisdiction over capital crimes throughout the town, the archbishop complete jurisdiction over clerics and the clergy. It was no longer a moral issue, but a practical question of the operation of lordship.

Seven years later, in 1119 (it is impossible to tell whether this is sheer chance or a survival of the seven-year cycle instituted by the peace of God for the renewal of agreements), the question was once more brought before a council. This time its sessions were held in far-away Rheims, at the other end of the French kingdom. The dispute had flared up once more; but this time it was not the *vicomte* who sought a judgement from the Pope, but Archbishop Richard, a product of the Roman curia and a papal appointment. The Papacy undoubtedly had the upper hand.

The calibre of the French episcopate had not been adversely affected by nepotism, nor by payments made to secular rulers with a view to influencing their choice of bishop. The case of Guifred himself – reformer and simoniac combined – demonstrates this. For secular rulers feared God and his wrath; they were worried about death and the life hereafter; some – possibly most – of them were fully aware of their duties to the Church, and almost all of them realized the advantages of an educated episcopate, if not a chaste one. They probably kept a less attentive eye on the bishops for whom they were responsible than on the monasteries whose prayers guaranteed their eternal salvation. We need not take the reformers' vituperative criticisms at face value. The bishops' actions are the best gauge of their moral worth, and the bishop of Marseilles was not alone in relinquishing his jurisdiction over a monastic house. They were all keen to improve the material fabric of their cathedrals, and this is often criticized as excessive concern with prestige and display. However, the same resources could easily have been directed to less praiseworthy ends. Many bishops worked for an improvement in clerical morality, following the example of Archbishop Adalbero of Rheims who, well before 1000 brought his cathedral clergy under the strict Augustinian rule, imposing silence and a temperate common life.

In northern France at least, the cathedral clergy displayed an enthusiasm for learning equal to that of the scholars of the Carolingian Renaissance. Evidence of this is to be found in the flourishing cathedral school at Rheims in the late tenth century and in the learning of Fulbert of Chartres in the early eleventh century, together with that of the canons of Orléans, whose meditations on the Holy Spirit displayed such intellectual audacity that they were accused of heresy. Then there was Master Bernard of the cathedral school at Angers, shocked by the materialism of peasant devotion in the course of his travels in the Auvergne; or the scholar Berengar of Tours, who had the confidence to advance his own new interpretation of the eucharist. Scholarship was stimulated by general progress. One consequence was a clearer view of what had bound society together in less troubled times. Finally, increased mobility was one of the prime consequences of the rise in population; mental horizons also broadened and endeavours were more co-ordinated. In short, growth enabled large-scale restoration to be set in hand.

In 1049 Pope Leo IX – who had been enthroned the previous Christmas Day by his cousin, the Emperor Henry III – decided to go on a journey.

As bishop of Toul, he had worked tirelessly for reform with his colleagues in Lorraine. His regional, family and household background all preserved Carolingian tradition in its purest form, and his notion of reform inevitably had an imperial basis. He believed there should be simultaneous reform throughout Western Christendom and that it was the duty of the Pope, as the successor of St Peter, to lead the reform movement. He travelled systematically the length and breadth of the Empire to instigate it. From Mainz, he reached Rheims in October. A council was to be held to reform the state of the clergy in northern France. The bishops of the region were summoned, not by the king, but by the Pope, taking upon himself the role of the secular ruler. Secular kingship – whose powers to act in ecclesiastical matters were already being whittled away by the reduction of regalian rights and the gradual separation of secular and ecclesiastical affairs – was further debased by this move. In the event, it was primarily bishops from Normandy and the region of the lower Loire who responded to the papal summons. There were a few from Capetian lands, but the majority would neither attend nor allow the king to go to Rheims. On this occasion the French bishops stood loyally beside their sovereign with the great lay magnates, zealous in the defence of royal prerogative. Following their advice, Henry I made his excuses and did not attend.

Support for the Papacy came mainly from the areas of the old kingdoms of Lotharingia and Burgundy, and included the archbishops of Trier, Besançon and Lyon and the abbot of Cluny. With their backing, the Pope launched his initiative for moral reform. The clergy were forbidden to carry arms or associate with women; simony and worldly corruption were to be rooted out. Secular rulers were no longer to contract incestuous or bigamous marriages. The council accordingly excommunicated a number of counts who had married their cousins; the bishops of Langres, Nantes, Beauvais and Amiens and the archbishop of Sens (whose morals were all notoriously lax) were deposed. This was a warning to other bishops of what might befall them if they were reluctant to acknowledge papal supremacy. So the reform of the French episcopate began without and despite the king. Many of the French bishops were shocked at the way in which this rigid, itinerant Pope ignored royal prerogative in pursuit of his imperial dream.

Leo IX had been brought up in the monasticism of Lorraine, a rule even more austere than the Cluniacs, preserving Carolingian attitudes to the Church and society. Most significantly it did not – unlike Cluniac monasticism – challenge episcopal supremacy. There was one exception: since of all men the monks – least tainted by worldly contact – were subordinate to their bishop, it was imperative that the bishops themselves should lead lives purer even than those of the monks. In the Pope's mind, reform of the episcopate was the essential prerequisite for reform of any kind. In his view, the French king could not carry out such a programme himself, even in the northern part of the kingdom, where he lived. It could only be done by the Papacy, itself recently reformed by an enlightened Emperor. Thus reform was set in hand by the Pope, not only without the French king, but in defiance of his authority, and it threatened to break the alliance between king and bishops, which had been effective since the 1020s. Leo IX did not make any direct approach to Henry I of France. His plans were steeped in Carolingian imperialism, however, and this encouraged him to copy the actions of one of his predecessors. At a council held in Rome in 998, the Pope had threatened to anathematize Henry's father, King Robert, for bigamy and incest (as other French princes were threatened at the council of Rheims in 1049), demanding that the king should separate from his wife and condemning the French bishops for their compliance. Fifty years before, the Pope was already claiming jurisdiction over the sexual morality of kings and the right to suspend bishops who proved excessively loyal to their temporal lord.

Claims to papal supremacy hardened as the Church adopted a more overtly monarchical form; one consequence was the hostility of the papal household to the French king. In the middle of the eleventh century, he seemed their principal adversary in France. The king straddled the spiritual and the temporal by virtue of the unction of his coronation. Half of the king's person was committed to the episcopate, and as such he could be seen as a major competitor; it was his royal office that was likely to prove a stumbling-block to ecclesiastical reform. However, the French king's sacerdotal role provided the Papacy with a pretext for keeping a careful watch upon him, and in particular upon the actions of the other half of the royal personage in the temporal sphere.

The Papacy had to fight for reform on all fronts at once. Leo IX travelled constantly. He drew up a team of delegates on the Carolingian imperial model, and sent the members out in different directions. One of these legates, responsible for moral reform in various regions and for the control of dogma, was the monk Hildebrand, who opposed Berengar of Tours and became Pope Gregory VII in 1073. He at once tackled the French king: Philip (son of Henry) was accused of predation, demanding payment – like all lords of the period – from the increasing numbers of merchants who travelled through his lands (Italians amongst them), who were beginning to journey across the Ile-de-France with the expansion of trade. The Pope also accused Philip of trading in the sacred, since he accepted presents from bishops recently appointed to sees which he controlled.

Gregory VII's stance became more aggressive once he was convinced of the decline of Capetian prestige. He tried to persuade the Frankish bishops, writing to them in 1074 that 'the decline of the once famous and powerful kingdom of France from its glorious state began a long time ago'. He decided to take advantage of this decline, working tirelessly to fill the French episcopate with reformed prelates in Gothia, the Narbonnais and in Provence beyond the Rhône. This was not because the bishops here were more corrupt than those farther north, but because the territorial princes in the south were particularly devoted to St Peter and responded more readily to papal influence; the expansion of Cluniac monasticism and in particular the influence of St Victor at Marseilles had eroded diocesan power more than in the north; above all, the king of France was an almost forgotten figure.

In some places there was an urgent need for reform. At Sisteron, for example, the see had been vacant for seventeen years: Raimbaud, lord of the region, had purchased it for his son, but had then decided he should have the bishopric of Vaison instead, while he exploited the diocesan revenues himself, as if they were part of his own domain lands. 'Raimbaud sold, his knights bought.' At the council of Avignon in 1060, the arch-bishop of Arles, the abbot of Cluny and the papal legates excommunicated Raimbaud and appointed a new bishop from outside the region, a canon regular from the collegiate foundation at Oulx. However, the new bishop 'could not even cross the city . . . he was repulsed on all sides'. It is clear from this that episcopal corruption was by no means universally frowned upon. Reform encountered opposition from the clergy themselves, as well as from the townspeople. In the south of France, they gave way before papal resolve. After 1050 a number of southern bishops were deprived of their office and replaced in a veritable cultural revolution. According to E. Magnou-Nortier, this policy dislocated 'one of the most important assumptions of the old social order, based on the complementarity of lay and ecclesiastical functions'. Political stability had also depended upon complicity between the higher reaches of the Church and the upper nobility, bound by close ties of kinship. The proponents of Gregorian reform tore these bonds apart, as they high-mindedly promoted absolute segregation of the laity and the Church. They succeeded in removing the episcopate from secular control, but the alliance between temporal princes and the Church was also killed at a stroke. Can we be confident that this alliance had been a positive socio-political force, or that there is any direct connection between its abrupt termination and the dramatic growth of heresy in the following century? I think E. Magnou-Nortier is convincing on this point, when she paints a picture of the bishops of Gothia bullied and humiliated by papal legates. I am not convinced that 'they never recovered their lost grandeur'. However, it is clear that these first thrusts were sufficient to influence the secular rulers. This region was henceforth one of the surest bastions of papal support. Long before the move to Avignon in the fourteenth century, if the Papacy was checked by imperial ventures in Italy, it could rely on the whole-hearted support of the Rhône valley and southern France. After the mid-eleventh century these regions served as a springboard for reform elsewhere in France.

In order to weaken the French king's position, the Pope aimed to isolate what he referred to as the *regnum Franciae*, reckoning on a loosening of the bonds that bound the other territorial principalities within the framework of the kingdom. He tried to encourage the autonomy of these other *regna*. First the duke of Aquitaine (in 1064), then the duke of Normandy (in 1066) received the *vexillum*, or standard of St Peter. When he gave it to them, the Pope blessed their military enterprises – in this case expeditions outside France against the infidels in Spain and the unreformed English Church – but by the same action he also made them his standard-bearers and auxiliaries, incorporating them into his household and extending his power and protection to them. We should not underestimate the significance of a symbolic gesture, such as the acceptance of a standard. It bound the recipient in the same way as the acceptance of arms. The scene in the Bayeux Tapestry showing William of Normandy arming Harold indicates that – by this ceremony – Harold became part of William's household. In the early twelfth century Louis VI raised the *oriflamme*, the banner of St Denis, to show – as he said – that he owed homage to the saint 'as his standard-bearer'. Guy Geoffrey of Aquitaine and William of Normandy could surely also be taken as St Peter's men?

The papal legates took more decisive action against the count of Anjou. This minor principality was indisputably a dependency of the kingdom of France. In 1067 one of the Pope's agents had the effrontery to dispose of this lordship. The count had violated the liberty of the Church, by attempting to control a number of monastic houses to an extent which they found unacceptable. The legates aimed to remove them from secular control. They confiscated Anjou from Count Geoffrey the Bearded, giving it instead to his brother (Fulk Rechin) 'on behalf of St Peter'. The scribe who drew up the relevant document did not want this ambiguous phrase to be forgotten. The words can be construed as meaning that by this concession St Peter, bishop of Rome, became the count's lord, in place of the king of France. The latter was by no means excluded from these arrangements: the new count was to reach agreement with him and hand over his ancestral lands at Château-Landon to the king. The Roman curia seems to have hoped to use the granting of a benefice and creation of personal dependence to extend papal influence over territorial principalities, as it had over Cluniac monasteries. This policy could be followed openly in the south, further from the centres of Capetian power. In 1081 the count of Provence did homage to the Pope; four years later the count of Mauguio formally acknowledged that his lordship was held jointly from the Pope and the bishop of Maguelonne, and henceforth he made an annual payment of an ounce of gold, a symbol of his subordination to the Pope, not unlike the payment which expressed Cluniac allegiance. The Pope at this point was Gregory VII, who carried the reforming offensive into northern France.

He entrusted this endeavour to two bishops appointed to recently reformed areas. Amat, bishop of Oloron, and Hugh, bishop of Die, making one archbishop of Bordeaux, the other archbishop of Lyons. Reform in the northern provinces was entrusted to them. In 1080 Hugh of Die was moved to the archbishopric of Rheims. Eight years later he appointed Ivo, a canon regular from Beauvais, to the see of Chartres, despite the opposition of the archbishop of Sens, who refused to consecrate the bishop-elect. In 1088 the Pope performed the consecration himself at Capua. The archbishop, however, was supported by Philip I of France, who summoned a council at Rheims in 1094 to drive out Yvo of Chartres. The Roman curia and the French king were now in open conflict.

Fulk Rechin, count of Anjou (whom the Papacy had substituted for his brother seventeen years before), was excommunicated for abusing his position, because he had kept his brother in prison until he went mad. This excommunication was at once annulled by Hugh of Die, who then summoned a council at Autun, where the weapon of excommunication was turned against Philip I of France. It had nothing to do with simony or the appropriation of ecclesiastical possessions; the issue was one of personal morality, for the French king had contracted a marriage that was both bigamous and incestuous. He had married the wife of Fulk Rechin, although his first wife was still alive. Moreover, the second wife (Bertrada of Montfort) was also his cousin. These were sufficient grounds to ensure that the French king's behaviour towards the Papacy would now be more submissive and circumspect. The legates were supported by Ivo of Chartres, the only French bishop to have criticized the marriage openly. Another ally was the repentant and submissive count of Anjou, who from this date onwards decreed that the deeds issued by his chancery were not to be dated by the regnal years of Philip, 'whose adultery sullies the kingdom of France', but by those of the Pope. Such alterations to scribal practice are a clear indication that the French king's transgression had resulted in a transfer of sovereignty to the Pope, Urban II, former grand prior of the Cluniac order.

Like Leo IX before him, Urban II travelled, demonstrating his power throughout the world and convening reforming councils in a few chosen places. One was held at Piacenza in the north of Italy, where canons were promulgated that further emphasized the gulf between priests and laity. Priestly celibacy became compulsory and lay rights to episcopal investiture were declared null and void: all aspects of the investiture ceremony which implied any ecclesiastical dependence on a temporal power were banned. Then the Pope went to France, first visiting the regions where his supremacy was uncontested. Letters summoning a general council were sent out from Valence and Le Puy. It was to be held at Clermont in the Auvergne, on the very borders of the Capetian domain and the ecclesiastical provinces whose bishops and archbishops had showed themselves unduly influenced by Carolingian tradition and over-respectful of the dignity and prerogatives of the French king, witness their blessing of Philip's marriage and the lone criticisms of Ivo of Chartres.

At the end of 1095 Clermont was the setting for a magnificent display of theocracy triumphant. The entire population assembled round the sovereign pontiff, who filled the place reserved in earlier assemblies for holy relics, in other words for God himself. Once he had turned his attention to the north, Urban II took personal control of episcopal reform there, amending and making further additions to the decrees passed at Piacenza, in order to detach the bishops further from the French king: 'All bishops and priests are forbidden to perform liege homage to the king or any other secular lord.' The word 'liege' implies overriding personal allegiance. By using this term, the edict was not forbidding all forms of allegiance; but it provided justification for any cleric who might want to debate a point, side-step his obligations, or betray his secular lord. Urban II's policy was to extend the prescriptions of the peace of God, so that they might be uniformly observed throughout Christendom – a fitting task for the uniquely responsible vicar of the omnipotent God. After these preambles, Urban II solemnly confirmed Philip I's excommunication. Then the Pope, consciously imitating the legendary Charlemagne and acting as supreme guide of the people towards the glory of the Second Coming of Christ, launched what we call the 'First Crusade' from this meadow outside the gates of the old city of Clermont in central France. The text of his appeal has been lost, but chroniclers put words such as these into the Pope's mouth:

Come to the aid of your brothers in the East. The infidel has advanced as far as the Bosphorus, just outside Constantinople. They have already defeated them seven times in battle; they wish to crush them entirely. Which is why I exhort you – or rather, our Lord himself exhorts you, rich and poor – to leave your homes and go to their aid. Those who die on the journey or in combat will have full remission of their sins. Let those who until now have been moved only to fight their fellow-Christians now take up arms against the infidel.

Urban II was taking up a scheme of Gregory VII's. Twenty years earlier, he had cherished hopes of responding positively to the Byzantine Emperor's appeal for help against the Turks. He saw this as an opportunity for reconciliation with the eastern Church and its possible submission to the authority of Rome. Nevertheless, all the fundamental characteristics of the papal appeal of 1095 were enshrined in the ideology of the peace of God: the internal aggression of the warrior class was diminished by turning it outward towards the enemies of Christ, working for the extension of Christendom, the succour of oppressed Christians and the protection of pilgrims. Henceforth, the sword which distinguished the warrior class was only to be used in the struggle against evil. The turbulent knights had been checked to some extent by the peace of God and by truces, but fighting a holy war under the cross of victory would give them the opportunity to practise their true vocation. A war of this kind had been fought in southern Europe for the past fifty years. The territorial princes of the south of France, together with knights from the kingdom of France, Aquitaine and Catalonia and others from more distant regions, such as Champagne and Burgundy, regularly fought the Muslims along the pilgrim route to the shrine of St James the Great at Compostella, supporting the efforts of the kings of Aragon and Castile to drive back the forces of Islam. In 1063 Alexander II had promised remission of sins to all participants, and this proved a great stimulus, resulting in a great increase in numbers. The very next year the count of Poitiers gathered a large force of mounted knights, which he led into Aragon. They captured Barbastro, with fabulous plunder. In 1073 a northern lord, Eble, count of Roucy, brother-in-law of the king of Aragon, also went south: according to Abbot Suger, he rode like a king in the midst of his huge army. Five years later the duke of Burgundy led a new expedition, with less happy results.

Every source emphasizes how lucrative these Spanish expeditions were. By risking their lives in expeditions to these thriving regions, which offered every kind of delight, these knights could save their souls. Who could imagine a more enjoyable form of penance? The Papacy had acquired control of these expeditions, blessing the forces, guaranteeing a form of spiritual wage and entitling them to the same protection as unarmed pilgrims and the poor. Like pilgrims, these 'warriors of Christ' were especially entrusted to divine protection. Clermont codified the institutions of holy war, the counterpart of those of the peace of God. This time, however, their goal was to be the Holy Sepulchre at Jerusalem, the tomb of Christ.

The appeal of Jerusalem was even greater than that of the shrine of St Peter at Rome or of St James of Compostella. For every pious Christian dreamed of visiting the holy places and dying there, close to the graves in the Valley of Jehoshaphat, ideally placed for the final resurrection. Fewer went on this pilgrimage, for the dangers and deprivations of the journey, to say nothing of attacks by the infidel, required a higher level of commitment. Nevertheless, the numbers of pilgrims increased about the year 1000. Fulk Nerra of Anjou and Robert, duke of Normandy, both set out on this perilous journey, taking leave of their friends and families as if they were close to death. Since then, the upheavals in the East had made the undertaking still more hazardous. On the other hand, cultural progress was gradually drawing Christianity away from quasi-superstitious and unthinking adoration, centred almost exclusively on the liturgy. Christian faith was now focused more upon the realities of the New Testament, and the accounts of the life of Jesus in the synoptic gospels became the object of more sustained attention. Jerusalem, Bethany and Calvary became increasingly real to Christians in the West. Finally, there was the continuing influence of an eschatological vision, in which all humanity moved towards the site of Christ's passion, resurrection and ascension, under the aegis of an entirely spiritual monarchical power, for one final redemptive journey as the Last Judgement approached. The Emperor had been replaced by the Pope; it was thus his duty to give the signal for departure, and this, accordingly, he did. Then, in the first months of 1096, he travelled into the Capetian domain as far as Angers and then Tours. Like all his ancestors before him, Philip I was abbot of the monastery of St Martin at Tours, and it was here that Urban II held his coronation, giving a golden rose to the count of Anjou and securing his allegiance with this magnificent gift. From Tours he wrote highly critical letters to the archbishops of Rheims and Sens, who maintained normal relations with their excommunicated king. Then he returned south, via Bordeaux, Toulouse and Nîmes. This extended tour was to have a considerable impact on the development of forms of government in western Europe.

It is important to remember that this was a period of expansion. Progress is most dazzlingly reflected in cultural achievements; and it was remarkably rapid in architecture. During Urban II's time at Cluny, for example, the master-craftsmen responsible for work on the great abbey church discovered they could use stone vaults instead of the wooden roofing originally envisaged. This rapid progress in all spheres explains the unexpected and disconcertingly enthusiastic response to the crusade in the kingdom of France.

The appeal was not made to the king: his excommunication automatically excluded him from this great adventure. He remained silent. His fourteen-year-old son could have gone, since he had reached the age of

majority. But since he was the only legitimate son and the king's heir, his
life could not be risked. However, Philip's brother Hugh of Vermandois
was deemed expendable. He took the cross, sewing the red pilgrim's badge
on his clothes, like the other participants. The house of Capet was thus
represented by one of its most important members. Nor was the crusading
appeal addressed particularly to northern France. In the minds of Urban II
and his advisers, this was a papal expedition. The south of France had
been under tight papal control for the past twenty years, and it was
therefore anticipated that this region would provide most of the men and
their leaders. There were to be two principal leaders, one a bishop, the
other a count, reflecting the bipartite structure of society and the purest
traditions of Christian imperialism. Adhémar of Monteil, the distinguished
bishop of Le Puy, would represent the Pope; Raymond de St-Gilles,
count of Toulouse, the secular arm. Consequently, the Papacy was stag-
gered by the positive response from the Capetian kingdom itself. It was so
intense and lasted for so long, that the word 'Franks' (*Francs*) was used to
describe all pilgrims to the Holy Land throughout the crusading era. The
title of Guibert of Nogent's account of the First Crusade was '*Gesta Dei per
Francos*' (The Deeds of God, as undertaken by the Franks).

The majority of participants in fact came from northern France. From
the spring of 1096, the 'poor' also made ready for their departure to the
East. Urban II had undoubtedly also called upon them, but no one had
imagined that they would actually come. In the event, they responded with
alacrity, and were the first to do so. It was as if there was a great
mobilization of all the marginalized members of society. There had been
similar movements during periods of famine, and sudden, spontaneous
waves of peasant migration had periodically affected different regions, to
the amazement of monastic chroniclers, who may have exaggerated them
somewhat. These were a by-product of population increase, but they were
also one consequence of successful ecclesiastical reform, which carried
within itself the seeds of social unrest. Although it was suppressed for the
time being, there was a distinctly subversive strain in reformist thought. In
its appeal for a return to the discipline and purity of the early Church, it
put a premium upon individual freedom and the spiritual quest. People
were encouraged to read the Acts of the Apostles more attentively, and it
was hoped that the highest members of the ecclesiastical hierarchy would
want to live a life of poverty amongst the poor, like the first disciples. At
the end of the eleventh century, the number of fanatical penitents on the
fringe of the Church increased rapidly. They disappeared into the forests
in the west and the mountains of eastern France; some had previously been
canons, and had become convinced that ecclesiastical reform in the towns
should go further; they had left the cities far behind them, living on herbs

and roots in solitude and silence, only to find themselves pursued by bands of fanatics. Others remained in the suburbs of the rapidly expanding towns, denouncing rich and worldly priests, preaching the way to the promised land and constantly reiterating the name 'Jerusalem'. It was by means of such agitators – Peter the Hermit was one of the most famous – that Urban II's crusading appeal echoed amongst the least stable sections of the population. Great hordes of them were on the move, in pursuit of the old millenarian dream, massacring Jews in passing and being massacred in their turn.

In northern France the knightly contingents made their preparations without undue haste, calmly organized by the territorial princes, of whom almost all took the cross. Within the kingdom itself, the descendants of Charlemagne were appointed leaders of the French, by virtue of their distinguished ancestry: they were Godefroy of Bouillon, duke of Lower Lorraine; his brother, the count of Boulogne, and the count of Hainault. The count of Brittany, the duke of Normandy and his brother-in-law, the count of Blois, went too. Count Robert of Flanders, who had only just returned from a penitential journey to the Holy Land, also joined them. At the end of the summer, the army of Christ was ready to set off. It was divided into independent sections, each consisting of great households similar to the itinerant courts which accompanied counts or dukes in their ceaseless travels through their principalities, on their occasional journeys beyond its frontiers to worship at a particular shrine, or to attend the king's coronation. Each of these companies consisted of knights from the region, but also included women, servants and all sorts of youthful hangers-on. They were essentially inward-looking and lost no opportunity to score points off the other French contingents. Three years' travelling did nothing to diminish their mutual hostility.

That was only the beginning. The 'expedition to Jerusalem' was prolonged indefinitely. For almost 300 years, groups of armed pilgrims continued to go out to join the 'Franks' already established in the Holy Land during the intervals between the major campaigns. The crusade was a powerful influence on political development throughout France; I shall single out two aspects here.

Above all, the crusade provided an outlet for chivalric energies. The restrictions on marriage in the warrior classes undoubtedly curbed the expansion of a predominantly military society but, as we have seen, this brought its own problems. These energies could now be expended primarily in expeditions to the East, which provided numerous younger sons with the opportunity of founding their own dynasty abroad, as well as – above all – being terribly massacred. The crusade strengthened the peace of God immeasurably and was in effect an extension of it. It was a powerful

influence for peace in France, encouraging the re-establishment and con-
solidation of secular states.

The crusade considerably increased the prestige of the territorial princes
who participated in this venture – with the exception of those who, like
Stephen of Blois, returned home covered in ignominy and shame, so
dishonoured that he felt himself obliged to return to the Holy Land to die.
Ideally, the French king should have been the first among them. By
excluding him because of the excommunication, the Pope had successfully
discredited Philip of France. The First Crusade proclaimed at Clermont
eased the conscience of Capetian France more than any that followed –
for none of the rest met such an enthusiastic response. This somewhat
tarnished the reputation of the French king and diminished his prestige, in
a way that would have afforded Gregory VII considerable satisfaction.

Nevertheless, the development of Philip's tangled matrimonial affairs
demonstrates the solid basis of the French kingdom in its opposition to the
Roman curia. For all his alleged bigamy and incest, Philip would not yield.
He made a fine pretence of doing so, accompanied by fair words, but kept
his wife. He realized he had widespread support within the kingdom. First
of all there were the territorial princes: as a loyal vassal, Duke William IX
of Aquitaine promptly dismissed the council which had assembled at
Poitiers in 1099 with a view to excommunicating the king afresh. Above
all, the French bishops stood by him, and this too was a surprise for the
Papacy. Apart from their reluctance to submit to papal control, with all its
rebukes and commands, they were very conscious of the personal tie
between their episcopal office and the French crown. This remarkable display of solidarity made the Gregorian reformers – notably Ivo of Chartres
– think again: the Carolingian model of the king acting in concert with his
bishops proved stronger than they had anticipated. As a result, once Philip
had performed the necessary penance in the abbey church of St Germain-
des-Prés near Paris in 1105 (where he appeared barefoot, in the clothes of a
penitent, to hear the Pope's letter and promised to put an end to his sinful
marriage – a promise that no one cared to check on), the Pope's attitude
changed dramatically.

The great threat to the Papacy now came from the Emperor, king of the
Germans, and this made the Pope adopt a less arrogant attitude towards
the French king. He was now ready to be satisfied with mere appearances
as far as the illicit marriage was concerned and to moderate his demands
for nomination procedures for the French episcopate. It was now politically expedient for the Papacy to make an ally of the French king. In 1107
Pascal II visited Germany, vainly attempting to reach agreement with the

Emperor Henry V; however, he had no problems with the two associated monarchs, Philip I of France and his son Louis.

Philip and Louis were ready to accept the free election of French bishops by cathedral chapters. In exchange, the Pope agreed that no election would be made without the prior agreement of the sovereign. In other words, the canons of a cathedral had to discuss the matter with the king and take account of the preferences he expressed. Furthermore, it was agreed that the regalian rights (the seigneurial prerogatives that accompanied the episcopal office) should be bestowed upon the bishop-elect by the king after an oath of loyalty and the traditional investiture ceremony – a further papal concession, since this also implied the reversion of regalian rights to the king whenever the see was vacant as a result of the death or deposition of a bishop. The sovereign was then fully entitled to exploit these revenues as long as the see remained vacant. Thus the 'Gregorian crisis' came to an end at the beginning of the twelfth century. It had posed a serious threat to the French crown, but also prepared the way for its recovery. There are three aspects that merit especial consideration.

Henceforth the Pope sought refuge in northern France rather than the south in his quarrels with the Empire, either to flout secular imperial authority or to negotiate. Historians call this conflict between Empire and Papacy at the end of Philip I's reign the 'investiture contest': it undoubtedly strengthened the bond between the Pope and the king of France, for whom it was an incalculable advantage.

The reform of the episcopate under Calixtus II was no less advantageous. Unlike his predecessors, this Pope did not have a monastic background, but had previously been archbishop of Vienne. He put an end to policies which deliberately favoured Cluniac monasticism, which continued to flourish quite independently of the Papacy. Foundations at Grandmont, La Grande Chartreuse and Cîteaux gave expression to new forms of monasticism, inspired by eastern forms of Christianity and responding to a new thirst for asceticism, one consequence of the assiduous study of the New Testament. Moreover, these monks had no quarrel with episcopal control, and their monasteries proved a fertile breeding ground for excellent bishops. Numerous French bishoprics were of course in the hands of other secular lords, who controlled appointments and had reversion of regalian rights, just as the king did, and who, like the king, benefitted from episcopal reform. However, vastly more bishops owed allegiance to the king than to any other lord. The Capetians never lost control of the crucial group of four metropolitan sees in northern France: Rheims, Sens, Tours and Bourges. The bishops of Le Puy and Mende also began to look towards the French king from their areas of undecided sovereignty, as the partition at Verdun began to take effect, finally acknowledging themselves part of the kingdom of France. The king's coronation naturally placed him at the centre of the college of bishops, making him – with their advice – the natural protector of the Church in France. As the process of ecclesiastical reform drew to a close, it led ineluctably back to Carolingian tradition and the ideal model which Adalbero of Laon had proposed at the beginning of the eleventh century, never dreaming that political reality would one day take this form.

Finally, Gregorian reform introduced rational thought into the exercise of power. In the thick of the struggle with secular powers over priestly celibacy and lay marriage, the Church had been forced to prepare its case by collecting standard texts and organizing them. This was done more rigorously once the first rudiments of Greek logic – translated from Arabic – reached France, another consequence of successful holy war and the conquest of Toledo by the Christians. Gregorian reform set spiritual and temporal powers against each other, but was also responsible for the growth of a third power, the *magistri*, or intellectuals. These *magistri* were distinct from the *domini* (lords), and their origins lay in the Church, directed towards her aspirations to power and liberty, but in no way limited to them. Secular rulers had no problems in making use of these men. It was impossible for all those who attended cathedral schools and studied holy writ or Roman law to make a career in the Church. Many found employment in secular courts, where they were able to deploy their skills in juridical debate. Patristic texts and conciliar canons were studied most intensely north of the Loire, close to those cathedrals which were repositories of Carolingian scholarship, around Paris and in Paris itself. Once again, the king was best placed to draw upon these resources.

8

King and Lord

Philip I (1060–1108) was the first Capetian king to be given this name, which had been brought from the East by Anna of Kiev (the bride who had been found so far away for Henry I, son of Robert the Pious). It was imperative that he married a royal princess and there was none nearer home to whom he was not related within the forbidden decrees, a point which had now become crucial because of the Church's insistence on the issue. Philip was king of France from 1060 to 1108, one of the longest reigns in French history. He was only eight years old when his father died and had already been crowned two years before. No one was surprised at the succession of such a young child, for this office was an 'honour', and as such passed from father to son according to the principle of primogeniture, like any other high dignity or title held by the French nobility. All that was needed was for the boy to have a guardian during the six remaining years of his minority. This responsibility was not given to his mother, for at this date power was exercised exclusively by men. In fact, no sooner was she widowed than one of the great lords of France, the count of Valois, snapped her up as a great matrimonial prize. The boy's closest male relative was appointed guardian, following the traditional practice of the nobility, and Baldwin, count of Flanders carried out this task with integrity. The six-year-long minority is a fair indication that, three generations after Hugh Capet's seizure of the French crown, the royal dynasty had nothing to fear.

Philip cuts a sorry figure in traditional history books. He is inevitably compared with some of his more colourful contemporaries – men such as Raymond of St-Gilles, count of Toulouse and hero of the First Crusade; Robert the Frisian, who did not scruple to rob his two young nephews of the county of Flanders while he was their guardian; William of Normandy, conqueror of England; or William of Aquitaine, who seized the county of Toulouse one moment, the next organized an expedition to the Holy Land single-handed after the conquest of Jerusalem, besides writing the earliest French love poetry to have survived in the vernacular. Many historians have seen Philip I as an indolent pleasure-seeker, 'wallowing in the pleasures of bed and table' while the reins of real political power slipped from his grasp.

Many factors influence such a judgement, but the king's excommunication was undoubtedly the most important. The writing of history was a clerical prerogative in the Middle Ages, and these authors presented Philip as the abductor of another man's wife and as a king whose uncritical acceptance of current lay attitudes to marriage, as well as his defence of royal rights to episcopal appointments, were an obstacle to reform of the Church. This was the view of the early twelfth-century monastic chroniclers, whose allegiance was generally to the Capetian's major rival, the king of England. It was also expressed by Abbot Suger, who painted an unduly critical portrait of Philip I so that the (undoubtedly exaggerated) virtues of Louis VI would stand out all the more in contrast with his predecessor. However, Philip I has also been severely criticized by nineteenth- and twentieth-century historians because of the way in which royal power declined in the course of his reign.

All the princes of the realm had been present at Philip's coronation in 1060, with the exception of the duke of Normandy. The cathedral church at Rheims had resounded to their cries of acclamation, symbolic of their right and duty to give the king counsel and military aid as the faithful servants of the kingdom. Fifty years later, Philip's successor had to be crowned hurriedly and furtively; speed was of the essence and Rheims too far away. The archbishop of Sens therefore performed the ceremony at Orléans, anointing the new king with oil which had not come from the holy ampulla, the sacred vessel which had descended to the kings of France from the time of Clovis. Henry I of England refused to pay the homage he owed as duke of Normandy; so did the dukes of Aquitaine and Burgundy. Royal power and influence had clearly declined. Without either prelates or the great lay magnates, the royal court had lost its splendour. The prestigious setting that had surrounded the kings of France since the Carolingian period had melted away. Nothing now remained of the convivial companionship which brought the king into direct contact for several days at a time with those who held power throughout the kingdom. These relationships and the royal setting are of cardinal importance in explaining the dramatic change in the attitude of the great nobles towards the king. It looks as if we should place in the 1060s the establishment of what we (in a form of shorthand) call the 'feudal' system, a crucial juncture in the history of power.

It was at this juncture that royal power retreated into a purely domestic context. The *curia*, or royal court, took on the appearance of a mere *curtis*, or enclosure where noble and peasant tucked themselves away. The sovereign's entourage was no more than his household, like that of any other noble. It is no coincidence that the most striking episode in the course of Philip's exceptionally long reign was an essentially familial and domestic one – his marriage – or that it should have been a woman, the adulterous queen, Bertrada of Montfort, who occupied the limelight. In 1100 Philip, now in his fifties, decided that his place on military expeditions should be taken by his eldest son. Like other good fathers of the period, he did not make this decision from weakness or cowardice or so that he could sit back and lead a quiet life, but because he realized that practical military control was the prerequisite of effective kingship. His eldest son was by then twenty-seven years old; he had been knighted seven years previously and had acquitted himself well during the intervening period. He was known as the 'king-designate', for he had not been crowned; his father had simply presented him as his associate to the assembled members of his household.

Detailed analysis of the witness lists to royal charters shows that bishops and lay magnates were gradually replaced by the king's relatives and knights garrisoned in royal castles or in the towns with royal palaces which the king visited regularly in the course of his continual peregrinations through the kingdom. Finally, there were the heads of the four different departments of the royal household: chancellor, seneschal, butler and chamberlain. The chancellor was always a cleric, since he was responsible for the chapel and royal ceremonies and all written documents. On the other hand, the seneschal (or steward) had to be a knight, for it was he who took his royal master's place in military affairs. He personally carved the sovereign's meat, and he was also responsible for the organization of banquets, where the lord king ate in public, demonstrating his role as the people's nurturer. The vital importance of wine in ceremonies accompanying negotiation and at assemblies of vassals explains the importance of the butler, who had charge of the royal cellar. Finally, there was the chamberlain, whose duties revolved around the king's chamber, away from the public gaze. He was also responsible for everything placed there for safe keeping: the royal treasury, with its reserves of coin and splendid ornaments, as well as the jewels which were worn by the king on feast-days to express his power and glory. Since royal power was essentially domestic, it centred on these household offices. The most powerful lords who still frequented the royal court (the *vicomtes* and castellans of the Ile-de-France) competed avidly for these influential posts. Rival parties formed and squabbled over petty responsibilities at court. Political power rested with

the major-domos of the royal household, as it had at the collapse of the
Merovingian monarchy.

Royal power was now derived essentially from what the king held as an
individual – his domain, his lands and those who served him, besides
forests, rights of justice, tolls and powers of exploitation over the inhabitants and travellers in the vicinity of particular castles and within the walls
of certain cities – all held within an area stretching from Montreuil-sur-
Mer on the Channel coast to the countryside south of Orléans. Maps
attempting to represent feudal France give the impression that the royal
domain was very compact, especially in comparison with Aquitaine or the
county of Toulouse. In fact royal possessions were scattered and fragmented within this area, just like those of any other great lord (or, indeed,
peasant inheritances), and their history is essentially a series of successful
boundary disputes. This lordship was the source not only of sustenance,
but of all services and firm ties of loyalty. It was administered by officials
called *prévôts*, more affluent members of the peasantry who farmed the
king's seigneurial rights, paying for them in advance. This system ensured
that the royal household was provisioned, while relieving the king of the
responsibility for the day-to-day running of the household. The king and
his servants lost no opportunity of increasing this patrimony to meet
increasing expenditure, the inevitable concomitant of a growing money
economy. They acquired neighbouring lordships: in 1068 the Gâtinais was
ceded by the new count of Anjou; in 1077 the Vexin was inherited from
the counts of Valois after their last remaining scion ('St' Simon) had retired
to a monastery, adamantly refusing to marry and produce children to
continue the Valois line; in 1101 the *vicomté* of Bourges – sold by its lord to
raise ready cash for his journey to Jerusalem – was added to their lands.
These acquisitions were made without fuss and absorbed into the administrative framework of the Capetian lands. Philip instructed his officials to
ensure that established custom was turned to good account on his behalf
and to collect what was due to the crown – thereby provoking accusations
of greed from the Pope.

When this retreat into a domain-based lordship is examined more
closely, it appears not only profitable but virtually inevitable. The presence
of the territorial princes at court had often been a problem for the king. In
the reign of King Robert II, the counts of Anjou and Blois had intrigued
against him with his household clerics and his relatives; not long afterwards, the Plantagenet count of Anjou claimed the office of seneschal,
because it would give him a foothold in the royal household. Contraction of
the royal entourage was not without advantages; there were no more counts
palatine or newly established counts to squeeze into gaps in the royal
domain and feed off it. Did they leave the royal court in a bid for
independence, or were they pushed out? The king's position was un-

doubtedly more secure surrounded by his own knights, their loyalty assured by the 'generous payments' mentioned by the chronicler Wace.

Moreover, royal profits from lordship were growing all the time. The Capetian domain was well placed, in a region which after *c*.1050 seems to have benefitted from the increase in pastureland and vineyards, as well as changing agricultural practice. Here the king, by and large, controlled cities, roads and rivers. The population of the cities increased; they became richer with the growing prosperity of the peasantry; more and more merchants used the roads and rivers, trading increasingly valuable goods over longer distances. The earliest, unmistakable evidence for the recovery of trade is to be found in the charters issued by the royal chancery in the reign of Philip I to towns in the royal domain around Beauvais, Orléans, Paris and Laon. Paris was one of the smallest cities of the region, but it was centrally placed, at the intersection of the busiest trade routes. In 1085 Philip bestowed the title *Archichancelier* (archchancellor) – traditionally granted to the archbishop of Rheims – on the bishop of Paris, Godfrey of Boulogne. During Philip's reign the royal court made increasingly frequent visits to Paris. There was thus a gradual return from Orléans to the town chosen by Clovis as his final resting-place.

There are in fact indications of the recovery of the French monarchy just as it appeared to have reached its lowest ebb. The Cluniacs wished to establish a house outside the city of Paris, and in 1079 received permission to incorporate the monastery of St Martin-des-Champs into the order. The bishops here remained loyal at the height of the monarchy's troubles, just as William of Aquitaine did, or even Fulk Rechin, count of Anjou – although at one point the papal legates succeeded in winning him over to the anti-Capetian camp. All the malicious accounts critical of Philip I ignore the negotiations that undoubtedly explain Fulk's lack of protest at the departure of his wife to marry the king and the fact that he may well already have formally repudiated her. (From the king's point of view, marriage to Bertrada was an astute political move, since she was related to the dukes of Normandy on her mother's side and was a member of the Montfort family, which held a castle of enormous strategic importance on the borders of Normandy and the Capetian domain.) Fulk's younger son was brought up in the royal household and received the *comté* from the king himself when his older brother – who had ruled in association with his father for some years previously – died in 1106. The duke of Aquitaine happened to be at the royal court ('by chance', say the chroniclers – in other words, he was not formally summoned) and his presence gave additional splendour to the scene. He led the new count to Angers, where Philip himself (accompanied by his wife) was welcomed by Fulk Rechin with magnificent ceremony, as his king and lord.

A similarly deferential attitude can be seen in the count of Flanders in a document usually cited to illustrate Capetian decline at this date. Henry I of England (son of William the Conqueror) was afraid of an invasion by his older brother, Robert Curthose, duke of Normandy. He made an alliance at Dover (on the boundary, or 'march', of his principality) in 1101 with Robert II of Flanders, which was very similar to the *convenances* (pacts, agreements) of southern France. Very detailed provisions were made to establish the basis of mutual aid for the two parties.

The ceremony of homage was used to guarantee the agreement. The terms themselves were put in writing, however, a reflection of the increasing administrative sophistication of northern France. By placing his hands within those of the king of England, Robert of Flanders accepted him as lord. Henry undertook to defend Robert life and limb: this was above all a pact of mutual defence. In addition Henry bought Robert's services. If the count was captured fighting with or for Henry, his ransom would be paid. Moreover, Henry would pay Robert of Flanders the substantial sum of 500 *livres* in silver annually. Here the 'benefice' (or grant) takes a modern form: as times changed, so money payments began to impinge on politics. With a wage payment, the English king was able to hire the services of a warrior in the same way that a monastery of the period retained a specialized craftsman with an annual payment. Whenever the count of Flanders was summoned (in writing, it should again be noted), he had to be at his employer's service for forty days, together with 1000 knights. This was a large number and Robert would obviously provide considerable military support. The agreement went on to stipulate that each knight was to bring with him two servants (one a squire and the other a youth not yet fully trained in arms) and three war-horses. Here we see another aspect of progress, for the horse had only been used in battle for a relatively short time: since it was now more exposed, replacement had to be anticipated, as with any other piece of equipment.

If he provided these combatants, properly equipped, the count of Flanders met the conditions for payment of what would at a later date be called a 'money fief', or *fief de bourse*. However, the document makes two specific exceptions. If Henry I was attacked by his brother Robert, the count of Flanders' role was only to bring re-enforcements to England; they were to embark at Wissant in ships provided by Henry. In other words, the form of service could change according to context, and this reveals the dominant position of the king of France. Philip I might very well support an attack by Robert of Normandy, who was his vassal, for hostility towards England was a primary characteristic of Capetian policy at this juncture. Immediately after he was knighted in 1097, Prince Louis fought the previous king of England, William Rufus. The French king was Robert of Flanders' liege lord, and had received his homage. What should he do?

According to our sources, he should first try and dissuade him from invading England. This, too, had to be done strictly according to form: not by evil counsel (for there was a whole ethical code relating to *concilium*, forbidding intrigue or evasions that amounted to treachery), nor by corruption and the offering of bribes. (Here again we see how money was acquiring an increasingly high political profile.) If these sincere and loyal efforts had no effect and Philip persisted with the decision to summon his vassals, there was no question of the count of Flanders ignoring the summons and laying himself open to accusations of felony. The agreement did not merely exempt Robert from any response to Henry's appeal; it assumed that he would respond to the summons of the French king. However, he should serve with the smallest possible number of knights. In other words, he was bound to serve Henry of England only if the king of France was not involved. In that case, however, he and his knights were to live as part of the king's household for the entire period; all his expenses were to be met, notably reimbursement of lost war-horses by himself or members of his contingents. Both illness and a summons to the 'host of the king of France' were grounds for dispensation. The claims of the French king, as his liege lord, were overriding. Was this simply a response to the feudal lord from whom he held the county of Flanders? Or was it that as God's representative on earth, the French king was the guardian of public order, summoning his host to maintain peace or restore it within the lands entrusted to him? I think that in the early twelfth century Robert felt bound to respond to the king not because he was his feudal superior, but because – as one of the territorial princes of the French kingdom – his primary loyalty was to the institutions of public peace.

The second exception in the agreement concerned the possibility of Henry attacking Robert of Normandy and campaigning on the continent. If the *comté* of Maine (claimed by both Normans and Angevins) were attacked, the count's service would be less because of the greater distance involved: here he was bound to bring only 500 knights for a month, once a year, with all expenses paid. Robert of Flanders was to respond to an attack on Normandy, however, with full service, and was to meet the expenses of the first week himself. That is, he would take part in the invasion of another country and the concomitant pillage, for a large part of warfare was simply a question of seizing as much as possible. Even so, there was a possibility that the French king might come to the duke's aid and enter Normandy in person: in this case Robert was to fulfil his primary obligations and join the French king with the twenty knights he was bound to provide whenever the king raised his banner. The remaining 980 knights were to remain in the service of the English king, loyal to him as their employer.

The agreement drawn up between Henry I and Robert of Flanders thus respected the system of obligations which (following Carolingian tradition) convened armed military leaders round the king whenever he deemed it necessary. Admittedly they were now obliged to serve with far fewer knights. But in the case of the count of Flanders the lord was bound to serve in person, and that was significant. In the event, Robert of Flanders followed the king of France into battle against the count of Blois, King Henry's ally, and died in combat near Meaux; his son, Count Baldwin, was mortally wounded near Dieppe in 1118, fighting beside the king of France against Henry I, then also duke of Normandy.

At this period 'service' and 'loyalty' were still general concepts not yet strictly regulated by a feudal code. Private contracts such as the one we have examined – which is not exceptional in its attention to detail – established different levels of mutual aid, sealed by an act of private homage between the two individuals. But the anointed king still had a pre-eminent claim on loyalty and service, fostered by long usage. Even the pusillanimous Philip I was well aware of the obligations to the crown of the territorial princes who had proclaimed him king at his coronation. His awareness of the dignity of the royal office is reflected in two particular areas. As Andrew Lewis has demonstrated, Philip was the first Capetian to operate a policy of dynastic territorial acquisition: new possessions (such as the Gâtinais, the Vexin and Bourges) were not inherited by the younger son on his death, but the eldest. When he left only a very small part of their patrimony to his younger son, Philip was making a complete break with contemporary noble practice. We do not know whether this stemmed from a new attitude to royal lands and the belief – not as yet clearly articulated – that they pertained to the crown rather than to the king. It may also have been a purely pragmatic reaction to the succession problems posed by his marriage. The younger son was not a bastard: the king's marriage to his mother (Bertrada of Montfort) had been celebrated with due form and universally acknowledged, even by the Pope.

The other fact is more convincing. Philip's first wife was no more directly descended from Charlemagne than the majority of French noble-women, but their oldest son was nevertheless given the royal name Louis, that is, Clovis. The nobility were always given family names, and it was unthinkable to use those of another dynasty. More significantly, no noble family closely related to the Carolingian kings had ever presumed to choose the names Louis or Charles. The decision of 1078 was a serious matter. Was it Philip's initiative or that of Louis' mother, who had for so long been barren? Or can it be traced to the future St Arnold, monk at St Médard, Soissons, whose experience in questions of infidelity was considered nothing short of miraculous by contemporaries and whom the queen had consulted? Had he perhaps insisted that she promise to give the longed-for heir this name? Whatever the case, the splendour of the first Christian king of France was inevitably reflected on the next prince to bear his name. After Philip's death it was said that his adulterous marriage had bereft him of the miraculous gift to touch for the king's evil (scrofula). Later, the monks of St Denis were to relate that, highly conscious of his lapses, Philip had not dared have his own tomb near the martyr's shrine, close to the Merovingian and Carolingian kings of France. If he was in fact responsible for this sudden break with accepted practice, we must see Philip I as deliberately reviving memories of the most elevated claims of the French monarchy.

Louis VI, nicknamed 'the Fat', is much better known than his father – partly because there was progress in all fields during his reign, but above all because Abbot Suger of St Denis wrote his biography. A hagiographic life of his great-grandfather, Robert II, had also been composed, but he never achieved comparable fame and popular renown. In school textbooks Louis was presented as a good king, endeavouring all his life to protect his people and check the wicked barons. This was exactly the image projected by Suger, when he described how, tired of his father's inertia, Louis finally took action in 1102, assembling a company of knights and marching towards Rheims against the 'baron' Eble, count of Roucy. E. Bournazel has defined a 'baron' as 'a man who is strong and free, whose territorial possessions [that is, his lordship] form the basis of his power, which re-enforces his social position [his noble descent, in this case usually of Carolingian origin]'. But this was an unruly baron (*tumultuosus*). Suger also frequently uses two other words drawn from the terminology of the peace of God: 'tyrant' and 'plunder'. Eble's exactions were excessive, well above the normal price of security. According to Suger, the churches were the principal victims of his policy. Louis took it upon himself to avenge them, and for two months he 'pillaged the pillagers', driving the inhabitants from Eble's lands, plundering and burning – justifiable actions in a just cause such as this. The operation continued relentlessly – except on Saturday and Sunday – with breaks for negotiations. The 'new lord' Louis (formally his father's associate, in practice his replacement) demanded the restoration of peace. (He was also in a hurry to ride off elsewhere.) The rebel lord finally acquiesced, and an agreement was made, guaranteed by oaths and the exchange of hostages. Even before he was crowned, Louis was presented as the scourge of injustice, restoring peace by the sword.

Louis had received his own sword from the hands of the count of Ponthieu five years earlier, a detail preserved in a letter of the count to the local bishops. It is evidence of what seems to have been the relatively recent importance of knighting ceremonies in the gradual development of chivalric ideology. But the fact of Louis' knighting should itself make us pause. For this was in the very thick of the crisis precipitated by Philip's remarriage. It seems likely that by this action Louis was deliberately distancing himself from his father, like almost every other older son of the nobility at this period, in an attempt to free himself from paternal control. Soon afterwards he took sole responsibility for the defence of the kingdom, as king-designate, anticipating an invasion from William Rufus of England who, if Suger is to be believed, dreamed of seizing it for himself 'if by chance some misfortune befell Philip's heir'.

Every spring he then regularly led a group of young knights of his own age, bachelors like himself, to indulge in this military pastime. For them it was a form of recreation, and we should banish all images of toil and hard labour or of the king pouring out all his youthful strength in the service of a harsh discipline. Louis enjoyed military activity, and was only too happy devoting his energies to it. In 1102 he enforced the peace of God; but the following summer he came to the aid of Thomas of Marle, a lord in the Laonnais. Suger and Guibert of Nogent described him as the stereotypical 'tyrant': for them he was a bloody, bestial and depraved monster, chopping off hands and feet, and castrating his enemies. In fact, Thomas was a brave crusader; soon afterwards he founded the abbey of Prémontré on his lands. But he was also cruel and brutal. That year Louis supported him in a family quarrel because it offered an opportunity for military exploits. In the epic poems (*chansons de geste*) which were popular at this period, Charlemagne offered comparable pleasures to his friends. But Charlemagne's friends were princes, and he led them to the edge of the known world. Louis only led his to the frontiers of the royal domain in Berry or the furthermost parts of Auvergne or Burgundy, and these companions were largely drawn from small garrisons attached to towns in the Ile-de-France, or well-fortified little strongholds such as Corbeil or Beaumont.

While Louis sought adventure in distant parts with his so-called 'army' – the band of youths that congregated round the rootless young king as the paladins of old had once congregated round the emperor 'with flowing beard' (as Charlemagne is described) – battles were fought at the royal court round the ageing king for the great offices of his household. They were contested by three closely related factions: one led by the Rochefort, lords of the castle of Montlhéry and long-established members of the nobility, like the Montfort, the Montmorency and the counts of Meulan; the two others by more recently ennobled warriors, the lords of La Tour de Senlis and the Garlande family. The most influential member of the

Garlande camp was a rising cleric, Stephen, archdeacon of Paris, appointed
to the see of Beauvais in 1101, but deposed by Ivo of Chartres on the
grounds that he was uneducated, frequented the company of women and
had been excommunicated for simony. Abélard and Héloïse were both also
members of the Garlande family.

Close examination of the competition for royal household offices dis-
closes much about the nature of royal power at this period. In 1104 the
Rochefort camp held sway and Guy of Rochefort was seneschal. He
succeeded in betrothing one of his daughters to the king-designate, Louis.
The shrinking frontiers of Capetian marriage alliances plainly demonstrated the way in which the crown was being smothered by the petty
concerns of its household officers – so plainly in fact that contemporaries
were scandalized by this alliance. When the Pope passed through the Ile-
de-France in 1106, he was asked to dissolve the union; he agreed to this,
although it was contrary to the precepts of canon law. Royal dignity
required an end to this unsuitable match. If this tie with the Rochefort
family was broken, the field would be left clear for their rivals, the
Garlande. Stephen Garlande was already chancellor, one of his brothers
seneschal and another butler. At this juncture Louis took his father's
household in hand. Henceforth the royal chamberlains were as devoted to
him as his own knights. This group of officials slept in the room next to
the king's and were bound to him by the strongest personal ties. Some
came from families of serfs: one such was the knight Henry, called '*le
Lorrain*' (the Lorrainer). They were all part of the 'family' of the royal
household, and it was as its head that Louis claimed the right to appoint a
successor on the death of the chamberlain Vulgrin. The French monarchy
was so weak that it depended on the loyalty of the lowliest members of the
household. For this was 1108, the year of Philip I's death and Louis' own
hasty coronation.

The Montfort family supported the second son, Philip (to whom they
were related through his mother, Bertrada), as did the count of Meulan, a
Rochefort ally; he was championed in turn by Henry I of England. Two
years earlier (1106) Henry had taken his brother Robert Curthose prisoner
and seized Normandy. From this point he constituted the major threat to
the Capetian kingdom. Louis at once renewed his alliance with Anjou and
supported Robert of Normandy's son, William Clito. This was the reason
for Henry's refusal to perform homage for the duchy of Normandy and
Louis' summons of the French feudal host in 1109 against Henry, whom
he regarded as a usurper. The matter was thought to concern the kingdom
as a whole, and the summons went out to all the lords of the kingdom.
Many responded, including the counts of Flanders, Blois and Nevers and
the duke of Burgundy. To prove the justice of Robert of Normandy's and

William Clito's cause and to demonstrate that (in his role as peacemaker within the kingdom of France) he was defending a just cause, Louis proposed to submit the issue to divine judgement in formal battle. He offered the English king single combat, but Henry prudently declined. Instead, they made do with a treaty and the French army ceremoniously withdrew. In this instance two intermingling spheres of political action can be discerned – one broadly based and involving the public exercise of royal power, the other an essentially private, family matter. Military action similarly operated on two levels – one where all the great lords gathered formally round the sovereign to help him re-establish public order, the other a local and domestic affair, offering knights their annual springtime opportunities for plunder and arson.

It was in the course of one of these plundering expeditions in defence of their just cause that in 1111 the French king's knights laid waste the lands of Henry I's vassal, the count of Meulan. The count retaliated. He held a lordship in Paris on the right bank of the Seine and a *bourg* there called Le Monceau-Saint-Gervais, administered by his *prévôt*, with its own market, levies and court of justice. He had only to cross the Seine to take reprisals and sack the king's palace at Paris, at the very heart of the royal domain. There was intense alarm and after this the king was resolved to stress as emphatically as possible the unique role accorded the crown by the institutions of the peace of God, which made him superior to all other lords. Writing soon afterwards, the Norman chronicler Orderic Vitalis – with no sympathy for the French king – anticipated this trend:

The dignity of the crown had suffered because of Philip I's age and illness, and royal justice had been weakened by the opposition of wicked barons. Louis therefore appealed to the bishops throughout the kingdom of France for help in checking these pillagers and troublemakers. . . . The prelates then decreed that priests were to accompany the king at sieges or into battle, with their holy banners and all their parishioners.

The king was no longer playing soldiers: he and his comrades-in-arms had come of age. The problems relating to investiture and ecclesiastical liberties had been solved three years before. Changing his role, Louis now assumed that attributed to him by Suger. When he raised his banner against the duke of Normandy after his coronation in 1109, he wanted it to be known that henceforth he was supported in his peace-keeping endeavours not only by the naturally predatory knights, but also by the 'poor'.

Suger's account concentrates on Louis' campaigns against the lord of Le Puiset in 1111 and 1112. In 1115 he carried out the most important of these expeditions to establish the peace of God, when he attacked Thomas of Marle. The king's hand was forced by the decisions of recent councils at Beauvais and Soissons. The habitual anathemas had been hurled against de Marle as a persecutor of the Church, and the papal legate had even gone so far as symbolically to divest him of his sword-belt. These councils called on the king to carry out their sentence. The feudal host was summoned; the count of Nevers responded with alacrity; and the king did his duty. Contemporary historians and chroniclers – who were not all clerics – heaped praise upon him. In 1136, however, Louis VI took up arms once more against the rebel magnate, not this time as the instrument of divine, but of family vengeance. Thomas habitually held the merchants travelling through his lands to ransom, but he made the mistake of killing the king's cousin, Hugh of Vermandois. Thomas himself was mortally wounded by Ralph of Vermandois. Family concerns had once more overtaken the anointed king, although he could use his exceptional position to justify his actions further.

In my opinion the rise of the Capetian monarchy should be placed at a slightly later date, in the crucial years between 1119 and 1124. On 20 August 1119 Louis VI was utterly defeated by Henry I at Brémule, and barely escaped with his life. In the confusion that followed, he called upon his knights and upon all available foot-soldiers right across the kingdom – from Gournay to Clermont-sur-Oise and from Nesle to Noyon, from Péronne, Tournai, Lille and Arras, as well as in Picardy, the Vermandois, Artois and French-speaking Flanders. Louis then journeyed to Rheims, where Pope Calixtus II was presiding over a council of peace. All the powerful individuals who claimed to have suffered as a result of the conflict appeared before it, including the archbishop of Narbonne and Countess Ermengarde, who made accusations against her first husband, the troubadour William of Poitiers. Amongst them was Louis VI, who re-established good relations by formally acknowledging papal authority (*auctoritas*). In a letter to Calixtus, Louis describes himself as 'king of France' (no longer 'king of the Franks') and the 'special son of the Church of Rome', words which conjured up the ancient ties between Clovis and the Catholic bishops and between Pippin and the Pope, ties which now bound the French king closely to the reformed Church.

In the same year Louis put his sword of justice at the service of the Cluniac order. The charter recording this merits special attention. It was granted 'at the request of the archbishops, bishops and territorial princes of the realm' for the 'stability' of the kingdom. The aim was to revive the memory of the great assemblies of the kingdom where the king had once sat enthroned above all the lay and ecclesiastical lords of the area entrusted to him. Declaring that he was acting for the public good, rather than merely for his personal salvation, Louis said that he would take the 'most noble member of his kingdom', the monastery at Cluny, under his 'defence, protection and guardianship', together with all the dependent priories in the kingdom of France. This marked the reintegration of the Cluniac order within the framework of temporal power. In 1119 Calixtus II had supported the reformed episcopate against Benedictine claims to independence, which had been the result of the imperial vision of Abbot Hugh's time. The Cluniacs now needed royal protection in the face of developing secular States. According to the prescriptions of the peace of God, the king owed them his protection, and its precepts were clearly the basis of the young Capetian State. By the terms of this agreement, the king and his successors would be at the service of the monastery of Cluny, intervening only when requested to do so. Nevertheless, they were entitled to enter and make use of 'fortresses, castles and ramparts' belonging to the monks, although only in the 'public defence' of the kingdom, not in the course of private war. Even so, this clause demonstrates the king's pre-eminent right to occupy all fortifications, one which he had already exercised six years earlier, when he forbade the count of Blois to build new castles without his consent.

The document does not in fact refer to the public defence of the king or the kingdom, but of the crown – and this is the most important historical evidence that it contains. When the king occupied these fortifications, he did not take them into his own hand; instead, they were held for the duration 'in the hand of the crown of France'. Here in 1119 we see the ancient concept of political power toppling over into the future. The old picture of a hand is still employed, but not a man's hand. This is a strange image – the hand of a solid, shining and imperishable object, of a crown which symbolized the transfer of power into the timeless and immutable. The State was no longer something constructed temporarily by the leader of a warrior band; it had become an abstraction. The shift in terminology from 'kingdom of the Franks' to 'kingdom of France' marked the arrival of France as a political entity.

This was indeed a prudent assertion. The agreement lists the Cluniac priories said by Louis VI to lie 'within his kingdom'; it does not include those in the *regnum* of Flanders or of the duke of Normandy. The crown symbolizes the delegation of divine power over the area defined by the treaty of Verdun (843). In reality, however, the king promised only to act in the part of Francia dependent upon his own domain, and also – and this is highly significant – in those areas where a territorial prince was not in a position to maintain the peace of God on his own. Royal protection thus extended to the Nivernais, the Auvergne, the Bourbonnais and the Brionnais, towards Souvigny, St Flour, Marcigny and Cluny itself, where it touched the old Carolingian frontier with the Empire.

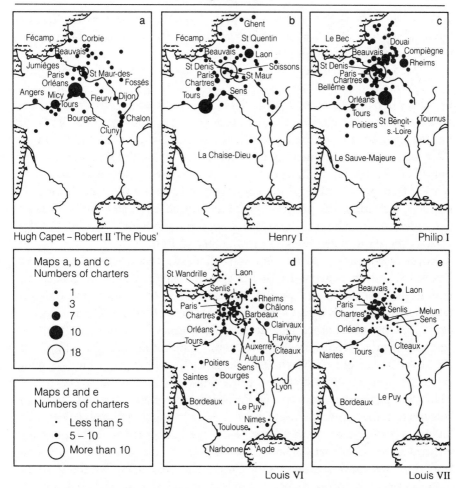

Figure 3   Churches granted royal charters from the reigns of Hugh Capet to Louis VII

At the same time there was a marked increase in the charters of franchise issued by the royal chancery to episcopal sees throughout the kingdom. Clerics at Bordeaux, or in the heart of Normandy at Rouen or Lisieux, were no longer indifferent to royal power. Nevertheless, royal influence spread mainly eastwards and southwards, extending over the suffragan bishops of Lyon at Autun, Langres and Mâcon and reaching Clermont, Le Puy, Mende, Lodève, Uzès, Nîmes, Agde and Narbonne. Direct contact between bishops and their sovereign now seemed appropriate, without the need for intervention by any power other than the Pope. Louis VI protested to Calixtus II over the archbishop of Lyons' claims to primacy over 'the Gauls', based on the precedent of his predecessor, Hugh of Die.

If there had to be such a primate, he said, it should not be a bishop 'from a strange kingdom', but the archbishop of Sens, who was metropolitan of the royal cities of Paris and Orléans.

Bernard Guenée has demonstrated how scholars replaced the old notion of the 'Frankish people' with a new picture of the kingdom. When Hugh of Fleury decided between 1110 and 1115 to continue his universal history – dedicated to his patron, the countess of Blois, and to Louis VI – he limited his narrative to the period between Charles the Bald and Philip I. This was no doubt influenced to some extent by Philip's decision to be buried at Fleury. Nevertheless, when it is compared with earlier historical writing from the monastery, the continuation reveals a remarkable shift in attitude, reflecting 'the progress of the territorial State and the historian's perception of it'. Hugh of Fleury was very conscious of its foundation by Charles the Bald, when he wrote his history of France.

Royal power preserved its essentially domestic character in the reign of Louis VI, and (as Andrew Lewis has shown) Capetian dynastic conscious-ness grew stronger in this period. As early as 1121 Louis – no doubt in response to a specific threat – appointed his son Philip an associate in the crown, as his own father had done. Like Philip I, he did this without coronation or any other ceremony, merely presenting his son as such to the royal household. Nevertheless, despite all these signs of innate con-servatism, the highly significant word *imperium* is used in a charter of 1119 exempting the cathedral of Paris from payment of a toll. It is no coincidence that from the pool of words expressing political power this highly evocative term should have re-emerged, expressing the supremacy of royal power over that of the territorial princes. The chancellor, Stephen Garlande, was also archdeacon of Paris, and this undoubtedly fostered links between the royal chancery and the cathedral school. The school at Paris was in a stage of intellectual expansion, with excellent scholars who attracted enthusiastic students from all sides. It was a major factor in any revival based on a reassessment of political theory.

This leads us to a different facet of political change. In 1120 the Capetians' main enemy, Henry I of England, finally agreed to perform simple homage for the duchy of Normandy, on the marches of their lands. He had meanwhile lost his only legitimate son (the 'Young King') in the shipwreck of the White Ship. (There were plenty of others, but none whose legitimacy was recognized by the Church.) Consequently the threat to France from this quarter was greatly reduced. Even so, the defeat at Brémule and the count of Meulan's raid were sufficient to ensure that Paris and the Vexin (a crucial buffer between the Capetian domain and the duchy of Normandy) remained strongly fortified. Renewal of Capetian links with the abbey of St Denis became a priority, because the county of

Meulan was held from them. Paris was a bulwark in the face of any Norman advance, and it was here that Louis took up residence. Of the charters of his reign, 120 were issued at Paris, only 32 from Orléans. There is a marked contrast with his grandfather, Henry I, who had divided his time between the two cities. The importance of Paris was not the result solely of its economic and geographical position and growing intellectual reputation. It also possessed the tomb of Clovis, with all its associations; while the sixth-century cathedral church of St Stephen was the largest in France after Trier, evidence of the city's magnificence at an earlier period. In fact the cathedral was in a very poor state of repair, and the town itself tiny, although R.-H. Bautier's estimate of 3,000 inhabitants may be too low. By all accounts, the left bank of the Seine was covered with vineyards and virtually unsettled, with the exception of the two abbeys of St Geneviève (on the site of the Roman forum) and the Cluniac foundation of St Germain-des-Prés, with its associated *bourg*. On the right bank, activity centred on the port (increasingly busy with the growth of river traffic) and three great churches dominating the marshy ground – St Gervais, St Jacques and St Germain-l'Auxerrois. The majority of the population lived on the island in the middle of the Seine, the Ile-de-la-Cité. On its eastern side were the bishop's palace and the houses of the canons (Archdeacon Stephen Garlande's was built on one of the towers of the old city wall); a new church, dedicated to the Virgin, was being built immediately behind the cathedral. The same rival factions clashed in this clerical sphere as in the royal household; only here they competed for the patronage of masters and their pupils. To the west was the royal palace, on the site of the Roman citadel and rebuilt by Robert the Pious in the previous century. The area between the seats of secular and ecclesiastical power was occupied by several small monasteries, the Jewish community, artisans and tradespeople.

The King first set about fortifying his own palace more strongly, particularly against attack from the right bank, almost all of which was held by other lords. He had the stone bridge repaired and built a small castle, known as the Châtelet, where it joined the bank. He also endeavoured to increase the town's vigour and prosperity. He established new religious foundations at St Victor and St Lazare; an annual fair was also instituted at St Lazare and another, jointly with the monks, at St Germain-des-Prés. However the biggest markets, the so-called Lendit fairs, were held near the abbey of St Denis in June.

St Denis was one of many monasteries founded near each Roman city. In the late fourth century, Clothar II (great-grandson of Clovis) decided to bury his wife close to the tomb of the martyr and evangelist St Denis, first bishop of Paris. 'Our special patron', the king called him. The church built over the martyr's grave was considered one of the most sacred sites in France, rivalled only by St Martin at Tours, St Médard at Soissons and St Aignan at Orléans. Dagobert I (son of Clothar) was buried there; then his wife and, later, his son. The abbey of St Denis had been one of Charles Martel's most important sources of support and he was also buried in the church. The son of Charles Martel, Pippin the Short, was educated there; he chose Fulrad, abbot of St Denis, as his chaplain, arch-priest of Francia and his principal clerical counsellor. Fulrad was responsible for the papal alliance that effected the change of dynasty. In 752 Pope Stephen II anointed Pippin, his wife and two sons with holy oil. Pippin wanted to be buried beside Dagobert, and he built a magnificent new church. After the division of the kingdom between Pippin's great-grandsons, Charles the Bald (who had been allotted Neustria) became lay abbot of St Denis. Like Clothar, he referred to St Denis as his 'patron'; but he also called him his 'lord', a word that introduced the idea of a devotion to the saint comparable to that which operated in a secular context. Odo, the first Robertian king, was also buried beside most of the kings of the Franks at St Denis. When he was king, Hugh Capet also made much of the abbey, appointing Mayeul of Cluny as a reforming abbot in 994. His son Robert displayed the same devotion and concern. His offerings were directed mainly to St Aignan (at Orléans), but in the preamble to a grant of an area of immunity round the abbey in 1008, he spelt out the importance of St Denis, protector of the Frankish kings: his predecessors, the last Carolingian kings, had ceased to reverence the saint, and this had caused their fall. He revived an old tradition for the good of the kingdom, and purged the monastery of worldly influences that would otherwise corrupt it afresh.

St Denis thus ousted St Martin. Tours was farther away, and the counts of Blois and Anjou were both influential there. Numerous legends sprang up round the tomb of St Denis, in which he was described as one of St Peter's first apostles and identified with Paul's disciple, Denis the Areopagite. The latter was also identified with an anonymous Syrian writer of c.500, who had written a work on the celestial hierarchies (*De Coelesti Hierarchia*). In the ninth century Louis the Pious, king of the Franks, had asked the Byzantine Emperor for a manuscript of the Greek texts attributed to Denis the Areopagite (the work of the so-called Pseudo-Dionysius). They were deposited in St Denis, and the abbot attempted to translate them into Latin. Since they believed that here was the tomb of the Areopagite, who had written an account of the hierarchies on heaven and earth, it seemed completely natural to place beside it the insignia of the individual whose coronation set him above all other holders of temporal office. When Odo was elected king, he went to receive his royal insignia at St Denis. Thus the monastery of St Denis acquired a significance within the symbolism of the Frankish monarchy that came to rival Rheims.

This explains what happened in 1052. The monks of St Emeram at Regensburg announced that they had accidentally discovered the body of St Denis, maintaining that King Arnulf had taken the body in the course of a plundering expedition. The Emperor Henry III gave them a hearing, well aware of the political advantage of having the patron of the Merovingian kings and Pippin the Short in his lands. The reaction in France was strong, and Henry I of France had the coffin at St Denis opened to confirm that the martyr's bones rested there.

Philip I's devotion was cooler, no doubt because the monks did not attempt to conceal their support for his son Louis, who had been brought up at St Denis. Abbot Adam therefore made strenuous efforts to re-enforce the links between crown and monastery, celebrating the anniversary of Dagobert's accession with great splendour and persuading Louis VI to entrust his father's crown to the monastery's safe keeping. The new king showered favours on the monastery, declaring St Denis not only the patron saint of France, but also lord of the Vexin. He was annoyed when Abélard (who had become a monk of St Denis after his misfortunes) questioned the identification of the French St Denis with Denis the Areopagite. The council of Soissons condemned Abélard's assertions in 1121. It is no coincidence that he was a member of the Garlande family, which the monastery of St Denis was trying, little by little, to displace from its influential position in the royal household. In 1123 the scion of a rival family, Stephen of Senlis, was appointed bishop of Paris. Suger had become abbot of St Denis the previous year.

Besides the *Life* of Louis VI, Suger wrote an *apologia* on his own account. It comprised two books (or parts), *De administratione* (*Concerning the Administration of the Monastery*) and *De consecratione* (*Concerning the Consecration of the Abbey Church*), reflecting complementary spheres of action. The monastery of St Denis was governed by essentially Cluniac principles. The monks' purpose – their *opus Dei* (work for God) – was to transmute the fleshly into the spiritual and worldly riches into the immutable, imperishable treasures surrounding divine glory. All the profits of temporal power should be devoted to the greater glory of God expressed in worship. Suger's first aim was therefore to relate his unprecedented exploitation of the monastery's lordship. His account sheds light on the economic development of the Ile-de-France at this period, as well as improved

administration, an increased area of land under cultivation and the creation
of new towns. The net result of this increased economic and commercial
activity was a consistent increase in revenue. But it is also quite clear that
this growth was dependent upon royal power: some of the rebel lords
(*tyrans*) whom Louis VI believed he was duty-bound to check and whose
rapacity he effectively bridled were men (like the lord of Le Puiset) who
claimed the right to exact payment from the abbey's dependents. In Suger's
eyes, these men were appropriating revenues for their own pleasures which
should have been devoted to the Almighty. The French king contributed
much more to the great church building programme by actively maintaining the peace of God than through his personal alms. The reassertion of the
monarchical State was directly responsible for the dazzling flowering in
Capetian lands of what we think of as works of art, but which contemporaries saw as a means to grace and a means of spiritual communication.
This is why the restoration of the abbey church, Suger's magnificent
offering to God and to St Denis, has a place in a political history.

It also finds a place because it indubitably reveals a political programme.
When he rebuilt the porch and the choir, Suger made a fundamental
assumption. Since St Denis was the patron saint of the entire kingdom, it
was essential to use the most recent methods from all over the territory
entrusted to the French king, north and south. In this way the sculpture
which had only appeared a short while before on the façades of churches in
the south of France was transplanted to the Ile-de-France. Meanwhile, as
the crusade rekindled interest in the legendary 'matter of France' and royal
clerks began to speak of the *imperium* of France, the figure of Charlemagne
began to replace that of Charles the Bald in the minds of the monks of St
Denis. It was said that Charlemagne had presented the relics of Christ's
passion preserved in the monastery, and that he had given the whole of
France to St Denis. Suger therefore decided that the new building should
be essentially Carolingian, and the stained glass is full of motifs from the
metal work of the Meuse. The windows' main purpose, however, was to
flood the whole building with light, an innovation made possible by the
systematic use of vaulting. Suger wanted the building to give outward
expression to the theology of Denis the Areopagite.[1] Rays emanating from
God, the source of all light, called every creature into being, one after the
other in their various degrees. Divine light shines, and returns by a series
of reflections to its source; by the operation of this light – which is love –
all beings are gathered into unity and peace, each established by its
outpouring in its own place in a hierarchy culminating in a single point.

---

[1] For a different interpretation, see (most recently) Peter Kidson, 'Panofsky, Suger and St
Denis', *Journal of the Warburg and Courtauld Institutes*, 50 (1987), pp. 1–17 – tr.

According to this model, it was God's will that power should be shared among men in all parts of the earth. So it was that architecture expressing a perfect political system was developed near Paris in the final years of the reign of Louis VI.

Aspects of this system were already evident in the Church. The earliest monastic reforms saw communities organized on the very basic hierarchical model of the family, united under the authority of their father, the abbot. The work of canon lawyers stressing the subordination of the entire episcopate to the bishop of Rome had simplified and strengthened this model. It was taken up by Suger to exalt the power of the French king, his friend and patron. He did so with reference to the practices of patronage, vassalage and feudalism which were gradually being formalized.

Three elements combined in Suger's concept of the monarchy. Its foundation was inevitably the ties of commensality forged between the head of the house and the knights who lived in his household, sleeping across the entrance to his chamber. Then there was love, for the beginning of the twelfth century in France witnessed a remarkable increase in and elaboration of ceremony and gesture, as well as a whole new vocabulary, all relating to love in every form – the love of God, of women and of youthful companions. At its heart lay the love between men of noble birth which secured peace and especially the mutual love between a vassal and the lord whom he had promised to serve. The third element was the gift, or price of this service – the fief.

When Suger first became abbot, a homogeneous system of formal written agreements was beginning to replace *ad hoc* oral understandings in the most powerful lordships. Previously there had been individual arrangements or painstakingly negotiated alliances, which were constantly challenged and amplified with reference to comparable arrangements. The process of change was very gradual and continued for most of the twelfth century. These developments occurred first in Normandy, which was now tightly controlled by Henry I of England after the earlier unrest in the duchy. He established the procedures previously used to regulate the distribution of land in England after the Norman Conquest. In order to establish the exact form of service owed to the king by each of those who received land in this fashion, the standard measure of the knight's fee was adopted. Obligations that originated in the quasi-paternal and quasi-filial love of lord and knight thus became attached to a material and concrete object, the knight's tenure. The Anglo-Norman example provided Suger with the basis for his vision of the French kingdom as a vast conglomeration of fiefs covering a huge expanse of land, subsuming areas which were *mouvant* (or feudally dependent) upon the kingdom. The term first appeared in chancery documents *c.*1130, and conjures up the image of a

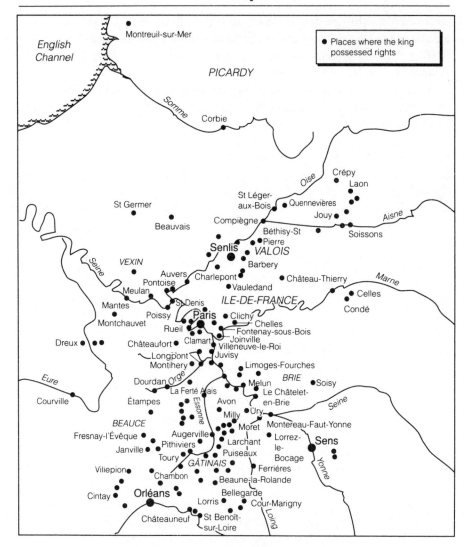

Figure 4   The royal domain in the reign of Louis VI (after W. M. Newman)

gearing mechanism, with large wheels turning smaller ones. For Suger, the
French kingdom was not unlike a machine of this kind, with large wheels
turning smaller ones.

'King Louis', he wrote, 'always takes precedence over the king of
England, because the latter is his feudal dependent as duke of Normandy.'
Traditionally Normandy had been an independent possession: there is a
marked contrast between Suger's attitude and that of Fulbert of Chartres a
century earlier, which carefully preserves the old distinction. For Suger,

Normandy is a fief like any of the other great fiefs that constituted the kingdom of France, an integral part of the larger structure. He also saw it as a land-holding, not unlike the plots of land taken from the abbey domain in newly cleared villages and granted to a peasant family in perpetuity in return for payment of taxes, especially upon succession. This was a revolutionary change and the territorial princes recognized it as such: hence their refusal to pay homage on the accession of Louis VI. Here, too, the concept of hierarchy was implicit: 'The count of Auvergne holds his lands from the duke of Aquitaine, who holds his from the king of France,' wrote Suger. One reason for Suger's development of the concept of the feudal pyramid was that the king held one of the cogs of the kingdom's machinery, the Vexin, from St Denis, whose agent the abbot was. The Vexin was a fief for which the king as its tenant also had to do service.

The year 1124 proved a turning-point. The Emperor Henry V had assembled an army in Lorraine in support of his father-in-law, Henry I of England, and threatened to invade France. Louis VI called upon the territorial princes. The counts of Vermandois, Troyes, Blois, Nevers and Flanders, together with the duke of Burgundy, came at once; the duke of Aquitaine and the counts of Brittany and Anjou prepared to join him. With contingents drawn from all over the kingdom, the royal host now resembled the army of Charlemagne. As Charlemagne had supposedly done before him, Louis went to St Denis and took from the altar the saint's banner of red silk, the *oriflamme*. Later, writing about the administration of the abbey, Suger explained the significance of this ceremony:

The noble county of the Vexin, between the rivers Oise and Epte . . . is the fief of St Denis. When Louis, king of the Franks and son of Philip I advanced against the Emperor of the Romans, who was invading his kingdom, he acknowledged before the abbey's chapter that he held the county from St Denis and that, as his standard-bearer, he owed the saint homage.

In a charter drawn up on this occasion, Louis VI acknowledged that the Vexin fell under the jurisdiction of St Denis and that he held it in fee from the saint and his two fellow-martyrs. At the same time, Guibert of Nogent wrote that St Denis was 'lord of all France'. The king was thus setting off to defend his lord's land, followed by his own vassals, who were in turn accompanied by some of their own feudal dependents. When Louis received the banner, the saint's relics were placed on the high altar of the abbey church, where they remained throughout the campaign. After the enemy had been repelled with ease, the king came back and placed the *oriflamme* beside them. The episode can be parallelled in a mosaic in the church of St

John Lateran at Rome, which shows Charlemagne receiving his banner from St Peter. By these actions the king of France declared himself the protector of St Denis, just as after the conquest of Jerusalem Godfrey of Bouillon had become the protector of the Holy Sepulchre. The king of France worked for the peace of the kingdom under the protection of his lord St Denis, the sub-tenant of God.

Louis VI continued with this task as long as he could ride. (In 1135 he handed this responsibility over to his second son, Louis, whom he had crowned at Rheims – where the Pope was presiding over a Church council – on the death of his older brother four years earlier.) It involved, firstly, the protection of churches, but also the maintenance of order throughout the kingdom, in particular in the towns, with whom the king developed a special relationship. He exerted his authority at Laon in 1128, for example. This was a big city rivalling Paris, with scholars, vineyard-workers and carters, who were a lucrative source of revenue. Seventeen years previously the clergy (led by the archdeacon in the bishop's absence) and the most important lay lords – joint custodians of the town's customary law – had been forced to accede to the demands of the citizens. According to Guibert of Nogent, they had 'sold to the people' authorization to form a commune. They were granted the right to group together and swear oaths of mutual aid, which implied the right to settle disputes amongst themselves. The profits of seigneurial justice were reduced as a result. According to Guibert of Nogent, these people were serfs: in fact, they made an annual payment in recognition of their dependence, because most had come from the countryside nearby, and the lord of their place of origin demanded this payment as a means of maintaining his control over them. The citizens had obtained a legal code which applied to the whole town, and offenders would henceforth be punishable by a 'fine in accordance with the law'. The various lords who had hitherto had jurisdiction over parts of the town had agreed to substitute a fixed rent for the income they had previously received from various sources; their subjects were to share the costs between themselves. Seigneurial rights were leased out to the inhabitants, and it was this which Guibert of Nogent and others like him found so objectionable. On his return in 1112, the bishop attempted to abolish this agreement, and was killed by rioters.

According to a document drawn up at Compiègne by Simon, the royal chancellor, when the king arrived, he established an 'institution of peace', for this was his function. He did not – any more than any other great lord – act on his own account: in this he took counsel not only from the 'great lords' of both the city of Laon and those who had accompanied him there, but also from the organized body of townspeople. What was referred to as the 'peace' was in fact a strictly demarcated area like those designated by the peace of God. Everyone living within it was strictly bound to keep the peace. If it was broken, violent reprisals were to be avoided, and there were to be no arrests. Justice would be invoked (here the term refers to the guardians of the public peace, who were responsible for the expulsion of the guilty party). This sanction – like that of excommunication – cut off the tainted member from the rest of the community. If, after two weeks and a formal summons from the bishop, he failed to appear, the entire town should bring him to justice. Indeed, if it was a case of 'mortal hatred', every form of ambush and pursuit was permitted.

After he had issued this ordinance, the king reasserted his rights over the city. He was to have right of lodging there three times a year, just as travelling magistrates in the remote past had done. Alternatively, they could make a payment of 20 *livres*, or 4,800 pieces of silver. The right to lodging would only be exercised three times a year, unless the king came there to levy the feudal host or hold solemn court, as he did at Christmas, Easter and Whitsun every year.

Agreements of this kind were gradually established, point by point, across the country by the king, one of the territorial princes or a lord of lesser importance, replacing vague and imprecise conventions with formal agreement. Throughout the hierarchy the use of written (rather than oral) agreements inevitably gave them a more rigid and artificial character. Writing did not supersede memory, but crystallized it. As in the text we have just examined (and the situation was the same with fiefs), the written form of custom was referred to as 'law', and it increasingly resembled the decretals of ecclesiastical canon law. The lord's power was usually strengthened by the progressive extension of writing, but it was also shackled by it, and in this way political power passed imperceptibly into the hands of lawyers.

The year before his visit to Laon, Louis VI had gone to wreak divine vengeance upon Flanders, 'to purge the land from sin', as Suger puts it. But he was also taking personal revenge and simultaneously demonstrating his sovereignty over one of the fiefs dependent upon the French crown. I shall examine this event in some detail because of the insight it offers into contemporary political structures and their functioning.

It was unleashed by an abominable crime, the murder of the count of Flanders in church, whilst he was kneeling in prayer and distributing alms to the poor. On 2 March 1127 Charles the Good died a martyr's death in the church of St Donatian in Bruges. It was at once recognized as such, and several accounts of his death were composed, of varying literary worth. One of these texts is of extraordinary historical interest. It was not written by a monk, but by Galbert of Bruges, a notary in the household of the count. In the very thick of the drama, he kept a day-to-day record of events as they unfolded 'on wax tablets', writing up this extraordinary record in its final form 'in moments of quiet'. His observations are remarkably detailed, and the evidence is admirably dated, classified and tested. Galbert of Bruges' main aim was to disentangle the intrigue surrounding the event and understand what actually happened. His work is a reflection of the high quality of scribes employed in noble households in the early twelfth century. It was clearly impossible for lords to manage without them, even in northern France, farthest from classical traditions. Scribes were the indispensable adjuncts of seigneurial administration. The importance of their work is reflected in the fact that after the murder of Charles the Good, his assassins immediately seized 'documents relating to comital revenues', and the new count had to summon the notary with all speed 'because shepherds and estate-stewards had arrived to pay what they owed him'. The written word was also indispensable for communication: when the knights of Oostkerke broke 'fealty and homage', they did not go and perform the necessary ritual in front of their lords; instead they sent 'a signed document' to Ypres. On 20 March 1127 two letters arrived at Bruges, one from the king of France summoning the lords to his side to choose a new count, the other – whose authenticity was contested – from a would-be claimant. The messengers sent to Louis VI with a reply returned ten days later with another letter from the king: Charles the Good's butler showed it to the citizens assembled in the field outside the town which they used for meetings; they saw that the document was sealed; it was then read to them and discussion commenced – initiated not by an individual but by a text. The written word was gradually impinging on political action.

In Flanders the count was the delegate of divine power, by virtue of his birth: the county passed from father to eldest son. There were occasional chance interruptions: in 1071 Count Robert the Frisian had ousted his nephews and taken their place. Charles the Good had himself succeeded a cousin without male heirs in 1119, but in very different circumstances: on the advice of his council, the dying count had bequeathed him the 'kingdom' on oath. The comital family was widely scattered, because the daughters had been married to nobles of the highest rank. Charles himself was the son of the king of Denmark, but he had been brought up in the traditional fashion in the household of his maternal uncle. As a result, he was regarded as essentially Flemish, which greatly facilitated the succession.

Charles was noble and virtuous, well endowed with the knightly qualities Galbert of Bruges terms simply 'chivalry'. He was also an excellent 'defender of his land', father and protector of churches, just to the powerful, generous to the poor. This was very apparent in the great famine of 1124, generally interpreted by contemporaries as divine punishment – for they thought only in these terms – for the usurpation of Robert the Frisian. Charles made strenuous efforts to check price rises. He ordered sowings of quick-growing crops and forbade the brewing of beer. Above all, he opened his own granaries and one hundred poor men and women were fed daily at Bruges during the crisis. In normal times, paupers were also permanently supported by the count's household and each of them received one *denier* whenever the count prayed in the castle's collegiate church. Redistribution of the profits of lordship amongst its inhabitants was a corner-stone of Charles the Good's vision of an ordered society. Above all, social order was synonymous with peace, which was his major concern. (Perhaps he dreamt of higher things, for he was a descendant of Charlemagne and – following Capetian example – was named after his illustrious ancestor. Galbert of Bruges tells us that he was offered first the Empire, then the kingdom of Jerusalem; he had taken the cross, and crusading had served only to strengthen his good qualities.) The count's primary aim was to contain the unruliness of the Flemish knights. He had no enemies beyond his borders, but he led 200 knights out of Flanders every year to tournaments elsewhere. Galbert's account reveals the political function of the tournament in the 1120s: it was a valuable arena for the practice of military skills and absorbed knightly aggression. Tournaments in northern France were largely organized by the territorial princes. Public order was not only threatened by the activities of knights, however. The rest of the population – below the knights and above the 'poor' and the peasants – contained individuals with a military role. These men lived in the *bourgs*, or settlements at castle gates, playing a part in the defence of these fortresses and providing protection for merchants on dangerous long journeys. These men had become increasingly restless. They were in a position to resist exactions or secure agreement over fixed money payments, as at Laon. The Flemish count wanted to disarm them. They made a verbal plea in defence of their rights. Galbert observes, however, that words are potentially more dangerous than weapons, because they can prevail by treachery. He wondered whether this measure, although intended to preserve order, was not in fact one of the major causes of the unrest that followed. A man of his times, he assumed it must have been displeasing to God.

Comital power was especially important on the Flemish borders. This area had been ravaged over a long period, first by the sea itself and then by the barbarians; the Roman cities had all been destroyed. Only Thérouanne remained an episcopal see; the earlier bishopric at Tournai had been absorbed into Noyon. Over the centuries the counts had assembled the people to repel first the barbarian invaders and then attacks from the sea. Their exposed position and turbulent history had also made the Flemings exceptionally violent and unruly. It was no easy task for the count to control them from his castles.

Galbert's narrative describes the comital castle at Bruges. The 'count's house' stood within its courtyard on raised ground, surrounded by a deep ditch. It was a three-storey building constructed of stone, transported from far away. The great hall occupied the middle storey, with the lodgings of the castellan and the castle knights on one side and the church on the other. This was also built of stone, and had recently been reroofed with tiles. It was octagonal, like the imperial chapel at Aachen, and possessed numerous relics.[2] As a collegiate foundation it was served by canons; their superior, the provost, had his own house with hall and chamber. A few married canons had independent households; the rest led a communal life that was disciplined, but still comfortable. Next to them were the notaries, responsible for comital documents. There was a massive fortified tower, or west-work, at the west end of the church, symbol of comital power. This had been built so that its walls were immediately adjacent to the masonry of the main body of the church, but structurally independent of it. 'It towered magnificently over everything else; like the throne of the kingdom at the centre of the country, it provided security and justice throughout the land, because it ensured peace and safety, right and the rule of law.' A vaulted passageway joined the count's quarters to a gallery in the church where – again like Charlemagne and many others – the count attended mass every morning. These architectural arrangements reflected the way in which military and liturgical functions were closely linked in the person of the count.[3] The townspeople lived outside the castle walls in simple wooden houses that were very susceptible to fire. Within this complex were various other churches and the market, also defended, but by a simple ditch.

Similar towns with comital castles were scattered throughout Flanders, at Ghent, Ypres, Bergues, Bourbourg, St Omer and Lille. The count travelled from one to the other, taking with him his household and the comital treasure. His control over these castles was considerably less than has often been assumed. For the previous sixty years, the two offices of castellan and provost at Bruges had been held by members of the Erembald family. Their position was very similar to that of the Garlande family at the court of Louis VI, where the head of the family was also a cleric. The count now wanted to demonstrate his authority by gaining

[2] In fact, an octagon within a sixteen-sided polygon; see J. Meertens, 'The Church of St Donatian at Bruges', in Galbert of Bruges, *The Murder of Charles the Good*, ed. and tr. J. B. Ross (Toronto, 1982), p. 167, n. 4 – tr.

[3] They can also be seen as a reflection of increasingly personal forms of devotion and a growing sense of responsibility for individual salvation – tr.

control of foreign merchants, relative newcomers to the political scene. In March 1127, 'on the feast of St Peter's Chair', they had come to Ypres 'from all the neighbouring kingdoms, to attend the great annual fair held there under the peace and protection of the count'. Among them were Lombards, from whom the count bought a magnificent silver cup for 21 marks. Merchants from elsewhere were the responsibility of the citizens. Bruges merchants themselves also sought business farther afield: some were in London at the time of the assassination of Charles the Good. They undoubtedly secured a considerable proportion of the wealth also coveted by the warrior class, and this was a further source of social tension.

Not all armed men were organized in groups around comital castles. There were also large numbers of much smaller fortified manor-houses where the citizens took refuge during disturbances, but which could also provide a base for the pillagers themselves. A few of these fortresses were owned by knights; but the majority belonged to richer individuals, referred to as 'princes' or 'peers' by Galbert of Bruges – in other words, equals of the count. Thus, although the count held one of the strongest and richest principalities in the kingdom of France, he was checked by rival powers within it, as well as the growing power of the castellan family at Bruges itself. According to Galbert of Bruges, Bertulf, the provost, was guilty of selling canonical prebends and treated the chapter's funds as his personal income. A rich man himself, his nieces married into wealthy families. His prestige was also increased by the exploits of his knightly nephews (Galbert names sixteen of them), whom he encouraged to participate in disputes and attacks. Relatives were also placed in the comital household: one of them was the chamberlain, another the butler, a third was a notary, while Bertulf held the office of chancellor. A high proportion of the county's knights were on occasion drawn into this influential web. One day, for instance, the 'provost and his nephews retired to a chamber and summoned the knights they required there.' Bertulf guarded the door and nearly 300 'swore oaths of mutual aid'.

Alliances such as these were the bedrock of military companies, and they were the scourge of the poor, for whom the count was the only hope of redress. Two hundred peasants came to him at Ypres and threw themselves at his feet. Men from Bruges, they said, had attacked a fortified manor-house nearby and devastated their lands in the process. They begged his 'paternal' aid, asking for restitution of their cattle, clothes and silver. The count took counsel and proceeded to vengeance, burning down the house of one of the ringleaders (one of the provost's nephews), then negotiating a peace settlement, sealed with a loving-cup. Resentment still seethed beneath this outward show of reconciliation, however, and it was to lead to the count's assassination.

The root of the problem was thus the discrepancy between the real power of the castellans (with their wealth and large retinues) and their legal status. It was one of the problems that stemmed from hereditary office-holding. The ancestors of the Erembald family, castellans of Bruges, had been recruited from among the count's serfs. They now made every effort to shake off this stigma through marriage into the nobility and dubbing, for knighthood was no longer just a profession, but also a social category. They were on the verge of success. The last vestiges of their servile condition had almost disappeared and their own personal ties to the count had simultaneously become looser. Throughout France, lords were adopting a tougher line in the face of declining revenues. At Cluny, for instance, the monks demanded more from their stewards. Charles the Good 'wanted to re-establish order in his kingdom and accordingly made thorough inquiries as to which men were his serfs'. His attention was drawn to the Erembald family, castellans of Bruges. In the face of such a threat, they decided to kill Charles the Good and appoint a new and tractable count who, owing his position to them, would not cause them any trouble. Charles had neither legitimate sons, brothers or nephews, only a multitude of cousins. There was the son of an aunt, Thierry of Alsace; the two sons of one of the nephews disinherited by Robert the Frisian; and Robert Curthose's son, William Clito. Finally, there was his closest relative, William of Ypres, who was generally considered a bastard, since his father (an uncle of Charles) had never married. The Erembald reckoned on his support. A disputed succession was inevitable; but all the interested parties hovered rapaciously in the wings, hoping for personal profit.

And so Charles the Good of Flanders was killed in the middle of Lent, during the office of prime, and others with him, including the castellan of Bourbourg and his two sons. The assassins cut them down with swords and axes. The count's body remained in the church at Bruges, which had been defiled by his murder. When he heard about the crime, the bishop of Noyon anathematized the murderers; funeral rites could not be performed. The canons who had not already fled in terror placed the body on a bier in the choir, and here the murderers also gathered, hoping to stay retribution for their crime. 'Like pagans and sorcerers they took a mug of beer and some bread; sitting round the tomb, they placed the food and drink on top, eating and drinking above the body of the blessed count, in the hope that this would shield them from vengeance.' Beggars also hovered near the body in anticipation of the customary meal provided for them from the dead man's estate at his funeral. Several early counts of Flanders had been buried in the abbey of St Peter at Ghent, and the abbot also came hurrying to claim the mortal remains of the count.

After a period of confusion, vengeance began in earnest, led by Gervaise of Praat, one of the dead count's chamberlains and closest friends and vassals, with some of the citizens. They besieged the castle, where the murderers had taken refuge. The canons had prudently removed the reliquaries and crosses, but there was still the count's treasury. This was a powerful lure, and it was sufficient to entice the castellans of Dixmude and Ghent, with their citizens and all the riff-raff from the surrounding villages. It was their greed, rather than the crime itself, which severed the bond between the castellan and the knights of the castle of Bruges. 'Taking straws, they broke them, thereby renouncing their homage, fealty and allegiance.' Then they broke down the outer wall of the castle and took possession of the count's house, searching in vain for the contents of the treasury, but pillaging all they could lay their hands on – corn, wine, hangings and even the nails from the doors.

At this juncture Louis VI entered the drama. Those who had initially avenged the dead count were summoned by letter to meet the king at Arras. On their return they informed the citizens of Bruges that the king of France had come to avenge his dead cousin and also as the agent of divine vengeance, 'sustained by God's power and the force of arms'. On the advice of Louis, 'emperor of the Franks', the barons of France and of Flanders had chosen William of Normandy as count. He was brave and had grown up amongst them:

We have promised him our fealty and allegiance and have done him homage according to the custom of the counts of Flanders. . . . He has given us the property of the traitors. Citizens, we advise you to accept Count William, who has been elected and invested with the county by the king. If you wish, he will abolish tonnage, as well as the ground-rents on houses within the city.

The citizens of Bruges replied that they and the inhabitants of the surrounding area had already agreed to meet 'to select a count'. The Saturday before Easter, twenty knights and twelve citizens of Bruges, together with some of the citizens of Ghent, accordingly came before the envoys of the French king, for 'the people of the Flemish towns and cities had agreed that they would respond unanimously to any proposal'. In this way William Clito was once more formally elected count.

He arrived in Bruges the following Tuesday, accompanied by the king. The canons came out to meet them, carrying relics, and escorted them in a solemn procession 'as befitted royalty'. In the field where the citizens habitually met, an assembly was held around the relics the next day, not unlike the assemblies of the peace of God. With their hands upon the holy relics, first the king and then the count swore to preserve the liberties of chapter and citizens. The citizens swore allegiance in their turn and formally acknowledged themselves the count's men. After that, the count's vassals each received their fief and dignity. Galbert gives a detailed description of the ceremony, which lasted three days, because each lord was presented individually to the new count. Each time there was first a dialogue: '"Do you wish to become wholly my man?" "I do." Then the vassal joined his hands together and placed them within those of the count, who enfolded them within his own and they sealed the mutual bond with a kiss.' Then, with his hand on the relics of the saints, the vassal swore, '"I promise faithfully that I will be loyal to Count William, and in all my dealings I will abide by the homage I have given him, in good faith and without treachery."' Finally, the count gave the man a rod, an act which formally invested the vassal with his fief. While Clito went from castle to castle receiving homage in this way, Louis VI stayed in Bruges. On 12 April he decided to attack the murderers. (Louis also had an eye on the comital treasury, for the county of Flanders was much wealthier than the kingdom of France, despite their relative size.) He had one of the conspirators flogged to discover the whereabouts of the treasure. The tower was finally captured by a great combined force of the 'most Christian knights of the king of France' and 'young men from the town'. But there was no treasure to be found. Louis VI wept over his cousin's corpse, which now received solemn burial. The church was ritually cleansed and reconsecrated by the bishop. All the assassins who could be found, as well as their associates, were condemned to death. After a final banquet in the comital hall, Louis VI returned to France. He had demanded the colossal sum of 1,000 marks of silver as relief for the fief. For all his high-flown talk about rapaciousness in others, Louis VI could be just as predatory himself.

The king had proceeded with extreme caution. He had halted at Arras, on the borders of Flanders, calling the Flemish 'princes' to him in the marches of the county, to decide upon Charles the Good's successor. Nevertheless, his own barons took part in these discussions and his candidate was chosen, William of Normandy, Louis' trump card in his dispute with Henry I of England. As with the appointment of a bishop, the king had effectively made his preferences known. The problem lay in the unprecedented role of the towns, and negotiations now had to be opened with them as well. So the king had to advance farther into Flanders and accompany the young count from town to town, where a formal entry had to be negotiated in each case. William already had the support of the great Flemish lords, but at every lesser castle he had also to establish formal bonds with all the important individuals in that particular locality, both the knights who served in the castle and the men from the *bourg* who also carried arms. It appears from Galbert of Bruges' narrative that the citizens as a body formally accepted the new count, but all those who received fiefs did homage individually. It is not clear why Galbert described the ceremony and the words exchanged there in such meticulous detail. One possible explanation is that this ritual had acquired its final form only recently. The transition from agreements with a great variety of clauses to uniform obligations fixed by custom may only just have taken place. In other words, it was at about this time that standard feudal practice crystallized in northern France.

Louis' expedition to Flanders had brought him no profit. Although the king no longer 'sold' bishoprics, he still plundered the houses of bishops whenever there was a vacancy. Now that he had failed to get his hands on the comital treasure in Charles the Good's castle, he levied a relief, which would cover the costs of his expedition. It was customary for every new vassal to make his lord a present of some kind. In England and Normandy it had been given a specific value, fifteen *livres* for a knight's fee. The king wanted very much more than this from the count of Flanders, and his excessive demands were to jeopardize the restoration of justice and social order which he had put in hand.

William Clito had been chosen count of Flanders because of his good qualities, and he wanted to carry out his duties as he should. But he was in desperate need of funds to pay the relief stipulated by Louis VI. He demanded payment of the toll he had promised to abolish: the knights permanently garrisoned at Bruges castle in fact held this levy in fee amongst themselves and constantly plagued the new count on the matter, alleging that he had no right to abolish payments due to themselves. The count could not afford to risk alienating this group of knights, and he also had a duty towards them as their leader and patron. He decided instead to put pressure on the towns, reckoning on support from the nobles because of the latent antagonism between this group and the towns. The citizens of Lille and St Omer rebelled first. Then, on 16 February 1128, the people of Ghent rose against their 'unjust' castellan as a result of his excessive demands for payment. The situation here was more serious because some of the local knights also opposed the count.

When the count arrived, he was met by two men-at-arms, one of them a 'peer' of Flanders, a great lord. The latter told him:

'You have broken the oaths which we swore in your name, when you undertook to defend the privileges obtained from previous counts by men of this land. Nevertheless, you are still our lord and lord of all Flanders, and we should come to terms without violence. Summon the great lords on both sides to a peaceful assembly at Ypres, together with the clergy and townsfolk.'

An assembly of the three estates was accordingly convened: the germ of the future Estates General can be seen at this early date at the very heart of the feudal system. The assembly itself was complex, combining remnants of Carolingian institutions in the shape of the *échevins* (town officials) with the unprecedented representation of the townspeople. The messengers proposed that the peers would judge the count before this assembly. 'If they believe you can hold the county honourably, we will accept their decision; if it transpires that you are judged unworthy, faithless and lawless, false and foresworn, let us choose someone from among those whose birth makes them fit to hold office.' William reacted furiously: 'I reject the homage you did me. I am once more your equal [for the formal act of defiance cancelled the loyalty implicit in homage] and I challenge you to a judicial duel, for I have acted within my rights. Everything that I have done in the county has been guided by justice and reason.' (It is interesting to note that there is already an appeal to reason in this context.) The speaker declined, but a day was arranged for a meeting at Ypres. The count arrived with his knights, armed and re-enforced with mercenaries. The men of Ghent advanced and when they were still some considerable distance away said, 'You have come against us armed, although it is Lent [a breach of the peace of God]; you are preparing to fight your vassals [a breach of the feudal code].' Their representatives then solemnly broke a straw, to symbolize the formal severance of the bonds of fealty and homage.

One after the other, the Flemish towns joined the rebels, for the citizens had nothing to lose. They admitted as much: 'The count has taken from us almost everything we had; we have been forced to use up everything else because we are cut off.' The townspeople of Bruges still hesitated. They made the decision to join the rebels on 30 March, with the arrival of Thierry of Alsace. In the great field outside the town, lords and people acknowledged him 'count of all Flanders'. The following day the relics of St Donatian were brought out and Thierry swore on them to preserve the liberties of the town.

Louis VI then returned once more to Arras and summoned eight wise men from every Flemish town to reconcile Count William and the rebels. They replied,

'The election and installation of the counts of Flanders is nothing to do with the king of France, whether the previous count has died with or without an heir. The peers of Flanders and the citizens have the power to nominate the individual most closely related, and the right to raise him to the office of count.'

Previously the counts of Flanders had always been blood-relations and the knights, lords and citizens had therefore accepted Louis VI's intervention the year before, 'but the obligations of kinship are quite distinct from what has been firmly established by tradition and in law.' 'The king of France would receive only a relief of arms for his rights over the land, which the first count had received in fee.' Here is a complete admission of the status of Flanders as a fief held from the kingdom of France, and that something had to be given in return for it. But the relief was to be purely symbolic.

Nevertheless, archbishops, bishops and abbots assembled at Arras, and William Clito did what was expected of him. He returned to the bishop of Noyon the dozen or so churches that he held in fee, emphasizing his role as 'protector and defender of the churches of Flanders'. The clergy then gave him their support. The bishop of Noyon declared an interdict; the archbishop of Rheims and his suffragans hurled anathemas upon Thierry of Alsace, who at once fell ill, proof to contemporaries of the injustice of his cause. Some priests supporting the rebel cause attempted to retaliate with excommunication, to the amazement of Galbert of Bruges: 'How can priests imagine that they can cast a spell on God, and influence his actions in this way?' In the event, God was not deceived, making his judgement dazzlingly clear when William was victorious in pitched battle. His was an army of penitents – the knights had cut their hair short and avoided elaborate costume, while the count had devoutly confessed his sins – and it had no trouble routing the forces of the wicked. The Flemings were held to be justly punished for presuming to choose a new count. But then the unexpected happened and God abruptly closed the whole affair with the death of William Clito before Alost on 27 July 1128. Galbert of Bruges' *Chronicle* ends suddenly at this point.

Galbert's work is remarkable both for the narrative it unfolds and the analysis that accompanies it, above all for the light that it sheds upon the transition from primitive to rationally based thought, the shift from a familial to a public role and from a fragmented, disparate feudalism to the essentially cohesive and nucleated structure of monarchic society. The *Chronicle* ends on an interrogative note: why this apparent reversal of God's will? Galbert's explanation was that God in his mercy had rid Flanders of a problematical count. William had in effect bought the county (through his payment of the relief to Louis VI), committing a kind of simony that had made him in turn a *tyran*, or unjust lord. God had merely used him as a tool to punish Flanders for the bloody usurpation of Robert the Frisian half a century before.

There was a dramatic change in the struggle for political power between 1125 and 1150. From this date onwards the political units were larger in size and they operated within the increasingly strict framework of feudal law which underpinned a hierarchical society. The territorial princes could dignify their lands with the title of 'kingdom'; they could cast themselves as defenders of their country; but no matter how powerful they were, their principality was feudally subordinate to the crown of France. The most powerful princes dreamt of crowning one of themselves, as William of Normandy had won the crown of England nearly two centuries before. They watched for every opportunity, hoping for the extinction of a royal dynasty. The practice of severely limiting the marriage of younger sons to avoid fragmenting the patrimony made royal houses vulnerable in the extreme. Since political power still operated within a domestic context, politics was inevitably a game of chance. It was pure chance that Henry I of England died without male heirs in 1135, just as Charles the Good had done seven years earlier. Two rival claimants for the English throne at once emerged: Stephen, count of Blois, and Geoffrey, count of Anjou, husband of the Empress Matilda. By chance, too, William, duke of Aquitaine, also died without a legitimate male heir in 1137. His daughter Eleanor had married into the Capetian dynasty shortly before.

PART III

Origins of State and Nation

9

The Great Age of Progress

In 1137 there were countless indications in western Christendom that the momentum sustained by generations of peasant labour was now yielding progress on a dramatic scale. It is doubtful whether the rate of progress between 1180 and 1220 in the lands which constitute modern France has ever been equalled. These four decades were a turning-point, and there was no comparable period before the mid-eighteenth century. Inevitably, this radically altered the conditions in which temporal power was exercised.

Military force was its mainstay, and warriors – those violent, pillaging members of society – were the first to profit from increased agricultural yields. Their surpluses were devoted first of all to better equipment; consequently, knightly accoutrements provide some of the clearest indications of progress at an early date. Swords (symbolic of the knights' role in society) were not affected, since Frankish longswords had for centuries had no equal: they were already prized by the Saracens in the Merovingian period, and neither papal nor imperial decree had any success in banning their export to the infidel. The impact was felt rather on defensive armour – hauberk, helm and shield – making the warriors whose exploits fill almost every page of contemporary poems and chronicles virtually completely invincible. It also resulted in better-quality war-horses, bred for greater stamina but still responsive in the thick of battle. Mounted combat was affected, too: after the mid-twelfth century the cavalry charge became the single most critical feature of medieval warfare. Its aim was to unhorse the enemy with the impact of the lance; once he was unseated and robbed of his mount, he could be captured. In other words, the encounter was an unexceptional joust, as described in countless romances. Warfare was essentially a team activity, like hunting, and squadrons of comrades-in-arms (termed *conrois* in the language of northern France) rushed towards each other at the critical moment.

Activity of this kind required constant training. This is why tournaments – chaotic and deadly practice encounters – were so important. Two sizeable teams confronted each other in a limited space, with injury and fatalities giving the occasion greater piquancy. The participants on each side did their utmost to break the united front presented by their opponents and scatter them in headlong flight, so that men and horses could be captured in the ensuing confusion. In the north of France, tournaments were arranged by mutual agreement between all the great lords, so that they were spread evenly throughout the year – with the exception of the brief periods when these mock battles fell under a total papal ban. The best knights were highly sought after, for each lord's individual reputation – and that of his land – depended on the military success of those who fought bearing his arms. This was the period which also saw the development of a formal heraldic system in war and tournament. When they were young, dukes and counts took part in tournaments; as they grew older, their teams were led by a son or nephew. Only the sacred personage of the king could never participate: it was not fitting for him to be part of such 'horse fairs', as the Papacy called them, for they fostered pride and corrupted knights whose first duty should be to God and the crusade.

Nevertheless, although the king of France did not take part in tournaments himself, they were almost always held outside towns in the French 'marches' (areas which had always been frontier lands) since time immemorial. In search of fame and booty, warriors from all over Europe came to test their strength against each other and against the knights of the Ile-de-France, the king's royal domain. Knights from Lorraine, Normandy and Anjou were all agreed that the French were among the best knights in the world. The superior calibre of these knights, combined with the exceptional fertility of his domain lands, were eventually to secure Capetian supremacy.

Still more important for the evolution of government was, in my opinion, the simultaneous rise of the chivalric ethos in precisely those areas where there were refinements in equipment and tactics. If they were to be victorious (or simply to avoid defeat), every member of the team had to be unswervingly loyal to his fellow-knights and to the lord under whose banner he fought. The mutual devotion between lord and vassals fostered by homage and fealty was really learnt on the tournament field. Because the best knights frequently fought in the retinues of different lords; because the tournament had to have rules and arbiters, and because the task of awarding the prize fell to a woman of noble birth, the strict rules and code of mutual obligation that were essential for survival in battle had to be adopted by all participants. In the writings of Galbert of Bruges, this code had already been given the name of chivalry. It was crowned by the 'chivalric' virtues. Besides loyalty, there was prowess – the ability to plunge headlong into danger without pausing to calculate the risks, always playing fair, never hitting below the belt or resorting to trickery; above all, never killing another knight. Then there was largesse, or generosity, since the champion at a tournament was not supposed to keep his winnings to himself, but share them amongst his friends and followers with gay abandon. Finally, the chivalric ethic was characterized by a particular code of behaviour towards women. Intertwined with this network of secular obligations, there was a strong religious element, rooted in the concept of the peace of God and the crusading ideal. This found expression in the rituals of dubbing or belting (the girding on of the knight's sword). These were the ceremonies which admitted the youthful aspirant to the order of knighthood, after he had proved his ability to handle a lance and control his horse and demonstrated his familiarity with the chivalric code. Its precepts had been learnt in the court where he was brought up from his earliest youth, in the sermons of household clerics there and in the poems which they composed for edification and entertainment.

These knights were able to serve their own lord and his overlord more effectively because of the constant improvements to horse and equipment and because of the high morale that resulted from a courtly upbringing. They owed service in the skirmishes of war, as well as in battle and at tournaments, where battle tactics were practised. In reality, however, it was highly unusual for a ruler to risk everything in a pitched battle. The Capetians only gave battle once before Bouvines (1214), and that was at Brémule in 1119, where they were defeated. Flanders saw only two battles in 150 years, and when Fulk Rechin, count of Anjou, related the exploits of his uncle, grandfather and great-grandfather, he could only find six in the space of four generations. War, by contrast, was simply an entertainment, a means by which the lord (through the profits of pillage and sheer enjoyment of the activity) could occupy his vassals and demonstrate his largesse; finally, it was also a means of forcing an enemy to start negotiating at the earliest opportunity. For war was the obligatory prelude to negotiation. Only the siege and successful capture of a stronghold had any political value at this date, and there were decisive improvements in this area.

The discovery of much more sophisticated fortification systems in the East, combined with the prodigious strides in masonry techniques that were made in the course of building great churches and cathedrals of stone, completely transformed the defence of towns and castles. Between 1180 and 1220 the old fortifications of earth and wood were rendered totally obsolete. In order to protect their lands from invasion, the rulers of principalities employed engineers and specialist craftsmen. Together, they had to make a comprehensive plan of defence, raise larger castles on carefully chosen and laid-out sites; finally, they had to build high defensive walls. The ditches of scarp and counterscarp had to be strengthened with a face of dressed stone; in the middle of it all, a great stone keep had to be built, even stronger than all the rest. Huge numbers of labourers had to be gathered in the shortest possible time, for this work was urgent: in contrast to cathedrals, which took decades to build, there are records of castles built to the highest specification and employing the most up-to-date techniques, which were erected in a matter of a few months. Such colossal ventures inevitably cost huge sums: the Plantagenet castle of Château-Gaillard (the strategic gateway to Normandy) cost 21,103 *livres* sterling, equivalent to the daily wages of 2,500,000 foot-soldiers. Every ruler was forced henceforth to spend vast sums on defence. According to the *Grandes Chroniques de France*, Philip Augustus had no doubts on this score, convinced that his ancestors had lost lands because their expenditure on fortification was too low. Between 1203 and 1214 he built round towers all over his lands. There is evidence for eighteen, all built on the same plan as the tower in the Louvre. The foundations there have been preserved unchanged since the sixteenth century (when the moat was filled in); excavations revealed high-quality construction. Each of these towers cost between 1,200 and 2,000 *livres*, enough to pay 1,000 foot-soldiers for six to eight weeks. Investment on this scale required income well above that generated by the royal domain before the annexation of the Angevin dominions. Town walls were being built at the same time, first of all at Paris (from 1190 onwards), then at Sens, Compiègne and Melun; their cost was borne by the town's inhabitants.

No sooner were fortifications improved than techniques of attack were developed in an attempt to overcome them. The besieging forces aimed to make a breach in the walls or break them down completely. They employed better-trained and better-equipped miners, as well as siege-engines like the mangonel and the trebuchet that hurled increasingly heavy projectiles with increasing force. Engineering ranked high among military skills, with laymen still borrowing here and there from techniques used in ecclesiastical architecture. For it had in fact been in buildings designed only to glorify God that the earliest techniques of carving and stone-dressing, drawing plans and measuring pressure had been developed. The remarkable balance of the choir of St Denis (consecrated in 1140) is based entirely on the rational application of the principles of geometry and arithmetic, which were being explored with such enthusiasm in the neighbouring cathedral schools. Classifying the different types of knowledge, the Parisian scholar Hugh of St Victor wisely added the 'mechanical' to the liberal arts. The efficiency of the heavy machines dragged jolting behind companies of knights stemmed directly from the experience of the builders whose job it had been to harness the winches and hoist the keystone arches in nave and apse higher and higher. Real experts ('master engineers', as they were called) were required to design siege-engines, calculating the required angle of strike, and then to supervise their operation. These men were not to be found amongst the knightly classes, but in the growing population of the cities, where church and workshop stood side by side.

The lower strata of society provided a different kind of specialist, the soldiers who were essential for effective warfare. Château-Gaillard was impregnable, but it was taken none the less. It fell because of the cunning of mercenaries in the pay of Philip Augustus, who crept like rats through the latrine shafts. Contemporaries found it particularly shocking, because this form of attack was totally devoid of prowess, operating at a distance and then striking without warning, like the plague, so that the victims were unable to see their attackers, much less identify them. Technical developments also played a part, since the crossbow was mechanically set, increasing both range and impact. In fact, it was rather like a light and easily handled catapult, firing bolts rather than stones with such force that they penetrated the thickest breastplates. The crossbow could kill a knight, and not even princes – with the best protection of all – were safe from them. Richard I of England was first wounded and subsequently killed by a crossbow bolt. From the very outset, the Papacy attempted to ban these deadly weapons. While he was making preparations for the First Crusade, Urban II vainly forbade their use against other Christians. In 1139 they were anathematized by the Second Lateran Council with just as little success. They became widespread after 1150; at the same time their operators sold their expertise in shooting down horses and piercing mail from afar to the highest bidder.

Such mercenaries were the drudges of war: they, too, operated in teams, grouped behind a leader, who negotiated with employers. The vast majority came from wild and impoverished regions, such as the Pyrenees, or the borderlands of Flanders or Provence; they were called 'Cottereaux' or 'Brabançons' after their place of origin. The foot-soldiers in an army (armed with knives, pikes, billhooks and crossbows) were not unlike the communal militias which assembled when the alarm was raised; but perhaps they had more in common with the heavily armed convoys of long-distance merchants going to fairs, who were bound together on oath. After them came the baggage train and camp-followers. They were a permanent grouping, and continued to roam, pillaging and living off the land, when they were not receiving wages. A recent arrival in the theatre of war, they were already quite incapable of leaving it, and spread fear wherever they went. Defiled by bloodshed, corrupted by money and by the gratification of their voracious appetites, these sacrilegious ruffians caroused from the chalices they had stolen from churches. Recruited from the very dregs of society and frequently illegitimate, they had known only penury and destitution. These men could not live without prayers and worship, however, and they had their priests, despite a papal ban. To the rest of the population these companies seemed like a terrible plague visited on them by the wrath of God, to be expelled from the land with all possible speed and might. The Lateran Council of 1179 called for their elimination, identifying them as heretics. Yet, in practice, a lord rich enough to employ these companies found it difficult to defend his lands without them. They were indispensable to anyone who wanted to offer effective opposition to the enemy, capture his castles, or simply correct the excessive balance in favour of mounted knights. In 1163 Louis VII and Frederick Barbarossa met on the Franco-Imperial frontier and agreed not to employ mercenaries within the area bounded by Paris, the Rhine and the Alps. But for all his piety, the king of France was not prepared to forgo the services of paid soldiers on the exposed western flank of his kingdom.

At the end of the twelfth century a number of mounted 'serjeants' were praised for their courage. Apart from the fact that they were sometimes armed with a crossbow, there was virtually no practical difference between these lowly born horsemen and the knights who claimed mounted combat as an exclusive prerogative, by virtue of their noble birth.[1] Had the ritual of dubbing to knighthood been developed partly in order to perpetuate this distinction? When mounted combat became a less exclusive activity, one of knighthood's major privileges was lost. As a result, knights placed greater emphasis upon titles, and stressed the overall sum of their noble and knightly virtues. This reaction speeded up the process by which the knightly classes became a true nobility, by fanning the flames first of fear and then contempt. This did not prevent knights from accepting money payments for their services, in precisely the same way as the much-despised mercenaries. They made great play of the fact that they did not hoard their wealth avariciously, but squandered it on conspicuous consumption, claiming that their wages merely represented the traditional largesse bestowed by a lord on his loyal followers. In the twelfth century money once more became the sinews of war and power, destabilizing relationships at every level of society.

Ever since the introduction of a silver coinage by Charlemagne, thin little coins called '*deniers*' had circulated in France. With the revival of a money

---

[1] In practice the 'serjeants' acted as a support group; they were not allowed to participate in the knightly charge or the tournament – tr.

economy shortly before 1000, these coins circulated more quickly, were made of baser metal, and were worth less. Ecclesiastical moralists were already worried about this state of affairs, which they ascribed to greed and covetousness leading men from the straight and narrow path. People became accustomed to this situation, however. The nobility found that they had a growing need for currency themselves; no doubt they suggested that the townspeople (who were situated at the centre of trade and handled a much greater volume of coin) use it to remit their obligation to provide their lord with lodging, and that the peasantry be able to commute by means of money payments the labour dues and services of cartage and watch which they owed their lord. The peasants in turn could sell their own labour, their livestock and the produce from their fields and vineyards.

Commutations of this kind gradually became standard practice. Seigneurial taxation became more flexible as a result. People became accustomed to the transfer of money from towns and villages into the hands of officials, all of non-noble birth. But it was not long before money affected the quality of relationships, which, until then, had been based on amity, devotion and uncalculating dedication. From the early twelfth century a knight in north-west France could absolve himself from military service by payment on a sliding scale. A little later he was also able to purchase divine forgiveness and God's favours in the world to come. For an annual sum, salaried priests would say mass for the souls of the departed on the anniversary of their death, and an entire system of accountancy evolved in this area. Laboriously recording payments and calculating the price of salvation, it overlapped with the world to come, encouraging theologians to think more deeply about the place of purgatory and indulgences, introducing the concept of time into the quintessentially timeless. Learning, too, had long had its price. After his castration in 1116, Abélard was able to earn a living teaching schoolboys; if he had wanted, he could have bought himself a good time with women. There was considerable justification for the preachers' comparison of tournaments with 'fairs', for knights did not merely seek fame there, but also the money which secured it. After the mêlée, shoals of horse-dealers, innkeepers and prostitutes were attracted by the certainty of fat profits, and the level of trade was undoubtedly higher than that of the best patronized fairs. While the victors were selling off the horses and armour they had captured, their unfortunate opponents explored all possible avenues to re-equip themselves and pay off their ransom. Money was always needed. Men were not driven to acquire it by greed, but from necessity; and this eroded the traditional values of honour, excellence, courage and loyalty. Monetary circulation affected the whole of society and made it much more flexible; but its impact was also profoundly destabilizing.

The simple and reassuring image of the tripartite division of society was no longer valid. People were forced to acknowledge that there were now very many more than three estates, and they were no longer rigidly demarcated. Immutable landed wealth transmitted by gift or through inheritance was being overtaken by fluctuating resources. The image of Fortune's wheel took root in the collective consciousness, turning faster and faster as it raised some and secured the downfall of others. The key themes were destabilization and emulation, and 'winning' (*gagner*) became a watchword for the period. The expression itself became much more common in the course of the twelfth century: it was used to describe land clearance, in trade, at war and even the course of university debates.

Towards the end of the twelfth century, the towns, whose expansion had been made possible by increased agricultural production, became more important than the countryside, which they were henceforth to dominate. Improved communications meant that the university at Paris (in the centre of the most prosperous region and at the heart of the Capetian domain) became a magnet for all keen students of theology, as well as for the scholars who were busy glossing the Scriptures for the benefit of those embarking on an ecclesiastical career. They also tried to make the meaning of the texts as clear as possible, to further what was recognized as the urgent need to bring the true word of God to the people, to educate and control them. Peter the Chanter and Stephen Langton both explored the nature of the secular powers held by both rulers and merchants. They were extremely worried about the impact of the money economy on established values and upon the social relations that ensured stability and cohesion.

This concern was fully justified. They were witnessing the progressive separation of individual elements in a society that had previously had a cellular structure, with small, enclosed units grouped round a clearly defined nucleus. The individual enjoyed a new-found freedom. He held his own purse-strings. A son's expectations no longer depended solely on his father, a monk's on his monastic superior, or a knight's upon the lord in whose household he was brought up. He could take his chance outside the established group. The power once wielded by the head of the family was diminished; old ties were loosened. Confusion was the order of the day. For the man who aimed to 'win' could not allow himself to be held back by social convention; he had to turn his back on a safe life and opt for danger, if he was to make his way in the beguiling world. Contemporary chivalric romances describe a world of adventure and opportunity, but with danger and treachery lurking in the forest and the wastelands, where the happy few made their fortune, but from which many never returned. So it was in real life. Anyone who decided to cut himself off from his roots became a stranger and, to some extent, an outsider, exposed and threatened. He could not seek any help from the narrow body of local custom which regulated the community he had rejected. In the course of his wanderings he needed to be able to refer to laws which operated outside the confines of household, village and castle, to rely on a more broadly based authority which could enforce obedience to these common customs. What he required, in other words, was the power of the State, and the money economy encouraged its development.

Increased monetary circulation also continually widened the gulf between peasant and town-dweller, already commented upon by Galbert of Bruges. After 1180 town and country were in effect two separate societies; and in each the successful had increasing power over the less fortunate. In the countryside money was needed to pay taxes and fines and to buy seed and replace livestock, as well as to purchase prayers and celebrate rites of passage in a fitting way. Consequently, those who were less clever – or simply unfortunate – had to resort to loans from their priest, local manorial official or neighbours with more productive farming techniques or better relations with their superiors. Rural debt gradually became more widespread and, as a result, most of the population in the countryside became increasingly dependent on a tiny peasant elite. A comparable but much larger gap between rich and poor in the towns emerged in the twelfth century, as the wheel of Fortune gathered speed.

The experience of acute poverty was probably one of the most overwhelming experiences for twelfth-century immigrants in the suburbs of the towns. Poverty was not new to them, of course. But misfortune had previously struck in waves during a period of crisis, induced by famine, ergotic poisoning or the fires regularly mentioned by chroniclers. Episodic plagues were met with resignation; for the peasantry were used not only to torture and the unspeakable atrocities committed by soldiers on the march, but also to a level of child mortality that took a quarter of their offspring before the age of five and another quarter before puberty. Family solidarity mitigated the effects of poverty to some extent, and lords – the traditional source of succour and sustenance – were forced to open their granaries and relieve this destitution. The rich were forced to practise charity. This was done routinely, mechanically; but it changed in the course of the twelfth century. The alms-giving of Charles the Good, count of Flanders, described by Galbert of Bruges, gave way to different attitudes and practices, typified by the count of Champagne. Not satisfied with merely symbolic gestures, he sold all his gold and silver plate and gave the proceeds to the poor, sending out his almoners to find out where there was greatest need and distribute aid accordingly. Hospices, almshouses and confraternities were founded in almost every town, specifically to cater for the needs of the indigent urban poor.

The confraternities were rich, but they were ashamed of being too rich; they had listened to the gospel, and wanted to avoid the sins that money brought in its wake. Pride crowned the hierarchy of vices, but avarice was a close second. Since the end of the eleventh century the quest for apostolic poverty had drawn troubled priests at the forefront of spiritual developments to hermitages deep in the forest and the adventure of life as an itinerant preacher. It had provided the inspiration for Cistercian austerity as a reaction to the splendours of the Cluniac order; indeed, it had been the exhortations of his friend St Bernard which had roused the count of Champagne to sell his plate and jewels. After 1170 there was a growing conviction amongst the urban patriciate that it was essential to renounce worldly goods and live a life of poverty amongst the poor, in order to enter the kingdom of heaven. It drove Peter Valdès, a prosperous merchant of Lyon, to sell all he possessed and begin to preach, urging his listeners, in the name of Christ, to follow his example. There was a new, spiritual force at work among the people, that of the '*bonnes hommes*' (good men) who had deliberately chosen to live like Jesus's disciples. The people listened to them, but they were roundly criticized by the priests, jealous of their own monopoly of preaching; in their eyes anyone who usurped that function was just as much a heretic as the lawless bands of mercenaries. It was not long before the '*pauvres de Lyon*' (poor men of Lyon) were condemned by the Church and hounded by the Inquisition. Twenty years later it was only the heightened spirituality of Innocent III (once a student in Paris) which kept Francis of Assisi and his fervent disciples within the fold of mendicant orthodoxy. (The Pope had himself been the author of a theological work on voluntary poverty.) True heresy unquestionably made great inroads at this period. It threatened the power of the prelates of the Church, whom it accused of robbing the poor. Its rapid and uncontrollable expansion was a direct consequence of the spread of a money economy and of a growing and troubled awareness of its social consequences.

Most of the men who handled money in the cities and the new settlements burgeoning at the intersections of trade routes – the money-changers and merchants, speculative urban landholders and employers who exploited immigrants desperate for work – devoted very little of their income to charity. They pocketed the rest, and their rulers encouraged their growing wealth, relying on these individuals to supply great sacks of money at a moment's notice, whenever they needed it. This was why they granted them the right to collect taxes from the lower ranks of urban society. One hundred years later, Philip of Beaumanoir commented that 'the rich are responsible for the administration of towns and, as a result, its costs are borne by the poor.' This was already true at the end of the twelfth century. The very rich – the butt of contemporary *fabliaux* – were in close and frequent contact with the unattainable world of the nobility (who did not sully their hands with work of any kind), and they attempted to enter it by the back door. They adopted a crude imitation of the life-style of their nobly born superiors. The old military aristocracy also derived considerable profits from agricultural expansion. This was not from customary dues: their level did not change and, since they were now paid in cash, depreciated in real terms. To compensate, they imposed an increasing number of direct taxes on the rural economy, exploiting mills and ovens, demanding a share in the fruits of newly planted vines, the produce of land in recent cultivation and the fleeces of their sheep. The lords were not personally involved in levying these dues; they delegated this task to intermediaries called *'fermiers'*. More money passed through these men's hands than their fathers had ever earned or their grandfathers had seen in a lifetime.

It was still never enough for the lord. There was always more modern equipment to buy, lost or exhausted war-horses to replace, the costs of a crusade or a ransom to pay, arrears to chantry priests, or simply the purchase of appropriate clothes to wear at court, where knights tried to outdo each other in conspicuous consumption. In this respect, money was a prerequisite of chivalry. One indicator of poverty amongst the upper echelons of society was the sudden appearance and rapid spread in the late twelfth century of the synonymous terms *écuyer* and *damoiseau* (squire). They had formerly been employed to describe the apprentice knight who had not yet been dubbed. Now it was the title used to indicate noble birth by the increasingly numerous sons of knights, whom their father could not afford to have dubbed, and who grew old waiting for the ceremony.

Driven by need, men of high birth ran into debt no less than the unlucky peasant. It was extremely difficult to find anyone in their own class prepared to lend money. They were forced to borrow from the townspeople whom they despised or, worse, from Jews, unshackled by the prohibition that applied to Christians and free to practice the usury for which they were universally hated. When their money ran out, the knights were forced to sell anything they could, and first of all their allegiance. Bit by bit they sold their allodial lands to their lord, and were reinvested with them as a fief. In this way the pattern of landholding among the knightly classes became markedly more feudal after 1180. Alternatively, they looked for a lord who would be their 'patron' and keep them as his retainers and members of his household, paying them an annual fief-rente, which they could only lose if they were convicted of treachery. They entered into service. In every case they abandoned their rights. Thus elements of the knightly classes that had been tumultuously independent a century before were now imprisoned in an increasingly tight web of obligation, because of the spread of monetary values throughout society. This also reduced military disorder in another way. Landed wealth became less important, and it was no longer so vital to preserve the integrity of an estate that younger sons were prohibited from marrying. Instead, all those who did not enter the Church could marry and start their own line of descent. There was a great proliferation of lineages, with a narrower landed base than before, and this enabled the ruler to control them more effectively. As a result, the group of young and celibate warriors who had been responsible for some of the most unruly breaches of the peace in the past were absorbed into the fabric of society. This was a major reason for the period of relative peace between the different orders of society in the thirteenth century.

Territorial princes were the net beneficiaries from shifts in the balance of power amongst the nobility, which widened the distance between the different orders. A memorandum of the military service on which Philip Augustus could depend, drawn up in his chancery between 1203 and 1206, distinguishes between four categories: dukes and counts, barons (this title became common in the twelfth century to designate men as powerful as counts, but without their Carolingian antecedents), castellans and, finally, *vavasseurs* – a portmanteau title to describe all other knights and squires. The essential distinction was no longer between the third and fourth groups, but between the second and the third, barons and castellans. The castellan class was disintegrating.

By 1200 the old castles had lost their original strategic importance. The castellans were in no position to refuse admittance to duke, count or baron. Moreover, the judicial authority which they had once exercised over the surrounding countryside was now fragmented, and operated instead within the newly strengthened unit of the parish. The lord of the castle retained this authority in some parishes. Otherwise it was entrusted to a man who, if he was a knight, had just as much right to be called '*sire*'; his house was also surrounded by a moat and was easily confused with the older castle. The castle no longer harboured the bands of household knights that had terrorized the peasantry around the year 1000. The castellan still assembled the local knights under his banner and received homage from them, but his income was scarcely larger than theirs and he was just as likely to be in debt. Technical improvements in warfare and the establishment of a money economy had reduced the castellans to the level of *vavasseurs*.

Documentary evidence is too sparse and insufficiently detailed for us to be sure exactly how the jurisdiction once exercised by the castellan became fragmented in the second half of the twelfth century. Many factors were at work. With the increasingly exact definition of feudal law, lords overcame their earlier reservations about breaking up their lordships: they agreed to enfeoff knights retained in castle garrisons, who demanded landed endowment, as well as their younger sons, who wished to marry. Another important consideration was the growing sense of identity in the surrounding community, and this also affected the final distribution of power. At the Fourth Lateran Council in 1215 the Church had strengthened the parish unit, so that it would be more effective as both a propaganda and a surveillance tool in the fight against paganism and heresy. It seemed quite natural to organize civil justice and the maintenance of law and order within the same parochial framework. Levying taxes and collecting fines fell within the jurisdiction of the local lord, who was also responsible for safeguarding roads, harvests and pastures, ensuring that local custom was observed and deciding the pattern of the agricultural year. A fundamental element of any system of control, his prime role was the introduction of a market economy into the countryside. Political decisions were made by those above him in the social hierarchy: barons, counts and dukes. Their role was to put an end to private war, by force and exemplary punishment among the common people and by arbitration amongst the knightly classes.

In practice, barons kept the peace over a huge area, for they had managed their inheritances more prudently than the knights. The barony of Coucy, built up of lands lying between ancient territorial principalities, provides an example. When he left for the Holy Land in 1190, Ralph I was careful to ensure that his estate would be kept intact: in his will he left three key fortresses to his oldest son; the two younger brothers were not forgotten, but they were to receive only a few small lordships, to be held from their older brother in liege homage and to revert to him if they died without issue. Arrangements of this kind were standard amongst the upper nobility; but families who concentrated all their holdings in the hands of the main branch were very susceptible to sudden disaster, which might end the lineage at a stroke. At this level of society the dominant trend was to amalgamate landed inheritances, rather than fragment them.

The barons exercised control over a large area, regulating the movement of population, encouraging new settlers, licensing assarts and founding new towns. However, the reclamation of forest and wasteland interested them less than new settlements and their markets or the large tolls they could levy on road- and river-traffic. These revenues enabled them to buy the homage and services of minor lords and squires and to pay the officials who were the indispensable concomitant of their sovereignty. They included administrative clerks, as well as the serjeants and marshals responsible for maintaining public order by means of regular patrols, ready to intervene in trouble-spots without delay. Money payments had enabled this protection to be extended to hundreds of parishes. Settlements were gradually making inroads into the great empty spaces of vast forests and marshes. In the course of the twelfth century, road- and bridge-building, better horses with better harness and the widespread distribution of blacksmiths and staging posts, all completely transformed transport and communications, especially in northern France. A threshold was reached in the early thirteenth century, surpassed only in the eighteenth century in speed and the twentieth in tonnage.

The structures of the barony and the even smaller county had consequently become too constricting by 1200. As old barriers were broken down, public peace and the pursuit of expansion required a more broadly based power, similar to that of the territorial princes. Their primary responsibility was to hold natural forces in check. It would have been impossible for each district in the Loire valley, for example, to protect its lands from flooding; a higher authority (that of the Plantagenet count of Anjou) was needed to co-ordinate the construction of dykes; under the aegis of the count of Flanders, work was put in hand to reclaim land from the sea. Only the territorial princes were in a position to protect foreign merchants bringing their wares to important fairs. The merchants' distress was clear for all to see in 1127, when the assassination of the count of Flanders deprived them of protection within his lands. As trade routes continued to grow longer, the problems posed by the many different standards of measurement increased, above all in relation to units of currency. In this sphere, too, it was only the territorial princes who could attempt a solution. There were times when circulation was sluggish, the coinage debased and fit only for empty gestures of largesse. However, mints to which an individual could bring his own silver for conversion into a few coins when he required them were distributed as widely as the centres of power. Marked with a cross, as if from a place of sanctuary, the coins struck there had something almost sacred about them; they strengthened the status quo. However, this was a disorganized activity and produced a proliferation of different types of coin; together with the inevitable effects of wear and tear as they circulated, it reduced the value of even the tiniest coins, until they were almost worthless. It was the job of the money-changer, on his bench near the market, to test and weigh coins and calculate their value. A good prince was expected to issue a sound coinage that would be valid for long-distance trade. Money circulated at increasing speed over longer distances, strengthening much larger political units in the process. It was their most powerful source of support.

The territorial princes had no scruples about involving themselves at every stage of the process of striking coin. First of all, they struck high-quality coin, in order to ensure that it was widely accepted and in demand; a proportion of the coin struck was levied by them at each mint. They also appointed tax-collectors to levy tolls on coin in circulation at all the important intersections of the major trade routes. When Philip Augustus seized Artois in the name of his infant son in 1191–2, he gained control of the castles first; but very soon afterwards he secured the lucrative toll at Bapaume, which dominated the immensely rich trade between Flanders and the Paris basin, where he set a new level of tariffs. The territorial princes held the strongest cities, and the fairs over which they had jurisdiction attracted great throngs of merchants. The influence of the lords of Montpellier grew steadily, because the simple manor given to their ancestors by the count of Mauguio was close to the port of Lattes, which they transformed into one of the most vital crossroads of Mediterranean trade. Merchants from distant lands, 'Lombards' and Jewish money-lenders were all vulnerable to some extent, because it was well known that their coffers were full of silver: so that they were in no position to refuse their ruler and protector anything. If a demand for a large loan was anticipated, they pre-empted the request, and suggested it spontaneously; they lent money at the slightest hint, at the first suggestion that a pogrom might otherwise be in the wind.

Although there was a general shortage of currency, it flowed copiously into princely households, where accounts were not kept by the *denier* or the *sou*, but in terms of silver marks and *livres*. It was the scale of income and expenditure which raised noble households so far above all those of 'knights, castellans, counts and even dukes', who were all irresistibly drawn there 'by the stink of money', as Peter the Venerable, abbot of Cluny, had already observed bitterly as early as 1130. Avarice made them tractable. In his *Dialogue of the Exchequer* of 1179, Richard Fitznigel (Henry II of England's treasurer) stated that money was as essential in peace as in times of war. In peacetime it was the vehicle for the ruler's charity. Significantly, he saw it as the ruler's primary duty to distribute money to clerks and monks whose prayers would ensure that divine favour smiled upon the State. He also believed that money should be spent upon church ornament and the building of cathedrals – one of the tympana of Notre-Dame at Paris depicts Louis VII holding in his hand a model of the church which his gifts were helping to rebuild, to the glory of God and for the greater prosperity of his people. When the ruler was at war, money had to be spent on fortifying castles and paying soldiers; but payments in connection with the defence of the realm had also to be made on many other occasions. Richard Fitznigel made a clear case. The revival of monetary circulation had enabled princes to employ companies of mercenaries, build impregnable castles, control the barons and so-called peers of the realm – in short, to gain political supremacy.

Revealing evidence on this subject is to be found in the work of Wace, the Anglo-Norman writer usually referred to as a chronicler. He was in fact a writer of romances (*romancier*) in the true sense of the word, since he wrote in the literary language of the French–speaking courts, known to contemporaries as '*romans*'. He was the '*clerc lisant*' of Henry II, the Plantagenet king of England, and his job was to entertain the court with readings of his own or others' writings. Henry II of England was also one of the most powerful French territorial princes: count of Anjou, duke of Normandy and (through his wife, Eleanor of Aquitaine) duke of Aquitaine. In his *Roman de Rou* Wace tells the story of the first dukes of Normandy, drawing heavily on an account in Latin written by the monk William of Jumièges a century earlier. Wace translated his source, revising it and making his own additions. I shall select pictures of the ideal ruler from two such passages. The first describes Duke Richard I shut up in a tower in Rouen castle. Although he would rather have spent his time hunting or engaged in other outdoor pursuits, he and his officials were reckoning 'his tallies and accounts'. Robert I, 'the Magnificent', comes later in the narrative. He is portrayed receiving gifts and levying taxes – or, to be more exact – the feudal relief imposed upon new vassals when they assumed their fiefs. Wace was writing at a period when this feudal due (still resisted by the Flemings in 1128) brought the ruler huge revenues: shortly afterwards Philip Augustus was to receive nearly 5,000 marks for Flanders and 20,000 for the fiefs held by King John of England. Wace thus presents Robrt engaged in precisely those activities which occupied Henry II. On the model of the ideal knight, he ensured a plentiful supply of food and drink for his household and his guests. Soon afterwards he distributed what was most greatly valued – horses, plate and, above all, money. Women were similarly distributed, although they do not feature in this context. Widows, orphans and wealthy heiresses were the most desirable presents Wace's patron could make to his loyal servants, holding them out in the hope of better service, but awarding them only after the most hard-headed calculation. Of course the moral of Wace's vignette is that money was the most highly prized of all gifts. The ruler could not hoard the revenues he received; it was his duty to redistribute them. For money was the life-blood and nourishment of the State, guaranteeing the ruler his subjects' affection. Like the supreme Christian virtue *caritas* (love, charity), expressed in friendship, self-sacrifice and mutual good will, the circulation of money ensured the stability of the established social order.

Wace describes three occasions when Robert I gave gifts. The first was a present of money to one of his knights, who was the first to follow him and offer alms at the altar; the knight immediately dissociated himself from the money and offered it to God. The second gift was a valuable jewel, which he presented to a clerk: it was so beautiful that the recipient died, consumed by greed. He deserved this punishment, because the clergy were not supposed to set their hearts on worldly goods, any more than knights. Robert's last gift was to a serf – not by any means a poor man, but a skilled metal-worker who made especially fine knives. In this allegorical scene Wace represents the armourers supplying a ruler with the weapons which ensured his military success. He is the only one of the three to keep the king's gift. In other words, it was acceptable for men of his kind to enrich themselves in order that they might be taxed. The *Roman de Rou* is an essentially political work: the three characters represent the three orders at the ruler's court, which underpinned the State.

During the same period John of Salisbury finished his *Policraticus*, a scholarly treatise in Latin and the first to be written on the theme of secular power. John was a churchman, but (like Wace) he was then in the service of Henry II of England and a close colleague of the chancellor, Archbishop Thomas Becket. They both worked within the most efficient administrative machine of the period. John had studied in Paris, and was eventually to become bishop of Chartres. At that point, however, he was preoccupied with the nature of secular power, which he described in terms of the human body, representing the knights as its hands, the peasantry its feet and the ruler its head. At its palpitating heart was the blood, found in the king's court (*sénat*) – and although he does not say so explicitly, I believe that money was seen as the life-blood of the State.

John of Salisbury was indeed right: the court was the hub of the State. Coin-carrying arteries converged there, and it was the focus for all the 'new men', the 'achievers' who sought to better their social status. An extremely diverse courtly society existed in this confined setting, separated from the common people in the same way as the households of the most insignificant squires. The ruler took great care to ensure that the court did not become homogeneous, preserving its hierarches (for which the heavenly Jerusalem provided a model) and ensuring that rivalry between the different social orders continued undiminished. For – as Wace's narrative demonstrated – each of the three 'estates' (or orders of society) had a distinctive, individual character.

Lowest of the three were the merchants, whose function was the creation of wealth: Philip Augustus's chaplain, Andrew (known as Andreas Capellanus), referred to them as 'plebeians'. Unrefined parvenus, they were objects of scorn: this was the section of society most valuable to the ruler; it also posed the greatest threat, because its members could rise with such speed. Other counsellors warned the ruler against the 'bad counsel' which they proffered. The ruler invariably listened, but he was careful to suppress the contempt which they expressed. By making use of them, the ruler ensured the merchants' support for his actions. The avaricious

nobility were inevitably jealous of commercial wealth. Their own achievements had been in feats of arms and courage, tested in the prince's
tournaments. In the ruler's eyes, they were ranged opposite that other
group of adventurers and achievers in a different sphere, the clergy. This
group was as valuable to the ruler as the merchants, since he needed
administrators capable of formulating sentences, keeping records and assessing the resources available to him at any given time. The clergy were
responsible for the final crystallization of the administrative structures
of the State, and introduced much more intellectual discipline into its
administration.

The Church was the guardian and repository of a written system of
government and administration. Restoration of this system – and a
'renaissance', based upon a return to true and uncorrupted forms of
government – had been the basis of ecclesiastical reform. The twelfth
century saw the flowering of this renaissance, above all in judicial practice.
Collating texts, resolving internal contradictions using the 'scholastic'
methods developed in the cathedral schools (the use of the *distinctio*, the
quaestio and the formal debate of arguments for and against the proposition), the reformers constructed a rational framework for canon law,
the code by which not only the clergy were judged, but also the laity in
matters that concerned the Church. Its sphere of action continued to
increase disproportionately all the time, because the clergy took the view
that everything to do with marriage and sexuality, as well as oaths – which
were taken on innumerable occasions – came within their purview.

Extending their sphere of jurisdiction still further, the clergy made
wider use of the practice of *inquisitio*, a rational inquiry whose conclusions
were preserved in a written report. The ambiguities of oral custom were
replaced by a written code, and documentary evidence substituted for oral
testimony and the judicial ordeal. In the late eleventh century the eminent
canon lawyer, Ivo, bishop of Chartres, called for an end to the practice
of ordeal by red-hot iron to determine the guilt of an endless stream
of women suspected of adultery, replacing it with written evidence. The
legal process became more sophisticated as the calibre of cathedral clergy
improved. It was strengthened by the powers delegated to bishops to
maintain the peace of God. Some canons became specialists in the administration of ecclesiastical justice. Diocesan courts were thus gradually
organized in the course of the twelfth century. The Fourth Lateran
Council of 1215 decreed that their sentences should be recorded, and
appeal procedures were established at the same time.

The Church thus provided the model for a legal apparatus that was
disciplined, efficient and sophisticated. With the exception of the king of
France (who was in effect a member of the episcopacy by virtue of the

unction of his coronation) and the great territorial princes, such as the dukes of Aquitaine, who had pretensions to be his equal, the lay nobility were illiterate. For them these pieces of membrane covered with incomprehensible signs had an almost magical significance, inspiring respect none the less. Written testimony had of course long been part of judicial procedure in comital courts and was soon resumed. In what had been southern Gaul the practice seems to have been interrupted only for a very brief period. It was only suspended for a generation in Catalonia. In the 1020s reference ceased to be made there to the ancient law of Toledo within the jurisdiction of the count of Barcelona, and quarrels between knights were invariably resolved by recourse to judicial duel; but from the mid-eleventh century new texts began to be consulted. The situation was not very different in the Mâconnais, where *c.*1020–30 village priests were required to record contracts relating to the sale of land and marriage agreements. The wording of Latin formulae dating from long before was certainly garbled; but there can be no doubt that these documents were preserved in case they had to be consulted in a lawsuit. From 1070 to 1080, moreover, the count of Mâcon had a clerical legal expert (*jurisperitus*) beside him when he passed sentence, and he considered himself bound to act upon the lawyer's advice. At this time in Provence and slightly later in the Narbonnais, legal experts assembled the remnants of Roman and civil law still operating in these regions, classified them, and cobbled together what was now believed essential to the secular laws governing public order.

Secular justice had ceased to rely on the written word at an earlier date in the old kingdom of the Franks; but there, too, it was reinstated. In the first three decades of the twelfth century the duke of Normandy had to find a means of controlling social disturbances (*inquietatio*), and he adopted the practice of appointing clerks without delay, who made inquiries on the spot, gathering evidence from witnesses and recording their depositions on the model of an episcopal court. A few years later some southern legal practices were also adopted. Louis VII had travelled across the south of France and spent some while at Montpellier on his return from a pilgrimage to the shrine of St James at Compostella in 1155. In 1170 a legal expert (*jurisperitus*) appeared in his retinue. At the University of Paris a 'master' – possibly the same individual – lectured on the new discipline of civil law.

Between 1180 and 1220 secular justice reorganized itself on the ecclesiastical model. Lawsuits were conducted with the formal sequence of supplication, inquiry and appeal, and the documents produced by the litigants were authenticated by a seal. The use of seals spread rapidly in northern France, while in the south, notaries (who validated documents) became increasingly widespread. Anyone who wanted to protect his rights and ensure that an agreement would be respected had to dig deep in his pockets, because he had to pay the scribe who wrote the document and the authority which authenticated it, as well as the lawyer who used it to plead his cause. At a stroke, a whole new, lucrative profession was born, that of the lawyers.

It was at this date in Provence, Champagne and Flanders that legal documents began to be drawn up in the vernacular rather than in Latin. At the same time, customary law began to be preserved in written form. In 1199 one of the clerks of justice of the seneschal of Normandy wrote down all the customary law he knew in his own region. It was no more than a memorandum, but twenty-five years later another clerk, versed in Roman law, transcribed the document and used it as the basis for the *Très Ancien Coutumier de Normandie* (*Most Ancient Custumal of Normandy*). During the period 1220–30 the principles of customary law in Paris and the Touraine were similarly defined, and – like Roman and civil law – glossed and refined. A cohesive and standardized body of law was as essential as a standardized coinage. A great swarm of lawyers and administrators were consequently employed in the courts of territorial rulers responsible for keeping the peace over an increasingly large area. Although scattered over a wide area, they were bound together by common procedures and by the need to base their work on a common body of customary law.

Mirroring the development of writing was that of numeracy. The Church did not take the lead here. For a long while numbers had been endowed with a mystical significance, and used by the Church as aids to meditation and spiritual exercises. In the 1140s, when Abbot Suger was so proud of the administrative progress made at St Denis and the monks introduced architectural innovations dependent upon geometry and the rules of proportion, there was no inkling of what Alexander Murray has called 'the emergence of an arithmetical mentality'. All numbers higher than 100 in Suger's biography of Louis VI are approximate and symbolic. In fact, there is only one exact figure over 10. Admittedly, this was a 'history', a genre in which exact numbers seemed not merely unhelpful, but positively incongruous. Counting was seen as a vulgar activity, the concern of peasants, servants and tax-collectors.

In fact, efficient administration of its temporalities forced the Church to adopt a new and practical approach to numbers, and arithmetical skills became widespread in the middle of the twelfth century. In 1155 the abbot of Cluny sent investigators to all the abbey's lands; they were instructed to make a detailed list of resources and work out a figure. The abbey was heavily in debt and an assessment of resources was essential if its finances were to be put in order. There is a clear connection here between minutely itemized lists of anticipated revenue, monetary problems and the impossibility of meeting current expenses, such as building projects which had been planned when money bought more and prices were lower. There can be no doubt that it was the unsettling influence of money at the very core of secular and ecclesiastical structures of power that made the introduction of exact calculation an overriding necessity.

This was no easy task. In the first place, the monetary system was extremely complex (as with the English pre-decimal currency there were twelve *deniers* in one *sou*, twenty *sous* in one *livre*); the Roman numerals used at this time were ill-suited to written calculations, and it was easier to add or subtract by moving counters over the squares of a chequer-board. Formal education was irrelevant here, and churchmen proved to be less adept than merchants and even knights, who at least had the advantage of playing chess. Numeracy was consequently more highly developed in towns and castles than in religious houses. In about 1170 William Marshal led a team of knights across France from one tournament to the next and wanted to record the profits of the undertaking. A man was recruited for this task whose sole function was to keep an exact record of their winnings. He had been responsible for purveyance in the kitchen of Henry, the 'Young King'(eldest son of Henry II), a post where arithmetic was essential. However, he was also literate (almost certainly a cleric), for he was expected to record the balance of profit and loss on a parchment roll after every encounter. As money circulated with increasing speed, written records superseded abacus and chequer-board. The earliest evidence of systematic accounting also dates from this period, in the efficient administrations of Flanders, Catalonia and Normandy. A volume entitled the *Gros Bref* was compiled in Flanders, for example, in which all the *brevia* (summary accounts presented by the county's forty receivers) were recorded, with payments in kind carefully converted into *deniers*, *sous* and *livres*.

It is always said that the French court was slow to adopt these practices; but was this really the case? We should not underestimate the role of chance: Philip Augustus was routed at Fréteval in Normandy by his formidable rival Richard the Lionheart in 1194; in the course of his headlong flight, he was forced to abandon his baggage train, including all his personal valuables. Chronicle sources tell us that his archive was lost, as well as his stock of coin. It is entirely possible that there were accounts among the lost documents, but there is no evidence of this. However, various hypotheses have been put forward to explain the possibly later development of methods of accounting in Capetian France. T. N. Bisson believes that the Capetian kingdom was so rich, with such vast quantities of coin flowing through the king's hands, that he simply had no need to count it all.

Whatever the case, any deficiency was made good with all possible speed in the reign of Philip Augustus. When the king left on crusade in 1190, part of his court remained behind in France: this was not to be itinerant, but to remain in one place. All receipts were to be brought to it in Paris. As a result of this innovation, the domain officials (*prévôts*) had to submit accounts regularly, and the treasury officials had to keep a record of them. This had been intended as a purely temporary measure, but the defeat at Fréteval four years later ensured that the arrangement became permanent. This catastrophe underlined the risk of travelling with documents and valuables and the subsequent difficulties of tax assessment. Permanence and centralization became the order of the day. The expansion of the royal domain and the resulting growth of income made them indispensable. First there was the annexation of the Vermandois and Artois, then the conquest of Normandy and Anjou, at precisely the period when these regions witnessed an increase in population and mercantile activity. As a result, crown revenues rose by 80 per cent between 1180 and 1203, then by another 80 per cent after the conquest of Normandy and Anjou. The relatively crude procedures which had been adequate for an unchanging domain were demonstrably inefficient in these different circumstances. The king's officials set about remedying the situation, drawing particular inspiration from the sophisticated Plantagenet administration in Normandy, which had been in place for some decades.

Budgeting was just as important as the rendering of accounts, however. Since the king wanted to know what revenues he would have at his disposal, it was imperative that his household were numerate. Inquiries into the revenues available from particular sources were held periodically. Their aim was to evaluate, or *priser*, as contemporaries called it. This was how the '*prisée des sergents*' came to be drawn up in 1194 and revised in 1204. It listed the numbers of carts and armed men to be supplied by eighty-three towns and royal abbeys when the king summoned the feudal host. The authors attempted to set a value on this assistance: 7,695 infantry and 138 carts were estimated at 11,693 *livres parisis*. The remarkable accuracy of these figures is an indication of the rapid spread of numerical skills in the royal household. Not only were they now adept at mental arithmetic, but they had also acquired the habit of thinking in terms of *livres*, *sous* and *deniers*, which was completely new to them. The duties of vassals were also calculated in relation to the fiefs they held. So that decisions were as soundly based as possible, Philip Augustus extended the scope of these inquiries beyond the boundaries of the royal domain. Among the surviving documents are a list compiled in 1207 of abbeys and bishoprics and another of the 'knights of the kingdom of France'. Finally, officials of the royal administration took the logical step towards balancing income and expenditure: the account presented at All Saints in 1221 was, in effect, an embryonic budget.

There was no longer any shortage of educated personnel. Whereas previously schools had virtually been cathedral annexes, they had now spread further afield and were scattered everywhere, teaching very considerable numbers. They offered an essentially professional training for the service of God. The liberal arts and numeracy were taught in order that they might pray better, and so that they might correctly interpret God's will in the Scriptures and the visible forms of his creation. Theology was the end of all education, but in order to reach this goal, other, highly practical disciplines had to be made available to those who would ultimately serve masters other than God and make their way in the world. A large number of educated men took service in princely households after they had studied the liberal arts and law, instead of continuing towards a high-ranking career in the Church. Towards the end of the twelfth century, the Church apparently began to realize the possible disadvantages of this trend, and considered taking measures to check the flow of graduates into secular government. John of Salisbury had been scathing on the subject of *curiales*, or courtiers, frequently clerics who had deserted the Church for the service of a prince.

He had in mind the men who had entered princely service inconspicuously, often when they had only completed the first part of their studies. From service in his chapel, they were drawn progressively towards the heart of his administration. In Philip Augustus's reign a number of household servants fell into this category: they included Andreas Capellanus ('Andrew the Chaplain') and William the Breton, as well as the clerk Adam, the first keeper of the royal accounts whose name has been recorded. Brother Guérin, the multi-talented administrator of the entourage which supported the king on his return from crusade, was a Hospitaller. The Order of the Hospital of St John was – with the Order of the Temple – responsible for the transfer of funds to the East; they were astute businessmen, as well as warriors, in close contact with towns and merchants. At the beginning of the thirteenth century, moreover, a growing number of masters and students started to group together in 'universities' (associations for their mutual aid) in the most active intellectual centres (such as Paris or Montpellier). They were one of the mainstays of the nascent French State; but the domestic institutions of household chapels and the collegiate churches beside the great castles were a far more important source of support. For the territorial princes devoted a proportion of any excess revenue to funding prebendaries and providing for new canons, who would not only pray for them, but would also play a part in secular administration. In the 1150s the count of Champagne with his friends and officials endowed more than 320 such positions. Every level of the secular ruling class created an intelligentsia according to their means, but they paid a fair price for it.

Surrounded by educated men, it was imperative that the ruler himself should appear competent; if he could not read himself, he should at least be familiar with the contents of books and know how to apply them to the business of government. Otherwise his prestige would suffer. By the end of the twelfth century no baron could afford to ignore the importance of education. All the great territorial princes took considerable pains to ensure that they could read. This is vividly demonstrated by the image of themselves and their ancestors that the counts of Anjou wished to project in the second half of the century and which is reflected in the anecdotes related by writers in their service. One of them describes the very early Count Fulk, who died *c*.960. The king's household was said to have laughed when they saw him chanting mass with his priests. The count wrote a rejoinder in his own hand: 'An ignorant king is a crowned ass.' The sovereign should realize that '*sapientia* (wisdom), eloquence and literacy were as essential for counts as for kings'. Thereafter Fulk was universally admired because, 'although he was very well educated in the liberal arts, in the rules of rhetoric and the arguments of Cicero and Aristotle, he nevertheless far surpassed all other knights in strength and courage'. From about 1180, the ruling nobility seem to have had to combine intellectual attributes with military ability. This is the moral behind a story about William Plantagenet, count of Poitou (who died in 1164). According to the chroniclers, when he was besieging the castle of Montreuil-Bellay, this 'educated count' sent to the abbey of Marmoutier for a copy of Vegetius, the Roman military theorist. He had it read to him – whether in the Latin original, or translated and glossed, is not clear. Whatever the case, upon reflection he put into practice the following day what he had heard, and succeeded in capturing the stronghold. The story is probably apocryphal, but it clearly reveals that a noble of his rank in the Touraine was expected to refer to classical sources, just like a churchman, before he took any action. It was this new serious streak that made the troubadours lament that the warriors from whom they anticipated financial reward now thought less about 'prowess and gaiety than justice and the law relating to individual rights'.

Writing shortly after 1200, Lambert of Ardres (who was in the pay of the counts of Guînes) presents a very detailed picture of this new-style prince. He was a priest in the count's household, proud of his education in the schools, with a position in the collegiate church (founded in 1069) that abutted the comital castle. His work clearly reveals the cultural change that was taking place in the courts at this period. Written in Latin like a scholarly treatise and adorned with the most pedantic rhetorical flourishes, it also has strong echoes of the rhythms of contemporary vernacular poetry composed for the entertainment of the knights. To illustrate the different virtues which the ideal lord should cultivate in youth and as an older man, the writer presents two contrasting figures. Count Baldwin is the older (*senior*), and his eldest son, Arnold, is still a bachelor. Baldwin comes from the middle-ranking nobility. He is proud to have been dubbed knight thirty years earlier by Thomas Becket; squeezed between two powerful principalities, he is also glad to have been able to preserve the autonomy of his own lordship. Although he cannot read himself, he makes strenuous efforts to acquire the *sapientia* (wisdom) which he knows can make him the equal of the princes on either side of him. He therefore accords passing scholars a liberal welcome, making full use of their brief stay so that he may learn more of God's purpose from them. As a simple listener, he takes pride in this approach to the true meaning of sacred texts and in being able to hold his own in formal debate. His greatest pleasure is to tell inquirers 'how he has acquired knowledge without a formal education'. His chamber is filled with books. His great thirst for knowledge makes him a generous patron of writers who translate into the vernacular Latin texts of the Song of Songs, the works of St Augustine and the *Life* of St Anthony, besides medical treatises which have given him a sound knowledge of physic. Arnold, on the other hand, is responsible for his family's reputation at tournaments, and has no contact with the written culture of his father. For entertainment in the brief interludes between campaign or tournament, he listens to the stories which all his fellow-knights know by heart – about the crusades, Charlemagne and King Arthur, or his own forebears. His taste was for the tales of adventure preserved in oral tradition.

A young knight was in fact expected to have an excellent command of language. This is well illustrated by a story about Geoffrey Plantagenet, who was welcomed by his father-in-law the night before his wedding and subjected to an exhaustive review of his linguistic skills. For while rulers certainly relied on strength and skill in arms to establish and consolidate their position, negotiation, good counsel and lucid analysis were just as important. It had long been the practice for the secular nobility to preside at judicial sessions, determining with reference to customary law where the particular rights at issue lay, a task that called for a good memory and a sharp mind. It was only as a result of very gradual cultural osmosis between this milieu and the learned world of the schools that attitudes previously confined to the Church were adopted by the nobility.

Already in the *Chanson de Roland* (*Song of Roland*), dating from the late eleventh or early twelfth century, the secondary figure of Oliver (embodying the cardinal virtue of prudence) plays an essential role beside the hero, Roland, the embodiment of courage. From 1090 onwards, there is increasing evidence that the sons of the lesser nobility, who were not destined for high-ranking ecclesiastical careers, were being taught by tutors at home, where they learnt to read and understand a little Latin. At the same time the epithet '*prudens*' begins to appear in eulogies of the good knight. It became increasingly popular and soon overtook other adjectives which stressed physical courage, such as *fortis* or *strenuus*. *Prudence* was the quality which enabled a knight to discern which course of action would find favour with God. It also enabled him to control his emotions and act rationally. It was a quality particularly fitting for a group of men who, despite their God-given sword and duty to uphold the divine order in the world, were always at risk from their own uncontrolled violence. The term *prudhomme*, to denote an individual who was not merely wise but in full control of himself, enjoyed enormous popularity in the mid-thirteenth century. Joinville tells us that Louis IX said that 'a *preudome* (*prudhomme*) is so grand and good a thing that even to pronounce the word fills the mouth pleasantly.'[2] It described the perfect knight in whom reason and bodily strength were perfectly balanced. A century earlier, *prudence* (which was above all a bastion against excess) already enjoyed a pre-eminent position among the qualities which set the knight apart from his social inferiors.

This value system was called '*courtoisie*' (usually rendered in English as 'courtly love', but in fact denoting an entire courtly life-style) by the contemporaries of Louis VII and Philip Augustus. S. Jaeger believes that it is to be found in its earliest form in the entourage and chapel of the Ottonian Emperors. The prototype emerged among clerics who were closely involved with the exercise of secular power at court; here, too, the idea of 'renaissance', or return to the customs and principles of a golden age, was a vital one. It was prompted by a rereading of classical writers like Cicero and Seneca, who exhorted the honest man to friendship, eloquence and self-control. Whatever its precise antecedents, this value system was gradually elaborated, and found its fullest development in twelfth-century France. It largely coincided with the twelfth-century 'renaissance' (which we have already mentioned), and *amitié* (love) was its principal weapon. But *courtoisie* was essentially a code of moderation. Bridling aggressive instincts and sexual passion, it provided a form of rational control for the physical impulses which otherwise threatened the established order. These strict rules constituted a political weapon for the territorial princes whose money underpinned the courts. Courtly love also proved an extremely effective means of strengthening the State. In fact, it was so influential that no study of the progressive rationalization of power can afford to ignore it, although at this period it is only documented in literary works, often centred on the theme of '*fine amours*', or refined love. There is some basis

---

[2] John of Joinville, *The Life of St Louis*, tr. R. Hague (London, 1955), p. 30.

for the term 'courtly love' and the concept of a 'courtly' mentality, since it distinguished this section of society sharply from the rest.

Like the tournament, courtly love was an elaborate, ritualized game. Its rules were not unlike those which regulated matrimonial law. The control of sexuality had been one of the reforming Church's main concerns since the eleventh century. When clerical marriage was prohibited, it was enjoined as a duty upon the laity. As a result, a solid juridical edifice defining acceptable matrimonial conduct came into being. Relatively soon afterwards, an analogous code was developed in the courts of secular rulers for the benefit of the large majority whom dynastic policy decreed should remain unmarried. Courtly love called for moderation in the young knight who wished to increase his reputation (among women, as well as men), following an ideal deemed prudent, rather than prudish. Courtly love demanded intellectual control of bodily excesses, exalting physical pleasure and simultaneously delaying its consummation. This code, which regulated behaviour between lovers, proved an exceptionally effective method of social control. Like feudal and customary law (and at the same date), it was eventually written down. The work embodying these precepts was an instant success. It was written in Latin, the language of conciliar decrees and Roman law, and in the form of an exercise in scholastic logic, reenforcing the distinctions between noble, less noble and non-noble in the enclosed and hierarchical world of the court. It was the only literary work listed among legal and fiscal books in the chancery registers of Philip Augustus. This treatise on *The Art of Love* (or, *How to Love Honourably*) was composed in 1186 by Andreas Capellanus, a member of Philip Augustus's household and one of his chaplains.

10

Louis VII

The concept of the State became increasingly widespread and accepted during the twelfth century. At the same time there were rapid advances in every discipline – literature, science and philosophy – and the scholars' view of the world was changing rapidly. They were no longer so mistrustful of nature, and they began to question the previously accepted idea that man was required by God to be his agent in a continual creative process. The concept of a vegetative creation gained ground, in which each generation took over the work of its predecessors, made its contribution, and passed it on to the next. As a result, history was no longer seen as an inexorable movement towards decline. The meaning of the word *renovatio* (renewal) also changed completely. Whereas previously it had implied restoration by contemplation of the past and withdrawal from the process of corruption, the term 'renaissance' was henceforth always to have connotations of progress and renewal. The scholars of northern France were the first to adopt this point of view; they were also responsible for the belief that reason was a precondition for the true peace (*vera pax*), which reigns in heaven. The most brilliant of these men were to be found at Paris, where the king had decided to establish his permanent residence. It was here in the reign of Louis VII (1137–80) that a new image of French kingship was created.

Historians are just beginning to realize that this king was not the feeble monarch of textbooks, whose weakness has traditionally been a foil for the achievements of both his father and his son – one, the champion of the French communes; the other, victorious over the Germans. Most chroniclers admittedly speak of Louis as 'young', immature and impassioned; demeaned by excessive regard for his wife, Eleanor of Aquitaine, who made a complete fool of him. His reputation was permanently tarnished when she left him, taking with her the duchy of Aquitaine. It was quite clearly Eleanor who took the initiative, securing an annulment of their marriage on the grounds that they were related within the prohibited degrees, and therefore the union was incestuous. It has never been satisfactorily established whether there was any truth in the widespread rumour that her uncle, the count of Antioch, had seduced her in the Holy Land. He was the head of the house of Aquitaine, and it is likely that he turned Eleanor's head – at the very least – persuading her to regain her freedom so that he could marry her if he chose. Eleanor was not hard to persuade: there was a huge gulf at this date between the customs of the north and those of the south, and she never felt at home in Louis' household, full of austere priests who strongly disapproved of her life-style. It is difficult to be sure whether Eleanor also had political motives. She was already a mature individual, although her second husband was to treat her as an object of constant ridicule. It is always assumed that Louis VII made a great mistake in letting her go. The evidence suggests otherwise, however. In the first place, Louis had excellent reasons of his own for annulment. It is significant that he accepted the episcopal ruling of 1152 dissolving the marriage, although the Pope was doing his utmost to reunite the couple with plans for another crusade. Louis was growing older, but he had no male heirs, because Eleanor had given birth only to daughters. The future of the Capetian dynasty was therefore in jeopardy. In such circumstances, lords with much lesser dynastic responsibilities repudiated their wives, in the hope that remarriage would produce a male heir.

Moreover, if Eleanor had remained queen of France, there would have been no question of annexing the duchy of Aquitaine to the royal domain. Inheritance customs were too rigid at this date, and the machinery of government was incapable of operating over such a distance. Aquitaine would have passed to one of their children; if a daughter inherited, there would have been no guarantee that her husband would have proved any more loyal to the French crown than Henry II of England. Henry II was the successful claimant – among many – for Eleanor's hand in marriage after her divorce. After many years' refusal, he eventually performed homage for Normandy to Louis, as his father had done before him. Finally, their divorce enabled Louis to marry into the house of Champagne (rivals of the Angevins), an alliance which was to bring the French kings incalculable benefits. Eleanor complained that marriage to her first husband was like marriage to a monk, rather than a king. Both his temperament and the education he had received from his father made it inevitable that Louis VII would be impelled to bind the French monarchy still more securely to the institutional Church. It was a decision that was to prove crucial for the development of government in France.

The French crown had been closely linked with the monastery of St

Denis for some while. Abbot Suger of St Denis was in effect the new king's tutor, and the new choir of St Denis was consecrated three years after Louis' marriage and his accession. This helped establish an ideology of monarchy which was inspired by the work of the Pseudo-Dionysius. Works recently composed in the monastery provided an important ideological foundation. They included the *Histoire du roi Charles et de Roland* (*History of Roland and Charlemagne*), attributed to Archbishop Turpin (one of the principal characters in the *Chanson de Roland* (*Song of Roland*)) and a forged charter, supposedly signed by Charlemagne. At the time, no one doubted the authenticity of these manuscripts, which purported to document an episode in which Charlemagne supposedly proffered his crown to St Denis, placing four pieces of gold on the high altar of the abbey and 'enjoining upon his successors the annual duty of bowing low before the altar and offering four bezants there'. The response of the twelfth-century French kings to this fiction was twofold: on the one hand, they exploited such ceremonies in order to reinforce their claims as the legitimate heirs of the legendary Charlemagne; while on the other, they accepted this obligation, and became the vassals of St Denis. However, since the power vested by Charlemagne in the patron saint was now delegated to the Capetian kings, it also ensured them supremacy over all 'the land which was once called Gaul and is now known as France' – called France (the text elaborated), because it was '*franche*': 'free, and without obligations to any other nations'. This was sheer invention, but it nevertheless guaranteed the liberty of the entire kingdom. Moreover, it did not refer to Francia (the old Frankish kingdom), but was synonymous with Charlemagne's Gaul, without an imperial frontier to the east. Finally, when the king of France became the liegeman of St Denis and accepted the *oriflamme* (the great red banner, supposedly Charlemagne's own in a state of miraculous preservation, that accompanied the kings of France into battle), it also became his sacred duty to exercise the rights of the saint on earth. Since these spurious texts also maintained that Charlemagne had made the abbey of St Denis 'head of all the churches of the kingdom', it also provided the justification for royal control of the French episcopacy.

Benedictine monasticism had been losing favour for some decades, and Louis VII gradually turned instead towards the Cistercians, who were supplanting the Benedictines by their austere life-style and rejection of all display. Alone with his grandfather Philip I, of all the Capetian kings, Louis VII chose to be buried in his Cistercian foundation at Barbeaux, rather than by the shrine of St Denis. The Cistercians were essentially episcopal servants, and the king had the sense to project himself likewise as the servant of the French bishops. All the Gregorian reforms relating to episcopal elections were applied to the letter. The king intervened only to communicate the identity of his preferred candidate and to invest the individual who was eventually chosen with the temporalities of his see. This respect for their autonomy, combined with his evident piety, made the king an object of genuine affection among the bishops, who were a major political force. As it was, the Capetians were extremely fortunate that their representative at that particular juncture was a man ridiculed at tournaments for his excessive piety.

Louis VII also welcomed with open arms all prelates from abroad who sought refuge in France and used the country as a base from which to continue their struggle against rulers who were less adept than the French king at manipulating ecclesiastical power. Most notable were Thomas Becket, the exiled archbishop of Canterbury, and Pope Alexander III, driven from Rome. Their support greatly strengthened Louis' position *vis-à-vis* his two great rivals on his eastern and western borders, Henry II of England and the German Emperor Frederick Barbarossa. Backed by the civil lawyers of Bologna University and the tenets of Roman law, the Emperor attacked the Capetian claim to the ancient kingdom of Gaul, alleging imperial superiority. According to the German case, Barbarossa was Charlemagne's legitimate successor; he had been responsible for the canonization of the Carolingian Emperor within the borders of the old kingdom of Burgundy at the diet of Besançon (1165); he had been solemnly crowned king of Provence in Arles cathedral, in accordance with ancient ceremony and – the most tangible threat of all – he maintained companies of Brabançon mercenaries on the banks of the river Sâone. Louis VII refused to be intimidated: when Frederick Barbarossa granted a golden bull to the archbishop of Lyon, for example, he issued one to the bishop of Mende. When he went to St Jean-de-Losne (at the confluence of four rivers) to meet this famous and formidable rival in 1162, his submission to the Church and the friendship of the true Pope (whose own aspirations to universal sovereignty ran counter to those of Barbarossa) proved invaluable. The following year, Pope Alexander III established the Roman curia at Sens, and with full papal authority formally granted Louis VII the golden rose, 'by which kings and justice reign'.

Things had gone less well for Louis at the beginning of his reign. In 1147 he made a desperate and unsuccessful attempt to secure the see of Bourges for his chancellor (one of his household chaplains), against the wishes of the canons. He also showed scant regard for the laws of marriage, which the Church was trying to strengthen, when he encouraged his seneschal, Ralph of Vermandois, to repudiate his wife and marry the queen's sister, for the sake of dynastic advantage. The spurned wife was the niece of the count of Champagne, who – like the count of Flanders and the count of Anjou – was politically independent, determined to reinforce his autonomy and check Capetian expansion at every possible opportunity. With this aim, he had helped the archbishop and cathedral chapter of Rheims to destroy the commune that the king had established in the city two years earlier in the hope of winning support from the townspeople. Encouraged by the vehement attitude of his friend, Bernard of Cîteaux, Count Theobald of Champagne opposed the king. The king reacted sharply and thoroughly defeated the count in a harsh campaign. But in pursuit of his own ends, the king had broken the peace of God and unfortunately burnt the church of Vitry, together with great numbers of the poor who had sought refuge there. This was sacrilege; the hands of God's anointed were defiled, and his enemies made great play of this betrayal of the coronation oath and rupture of the mutual bond between king and people by such tyrannical behaviour.

But when Louis VII decided to go on a crusade in the East (doubtless in the hope of absolution from his sins), everything was completely changed. At this time, the Latin kingdom of Jerusalem was beginning to crack under the pressure of Islam. When he held solemn court at Bourges at Christmas 1145, the king announced his intention of taking the cross and leading a second general passage himself. No king had ever joined a crusade in person before, but this one (preached by St Bernard at Vézelay) would be led by the king of France himself. He planned to lead the army of Christ towards the Jerusalem of their dreams and to save Christendom from the threat of the infidel. During the preparations the king was surrounded by groups of bishops and counts, as Charlemagne had been of old; the royal court suddenly recovered a brilliance that had been absent since the reign of Robert the Pious.

During the king's absence, the entire kingdom was placed under divine protection, as stated in the indulgences granted to the crusaders. During the two years of campaign, the mantle of regent fell upon St Denis – in other words, Abbot Suger – rather than upon officials of the royal household. Their responsibilities became purely honorary. This development enabled the king to enhance his prestige by granting these domestic offices to the highest-ranking princes in the land. This policy was not entirely free from risks: Geoffrey V Plantagenet, count of Anjou, had claimed the office of seneschal, and boasted that he had abused the king's trust and seduced the young queen in her chamber. But in 1169 and 1179, when his grandson (Henry, the 'Young King') carved before the French king at his table, the count of Anjou was merely part of the outward trappings of power. Real power now lay in the hands of the king's trusted counsellors and 'familiars', knights and clerics as utterly devoted to the crown as the comrades of Louis VI had been. They showed themselves increasingly capable of the unobtrusive management of day-to-day administration.

In the next reign the practical experience in government of these same individuals, now old men, was to be an invaluable support to Philip Augustus.

The French army failed in the East. Contemporaries believed this was because they were defiled by the women who went with them. (Louis VII set a poor example in this respect, taking Queen Eleanor with him.) Yet although God had withheld victory, when he returned to France from Rome (where the Pope received him like his own son), Louis' stature had been increased by his sacrifices and the tribulations he had endured. Soon afterwards, he abandoned his incestuous marriage, and was completely absolved. He was the first Capetian king to fight bravely far from his own lands. Further pilgrimages to the Grande Chartreuse (near Grenoble) and to St James of Compostella also took him beyond the frontiers of the French kingdom. These pilgrimages gave his subjects an opportunity to see, hear and touch the king in regions where he had not been seen for centuries. Even if it resulted from an excess of piety, the king's power was recognized throughout the kingdom, and its unity was sanctified by divine grace and the intercession of France's patron saint, St Denis.

This claim was repeated by Robert, abbot of Mont-Saint-Michel, when he stated that Normandy was part of the kingdom of France. In 1166 Odo, abbot of Cluny, wrote to Louis VII that, 'Your kingdom is not merely Francia, although the royal title refers specifically to that land. Burgundy is also one of your possessions.' A few years earlier, his predecessor, Peter the Venerable, had asserted that the land was 'kingless'. Odo added: 'Think of your entire kingdom as a whole body.' During this period the Capetians adopted the fleurs-de-lis as their emblem. Like the constellations on the sacred vestments worn by the Emperor Henry II in the early eleventh century, they were gold on a blue ground. The Capetian heraldic device was intended to express their unique position above the rest of mankind, where divine and terrestrial met: the place claimed for them one hundred years before by the great abbots of triumphant monasticism. It had been Suger's idea that each of the 'florets' on the French crown represented a fief, and that it therefore symbolized all the provinces of the kingdom. When the French king – at the very apex of the hierarchies described by the Pseudo-Dionysius (believed to be Denis the Areopagite) – held solemn court with this crown upon his head, he affirmed his duty to preserve peace throughout the kingdom of France.

At Soissons in June 1155, Louis VII instituted a ten-year-long general peace, 'at the request of churchmen and on the advice of his barons, to check the ardour of the wicked and contain the violence of pillagers'. The archbishops of Sens and Rheims were there with their suffragans, as well as the abbots of all the great monasteries. One after another, they swore to observe the peace; and they were followed in their turn by the duke of Burgundy, the counts of Flanders, Champagne, Nevers and Soissons and all the barons who were present. This was the wording of the king's oath: 'In full council and in front of everybody, we have given our royal word that we will keep this peace unbroken and do everything in our power to bring all who violate it to justice.' The assembly was in some ways very like those which had gathered about reliquaries *c*.1000. The peace of God was once more the subject, but this time the responsibility for preserving the peace no longer fell within the remit of the bishops in their dioceses. It was the sacred duty of the consecrated king, God's vicar on earth, to keep the peace in the entire kingdom.

In the last years of his reign, Louis VII directed all his energies towards the preservation of peace throughout the kingdom. In 1166 and again in 1171, the bishop of Mâcon and the abbot of Cluny both called upon him for aid. Both were being harassed by bands of mercenaries in the pay of malevolent lords. The king was at the abbey of Vézelay, which he had once protected against the count of Nevers, and hurried to them with all speed. All lawlessness ceased at the mere approach of his army. In the preamble to the peace charters issued at the courts over which he presided, Louis declared, 'We came because the long absence of a king in this land of Burgundy has left its inhabitants without the discipline of a just ruler. Consequently lords with any power at all could fight each other, oppress the weak and ravage the possessions of the Church.' Now that the king was amongst them, these activities would cease. 'We were moved to divine zeal by these wicked excesses to come with our army to Burgundy to exact vengeance, reform the land and establish the peace of God.' Shortly after these expeditions, an altarpiece was carved for the church of Avenas-en-Beaujolais. On one side, Christ in glory is surrounded by his apostles; on the other, with perfect symmetry, there is a statue of his earthly counterpart, the peace-loving king (*rex pacificus*) with a model of the little church in his hand. In fact, of course, it is a symbol of the whole Church: the king of France was a member of the priesthood by virtue of his consecration, and he was also the Church's supreme protector in the God-given land over which he ruled. The king of France was not a second David, on the pattern of Charlemagne; rather, he was another Melchizedek, for Melchizedek had been both king of Salem and priest. One of the Old Testament prefigurations of Christ, he had offered God a sacrifice of bread and wine. The exceptionally devout and ascetic Louis VII also claimed to be king and priest, as only the Pope had done since the days of Leo IX.

Louis was richly rewarded for all his exertions when he returned from a peace-keeping expedition to the most distant parts of his kingdom in 1166: the long-awaited son was born to him, and called Philip, after his grandfather. A prophetic dream was later credited to Louis VII, in which he saw the God-given child, another Melchizedek, 'holding a gold chalice filled with human blood and offering it to the princes of the kingdom, who all drank with him'. Following the earlier example of Abbot Suger at St Denis, a monk of St Germain-des-Prés wrote the *Histoire du très glorieux roi Louis* (*History of the most glorious King Louis*) to celebrate the birth of a male heir. He described the anxious period of waiting before the prince was born, his birth and baptism, and the subsequent eruption of joy in the city of Paris. Henceforth Paris was the capital city of France, and clerics from all parts of the kingdom flocked to it in search of knowledge. We do not know if the king played any part in assembling the best theologians in his capital, but it seems unlikely that sheer coincidence was responsible for their permanent establishment close to the king's palace, rather than, say, in Laon, which housed the library of the scholars patronized by Charles the Bald in his palace at Compiègne. There is certainly evidence for Louis VII's patronage of the rebuilding of the cathedral of Notre-Dame in Paris. He actively supported the plans of Bishop Maurice of Sully against Peter the Chanter and his supporters, who condemned expenditure on church building as a manifestation of pride, arguing that the money would be better spent on the poor.

The great age of cathedral-building in France began in the reign of Louis VII, with the development of the style we think of as Gothic, but which contemporaries called *opus francigenum* ('work in the French style'), referring to the place where it was first developed. It had indeed emerged at the very heart of the old Frankish kingdom, in the abbey of St Denis. The building undertaken there under the auspices of Abbot Suger supplied the prototype. As I suggested (in chapter 8), the abbey church was intended to give outward expression to the ideas of St John and the Pseudo-Dionysius. Since – they said – God is light, a church building should be filled with light, revealing through the lavish provision of rose and lancet windows that every facet of creation reflects God's grace and is an expression of divine love. The fact of the incarnation – that God had become man and had lived as man upon earth – dictated that the western façade (seen by the people as they entered the church) should be like a permanent sermon, carved with images representing Christ as their influential brother and friend. This model was adopted after 1140 by bishops throughout the royal domain, who often engaged the workmen who had been in Suger's employ at St Denis. The sculptors, for example, also worked on the so-called *Portail Royal* at Chartres, while the glaziers made a window for the old church of Notre-Dame. From now on, building work was concentrated around cathedrals, rather than abbey and monastery churches.

This shift was the result of a threefold alteration in the balance of power. First of all, it reflected the success of the ecclesiastical reformers, with monasticism emphatically subordinate to the episcopate; but it also gave expression to a much more profound change, in which prescribed rites around miraculous relics were replaced by a highly moral faith, whose precepts had to be conscientiously instilled in each one of the faithful. This duty fell to the clergy, above all, to the bishops. It was the cathedral's function to disseminate teachings and give visual expression to the learning of the schools. Another novel and important factor was the growth of power in the cities, which lay within the lordships of bishop and cathedral chapter. Neither hesitated to exploit this new source of wealth, drawing heavily upon urban resources to rebuild town churches. Indeed, their demands were sometimes so heavy that the townspeople rebelled. This happened at Rheims, where an uprising halted building works in the cathedral at one point. Nevertheless, the walls and belfries towering over the hovels around them were also a celebration of urban power and strength. Merchants acknowledged episcopal lordship at fairs, and paid the bishop the necessary dues; they were reluctant to pay – but they contributed none the less. However, they wanted some tangible witness to their financial contributions, so that there could be no doubt which guild had contributed which stained glass window, for example. These small tokens of their pious munificence often survive, witness to the involvement of the city's inhabitants with the work of the clergy, on which they spent a considerable part of the fraudulently acquired wealth they had tapped from the surrounding countryside.

Finally, the magnificent buildings that sprang up all over the Capetian domain reflected the renaissance of the French monarchy. After the conversion of the Roman Empire, cathedrals had been built in Gaul in all the major cities, and consequently the attributes of public power had been focused upon them. Moreover, secular power was sublimated to ecclesiastical, for the cathedral was designed to prefigure heavenly Jerusalem, and the rectitude of its stone walls, the towers that rose up like a fortress and the great doors which opened (like the gates of the town) upon a more rigorously organized space – all these characteristics presented a pattern of the eternal State. Louis VII had delayed his return from the Holy Land in order to make pilgrimages to all the shrines associated with the life of Jesus; and since his return, he had always been surrounded by the episcopate. Indeed, it would have been easy for contemporaries to mistake the bishop's throne in every cathedral for the king's own.

Besides, the virtues impregnated by the unction of coronation destined the French king to be a patron of church-builders. One hundred and fifty years earlier, the bishop of Laon had reminded another French king of his unique duties: 'Remember that the king of kings has bestowed great glory upon you. In his mercy he has given you the most precious gift of all . . . You are destined to know the heavenly Jerusalem, its stones, walls and gates – all the details of its buildings.' Uniquely endowed with such a vision, it was inevitable that the French king would be called upon to contribute financially to the rebuilding of the cathedrals. Louis VII was well aware of his obligations in this sphere, and the 200 *livres* of silver he gave to the bishop of Paris paid for the remarkable choir of Notre-Dame, which was vaulted with arches taller than any built before. The king lived to see the project complete, but died before the high altar was formally consecrated by an envoy of the Pope in 1180. He was buried in the Cistercian abbey of Barbeaux where, for the first time, the distinctive insignia of the sovereign – crown, sceptre and the seal that authenticated the decrees of a general peace – were placed beside the king's body. Most important of all, however, the funeral ceremony was presided over by Louis VII's heir, the son whom he would have regarded as God's reward for the just and conscientious way in which he had fulfilled his royal office.

The upper echelons of the Church perhaps dreamt more of unity at this period than at any other. It was a period of unprecedented harmony in ecclesiastical affairs: the Pope was now able, through his legates, to ensure that his decrees were observed in the furthermost corners of western Christendom, while the abbots of hundreds of Cistercian monasteries scattered the length and breadth of Europe met annually (at a general chapter in the mother-house) to discuss the order's business and share their spiritual experiences. At the same time, the clergy – the best of whom had studied together in Paris – prayed for the unity of God's people. This was essential for the deliverance of the Holy Land, which stood in great jeopardy. The king of Jerusalem was a leprous adolescent; Saladin was gathering together infidels from every country, calling them to a *jihad*, or holy war; and there were grounds for believing that he might capture the Holy Sepulchre before long. It was vital for the unruly might of individual princes to be subordinated to the rule of kings and their wisdom and discipline. It was no coincidence that the seals of kings depicted them seated, throned in majesty and the stability of heavenly peace, while those of lords showed them on prancing horses, the embodiment of uncontrolled strength.[1] There was ecclesiastical support for monarchies in their struggle

---

[1] Royal seals might sometimes also depict equestrian figures on the reverse – tr.

with the principalities, because it was in the Church's interest to have strong kings – ideally, united beneath papal authority.

The Pope himself was in bitter conflict with the German king, and worked tirelessly to check his expansionist ambitions. He was reluctant to become reconciled with Henry II of England, who had been excommunicated for allowing his blind hostility to the Church to countenance the murder of Archbishop Thomas Becket of Canterbury on the very steps of the cathedral. The tractable king of France was therefore somewhat inevitably the object of papal favour. Moreover, his rule seemed to be very securely established, supported on the one hand by the produce of the fertile Ile-de-France, on the other by the city of Paris which, after a period of slow change, had now developed into the most sophisticated cultural centre since classical times. It was not merely by chance that the French kings adopted the Latin term *imperium* with reference to their administration of peace and justice. Stronger feudal ties ensured that the most powerful lords of the kingdom were closely bound to him. It was no longer absurd to imagine the French king accomplishing his mission of peace accompanied by twelve supporters (on the pattern of Jesus's disciples or the twelve peers of Charlemagne), the peers of the realm of France, each equal beneath his royal patronage. This role was already adopted by the six bishops of the cities of north-east France, and it was reasonable to hope that they would soon be joined by six lay princes: the three dukes of Burgundy, Aquitaine and Normandy and the three counts of Flanders, Champagne and Toulouse.

Reality ran counter to this dream, however. France remained a medley of rival political entities. The king could, of course, exploit disagreements amongst his vassals. In return for effective royal protection of a diocese or a monastery, the sovereign obtained the right to participate in the government of the lordship; he used these agreements as a pretext for appointing royal officials (*prévôts*) to places far outside the old Capetian domain. These were only the first steps in the complex process of expansion, and they resulted in conflict with other States likewise supported by money, administrative efficiency and the shrewd exploitation of feudal custom, which all combined to strengthen the monarchic State.

Of all Louis' vassals, Henry Plantagenet was undoubtedly the most formidable. First of all, he was king of England; but modern historians all too easily overlook the fact that he saw himself first and foremost as count of Anjou. He chose to be buried at Fontevrault, where both his wife, Eleanor of Aquitaine, and his son, Richard the Lionheart, were also to have their tombs, in the land where his ancestors had made their mark. The roots of Henry's power lay in the area between Chinon, Loches and Angers; through a combination of his own dynamism and a good measure of luck, Henry was able to extend his influence over almost half the kingdom of France. Evidence of the central importance of his Angevin lands is reflected in Henry's predilection for the majestic figure of his father (Geoffrey of Anjou, second husband of the Empress Matilda) on the enamel plaque on his tomb at Le Mans and in a biography and dynastic history written at Tours in the 1180s. No sooner was the hero of this panegyric knighted and married than he was victorious in arms. Significantly, this did not occur in battle, but at a tournament held on the sands of the Norman-Breton border before Mont-Saint-Michel. A team of Bretons met one of Normans, not led by the duke, but by his three nephews, the counts of Mortain, Flanders and Blois. Geoffrey of Anjou chose to fight on the Breton side. From the very outset, the notion of support for Brittany, land of Arthurian legend, was calculated to appeal to Henry II. The team encounter proved inconclusive and was followed by single combat. The Normans chose a huge English warrior for their champion. Geoffrey unhorsed him, and – like a second David triumphing over Goliath – cut off his head. This was naturally also a symbolic victory, affording dazzling proof of Angevin superiority; for the victorious count of Anjou had already married the wife whose son would inherit Normandy, and his victory foreshadowed that of Henry himself over Stephen of Blois and English submission to Angevin rule.

Henry succeeded his father in 1151 and laid claim to Normandy through right of his mother. The following year he became duke of Aquitaine in the name of his wife, and was crowned king of England in 1154. At the same time he gained a foothold in Brittany in the name of his son Geoffrey. This was an extraordinary series of achievements. However, it is important to remember that the collection of lands assembled by Henry within these dozen or so years, the so-called Angevin 'Empire', was never a single State, but a conglomeration of separate States.[2] Each retained its own judicial system and administration; Henry moved continually between them in order to demonstrate his authority, and to contemporaries he seemed to be in perpetual motion. This is a description by one of his notaries, Peter of Blois:

He does not sit down from morning until night; and even if his legs are black and blue from spurring on his recalcitrant mounts, he sits only to eat or to ride. [Sitting was a posture which, as we have observed, might be associated with kingship.] If necessary, he will walk four or five leagues a day.

His life's energies were spent in the constant demonstration of authority in his scattered dominions. Since he was almost always absent, a seneschal

[2] For a different view, see J. Gillingham, *The Angevin Empire* (London, 1984); J. Le Patourel, *Feudal Empires: Norman and Plantagenet*, ed. M. Jones (London, 1984) – tr.

invariably represented him in one or other of his lands. Virtually all had firmly established administrative and judicial structures. Normandy was foremost in this respect: here, circuit judges succeeded in preserving the peace to an extent comparable to that praised by the Cluniac monk Ralph Glaber in the mid-eleventh century, and closely scrutinized *prévôts* exploited the duke's resources to the full; the network of feudal loyalties was closer here than elsewhere. Henry's weakness lay in the south, where the duchy of Aquitaine was perennially restive and intractable.[3]

Ducal power relied heavily upon the support of the towns to crush rebellion. La Rochelle was particularly valuable in this respect, since it was a recent foundation, strongly fortified and very affluent. Convoys of great ships came across the North Sea and the English Channel for cargoes of wine, and the huge quantities of stones used for ballast on the outward journey (which are still to be found in the shallows) are some indication of the volume of this trade. Henry also attempted to establish the constraints of feudal law south of the river Loire, in the hope of controlling the nobility of Aquitaine in the same way as the English and the Normans. This was too ambitious and too great a divergence from regional custom. The attempt to impose feudalism by force resulted in an endless series of revolts, ruthlessly suppressed, then flaring up once more. Henry's other problem was his four sons: once they were into their teens, they constantly laid claim to various parts of the Angevin dominions, and plotted to secure them. Their earliest attempts were directed towards Aquitaine, supported and encouraged by their mother. Their cause attracted all the discontented and avaricious elements in Henry's lands and, inevitably, the backing of the French king. As their father's natural lord, he was their appointed protector, and did not hesitate to exploit their insubordination to the full. Henry II found himself in a cleft stick as far as Louis VII was concerned, since he could not afford to set his own vassals an example of treachery to an overlord. He died in a state of combined rage and misery when he discovered that Richard – the son whom he had believed most loyal – had also betrayed him. It was clear that the haphazard collection of principalities united under Henry's personal rule was doomed to fragmentation. Maps purporting to show 'feudal France' at this period are misleading. Henry II's possessions cut a great swathe across the country, posing a serious threat to the French crown from the west; but the situation was less grave than it seemed.

Capetian rule was also under threat from a union of counties to the south and west of the domain. Like his grandfather, Odo, Theobald of

---

[3] For a different analysis of the situation in southern France, see M. G. A. Vale, *The Angevin Legacy and the Hundred Years War* (Oxford, 1990) – tr.

Champagne was also count of Meaux and Troyes, as well as of Blois, Chartres and Châteaudun. He also had a claim to England and Normandy by right of his mother, but had allowed this to pass to his brother Stephen (king of England, 1135–54), who had pursued it to a successful conclusion. Theobald's death in 1152 demonstrates all too clearly the impact of the natural progress of family life upon political history, for the custom of partible inheritance (dividing the inheritance equally between all the sons of the deceased) operated, one of the major reasons for the essentially transitory nature of unions of lordships and principalities at this period. Theobald had two sons: Blois passed to the younger, while the older inherited the more substantial lands in Champagne. The rapid progress of assarting in Brie and, above all, the success of fairs at Troyes, Provins, Lagny and Bar-sur-Aube meant that Champagne was becoming increasingly wealthy. Over the previous two decades or so, a system of protection and guarantees for merchants had been established, and this had attracted long-distance trade away from the much older, episcopally controlled fairs at Rheims and Châlons to those of Provins and Lagny, which were close to the crossroads of the rapidly expanding Paris basin. This was the origin of the remarkable success of the commercial syndicates of Champagne, which were to become the principal point of contact between merchants of the south and those of northern France, once the fairs in Champagne were organized on a regular basis. The guard supplied by the count was granted extended jurisdiction, and Italian and Provençal merchants travelling to the fairs organized themselves into associations for mutual defence. None the less, feudal law was the primary foundation for the reconstituted State in Champagne. The count's domain lands were vast, administered by some twenty *prévôts* and provided with close on ten fortresses; the count's officials began to keep careful records in the reign of Philip Augustus, primarily as a means of recording feudal obligations. The count himself owed homage to the king of France, but not for all his lands. Some were held from other lords, notably the king of Germany: turning to the Empire for support was an effective means of putting pressure on the French king. In the 1160s, Henry 'the Liberal' of Champagne was to exploit his singular position, and played Louis VII and Frederick Barbarossa off against each other. Nevertheless, the bishoprics followed an independent line, with the exception of Troyes, where there was already considerable royal influence. In this narrative, however, we are only concerned with the way in which the laws of inheritance ensured that principalities were always less powerful than the crown. The count could at least rely on the support of the growing numbers of monastic and collegiate foundations scattered throughout his lands, praying for his safety and success in arms. The ablest of these clerks were to be found in his household, advising on the most effective means of exploiting feudal prerogative. They also served him in other ways, which enhanced his prestige still further. His wife Marie of Champagne (daughter of Eleanor of Aquitaine) presided over a court, where she commissioned the romance *Lancelot* from the famous poet Chrétien of Troyes. His works gave sophisticated expression to the rapidly developing chivalric culture of the late twelfth century which found dazzling expression at the court of Champagne.

For it was above all in cultural developments that the territorial princes were able to express their identity most forcibly and offer a vigorous challenge to Capetian kingship. This was the case, for instance, in the church-building projects to which the nobility contributed. The Gothic style that had emerged in the royal domain was admired in Anjou, Poitou, Burgundy and Lyon. It was the inspiration for new church buildings there, because people wanted cathedrals and great churches filled with light like those at Noyon, Laon and Paris. Nevertheless, the prelates and nobility who patronized these schemes took care to ensure that these new buildings retained distinctive stylistic detail that was typical of local tradition. Further south, native culture was strong enough to hold the Gothic style of northern France at bay; architectural forms which we label 'romanesque' continued to flourish. Indeed, when Gothic churches were built at Clermont in the Auvergne (modern Clermont-Ferrand), Narbonne and St Maxim in Provence a century later, they were generally interpreted as marks of colonial appropriation, the seal finally placed by the Capetian kings of France upon the region whose resistance had at last been broken by force of arms.

The Capetians emphasized the superiority of royal power, by conscious reference to the Carolingian past and the form of the new coronation liturgy. It is not surprising that the territorial princes felt a need to balance the ascendancy of the austere Parisian court, with the European centre of theological inquiry at its very gates, by their own patronage of secular and chivalric culture. In the early twelfth century, for example, William IX of Aquitaine (count of Poitou and duke of Aquitaine, the grandfather of Eleanor) patronized the troubadours – secular Provençal poets whose work would more than bear comparison with the sophisticated Latin verse composed by ecclesiastics in northern France, although it was composed in a different language and on different subjects. In so doing, he was consciously expressing the unique character of his own dynasty and signalling his opposition, both to the Capetians and to the Frankish house of Anjou which at that time constituted a direct threat to his own power. This poetry was deeply rooted in the culture of the Limousin, which – of all his possessions in the region – was least susceptible to the influence of northern France. Its source is believed to have been the tropes (liturgical phrases) chanted by the monks of St Martial at Limoges. The poets themselves were knights – William IX may in fact have composed the poems which were later attributed to him – and the poems which they wrote in the *langue d'oc* celebrated the values of *cortezia* and the delights of courtly love, in conscious opposition to the austerity of Fontevrault. William IX hoped that the rituals of courtly love, which provided a tranquil interlude in an otherwise tumultuous existence, would control the nobility more effectively than the uncertain ties of vassalage which operated in this area.

His example was followed by his successor, Henry Plantagenet. He, too, welcomed courtly poets; indeed, he patronized poets of all kinds, troubadours from the South, but also clerics whose literary abilities were responsible for elevating the dialects of the Norman and Angevin nobilities to the status of a literary language. To a man, they dedicated their compositions to Queen Eleanor; but it was Henry whom they served in reality and upon whom they depended for their livelihood. His household clerks produced their own versions of the *matière de France* (tales of the history of France), designed to please the king in their emphasis on the exploits of William of Orange (the good vassal without whom the king would have been totally lost), rather than Charlemagne. The better-educated produced 'romance' versions of classical writers and texts, such as Statius, the *Æneid* and the story of Troy. Both poets and patron had a clear preference for 'the matter of Britain', the legends preserved in oral Celtic poetry and sung by travelling minstrels from Wales and Brittany, who were also sure of a warm welcome at Henry's court. In the misty outposts of the territories he strove so hard to control – Cornwall, Wales, newly conquered Ireland and the Armorican peninsula – there was an enchanted 'other world', through which chivalry could express its fantasies and its longing for individual freedom. They were embodied in a galaxy of heroes, whose wonderful adventures far outshone those celebrated in Carolingian epic. They were knights errant, making their way through the perils of the wasteland, defeating unknown knights, winning the love of ladies in enchanted castles, heiresses to great lands and titles. They also encountered naked fairies as they bathed in fountains, and savoured their fleeting charms, before returning – sometimes broken in spirit, but glorious in their defeat – to share their joy with the court of King Arthur and to take their seat amongst their equals, the knights of the Round Table, supreme champions of chivalry. Henry naturally hoped that some of this renown might reflect to his own advantage. He presented himself as the heir of Arthur, a counterbalance to the king of France, who emphasized his inheritance from Charlemagne.

When he succeeded to the English throne, Henry commissioned Wace, one of his clerks, to write an account in French verse of the history of Britain. The *Roman de Brut* (*Romance of the Brut*) drew substantially on Geoffrey of Monmouth's Latin *History of the Kings of Britain* (an accepted practice at this period), which related how the Britons were descended from the Trojans, in the same way as the Franks and the Normans. The house of Anjou had defeated the Normans and the Saxons, and this triumph was articulated in the figure of King Arthur, the civilizing monarch whose return was still anticipated by the Celts. Henry intended to take his place and he staged an elaborate 'discovery' of the tombs of Arthur and Guinevere at Glastonbury Abbey, to provide conclusive proof of the impossibility of Arthur's return. Cloaked in these glorious secular legends, he defied the majesty of the French king.

This defiance was found above all in the support for chivalric rather than ecclesiastical values expressed in the works written for him. When they celebrated the bravery of knights in the 'other world' of Breton romance and displayed chivalric virtues triumphant amid the dangers of pagan magic, as well as in the delights of courtly love, the writers whom Henry patronized were also expressing a sense of identity consciously independent of the French king and his priests. In 1159, Henry II's chancellor, John of Salisbury, explained how 'the divinely appointed order of chivalry' could be incorporated within the body of the State (on the model of ancient Rome in newly discovered classical texts) by directing the knight's oath of allegiance to the public good, 'protecting the poor from injustice, keeping the land at peace and, if need be, laying down his life for his brother'. When Henry II found himself in difficulties *c.*1175, with uprisings in Aquitaine and the adverse effect of Becket's canonization upon relations with France, he commissioned a *History of the Dukes of Normandy* (*Estoire des ducs de Normandie*) from Benedict of St Maure, in the same octosyllabic rhyming couplets employed by Wace. Benedict was Henry's faithful servant and eager to please. He altered the structure of an imaginary discussion between the tenth-century duke, William Longsword, and Abbot Martin of Jumièges on the various duties of the three divinely appointed orders of society. In the original version of Dudo of St Quentin, the ecclesiastic replies to the questions of the duke; while in Benedict's work, their positions are reversed, with the prince explaining that there are three orders of society, 'knights, clergy and peasants'. The traditional tripartite order did not appear in the original, with its emphasis on the priestly role of the king, intermediary between God and his people, propounded by the Frankish bishops in the year 1000 to shore up the enfeebled French monarchy. In Benedict's version, the ruler is scrupulously desacralized.

It was no longer appropriate to place the duke of Normandy in one of the three traditional categories, as his distant ancestor had been. His place was apart from other men and above them, since he claimed lordship in his household over all conditions of men, and made use of their different talents. Moreover, it is no longer a churchman who communicates divine wisdom to other men, but an unconsecrated prince. It is for him to establish temporal justice and keep the peace in his lands. He is responsible for seeing that tasks are fairly divided and services exchanged on an equitable basis, for the common good. Finally, the knights precede the clergy in this schema of society, for they were a far greater source of support to Henry than the clergy, the mainstay of the French monarchy. Cloaked in all the panoply of chivalric virtues and their attributes, he hoped to outshine his Capetian rival. It is clear that in the last quarter of the twelfth century, the most powerful of the French king's barons was the instrument of decisive change: Henry himself was responsible for a reversal which gave the secular nobility primacy over the clergy, valuing prowess and pleasure more highly than charity and penitence, secular power more than the liturgies of royal consecration. Poets quickly disseminated this ideal to all the other courts of the French kingdom. Chrétien of Troyes went from the service of the count of Champagne to that of another powerful territorial prince, Philip of Alsace, count of Flanders, and in his *Perceval* (written ten years after Benedict of St Maure's *Estoire*) he declared, 'The highest sword-bearing order, created and ordained by God, is the order of knighthood.'

At tournaments knights were divided into increasingly large teams on the basis of the land from which they came. The jealous members of a tournament team, who accused William Marshal of trifling with their lord's wife, were Normans; they could not tolerate an Englishman vaunting his success in this way. The territorial princes were able to exploit the growing sense of regional identity – the germ of national sentiment – and use it as a bulwark against the centralizing tendencies of the French crown.

The Latin word *natio* (nation) is rare in contemporary texts. It was used in the schools at Paris for the associations of mutual aid which were formed between clerks of all ages who came from the same region and spoke the same dialect. However, the word is found in a eulogy composed in the Touraine in the reign of Philip Augustus: it occurs in a passage about Paris, where the author says that the city has a position far above all others, 'through the operation of Mars and because she has dominion over all the "*nations*"'. The expression may have come naturally to the pen of this canon of Tours, author of the exceptionally clear *Présentation de la province tourangelle* (*Description of the Touraine*), who would have been familiar with such associations in the student community in the capital. But it seems more likely that when he used it to refer to Paris, which was for him the 'seat of monarchy', he was deliberately alluding to the different peoples of the kingdom who were gathered together under the aegis of a king who had led the movement for a general peace in the constitutions of Soissons of 1155. In that year, another native of Tours – or conceivably the same individual – composed a work in very elegant Latin, which I propose to examine in some detail, for the light it sheds upon contemporary awareness of 'national' identity.

This narrative (the *History of the Lords of Amboise*) was also written for Henry II, shortly after he had been crowned king of England. The author was not a member of the royal household, however, but in the service of the orphan sons of the lord of Amboise. A faithful vassal and trusty warrior of the count of Anjou, the lord of Amboise had been betrayed and defeated, dying in captivity in the hands of the count of Blois. His young heirs were beset with dangers, for their enemies would attempt to exploit the situation and use every possible means to deprive them of their rightful inheritance. As liege lord, it was Henry's duty to defend these Angevin vassals, and an extremely well-informed scholar – probably a relative – was commissioned to write a history of this minor lordship, in the hope of urging Henry to prompt action. He recounted the exploits of their valiant ancestors, who had protected the lordship down the ages, and set out 'the lineage of the lords of Amboise', showing 'at what time and by which count' (his own ancestor) 'they had settled in this land, by virtue of their merit', and stressing throughout the family's close ties with the Angevin house and the mutual obligations that stemmed from this tenurial bond. The work presents a parallel history of successive lords and vassals, and its author stresses the unswerving loyalty of the castle and surrounding town of Amboise to their overlords, the counts of Anjou. Packed with quotations from Cicero, it is first and foremost an apology for vassalic friendship, which unites the might of the counts with the loyalty of the lesser lords for the good of the region.

The anonymous author chose to begin 'with a brief description of the situation of the town (*oppidum*) of Amboise'. To do so, he made full use of the exceptionally fine library at Tours, drawing upon the *Life of St Martin*, Ratbode, the *Gestes des Romains* (*Deeds of the Romans*), Geoffrey of Monmouth and a history of the Franks which had also been used by Hugh of Fleury. But he also incorporated what he could see around him – scattered classical remains, sections of walls, carvings and surviving place-names which reflected previous Roman occupation. Rome was also the mainspring of his historical narrative. He informs us that Caesar decided to use this hill dominating the valley of the Loire as his base for the conquest of western Gaul, from Tours to Le Mans, Angers and Brittany. Caesar is shown as prefiguring contemporary reality and constructing a wooden bridge and a few huts for his soldiers at the foot of the hill. Lastly, he also had a palace built, which was comparable to that of the lords of the eleventh century, with wooden buildings and a great hall of stone for display, with a tower originally surmounted with an idolatrous statue of the god Mars for a banner, later destroyed by St Martin.

No trace of this first settlement from the golden age of pagan antiquity now remains, he tells us. It was completely destroyed by the new invaders. But at the end of this disastrous period, the author places a second heroic founder of Amboise: the most liberal and devout King Arthur, a detail that was surely also designed to secure Henry II's good will. Arthur supposedly appeared on the scene forty-seven years after the Breton invasion of the Armorican peninsula, and freed the people of Gaul from Roman subjugation. They accepted his lordship willingly, and he killed the Roman general in single combat before Paris. Arthur then supposedly took possession of the city, which – as in the other Touraine text we have discussed – was accredited with the status of capital city. Here the victory was celebrated; here he was crowned, and shared the newly conquered lands among his followers. Angers and the Touraine were granted to his seneschal – another detail calculated to flatter Henry II, since he claimed this important office at the French royal court. Henry would also have been pleased to find the king of Franks unambiguously Arthur's satellite and subordinate, even if he was styled '*amicissime*' (very dear friend) – friendship being one of the narrative's major themes. After the departure of the Bretons, it was the Franks who led a war of liberation against the Romans, whom they forced to retreat towards Angers, destroying the 'Roman buildings' there and pushing them back as far as Amboise. Here there lived a woman who was descended from one of Arthur's warriors on her father's side, but was an heiress through her mother to a prominent Roman landowner. She was a widow and a follower of St Martin. After the death of her own sons, she was said to have adopted Clovis and bestowed all her rights and property upon him, and it was in this way that 'from that time on until the reign of Charles the Bald, the town of Amboise was held by the Franks'. This was the place collective history accorded the Franks, in relation to the Romans and the Bretons.

At this point the author included the genealogy of these kings, from the Merovingians and Carolingians to the Capetians, ending with Louis VII and a judgement on the recent failure of the Fourth Crusade. This was a treacherous allusion to Raymond of Antioch and his niece Eleanor of Aquitaine, but the author diplomatically, if somewhat hypocritically, refuses to pursue the point, since Christendom was in such dire straits.

'This unfortunate state of affairs was the result,' he continues, 'of the habitual arrogance of the king of the Franks.' It is important to remember that the counts of Blois (supported by the French king) posed the main threat to Amboise in the middle of the twelfth century. There is an abrupt break in this historical summary with the onset of decadence at the end of the reign of Charles the Bald, when Louis 'the Fainthearted' yielded to the Normans. The Franks had been presented in an admirable light up to this point, but Charles the Bald's successors are little more than contemptible. This break is presented as the direct consequence of what we know as feudalism; for it was in the final years of the ninth century that the Angevin dynasty, which was to settle the lords of Amboise in their fief, was established in Anjou. The old Frankish kingdom was parcelled out in fiefs and *arrière-fiefs* (fiefs held by subtenants), so that power and 'national' (or regional) identity were divided like the interlocking pieces of a jigsaw.

People were still proud of their Frankish antecedents in Amboise, however. Whenever there is a question of glory or cultural achievement, the author refers to the people as *'populus francorum'* (the Franks) courageously withstanding all aggression, while Tours is called *'Martinopolis'*, the town of St Martin (the Franks' first patron saint and rival of St Denis). The author also gives a broad outline of the historical division of Gaul between the different races. He distinguishes four peoples in addition to the Bretons.

The Romans [he writes] were driven from this kingdom by the courage of the Franks and the Goths. All the nobles of the kingdom are descended from them and from the Suevians and the Dacians who drove out the Franks from Normandy and much of the area between the Seine and the Loire. After the Franks had defeated the Goths and crushed their king, they made peace with many of the Gothic nobility, and allowed them to rule Aquitaine under Frankish sovereignty, intermarrying with them.

A few leagues south of Amboise was the frontier with the Poitevins, marked by a line of *tumuli* said to have been placed there by Childeric to mark the boundary; Frankish superiority was established here, too, so that they controlled all of Touraine. But the Franks here were particularly vehement in asserting their superiority over the other Franks whom they encountered beyond Tours in the direction of Orléans.

The scholars of northern France were well aware that Charles the Bald had peopled Anjou and the Touraine with the noblest Franks, as a bastion against the Aquitanians (generally dismissed as treacherous and cowardly half-castes), the Bretons and pagan newcomers in the north. When the count of Anjou thought of the origin of his dynasty, he looked therefore to Charles the Bald. When he dictated an account of the origin of his own dynasty to his notary in 1096, Fulk Rechin, count of Anjou, went back as far as Engelgerius 'who first received the county of Anjou' from the king of the Franks – a fine warrior, he added, 'not of the race of Philip the Impious, but of Charles the Bald'. The genealogy of the counts of Anjou in our source records that their earliest predecessor came from the Orléanais, acquiring the stone castle of Amboise by marriage, rather than from his lord. As a good historian, the author was keen to associate Charles the Bald with the ninth century, and accordingly pushed back the foundation of the dynasty two generations. Engelgerius is therefore given a native grandfather, a descendant of the Armoricans driven back to the scrubby wastelands by the Breton invasion. Charles the Bald made him his forester 'the year that he drove the Normans from Angers'. This man had a son, who went to seek his fortune – and wherever we find the twelfth-century territorial princes defending their autonomy and preserving the memory of their ancestors, deep in the mists of invention, we also ultimately find the figure of a knight errant set against the ideology of the Capetian monarchy. In this case the young hero is described joining one of the warrior bands fighting for the king of the Franks against the Normans. He enters the Frankish king's service, his marriage is arranged by the king and he settles in the Orléanais. The author deliberately flatters Henry II, encouraging him to see himself, as it were, as an *émigré* Frank, linked to the Armoricans (the original inhabitants of Brittany) through his distant ancestor, but also invested with the right to subjugate the Bretons.

Once they had become lords of a land which, according to Fulk Rechin, 'they had rescued from pagan hands and then defended against neighbouring Christian counts', the counts of Anjou defended themselves valiantly on three sides, consistently loyal to the Frankish king. Nevertheless, their very bravery put them in a position superior to their liege lord when his power began to decline. The seneschal Geoffrey Greymantle found himself having to defend an extremely weak overlord, just like William in the *Couronnement de Louis* (*Coronation of Louis*). At this juncture, the count of Anjou invested one of his warriors from Orléans with the castle of Amboise and found him a wife, just as his own lord had done. From him all the future lords of Amboise were descended. It is also significant that when a fourth enemy – the count of Blois – comes on the scene in the early eleventh century, neither *gallus* nor *francus* are used to describe this new threat. National communities are now more narrowly defined, and the author identifies the small group of *Ambazienses* (the men who fought for and were in turn protected by the master of Amboise castle) among the *Andegavenses*, or knights of the principality of Anjou.

The *History of the Lords of Amboise* undoubtedly reflects attitudes that were widespread in France at this period, when – as the bonds between lord and vassal gradually loosened – there was a growing sense of identity with the region in which they lived (*patrie*). Men were proud to serve their land now and good knights were (as John of Salisbury said) ready to die for it, if need be. In the Rouergue or Gévaudan or other areas of southern France where brigandage was a particular problem, this affiliation was with the diocese, where the institutions for the peace of God formed the basis of an effective framework for self-defence. Elsewhere, loyalty to *patrie* and local lord were synonymous, centred on the castle lordship held by the latest in a long line of defendants and from whom the knights of the area held their fiefs. Military and dynastic interests combined in these first stirrings of what would later be identified as national consciousness, built on the dual foundation of past military successes under their lord's banner and recollections of the sequence of individuals in the dynasty of the same lord, who had passed their banner from generation to generation. Their memory was kept green by the recitation of ancestral romances not far from where those same authors were buried.

In the course of the twelfth century the upper nobility began to bury their dead in one place, following the example of the kings of France at St Denis. In 1096 Fulk Rechin professed to have no knowledge of the burial place of his distant forebears, while the tombs of more recent ancestors were all to be found in different locations. The strengthening of centrally controlled structures on a royal – and therefore dynastic – model gave rise at a slightly later date to funeral ceremonies in the church or chapel closely linked with the dynasty, which would become their mausoleum. From 1119 the abbey of St Bertin became the burial-place of the counts of Flanders, and from 1133 onward the counts of Hainault were laid to rest in the collegiate church at Mons. In 1157 the count of Champagne decided to turn his palace chapel at Troyes into a collegiate church dedicated to St Stephen, after whom many of his ancestors had been named, including the most famous, the English King Stephen. His descendants were all buried there. This was also the period when a number of emblems appeared on ancestral tombs, all designed to ensure the continued glorification of the lineage. Noble tombs had previously been characterized by humility, and Louis VI was interred beneath a plain slab at St Denis. At the same time, however, the mortal remains of Geoffrey Plantagenet were placed in a tomb-chest covered with a brightly coloured enamel plate which depicted him on his feet, with the sword of justice in one hand. Louis VII's widow had wanted to cover his tomb with gold, silver and jewels. The splendour of this sumptuous decoration, which completely transformed the austere architecture of its Cistercian setting, transported the body of the pious king to the joys of heavenly Jerusalem, reflecting recent developments in the ideology of kingship.

This period also saw the first recumbent effigies of the higher nobility, presenting them larger than life, in a sublimated form comparable with the figures of the saints and the Old Testament kings and prophets which decorated cathedral porches. Like the corpse on its magnificently decorated funeral bier, however, these noble effigies waited in sleep for the final Day of Judgement. So, in St Stephen's, Troyes, for example, there was an effigy of Henry the Liberal, count of Champagne (who died in 1181), on a beautifully worked sarcophagus of silver and gilded bronze, quite as dazzling as that of his father- and brother-in-law, kings of France. The effigy of his successor, Theobald, who died in the course of the Fourth Crusade twenty years later, is supported by eleven 'weepers' on the sides of his tomb (small statues of his illustrious relatives), among them three kings – Theobald's brother-in-law, the king of Navarre; his grandfather, king of France; and his great-uncle, the king of England. The undisputed prestige of the monarchy was never questioned by the nobility. However, the memory of royal ancestors was also preserved in order that the rights of the territorial princes could be defended against the current king.

Only a tiny proportion of the great wealth of dynastic literature produced in northern France in the second half of the twelfth century has survived today. These narratives record events that could not be expressed in funerary monuments. Going back beyond living memory, the scholars commissioned to preserve the origins of noble lineages had no hesitation about providing them with an imaginary, heroic founder, a youthful adventurer who had acquired the land through marriage at the beginning of the feudal period. From his wife came the 'blood of kings' which it was vital to demonstrate flowing in the veins of the present lord. In fact, all this vast noble cousinage – for they all intermarried despite the taboo on incest – could boast Charlemagne as an ancestor, starting with the Capetian kings of France. It is significant that the nobility invoked the spirits of their ancestors at the very moment when they were threatened by royal expansion.

Count Baldwin of Hainault instigated searches in the libraries of St Denis, Troyes and Cluny for a copy of the history of Charlemagne attributed to Archbishop Turpin. G. M. Spiegel has found six translations of this Latin text made in eastern France (in lands near the imperial border) between 1200 and 1230. One was made for Baldwin's sister, the countess of St Pol, another for the grand justiciar of Flanders, others for the lord of Béthune and for Renaud of Dammartin, count of Boulogne. In the prologue to each of these narratives, Charlemagne – whom the patron claimed as an ancestor – is portrayed as the very embodiment of knightly virtues, a model for those who lament the decline of chivalry. It was also during the growth of Capetian power in the twelfth century that the clerics employed in the households of territorial princes began to recall how Hugh Capet had usurped the crown. They also found favour with their patrons by repeating the 'prophecy of St Valery'. According to this story (invented at Montreuil-sur-Mer in about 1040), Hugh Capet had transferred the relics of St Valery there from St Bertin, at the saint's request. In return, the saint was said to have promised him the crown of France, saying that it would be worn by seven generations of Capetian descendants after him. The author meant 'for ever', since the number seven symbolizes infinity; but in the twelfth century some careful reckoning was made in the households of the nobility. In the reign of Louis VI, Orderic Vitalis had noted that 'four kings had reigned before him'. When the legend was transferred from Hugh Capet to his father, Hugh the Great, Louis VII became the seventh Capetian king. On his death, according to the prophecy, the usurpation of the throne of France would be at an end, and the crown would revert to the heirs of Charlemagne, its rightful inheritors. This was naturally of considerable significance for Louis VII's young heir. Perhaps it would be his lot to cede the crown to another claimant (a view possibly held at one juncture by Philip of Alsace, count of Flanders); or possibly he would have to present himself as a second Charlemagne – as his father-in-law, Baldwin of Hainault, undoubtedly believed. The monk Andrew of Marchiennes praises his patron, the count of Hainault, for marrying his daughter to Louis VII's young heir, thereby giving the French monarchy a new lease of life.

11

Philip Augustus

King Philip II of France is known to us as Philip Augustus. The epithet was bestowed upon him during his lifetime by the southern French monk Rigord, who completed his history of the new reign in the abbey of St Denis in 1196. To call him 'Augustus' of course identified the king with Caesar; first and foremost, it celebrated his achievement in extending the boundaries of the state – '*augebat rem publicam*,' to quote the classics. For Philip had just added the county of Vermandois to the royal domain and further extended it before his death; meanwhile feudal resistance to royal authority was very substantially reduced.

A mere, unkempt boy, he had been crowned on All Saints' Day 1179; he was barely fourteen years old and his father's only son. For seven years the Church authorities had pressed Louis VII to announce his heir publicly. He finally made this decision and informed the lords spiritual and temporal gathered at Paris that the coronation would take place on the feast of the Assumption, 15 August. The future Philip II was hunting in the forest of Compiègne; two days later he was found half dead: had God finally given the king an heir, only to snatch away his young life? Stiff with age, Louis VII took up his pilgrim's staff and went as a penitent to the tomb of Thomas Becket at Canterbury, to intercede with the martyr (whom he had protected from the violence of the Plantagenets a scant decade before) and to ask for the recovery of his heir. The saint answered his prayer. St Denis bestowed a further blessing on the young Philip, striking his father down with paralysis as he prayed at his tomb on his return from Canterbury. Louis VII survived another year, but he was as good as dead already.

According to contemporary custom, Philip was of age, but he was an only child. Moreover, it was a period when many youths died hunting or in military pursuits, in tournament and warfare. Certainly he was insufficiently mature to escape the influence of older relatives and the great feudal lords, who were bound closely to the king by virtue of the homage they had performed. The great vassals gathered at Rheims for the anointing of the king, the count of Flanders carrying the king's sword, the count of Hainault, Henry the Young King, joint ruler of England and his father's representative, bearing rich gifts. His four maternal uncles from Champagne were also present, duty-bound to protect their nephew: the consecrating archbishop, Count Henry 'the Liberal' of Champagne, Theobald, count of Blois and Chartres and seneschal of France, Count Stephen of Sancerre – all these powerful individuals hoped to manipulate the adolescent to the advantage of their own house. To this end, the childless Philip of Alsace, count of Flanders, lost no time in betrothing the young king to his niece Isabella, thereby breaking an earlier marriage contract with the house of Champagne.

However, this policy set the great lords against one another. And they soon found that Philip was not of a disposition to be easily led. Immediately after the coronation, the king had displayed his resolve by seizing the castles that had been part of his mother's marriage portion. He played the Champagne interest skilfully against the count of Flanders. In 1184, for example, he summoned a council at Senlis to dissolve his as yet unconsummated marriage on the pretext of consanguinity. This was merely the politics of intimidation: he kept the young queen, for she was useful to him, and gave him the heir he needed three years later. After Isabella's death, he took possession in their son's name of the lavish marriage portion with which the bride had been provided by her uncle and aunt – Amiens, Artois and the Vermandois. Having thus, like Caesar, 'enlarged the state', he confronted the magnates ranged against him.

The king held two trump cards. In the first place, he benefitted from the recent strengthening of the chivalric ethos, with loyalty as its corner-stone. As a good knight, for instance, the ageing Henry II of England remained loyal to his young lord, and refused to join the forces of the princes who were attacking the French king, an action which would have tipped the balance irredeemably against him. Philip could also rely on the much more solid and incorruptible loyalty of his own household knights. The second and more important source of support (which enabled him to skirt the hazards of the beginning of his reign) was the royal household itself, the *familia* he had inherited from his father. This was quite different from the disparate mob of swashbucklers and mountebanks at the court of Eleanor's husband in England. The French royal household numbered men of solid worth, whose sons would serve the king after them, such as the marshal Robert Clément or Walter, the chamberlain. Philip completed the team with a discerning eye. On his return from the crusades, he selected men such as William of Les Barres, Matthew of Montmorency and the

Vermandois knight Bartholomew of Roye from among his most trusted companions-in-arms. Educated young men were appointed to his chapel, such as Andrew (brought up at the court of Champagne), William (who had come from Brittany to study first at Mantes and then at Paris) and finally the Hospitaller Brother Guérin, 'King Philip's special counsellor in the royal palace by virtue of his wisdom and incomparable gift of counsel, with responsibility for royal and ecclesiastical affairs second only to the king'. Philip was a good and generous master, rewarding these men with robes, money and jewels. Fiefs confiscated in newly conquered provinces and rich heiresses were the king's rewards for his household knights, fat livings for his clergy. For those who had served him well, or for their young kinsmen, Philip found bishoprics – Brother Guérin at Senlis, Bartholomew's nephew at Evreux, Walter's sons at Noyon, Paris and Meaux and Robert Clément's at Sens. Between 1190 and 1200 these servants of the crown (both soldiers and clerics) performed a very wide range of duties. As they made lists, kept records, checked estimates for town walls and other fortifications, they completed the military and administrative framework which was to prove the monarchy's greatest strength.

For the contemporaries who sang its praises, however, divine grace was the source of all royal power. As they saw it, God showed favour to Philip because he had kept the promises made at his coronation. This was Rigord's favourite theme. His successor as royal historiographer at St Denis, William the Breton, described the king blessing the army before the battle of Bouvines, from which he emerged victorious because he was fighting to defend the Church. The sacred image of the French monarchy had been firmly established by Louis VII, and from him Philip inherited the whole-hearted devotion of the French Church, a crucial factor in the balance between king and Papacy. Philip's devotion was no more than conventional, but the strength of his position was such that he could brave the anger of the Pope – the acknowledged arbiter of kingly behaviour – who vainly attempted to make Philip respect the laws of marriage.

Philip sent his second bride back to her home the day after their marriage (15 August 1193). She was Ingeborg, the king of Denmark's sister. 'Prevented by sorcery', as Rigord puts it, the king had been unable to consummate their marriage. His first marriage had produced only one son, a sickly infant. It was the king's dynastic duty to provide other sons and he would therefore have to take another wife; to this end, the solemn marriage vows he had just made would lawfully be broken. If it could be proved that the marriage was incestuous, they would be null and void in any case. Accordingly, fifteen witnesses (twelve of them from the royal household) swore before an assembly of bishops and lay lords, presided over by the king's uncle, the archbishop of Rheims, that Philip and

Ingeborg were related within the prohibited fourth degree. This was quite untrue, but it enabled the king to embark upon a third marriage. The bishops solemnly blessed the union, but in 1198 the new Pope (Innocent III) decreed the French king guilty of bigamy. The papal legate did not go so far as excommunication, but he pronounced the fearful sentence of interdict on the kingdom – no masses were said and burials in consecrated land were suspended. But two-thirds of the French bishops were dependent on crown patronage and in these dioceses the sentence was ignored. And so Philip's luck held – for fifteen years. The Pope had to acknowledge the legitimacy of the two children of the suspect marriage. He was forced to give way before the alliance of crown and bishops that had been forged so strongly in the previous reign. Blessed with wise counsellors, the son of the most Christian King Louis VII was careful not to disrupt the *status quo*. Its regular working ensured that the king could safely appoint his own supporters to bishoprics. Moreover, although Philip intervened only to calm relations between students and townspeople, the University of Paris continued to flourish in his reign and – although this natural expansion was encouraged by the Papacy – the success of the university only added to the prestige of the French crown.

It was quite true that from the very outset of his reign, Philip had put the power of the secular state at the service of the Church. His first campaign (in the Mâconnais in 1180) completed the pacification of the area begun by his father. But at the beginning of the reign, Rigord praises him above all for ridding the kingdom of corruption. He began in the royal town of Paris, cleansing it of filth and stench, then removing merchants and prostitutes from the church of the Innocents: he enclosed the cemetery with a wall, then had market-halls built outside. Heretics in the Ile-de-la-Cité who preached false doctrine were burnt at the stake. The king cleansed the city with fire and the sword. He did not hesitate to employ mercenaries, although his enthusiastic chroniclers did not say so explicitly. They seem to have been critical of this policy, mistrusting the Brabançons. The peace-keeping leagues caused carnage at Dun-le-Roi in Berry, allegedly massacring more than 10,000 *cottereaux* and their companions, 'between 500 and 900 whores, whose attire was worth vast sums'. Philip was believed to be the author of this salutary purge.

His treatment of the Jews was the king's great glory. Aware of his obligations, his father had protected them. 'Out of respect for him', Rigord tells us, Philip checked his zeal and reined in his temper. However, he did not wait for the death of Louis VII, but had the Jews seized in their synagogues in February 1180. According to English chroniclers, 31,000 *livres parisis* were extorted from them before their release, one-and-a-half times the annual income of the royal domain. Confident of support in the bitter climate prevailing in the aftermath of crusading defeats in the East, Philip cancelled all Christian debts to Jewish creditors, keeping a third of the debtors' bonds for the crown. Then the Jews were expelled as deicides and their lands and property confiscated. Their return was soon countenanced, so that they might be taxed – but at a modest rate: in the accounts of 1202–3 these sums represent only 1 per cent of the receipts of the crown. And so the mechanism for the rational exploitation of Jewish wealth was adjusted and, by fits and starts, vast sums of money found their way into the French royal treasury, the result of more than a century of alternating protection and periods of violent repression. An ordinance of 1206 tightened the king's grip further, extending the regulations of the duchy of Normandy concerning Jews to the kingdom of France. It limited the interest on usury to 2 *deniers* per *livre* per week, an annual rate of 43 per cent; more importantly, officials to control credit transactions were appointed in every town and their prime task was to make an exact assessment of reserves of Jewish liquid capital.

Overflowing with zeal, Philip was also rewarded by providence for having played his part in the perilous adventure of the crusades. As soon as news came of the crushing defeat at Hattin and the fall of Jerusalem, a new crusade was preached. At Gisors in January 1188, the two kings Henry II of England and Philip II of France exchanged the kiss of peace and followed the example of Frederick Barbarossa (the third sovereign present) in vowing to lead the crusade. A general tax (the *dîme saladine*, or Saladin tithe) was levied to cover the costs of preparing for the expedition. In 1190 Philip left on crusade. The queen had just died and his son was only three years old. The fact that he was prepared to hazard everything in this way forces us to consider the possibility that this man – described as wily as a fox later in his reign – really was prepared to place the service of God before political expediency, and that he was guided by the Christian virtues of faith, hope and charity. Admittedly, the new head of the house of Plantagenet, Richard the Lionheart, was also going, and Philip himself was followed by all the great lords of his kingdom. To strengthen his position still further, he took serious precautions before he left. In a will (the first document to deal with the French royal succession) he laid down the way in which royal power was to be exercised in his absence and, in the event of his death, how his counsellors should maintain 'the royal office whose duty is to secure the subjects' welfare by all possible means, and place public good before private gain'. This ordinance established Paris as the seat of central government and especially of justice. The king's closest relatives, the queen mother and his maternal uncle, the archbishop of Rheims, 'were to hear the pleas of the men of the kingdom and settle their quarrels to the honour of God and the good of the realm' in Paris every four months. Philip left representatives behind him who were to be present at these general assizes and were to 'give an account' of the affairs of the kingdom. These men were called '*baillis*' (from the French word *bail*, meaning 'lease'), because some royal powers had been temporarily delegated to them. Neither the queen mother nor the archbishop could deprive them of their office unless they were proved guilty of a capital crime. He had placed them all over his lands, distinguishing each region by name – and here the king acknowledged their individual character – to exercise justice each month in his name, safeguarding individual rights without infringing the king's own, and keeping a written record of the profits of justice that accrued to him.

Philip was anxious that justice should be done, but he did not overlook the financial side. In each lordship the *baillis* were to ensure that their subordinates (the *prévôts*) appointed four trustworthy local men, 'prudent, lawful and of good repute', who were to be present whenever local affairs were discussed. The king himself chose the six at Paris, townsmen and the richest merchants and money-changers – numerate men, who could probably also read. Three times a year, on the feast of St Rémy, at Candlemas and Ascension, 'all their rents and revenues and receipts of extraordinary income are to be brought to Paris', to the exceptionally thick-walled strongroom the king had ordered to be built.

Philip reached Syria via Sicily. One of the first of all French kings to go overseas, he fought valiantly in the East, destroying his health in the process. But he returned at the earliest opportunity – possibly too soon, for Jerusalem was still in the hands of the Saracens. In his *Life* (*c.*1309) Joinville describes how Louis IX was forced to admit that his grandfather's conduct had not been entirely blameless. At the end of 1191, Philip was at St Denis, giving thanks to the martyr, both for watching over the kingdom and for preserving his own life during the rigours of voyage and campaign. He was now ready to derive every possible temporal advantage from his crusading activities.

These were substantial. The crusade had removed his principal rivals, and put the most dangerous of them out of the way for three years. For Richard the Lionheart stayed in the East: of the three crusading kings, he alone was prepared to follow in the steps of the Magi toward Bethlehem, breaking his journey for formally regulated tournaments and single combat with the Saracens and achieving great feats of arms and adventures, like the heroes of Arthurian romance. On the way back he was captured by his German enemies and kept in prison for many months, as his captors demanded ever increasing sums for their splendid prize. They justified their conduct in ransoming a crusader by citing the violence and treachery of which Richard himself was guilty in the Holy Land. This rumour spread, and in the bitter aftermath of the Third Crusade people began to see that, for the rich, a crusade was not merely a question of piety, but much rather one of pleasure and profit. Just as he had previously plotted with Richard against his father, Henry II, so Philip now plotted against Richard with his younger brother, John 'Lackland'. Philip easily exploited the young prince's desire for territories of his own, promising Normandy, Maine, Anjou, Aquitaine – everything. For his own part, he seized estates all along the river Epte on the borders of the domain lands, beginning with Gisors, potentially the most dangerous. In anticipation of Richard's return, he acted with all possible speed.

These manœuvres brought only a precarious advantage. The French king undoubtedly derived longer-term benefits from the wholesale slaughter of his great magnates. He had returned almost alone from the crusade. Virtually all the lords who had accompanied him fell at the siege of Acre, ᛫mong them the most powerful – the three brothers of the house of Champagne and the count of Flanders. This last died without a direct heir, and the king (whose claims through his dead wife were strong) had his eyes on part of the inheritance. As the crown became more powerful, so had the principalities: now their weakness stood revealed. These political units needed a warrior at their head, someone physically capable of wielding a sword. This was also true of the monarchy. But the principalities were infinitely more vulnerable when there was an abrupt break in the line of succession, as there was after the Third Crusade. This was because they were *fiefs mouvants* (that is, held directly from the crown) and also because the practices which placed the king at the summit of the feudal pyramid and made him the ultimate focus of homage gave him endless opportunities for intervention that transferred lands into royal possession or, at the very least, ensured that they posed no immediate threat to the crown.

When Philip Augustus succeeded to the throne, the judicial system envisaged by Abbot Suger was already established. Indeed, it was in place in 1169 at the assembly of Montmirail, when Henry II of England (who had decided to divide his inheritance) led his sons Henry and Richard to place their hands between those of the three-and-a-half-year-old infant Philip, the first performing homage for Normandy and Anjou, the second for Aquitaine. No one could now refuse to acknowledge that homage must be paid to Philip in person, simply because he was the king. This principle was applied in 1185 to the town of Amiens, when powers held by the archbishop fell into Philip's hands. In the course of the reign his legal experts helped ensure that the rope effectively holding the great lords prisoner was tightened. When the king invested new lords with these principalities (which were now treated as fiefs), his lawyers advised him to demand sureties who, when the vassal took his oath, were to swear to

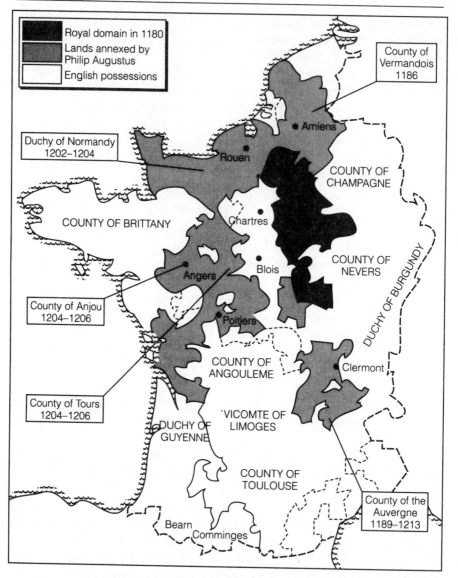

Figure 5   France under Philip Augustus, 1180–1223

indemnify the king if the prince failed to carry out his obligations. After 1202 this custom was also applied to subinfeudation: when a vassal swore an oath of loyalty to his immediate lord, there was a clause specifically reserving the first claim on his allegiance to his sovereign, the lord king. Staying near the newly built keep of Villeneuve-sur-Yonne in 1209, Philip issued an ordinance decreeing that, if a fief held in liege homage was

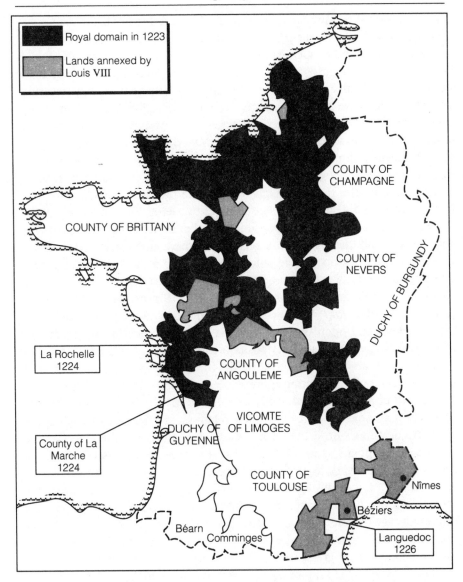

Figure 6   France under Louis VIII, 1223–1226

divided, the heirs should pay homage to the immediate lord, rather than to the head of the house. Military service was henceforth also owed to him. The duke of Burgundy, the count of Nevers and other great lords welcomed these changes with enthusiasm, realizing that they stood to gain from them. These men were not allowed to abuse the new situation, however.

It is important to understand that it was because the fief had become the means by which a noble held land and arranged his inheritance that feudal law was defined with such speed; equally, the reversion of a fief had become a hotly disputed legal issue. Vassalic friendship had long held sway, placing loyalty at the summit of all the noble virtues; but swearing an oath of allegiance had increasingly become a mere formality, a ceremony performed because it was the accepted means of entering into possession of land. Hence it became admissible for dowagers and female heirs to perform homage, although, since they were women, they could not perform military service in person. Service in war had become of secondary importance. Undoubtedly, the king expected that the men who knelt before him in homage would also fight beside him. He ordered his household clerks to make lists of knights responsible for the defence of specific towns and castles, and the documents relating to these fiefs carefully specified those who owed service to the feudal host in each area. They were bound to serve at their own expense for forty days. Alternatively, they could commute the military service owing to the king. But on campaign, in both private and public war, he relied more on the devotion of his friends and his household and upon the ability of the men he hired. In every lordship where the king consolidated his position as sovereign – whatever its size – he anticipated, above all, financial profit (from the levy of feudal dues) and political advantage, exploiting the weakness of the French nobility.

The lord of a fief was now firmly established in a position of unassailable superiority amongst the dead vassal's relatives, authorized to claim paid wardship of minors until they were of age and to arrange the marriages of widows and orphans as he wished. From the very beginning of his reign, Philip exploited every aspect of these prerogatives. The count of Nevers and Auxerre, for example, died in 1191, leaving an only daughter; for three years the king pillaged the fruits of the lordship of which he was supposedly guardian, then gave the child in marriage to his cousin of Courtenay; no sooner was she widowed than she promptly returned to royal custody, to be given (with the lordship of Nevers and Auxerre) to Hervé of Donzy – the king of course profiting from the levy of the relief on this second marriage. Philip did not turn a blind eye to the daughter of the second marriage, either, securing her for his own grandson and wringing a promise from Hervé that, should this contract of betrothal founder for some reason, no other marriage would be arranged for her without royal consent. In 1201 chance decreed that the house of Champagne should fall under the heavy tutelage of the king. Blanche of Navarre, the countess of Champagne, had one daughter; when her husband died, she was pregnant and close to her confinement. Philip precipitated matters and agreed to receive the widow's homage, but only on condition that she promised not to remarry nor to marry her daughter without royal approval; furthermore, the child she was expecting was to be a royal ward. Philip seized two castles as security for this undertaking, to which all the principal barons of Champagne were also bound. From a written complaint Blanche made to the Pope in 1215, we know that one fine day the king's eldest son, Prince Louis, burst into her hall with his knights and serjeants to try and wheedle money out of her as she dined with her son; she took refuge in her own chambers, while her servants successfully repelled the intruders. The episode provides an insight into the way in which Philip's right of wardship was exercised in practice. By virtue of the same right, Philip had complete control over the two daughters of the count of Flanders, who had died in the East, and also of the heiress of Brittany.

Most importantly of all, it was by exploiting his feudal rights that Philip was able to destroy the Angevin Empire. When Richard returned from captivity, he no longer considered himself bound by the ties of vassalage, since Philip had broken his obligation to Richard by plotting against him with his brother John. For five years he waged a brutal war against Philip. In September 1198 he sent a newsletter announcing victory to his subjects. Here we see the written word playing a vital role once more, this time as an instrument of political propaganda, moulding an event, exploiting it and exaggerating its importance.

I attacked the enemy fiercely outside Gisors [Richard wrote]. The bridge over the Epte was broken by the impact of French knights in full retreat. The king fell into the river and twenty of his knights were drowned; I unhorsed Matthew of Montmorency, Alan of Roucy and Fulk of Guilleval with my lance; they were taken prisoner with one hundred others; I am sending you most of their names – I do not yet have details of the rest, who were captured by Mercadier [a mercenary captain]. A great crop of prisoners and 200 war-horses were taken, forty of them with iron horse-armour.

Philip Augustus had not been defeated in pitched battle; technically Fréteval was no more than a skirmish. But it was a substantial defeat and might have had serious consequences had the situation not been completely changed by Richard's accidental death from a crossbow bolt the following spring. He left no legitimate male heirs, and there were two main claimants to the English throne: his nephew Arthur, count of Brittany, and his youngest brother John, who took England and Normandy into his own hands without delay. This was a godsend for Philip – an opportunity to act as his grandfather, Louis VI, had done in Flanders after the death of Charles the Good, but far more effectively, because by this date his rights of lordship were defined with much greater clarity. He marched with all possible speed to Le Mans and took charge of the young Arthur, investing him with Anjou and Maine and escorting him back to Paris. Philip used the boy as a trump card in the tense political game he played with his uncle: Arthur was abandoned at the crucial moment when Philip took the two great fiefs, Maine and Anjou, into his own hands once more and invested John with them in return for a huge sum. He also agreed to a marriage between his own son and Blanche of Castile, the niece of his new vassal. As far as Philip was concerned, it was imperative that the Plantagenet ruler of England should become his liegeman once more for the lands he held in France.

Just a few months later, two of John's vassals in Poitou, Hugh, lord of Lusignan, and the count of La Marche, defied their lord. Striving to keep the loyalty of their unruly ancestors had been a full-time job for the duke of Aquitaine at the beginning of the eleventh century, and they needed tactful handling. John made a disastrous mistake when he took Isabella of Angoulême as his own wife, although she was already betrothed to the son of one of the Poitevin lords. This was treason and her relations appealed for justice to John's overlord, the king of France. Such an appeal, climbing right up the feudal ladder, was in accordance with the new practices. Philip naturally welcomed the appeal with open arms and summoned John as his vassal to appear before the royal court in Paris, so that peace might be made between the two parties. John did not present himself, arguing that he was liable for service as a vassal only in the marches of Normandy. Philip retorted that he had been summoned as duke of Aquitaine. John stood his ground. Then, in April 1202, the court passed judgement. The French barons pronounced the *commise*, or sentence of confiscation, of all fiefs held from the king, using John's non-appearance as the pretext for their decision. They were referring to customary law. It sometimes happened that a lord who had been betrayed threatened to seize the land of his unfaithful vassal, but it was extremely rare for anyone to risk putting the sentence into practice. In any case this sanction had never been applied to a principality.

It was quite revolutionary to apply the law relating to seigneurial prerogatives in this way. Philip judged his position strong enough to pass such a sentence and to execute it. He reckoned once more on Arthur, formally knighted him and received his homage for Brittany, which by this act became in its turn a fief held directly from the crown. He promised Arthur that when he was in a position to do so, he would invest him with Aquitaine, by right of his grandmother, and with Maine and Anjou, inherited from his grandfather. Normandy, however, was not to be his. This province was to be ceded to the crown as the relief for Arthur's other lands and Philip's conquest of Plantagenet lands began there. In desperate straits, John had turned to the Pope, complaining of the injustice done him. But in response to papal claims to act as an intermediary, Philip asserted that this was a case for lord and vassal, a temporal affair that had nothing to do with the court of Rome; he would find it 'insulting to the dignity of the crown' to submit the case to papal arbitration. He had the full support of the French lords and bishops. When it was rumoured that King John had killed his captive nephew at Rouen with his own hands, Philip exploited the situation to the full. The great French lords were sickened by this murder and with their help Philip seized Anjou and Maine, since – he maintained – the lawful heir had forfeited his rights to them. However, he left the seneschal of both counties in office, the man upon whom power devolved in the absence of the count. He did not chance his hand beyond the borders of the old Frankish kingdom. Poitou was too far away and simply too foreign to be sequestrated. But the king kept Tours for himself, besides that choice morsel, Normandy. There was no question of seneschals there any more. The province was administered directly by royal *baillis*. Henceforth Normandy was part of the royal domain, legitimately annexed by virtue of custom, or rather, feudal law.

The miscreant vassal was still at large, nevertheless. In 1213 Philip made as if to cross the Channel and pursue John to England. The Plantagenet king had been excommunicated for having pressurized the Church too insistently. The French army advanced into Flanders. At this point John – distributing largesse with a ready hand – roused the counts of Boulogne and Flanders against Philip, as well as the Emperor Otto, king of Germany. Renaud of Dammartin, the count of Boulogne, was an old comrade-in-arms of Philip's: the French king had knighted him with his own hand, but he was an ambitious member of the royal household who had risen fast as a result of the king's favour, and then forgotten the obligations of friendship in pursuit of his own political ends. Ever since he repudiated his first wife (Philip's cousin) and married the heiress to the county of Boulogne, Renaud had adopted the claims of the counts, her ancestors. Proud of their descent from Charlemagne and their connection with the crusading hero, Godfrey of Bouillon, the counts controlled the great Channel port of Boulogne. Renaud changed his allegiance and Philip's affection turned to mortal hatred. The French court decreed another confiscation (*commise*), that of the powerful lordship of Mortain, which the king had given to Renaud a short while before, when he took possession of Normandy. The very next year Renaud of Dammartin became the king of England's liegeman. Ferrand, count of Flanders, was stung by the excessive relief that Philip had wrung from him when (by right of his wife) he took possession of his great lordship. The Flemings shared his resentment; he could count on them. So Ferrand's service to his overlord was stingy, performed as perfunctorily as possible without risking sanction;

and when the king crossed the border into Flanders, he rallied the opposition. Finally, the Emperor Otto of Brunswick was entirely dependent upon King John, his maternal uncle. Four years previously he had also been excommunicated, because his policy in Italy ran counter to papal interests, and Pope Innocent III had the young Frederick of Hohenstaufen elected and crowned king of the Germans. Otto therefore regarded the Papacy's natural supporter, the 'most Christian' king of France, as his most dangerous opponent. The coalition forces of Flanders and Boulogne attacked Philip from the north, while King John embarked upon the reconquest of his inheritance from the south.

In February 1214 John disembarked at La Rochelle; his army advanced, captured Angers on 17 June, then laid siege to a neighbouring castle, La Roche-aux-Moines. Philip Augustus had charged his son Louis, count of Artois, to hold this front with all the knights levied from the southern part of the domain. The knights from the northern domain lands were with the king himself in Flanders, where he laid waste and destroyed the land of his contumacious vassal. His barons advised him not to confront the enemy, however, and he drew back in a weak position to Lille. On 2 July the king of England raised the siege, and took sudden flight at the approach of Louis and the French forces. On 27 July Philip won a dazzling victory at Bouvines, in a battle which historians have rightly judged of fundamental importance.

We have an eyewitness account by William the Breton, the king's chaplain, who stayed at his side throughout the battle. This seems to be the gist of his narrative, clearly written to glorify the French crown.

Bouvines was a true pitched battle, one of those very rare encounters between medieval armies, where all the rites were observed, so that a political conflict might be definitively resolved by the hand of God. Three aptly named '*batailles*' (battles or battalions) of knights were lined up facing each other at opposite ends of the chosen ground. The kings of France and Germany were in the centre of their armies, each displaying aloft the emblems of their power. On one side were the two banners of the kings of France, the great red one called the *oriflamme* and another decorated with fleurs-de-lis, their sacred emblems. On the other – across the open ground, like the empty space on the chess-board separating the black pieces from the white at the beginning of the game – there were very different emblems: a chariot (replica of a *caroccio*, or battle-chariot, which the Milanese had taken with them into a famous battle in *c.*1000) and, placed upon it, the imperial eagle and a standard in the shape of a dragon – profane and arrogant emblems that seemed to William the Breton to verge on the demoniac.

Philip was nearly fifty years old, an age when few lords played an active part in battle. But he did not hesitate to risk his own life. He went into battle supported by his household, a cohesive group who all came from his own kingdom. The enemy, on the other hand, were drawn from a variety of nations and they found it impossible to present a united front. Philip did not rush to give battle, for the good Christian does not tempt his God and 27 July 1214 was a Sunday, when no Christian should carry arms. It was the wickedness of his enemies – declared William the Breton – which forced him to do so.

Pitched battle was a quasi-religious ceremony. The French king played his part fittingly; he had two priests beside him continually singing the psalms of David in the thick of the fighting. In the silence before the onslaught, he turned towards the Lord and prayed for mercy; then, extending his hands towards the kneeling host, he blessed them. Afterwards – still adhering strictly to the ritual of battle – he addressed them. The men they faced, he said, were henchmen of the devil; the Emperor had been anathematized because of his attempts to destroy Holy Church. William added that the warriors who fought for the Emperor were mere mercenaries, hired men who had sold their service for money – money, moreover, that had been seized from the poor and the clergy – those same priests and poor people whom Philip was at such pains to protect. What is more, the enemy carried weapons which no true knight would stoop to use, long knives which could penetrate mail. The enemy clearly aimed to kill. Lawless and godless, they would even kill their own brothers, denying the closest ties of friendship. And many of them had come to attack their liege lord. The old countess of Flanders (who enjoyed heaven knows what commerce with the devil) aided them with her witchcraft and promised them victory. The king of Germany was surrounded by corruption, Philip continued; by contrast, the king of France gathered round him priests who respected papal authority, loyal knights and the good serjeants of Soissons, who performed wondrous deeds, and the valiant people of the communal militia to whom, in a symbolic gesture, the *oriflamme* was entrusted.

Philip's enemies had sworn to share the Capetian lands, but to kill the king first. The count of Flanders went so far as to lay hands on the king; but he drew back at the last moment, stunned by the horror of what he was about to do and by fear of committing a mortal sin if he tried to kill the man who was not only his natural lord, but was also placed under God's especial protection (by virtue of the unction of coronation) like bishops or the martyred Thomas Becket.

Philip was not vanquished, even when enemy soldiers armed with hooks rode through his household knights and pulled him from his horse. His most faithful comrades, the hard core of the *familia*, protected him with their own bodies and helped him regain his saddle. It was at this juncture, amid clouds of dust from the harvest they were trampling underfoot, that the rout was suddenly unleashed. God marked out the loser, the wicked ruler. He escaped death by a whisker, as a blow dealt him by one of the bravest French knights turned aside and slid off his hauberk, killing his horse beneath him. The Emperor jumped onto a fresh mount and fled at a gallop, not to be seen again. He left on the battlefield the broken chariot and the eagle with its broken wings. It was beneath Philip to assume those signs of imperial power. An obedient son of the Church, he had them sent to the anti-king Frederick – in other words, to the Pope.

There was carnage amongst the foot-soldiers: the Brabançons in the pay of the count of Boulogne were totally annihilated. In William's view, these heretics met their just reward. Fatalities amongst the knights were far fewer. William names only two, both killed by accident. On the other hand, there was a huge number of prisoners, amongst them the two traitor-counts. According to the custom of the land, they could have been put to death, for plotting regicide. But Philip was God-fearing and demonstrated his clemency, content merely to lead them in chains to a secure prison, for they were extremely valuable captives. The king refused to negotiate over Renaud of Dammartin, who spent the rest of his life in strict confinement in the castle of Péronne. All the rest were ransomed and carefully catalogued for the purpose. A 'catalogue of prisoners' drawn up at the beginning of August listed 110 knights transported to Paris in village carts, 16 handed over to great lords and 3 to officials of the royal household. Three times this number had been taken prisoner; the rest had been exchanged or left well guarded along the way.

All the people, 'high and low, men and women, old and young', gathered at crossroads to cheer their victorious sovereign. It was harvest time, and peasants carrying on their shoulders sickles and hay-forks (the tools that marked them out as workers of the soil and providers of food) flocked to see Count Ferrand of Flanders chained to the cart and no one, serfs, villeins or children, hesitated to insult him. Under the gaze of the victorious king and surrounded by his warriors, public rejoicing allowed the common people to give free rein to their resentment of the wicked lords who were being punished for disrupting the natural order of society. In the towns there was more derision and more taunts, as well as formally organized public rejoicing. Bells pealed and streets were strewn with branches and wild flowers, as the clergy greeted the victorious procession with shouts of praise, and the townspeople danced. The celebrations reached a climax in the walled city of Paris, where the king went to recover. Here, William the Breton tells us, they lasted seven days and seven nights. According to his account, joy knew no bounds, and the festivities seemed timeless, because artificial lighting chased away the shadows and made night 'as bright as day'. The victorious king entered his capital city as if it were Jerusalem on the Day of Judgement. God had just blessed him, demonstrated the justice of his cause, and re-established peace in the land, inviting the two parts of Christian society (*ecclesia*), clergy and people, to praise him and rejoice. Indeed, 'the university of scholars', on one hand, and the citizens, on the other, 'rejoiced whole-heartedly with banquets, singing and dancing'. Reckless expenditure was the order of the day, with the same outpouring of joy that characterized wedding feasts. In the aftermath of victory, Paris celebrated the union of crown and people.

William the Breton used the substance of this preliminary account to compose a Latin poem nearly 10,000 lines long, a splendid monument to the glory of the monarchical State. This took some while – too long for him to be able to present it to his master, Philip Augustus. In 1224 he presented it to the new king, Louis VIII. Modelled on the *Æneid* and using many of the rhetorical devices of the classical epic, the *Philippide* celebrates Philip, king of the Franks, and Bouvines becomes a national victory of the Frankish nation. Outnumbered three to one, the warriors did not hesitate to face the dangers of battle 'with burning courage', and their bravery secured the victory. Before they hurled themselves into the fray, Brother Guérin, striding about in front of the lines of serried troops, reminded them that their race, 'victorious in all encounters, had always defeated its enemies'. On that fateful day – and this was what made the battle so cruel – the same blood coursed through their enemies' veins. They, too, were Franks and this in itself sufficed to save them from dishonour, even the treacherous Renaud of Dammartin. 'The courage he displayed in battle was natural in the fullest sense of the word; it proclaimed that he was indeed of Frankish birth and however his crimes sully him in your eyes, O France, do not be ashamed or blush for him.' All the other combatants were forced to yield, 'the sons of the Empire for whom the pleasures of debauchery and the rewards of Bacchus were sweeter than the gifts of redoubtable Mars', and this was especially true of all Teutons who spoke in Germanic tongues, the Germans and the northern Flemings. Their defeat proved 'that they are essentially inferior to the French, for there was no question of comparison in battle'. Their savage and almost bestial fury was powerless against the valour of the 'children of France'. The most remarkable feature here is that 'France' is no longer confined to the Francia of Clovis or Robert the Pious. Later, William the Breton says that 'the children of Gaul' were united in the forces of Philip Augustus. He is talking about the Gaul of Caesar's *Commentaries*, an area far larger than the kingdom of France.

He presents France as a single nation, a body with the king at its

head. Seething with rage like his warrior subjects, the king of the *Philippide* is no longer the watchful figure slipping away from the heat of
the battle. Despite the advice of his barons, he burned to engage the
Emperor in combat, and was bitterly disappointed when the press of battle
prevented him from killing his opponent with his lance, a second St
Michael crushing Satan beneath his feet. Raising the *oriflamme*, 'which was
exactly like the banners carried in religious processions', he had set out as
the avenger of all Christendom, his purpose to purge it of the heresy which
originated with Otto of Brunswick. For Otto had robbed pilgrims in
Rome; it was his fault that God's people had failed to raise troops for
another crusade to free the Holy Sepulchre from the hands of the infidel.

In the speech which William the Breton gives the Emperor before battle,
Otto calls on his men to 'put to death or capture the clerics and monks who
mean so much to Philip and whom he will defend with all his might'. He
maintained that there should be fewer of them, their numbers reduced to a
more realistic level, 'so that the knights, who are the custodians of the
public weal and responsible for the safety of clergy and people in war and
peace, should own the land and levy the greater tithes'. It was the Emperor
who had promulgated a law stipulating that 'churches should only have
lesser tithes and offerings,' and that ecclesiastical lordships were to be
surrendered to the Emperor, so that he could provide for the people
and pay for his soldiers. 'The Church will be so much more useful and
effective,' added Otto, 'after I have restored justice in this way. Much
better for the good knight to have well-cultivated fields of his own, lands
running with milk and honey, than this lazy lot, born only to guzzle the
harvest and pass their lives idly withering in the shadows.' The French
king was presented as the champion of the established order of things,
against anticlerical princes and the errant preachers who provided them
with biblical justification for their greed and against all forms of subversion
and encroachments of temporal power. He was the supreme defender of the
Church, corner-stone of the sacred institution of monarchy. The alliance
between throne and altar had been sealed by God-given victory in battle.

The *Philippide* did not omit the description of the victors' journey
through the French countryside. But there is no mention of jeering
reapers. Instead, the narrative focuses exclusively on the triumph celebrated in the capital city, emphasizing parallels with imperial Rome and
especially the triumphs of the Emperors Titus and Vespasian, since the
Capetian king was, like them, the scourge of the Jews. But his triumph
was in another league; for the Franks had defeated the Romans and freed
Gaul from their yoke, while the highest forms of knowledge studied in the
Paris schools had been transmitted from ancient Greece. Rather than a new
Caesar, Philip was a new Alexander. (A Latin verse life of the Emperor

Alexander had recently been composed by Walter of Châtillon, notary to the archbishop of Rheims.) The joy of victory resounded from Paris to the very edges of the kingdom, throughout the body politic with the sovereign at its heart, pulsing 'through cities, towns and boroughs', the financial centres that now dominated the feudal world and were the tools of centralized power. And so 'a single victory ushered in a million triumphs.' France began to look like a great nation and a fully fledged State.

Unanimity was the theme of the festivities which France in her gratitude offered to Philip. Like the water of baptism, the blood spilt on the field of Bouvines purified all the 'children of Gaul', re-endowing them with the innocence of the first days of creation. From innocence it was a short step to equality. For the triumphal ceremonies abolished for a while all distinctions 'of rank, fortune and condition'. Knight, townsman and even the peasant each shone with the same splendour, bestowed directly by God to the clergy, but reflected to the people through the person of the king, himself clothed in additional splendour by his God-given victory.

The *Philippide* distinguishes four social categories: men of prayer, men of arms, townsmen and peasants. William the Breton intended that his poem should reflect the contemporary situation with some degree of realism and he puts the peasant unambiguously in his proper place – last of all, at the bottom of the heap, furthest from the source of light and power. He alone was stunned by the glory that surrounded him. He had the effrontery to believe himself 'raised up to the level of the greatest kings'. The stupid creatures forgot that the marvellous trappings would last only a few hours, and thought that they were being removed permanently from the uncouth and ignorant state of submission and toil that was their lot. They thought that '[they] could change [their] appearance merely by putting on another set of clothes', forgetting that peasants were no more than the feet of the body politic and that entry into the joy of the royal court was granted to the other three estates alone. After Bouvines, the French monarchy laid claim to the chivalric ideal which rival princes had used against them a short while before. Supported by the three orders of society (clergy, nobility and the third estate), the 'most Christian king' placed himself at the head of the assembled nation for centuries to come, loving it like a father and expecting filial devotion in return from each one of his subjects. After Bouvines, 'you could well ask whether the king loved his people more than the people their king. It was as if each tried to outdo the other in their love. You could not say which was dearer to the other or whose love was the stronger, such tender affection united them with ties of perfect purity.'

For once it is entirely justifiable to close one of the periods of very gradually evolving political and administrative history with a specific event and a precise date. On the evening of 27 July 1214, a change took place which was to last for two centuries. The battle decided everything. 'After that day no one dared to wage war on King Philip, but he lived peacefully for ever after, and the whole land was at peace for a long while,' observed an anonymous chronicler in the service of the lords of Béthune. He was right. After Bouvines, the king of France could sit calmly on his throne, as befitted one of his age. If action was required, his son went in his stead. Whether he went meekly is open to question. In those days relations between long-lived lords and their heirs were generally strained. Numerous sources suggest that Prince Louis (count of Artois through his mother) took his own political decisions; and his trouble-making wife, Blanche of Castile, undoubtedly encouraged his efforts towards independence. The fact that Philip, the first Capetian of that name, did not have him consecrated in his own lifetime proves nothing. His own father had only decided to share the crown when confronted with increasing disability. It would be wrong to assume that even after his historic victory Philip thought the future of his dynasty any more secure than that of his predecessors. Succession was a risky business in any family, and Philip Augustus may have thought it wiser not to have his appointed successor crowned, when he allowed him to become involved in hazardous undertakings from which he himself held aloof, such as the conquest of England in 1216 (despite Louis' excommunication) and then – with the Pope's blessing this time – the Albigensian Crusade.

He was at least careful to instil in his heir the moral values which would fit him for the throne. A Parisian cleric called Giles composed his 'mirror for princes' for Louis' benefit, and presented it on the prince's thirteenth birthday, in 1200. In this work, the *Karolinus*, the example of Charlemagne demonstrates to the boy the four cardinal virtues of courage, justice, wisdom and temperance. In the book, Philip Augustus is made to say that his successor should be less quick-tempered than he has been and should avoid marital problems. On one page of the manuscript 'the modern kings of France' are found in a genealogical table. From Robert 'the most pious and well-read', all the rulers of the house of Capet are there, their names in red ink, decorated with fleurs-de-lis. It was not apparently thought necessary to mention the fact that both his mother and grandmother were descended from Charlemagne. For neither the author of the *Karolinus* nor anyone else could possibly doubt that Louis was the legitimate heir – just as his ancestor Robert Capet and his father had been. 'It is common knowledge', proclaimed a bull of Pope Innocent III, 'that the king of France is descended from the lineage of Charlemagne.' Two years earlier, under the supervision of Brother Guérin, Stephen of Gallardon had inserted the prophecy of St Valery in one of the registers of the royal chancery. There was no reason to fear a disputed succession: the son of Philip Augustus would undoubtedly wear the crown of France and would take possession of the royal domain that, to general amazement, his father had so zealously extended. For, crowning all the vagaries of fortune that had favoured Philip, was the fact that Louis had no brother with a claim to some share in the inheritance. He could leave everything to his older son. Inheritance customs would undoubtedly have forced him to leave one of the great lordships he had acquired – perhaps Normandy – to his second son, Philip Hurepel, had the boy's mother not been one wife too many. His legitimacy was unquestioned, thanks to the Pope; nevertheless, he was half-bastard in everybody's eyes and would never be able to claim more than a few scraps of his father's inheritance.

In September 1222 Philip fell ill. He started to give away his worldly wealth for the good of his soul. He gave the money in his privy purse to knights who had fought in the Holy Land and to the Paris poor; to the abbey of St Denis a cross, a reliquary and the jewels from his personal treasury. A few silver dishes, three dozen goblets, a sackful of Byzantine coins, some precious stones given to him by his mother and his household and by prelates and the chamberlain, Walter – but only a very few: the inventory drawn up by Guérin in 1206 demonstrates that the Capetian court still eschewed ostentation. The king survived until the following summer. He was at Pacy-sur-Eure when he realized that he was dying, and wanted to return to Paris, where the council was in session making preparations for a new crusade. He died on the way there, at Mantes. The *Grandes Chroniques de France* gives him the funeral oration he would have wished for:

He increased and wondrously multiplied the kingdom of France [the words 'domain' and 'kingdom' are still interchangeable]; he defended and most wonderfully protected the lordship, rights and nobility of the crown of France . . . He always made himself the shield of Holy Church against all enemies. As a special devotional privilege he guarded and defended the church of St Denis of France above all others, as if it was his own chamber, and on many occasions his actions displayed the especial love he had for the martyrs and their church. He was a jealous and impassioned defender of the Christian faith; he took up our Lord's cross and bore it on his shoulders to the Holy Land; in the East he went at the head of a great army against the infidel and laboured loyally and noble-heartedly until the city of Acre was taken. . . . He gave alms generously in many places.

The body of the dead king, clothed in a dalmatic as on the day of his coronation, crowned and with a sceptre in his hand, was escorted across Paris to the royal burial-place at St Denis. It was met by a great throng of bishops and archbishops. The son of Louis VII was returning to establish himself at the centre of the institutional French Church for all eternity. Miracles sprang up along the route of his cortège and men said that he, too, was a saint. Philip had assured the permanency of the French monarchy by force of arms and by the skill with which he exploited feudal law, but above all because – as the chronicler tells us – he had faithfully fulfilled his obligations as a Christian king.

During the reign of Philip Augustus the new symbols placed upon the façades of French cathedrals became the primary vehicle for the expression of royal power. Two themes were developing at that period, both products of movements in academic theology on the incarnation. Half a century before, Suger had been the first to express Christ's humanity by placing on the portal of the abbey church of St Denis statues representing the ancestors of Jesus. According to Scripture, they were kings – Jewish kings. But who would fail to think of the kings of France as they stood before these crowned figures? The concept was expressed on a larger scale in the design of the new façade for the cathedral of Notre-Dame in Paris at the beginning of the thirteenth century, where the schema of the kings of Judah is set out above the three porches at the base of the towers. The statues were sculpted long after 1223, when the alterations were first planned. Their heads have only recently been found, for in 1793 they were decapitated by revolutionaries. This action reflects the power of these symbols: the vandals who wanted to do away with the monarchy made straight for these images which had for centuries celebrated the living kings of France in the heart of the royal city and on the façade of a building whose massive stones and fortress-like aspect were in themselves the very embodiment of power. The statues clearly stated that this was the power of the French monarchy.

The second image is the coronation of the Virgin, both richer and subtler, which communicates the results of an entire debate on the nature of power. First sculpted in 1190 on the portal of Senlis cathedral, the motif reappeared in Paris some thirty years later, on the tympanum of the northern portal of the façade of Notre-Dame. For its southern counterpart a bas-relief some fifty years old was reused. This also showed the Virgin, seated and holding the baby Jesus, her whole body a throne. On either side of this central figure two additional, related characters, king and bishop, endow the whole scene with significance. Although by no means of equal importance, they are carved on the same scale. Louis VII kneels on the left, dominated by the standing figure of the bishop on the other side. In this way the people were presented with the success of ecclesiastical reform, which had assured the superiority of the spiritual over the temporal and which – in the reign of Louis VII at least – had tried to subordinate the monarchy to the Church.

The figures of the coronation of the Virgin on the north portal bear an entirely different message. The Virgin is no longer in the centre. She sits beside Christ, on the same bench. Crowned, and slightly taller than his mother, Christ is about to place the crown on her head. Here again, the crown is the dominant symbol, the image of royalty, worn by the Capetians when they held solemn courts. Here, of course, the crown is clearly associated with Jesus and Mary, outside historical time, at a point after the death and assumption of the Virgin. But the very representation of Christ as king exalted the monarchy and gave it a divine aspect, heightening the prestige of God's representative on earth. It should be added that, reduced to its starkest terms, what is seen is a man crowned and a woman whom he is about to crown. The scene expresses male domination and the fact that any power wielded by a woman proceeded from power exercised by a man: it is a question of delegation and subordination. When it was carved, theologians believed that in this scene the Virgin represented the Church; and this was the theory which preachers expounded to the faithful. Similarly, the carving on the porch of the cathedral lauded the power of the Church in the crowned image of Mary the mother of God. But it also clearly stated that this power was subordinate. Superior power rested with the actor in the scene, Christ the crowned king and, by implication, with the king who was his delegate on earth.

The diffusion of such a theme at the very beginning of the thirteenth century in the royal domain, close to the university where the future propagandists of the monarchy were being trained, is evidence of a return to Carolingian structures. Here below, supreme power lay in the hands of the king and was held directly from Christ. Beneath him were the three orders, or estates, of society. In particular he towered over the highest of these, the Church. Bishops were delegates of royal power; the king appointed them so that they could adorn their cathedrals – but they did so in his name. These carved figures are a powerful reminder that henceforth the king was in command of the work, just as he was the defender of the true faith when he led his knights on crusade, against either the infidel or the heretic.

12

The South

In reality by no means all of the 'children of Gaul' were obedient to Philip Augustus. His annexations had certainly reunited around Paris the ancient territories of the Franks and the duchy of Normandy, while the king's feudal prerogatives also enabled him to keep a tight grip on Champagne. He had no ambition to seize the Burgundian lands (from which the crown had long since detached Sens, the Auxerrois and the Nivernais): the duke was his cousin and an exceptionally loyal vassal, who had fought like a lion at Bouvines. Other knights from imperial lands had also fought for him there, beneath the *oriflamme* of the kings of France. They included the count of Bar, 'a young man with the courage of a veteran', and several Lorraine knights, most notably Gerard La Truie, who fought in the central battalion shoulder to shoulder with Philip. South of Burgundy, Capetian power made gradual inroads, pushing the old frontier of the kingdom almost imperceptibly towards the east. In the reign of Louis VI, the lord of Beaujeu had already accompanied the king on his campaigns in the Auvergne. Louis VII had extended royal protection to the dioceses of the Central Massif and established outposts of the royal domain along the Saône. Ever since the seafarers of Genoa and Pisa had freed the eastern Mediterranean from Saracen control, trade had flourished with renewed vigour in these areas. Business prospered at St Gilles, Montpellier and Arles. Marseilles was soon to follow, and Lyon was already flourishing. When Philip and Richard the Lionheart took the cross, the Rhône and the Mediterranean offered the best route to the Holy Land.

In south-west France, on the other hand, the advance of the French monarchy was blocked by what remained of the Angevin Empire and, above all, by the hostile character of the former kingdom of the Goths in the Toulousain. No echo of Bouvines sounded south of the Loire. Philip had made virtually no impression on Poitou. Moreover, he shrewdly avoided involvement at such a distance, realizing that considerable military risk would achieve only the most precarious of loyalties. He never seriously considered annexing Aquitaine: his father had been fully aware of what he was doing when he disentangled himself from the principality; Henry II had exhausted himself there to no avail; and it had cost Richard I his life. The French king turned a deaf ear to requests that he should fulfil the obligations of his coronation oath and stamp out heresy in the south of France. All he did was to give Prince Louis permission to try his luck in those distant lands, for which the *Grandes Chroniques de France* praised him in fulsome terms: 'When he was older and not so strong himself, he did not spare his son, but sent him twice at the head of a great army against the Albigensians to crush the heresy that was rife there.' Philip had no idea that these expeditions against the Cathars (often called Bulgars because of the geographical origin of their beliefs) would eventually lead to the extension of the French kingdom to the shores of the Mediterranean.

Several fundamental misconceptions about the south of France at this period need to be dismissed before the role of the French king can be examined: there was no deliberate attempt at colonial conquest by the French; these regions possessed neither political nor cultural unity; Catharism affected the whole of Christendom at this period, and was not confined to this area.

However, it was an incontrovertible fact that the French kings were charged by God at their coronation at Rheims to maintain peace and the true faith throughout France at all costs, as far as the borders of the adjacent kingdoms of Navarre and Aragon. At the beginning of the fourteenth century the shepherd-heretics of Montaillou knew very well where the boundary lay, and acknowledged themselves French subjects during the Inquisition proceedings against them. Apart from these sovereign boundaries between the kingdoms, which no one dreamt of changing, the south of France was divided into a large number of regions (each acutely conscious of its identity) and between peoples who did not even speak the same dialect. From this linguistic diversity sprang the language of troubadour poetry, admired not only from Toulouse to Orange and beyond, but also at Caen and, soon afterwards, at Florence and Naples. This common court language undoubtedly bound together the noble classes in the face of northern attacks and depredations; it united them and later fostered nostalgia for their lost liberty. Stimulated by external aggression, this sense of national identity was also to play a part in influencing the political development of the region.

As in the north, the great territorial princes had become increasingly powerful in the twelfth century. The lack of good chronicle sources makes it more difficult to trace this trend: in these regions, law and poetry were the highest forms of cultural expression and there was relatively little historical literature. Increased princely power did not have its roots in the feudal systems that operated in the former Frankish kingdom in the north: according to native tradition (which the Plantagenets had attacked, but failed to displace), relations between men were based on freely made contracts. Here, the term 'fief' referred to the profit derived from a particular property by the individual, noble or otherwise, who held rights to it under currently valid agreements.

Two particular factors determined the unique political development of this part of France. In the first place, it was the favourite haunt of mercenary companies throughout the Middle Ages. The particularly high incidence of brigandage in these areas stemmed above all from the high proportion of unproductive mountainous land, which was unable to support more than a tiny proportion of the young male population, whose only resources were their physical strength and fighting ability. The majority came from knightly families; bastardy and the low value of patrimonies fragmented by successive divisions which continually reduced the value of an inheritance forced them to seek their fortune elsewhere. The profession of arms was the only means by which they could do this; so they grouped themselves into companies, and offered their services to anyone who would employ them. These ruthless warriors with their incomprehensible speech were known as 'Aragonese', 'Navarrese' and 'Basques' to the people whom they terrorized. The great lords of the region may well have been over-hasty in employing bands of them to achieve their political ends; but the fact that for a long while larger quantities of liquid capital had been available in the south was undoubtedly also a decisive factor. You have only to look at the memoranda drawn up in the assemblies arbitrating noble disputes in Poitou and the Narbonnais in the first half of the eleventh century, where the sums involved run into thousands of *sous*. This was the scene of large-scale financial operations, as in England, where trade and commerce developed at an early date. Financial experts were called 'Cahorsins' in the twelfth century, whatever their origins: an epithet that reflected the prosperity of the southern city of Cahors. The proliferation of mercenary companies in the south of France can therefore be explained by the juxtaposition of impoverished mountain areas and rich cities where wealth was steadily increasing.

The second crucial factor in the political development of the south was the stability of social structures in the towns, where political power was rooted in municipal institutions. This was the case not only in towns of Roman origin, but also in the secondary settlements that had grown up around them, called 'castrum' in local documents – a term that referred both to defensive keeps and to the groups of closely built stone houses that also played an important strategic role. Because inheritance laws stipulated that seigneurial rights were to be divided equally between all children, male and female, and because the nobles did not consider it beneath them to engage in trade, both in *castels* (fortified villages) and towns, power lay in the hands of a large group of associates who held the lordship in common. These co-seigneurs dominated the less affluent urban families, but were prepared to take their advice, and delegated the running of the town to the magistrates. Authority was thus shared between knights and citizens. The former took precedence, but, unlike the nobles of the north, did not crush the latter with their overweening pride: the townspeople fought with them to defend the collective interest. Equally at home with the written word and as accomplished in debate, knights and citizens shared a common secular culture, based on *cortezia* (courtesy), which was more vigorous than its ecclesiastical counterpart. The political poems of the troubadours, the *sirventes* and the *tensós*, are ample testimony to this. Nobles and townsmen attempted to form an organized body to control disorder in the hinterland. From the tiniest *castelnau* (fortified village) to the great city of Toulouse, they all attempted to subjugate the surrounding countryside to urban power with a combination of bribery and force.

Obviously, the cities had the upper hand over the *castra* because of their wealth and superior defences (with town walls as well as castles built on Roman ruins), to say nothing of the presence there of a bishop, responsible for maintaining the peace of God throughout his diocese. In the course of the twelfth century, this ancient system of security had been perfected in the Vivarais, Gévaudan, Velay and the Rouergue. The bishops gathered the people together periodically to re-enforce their peace-keeping mission, demanding promises of non-aggression from nobles and knights, prayers from the clergy and money from the merchants. Endless deliberations, discussions and legal proceedings were conducted by the lawyers. Finally, all the money for the *pezade* (a tax to fund the common peace) was collected. If there was an alarm, the knights and all 'the men of the area' under their guild banners made a concerted attack on trouble-makers, especially the mercenary companies. Lords could not afford to ignore these powerful municipal organizations, and made a point of calling them to the assemblies over which they presided and including them in the decision-making process. The support of the town was an essential element in the rebuilding of the State in the south.

The process was complicated by the emergence of three centres of political development. One was in Poitou, far to the north, where the Plantagenets applied considerable pressure to establish their authority; but their efforts ran up against revolts in the mountainous regions to the east. They were more successful in the western maritime provinces, but south of

Bordeaux encountered resistance in Gascony; before Toulouse, ancient capital of the Gothic kingdom, they failed completely. This was the second and central focus of political change. The counts of Toulouse were also of Frankish descent, and claimed sovereignty over the dioceses of Périgueux, Cahors, Agen, Albi and Rodez, as well as the Narbonnais and the great cities of Toulouse and St Gilles, an important trading-post for overseas merchants. Beyond the Rhône, they had recovered some of the rights of the marquises of Provence. The dynasty's prestige lay in the memory of their ancestor Raymond, the first count, who had been charged by the Pope with leading the First Crusade. In the reign of Philip Augustus, of course, the count of Toulouse (who was a relative of the king) acknowledged that he was the French king's vassal. But his lands were so far from the capital that he alone had dispensation from attending the king's coronation or solemn courts – in fact, from all outward forms of service. This independence was threatened by the kings of Aragon to the south-west. King Peter II of Aragon was count of Barcelona; his brother held the *comté* of Provence according to Catalan custom, that is, he simultaneously exploited Roman and feudal law, ensuring that power remained strictly in his own hands. In the Iberian peninsula, Peter II adopted the role of Christian champion, fighting the Moors with the king of Castile and inflicting a defeat on them at Las Navas de Tolosa that was no less dazzling than Bouvines. He then attempted to extend his influence north of the Pyrenees. First the *vicomte* of Béarn, the count of Bigorre and the counts of Foix and Comminges, then Trencavel, *vicomte* of Béziers and Carcassonne, all became his vassals. In 1204 he married the daughter of the lord of Montpellier, who – like Philip Augustus – was bigamous. To please Peter II, the Pope refused to legitimize Montpellier's sons: as a result, the daughter was sole heir to this extremely important lordship. Here a fourth element in southern politics is revealed: namely, the religious factor. As in northern France, it was intertwined with secular developments; but here their relationship was very different.

Gregorian reform had exerted a more profound influence on the power-structures of this region, which had witnessed the earliest assemblies of the peace of God. The reforms of the upper echelons of the Church had effectively destroyed the unity of the upper classes, abruptly denying the great families of the region any say in episcopal appointments. Here the Pope was no mere visitor, as he was in Capetian territory: this was also his land, for the *comté* of Mauguio was a fief of the Holy See. In 1204 Innocent III persuaded Peter of Aragon to come to Rome and offer his kingdom on the high altar of St Peter's, receiving it once more only after he had done homage to the Pope for the realm. The Papacy, like any other monarchy of western Europe, was flexing its political muscles by means similar to those employed by the secular powers; but in this case they were employed with far greater consistency and in the context of wider schemes. Southern France, which had been without a king for so long, offered an effective springboard for papal expansion. Here there was no close alliance between the ecclesiastical and the secular arms of government, as there was in the north. Instead, they wrangled over the exercise and limits of their powers. These continual disagreements favoured the spread of religious beliefs which were universally condemned as heretical by the Church. The liberation of the individual conscience from sheep-like conformity, greater concentration by academic theologians on the teachings of the New Testament and more direct lay contact with the Scriptures were significant twelfth-century developments. One consequence was a widespread increase in heretical beliefs of every kind. It is difficult to distinguish between them, because almost all our evidence comes from their persecutors in the established Church. Blinded by zeal, they could not separate the wheat from the chaff. Moreover, members of persecuted sects remained silent under interrogation, or gave only evasive replies. However, it seems certain that the majority of the men and women forced into hiding to escape punishment for heresy were seeking a form of Christian belief that was free from ritual, and a more spiritual way of life. Soon after the year 1000, these priorities were expressed with greater urgency: denying the need for priestly mediation, convinced that man had no right to invoke God in an oath and that sexuality was evil, they were repelled by the notion of God incarnate in human flesh. Their essential preoccupations were little different from those of the reformers within the established Church, and they had been stimulated by the success of ecclesiastical reform. These ideas were reformulated at the beginning of the twelfth century by recalcitrant and independently minded individuals, such as Henry of Lausanne and Peter of Bruys, who preached throughout Provence and Toulouse, burning crucifixes wherever they went.

Nevertheless, most of those who dreamt of a better Church did not go this far. They were horrified above all by material wealth. Clerics and laity renounced all forms of wealth, a gesture which led them to denounce the riches of prelates, as well as the undue influence of contemporary equivalents of the biblical scribes and publicans. This was the attitude of the Waldensians, disciples of Peter Valdès. Their austere life-style emphasized the shortcomings of all churchmen who saw the office(s) they mechanically performed as a lucrative trade. The people admired these *bonshommes* (good men) and listened to them, attracted by their appeal to less formal religious practices and a less complex path to redemption. Nor were they put off by sermons, for the heretical preachers used the same words and images and the same exemplary figures as the churchmen, focusing above all upon Christ the Saviour. In this way small groups grew up, not claiming to be separate from the Church in any sense, but on the contrary, eager to demonstrate that reform from within and a return to the early Church was possible. Their attitudes disturbed the established authorities, however, who harassed them, forcing them to adopt a more intransigent line and declare that it was more important to obey God than earthly authorities. From here it was a small step to clandestine rebellion.

At the same time quite different forms of belief were adopted. These were preached by the Premonstratensian Evervin of Steinfeld in Cologne in 1143. Their origins lay in the East, and contemporaries accurately called adherents to this form of belief '*bougres*' (Bulgars) or Cathars, a Greek word. These were essentially Manichaean heresies, with belief in a second god, of evil and the material world, who was continually struggling with the good god in a combat whose eventual outcome still hung in the balance. These beliefs were quite foreign to Christianity. They were accepted because their supporters used the same vocabulary and even the same allegories as the priests of the Christian Church. They were the somewhat paltry weapons of a new religion which (if we are to believe the documents, of doubtful authenticity, from a council supposedly held at San Feliú de Lauraguais in 1169) intended to become a formally established Church, with sacraments, a hierarchy and its own dioceses and bishops. Thus, at the end of the twelfth century, two principal bodies of heresy were ranged against the established Church. They were carefully distinguished by the theologian Alan of Lille: on the one hand were the Waldensians, on the other the Cathars. In the south of France, the Waldensians attacked the Cathars in defence of Christianity.

Heresy flourished equally in the towns of northern France, where there had been considerable heretical activity since 1135. From the mid-twelfth century, the ecclesiastical authorities were convinced that it posed a real threat to the established Church in Lorraine, the Rhineland and the kingdom of France. In 1153 Pope Eugenius III called on the bishop of Arras to be especially vigilant. Ten years later, Louis VII anxiously asked Pope Alexander III for guidance. The bishops of Nevers and Auxerre did their best to limit what they saw as the harmful influence of preachers and their followers. Once the sources of heretical teaching had been identified, the purifying fire of the stake swept across the French kingdom. But it was only at a later date that these measures were used in the Languedoc, where heresy was more widespread.

Here, as in the north, it spread out from large towns, where merchants (convinced that usury was a crime) were particularly susceptible to preaching on the theme of apostolic poverty. Like Cologne or Lyon, where trade was expanding, Albi and Toulouse were centres of the so-called

Waldensian heresy. It is possible that the urban elites may have sympathized with the more reassuring Cathar beliefs. The *bonshommes* professed to despise money utterly, but this did not prevent them from accepting it or making loans themselves. They persuaded those of their followers who made no claim to lead a 'perfect' life that, whatever they had done, as death approached, they could cleanse themselves of all sins solely by the rite of *consolamentum*, or the laying on of hands. In the countryside the spread of heresy was undoubtedly encouraged by the eagerness with which tithes were exacted by the reformers of the established Church. In Frankish and Burgundian lands (in the north as much as in Aquitaine), regions where the prescriptions of the Carolingian Church had been strictly applied, this levy on the produce of their land was clearly unpopular with the peasantry. Their anger was directed primarily at the tithe barns of ecclesiastical lords in the periodic uprisings that shook the region. Tithes had been collected since time immemorial, however, and the practice was entirely legal.

The situation was very different in the Languedoc and in Provence, where there was no history of tithing. This did not prevent the clergy from levying an equivalent tax (the '*restitution*') from the middle of the twelfth century onwards, a period when trade in agricultural produce was growing, and increasing sums of money devoted to the construction and decoration of ecclesiastical buildings. To justify this imposition, the bishops and abbots did not refer to custom, or even the practices of the Old Testament, but to Roman law. For them the tithe was a symbol of the supreme power claimed by the Roman Church. The strong resistance provoked by these demands was also attributed to heresy.

Nevertheless, it was principally the distinctive political and social structure and secular culture of these regions that made the population so receptive to the doctrines of the Waldensians and willing to protect them from persecution. It also explains why heresy was so strong and difficult to eliminate here. The ruling class was split into two camps. Anything which reduced the temporal power of the Church was automatically supported by rivals, the secular nobility and the knights. There was undoubtedly some justification for the belief of bishops and papal legates that heresy received some support from secular lords. Knightly households and those of the urban patriciate were natural breeding grounds for heresy. Preachers were sure of a warm welcome there; in the course of shared meals, they taught that there was no sacrament of marriage, no need for priests – or at least, not for those whose greed made further inroads into dwindling family fortunes. Women were particularly likely to lend a sympathetic ear: unlike orthodox Christianity, heretical piety did not relegate them to a marginal position: they, too, could be *perfecti*, lay on hands, and transmit the Holy

Spirit. I am not convinced that the position of women here was any worse than in the north; but this is an area which requires more research. However, it is undoubtedly true that women helped to spread religious practices which released them from the lowly position accorded them by the established Church. The close associations between houses squashed together in the *castrum* also played a part, since heretical practice and doctrine could easily spread from the most affluent households to their neighbours. For it was the *castels* (fortified villages), rather than the towns, which proved the most fruitful seed-beds of heresy. The organizers of the Church's counter-offensive soon became aware of this fact, and treated them accordingly.

I have already referred to the vigorous secular culture of these regions, based on free and open discussion. The inhabitants of town and *castel* were accustomed to debating legal matters freely, and now they discussed religious matters with the same lack of inhibition. The distinction between the sacred and the profane was not absolutely clear-cut. Like all other municipal affairs, it was the subject of endless discussion. The people gathered in the market-square to listen to the arguments propounded by both orthodox and heretics, for all the world as if they were listening to opposing sides in a debate between troubadours on a political issue. With the lords of the community presiding, the laity passed judgement. The chronicler William of Puylaurens has left us a lengthy description of one of these meetings, held in 1207 at the *castrum* of Montréal in the Carcassès. The papal legate Peter of Castelnau was on one side, Cathar *perfecti* on the other. 'They disputed for several days before the chosen arbitrators [knights and townsmen], and the two sides put their case in writing before the appointed laymen.' The latter prudently decided not to debate the matter (since it was on the eve of a crusade), and the assembly broke up without any final decision. This appeal to free reason and the explicit conferral of responsibility for the sacred upon individuals who (according to the accepted analysis of society) had no remit in this area are highly significant. It is some measure of the alienation from the established Church experienced by the local community at the beginning of the thirteenth century.

The Church closed ranks in the face of this threat, however. In the second half of the twelfth century, when the exact nature of the menace became clearer, Church leaders realized that it was imperative to take action in the towns. In the countryside the peasants still clung silently to their age-old and ineradicable superstitions, propitiating the supernatural by rites presided over by their priests, as well as in secret rituals which they no doubt considered more effective. The Church employed both word and image in its defence. In about 1170 the great monumental sculpture on the west front of the abbey church of St Gilles was one means by which the incarnation and redemption of Christ, the importance of the cross and the eucharistic sacrament, as well as the power of the apostles and their successors (the bishops), was preached to the people. The majestic tone of the message was like that of a Roman triumphal arch. The Church also realized heresy would have to be fought with argument, as in a lawcourt, and victory would ultimately depend on rhetoric and dialectic. The diocesan schools used the repeated exercise of formal disputation as preparation for the great fight for the minds of men. But it took two generations to hone their weapons and take aim.

At first, Cistercian monks were sent to combat heresy in the south, since they were thought to lead the most 'perfect' life, according to their own rule. But for all their professed poverty, the Cistercians' reputation for driving a hard bargain in the land market and for collecting every *sou* of their tithes told against them. Confident of their superiority, they failed in this task, nevertheless. In the confusion that followed the preaching tours of Henry of Lausanne, St Bernard, the most famous of all Cistercians, arrived on the scene. He had preached in the larger towns, including Toulouse and Albi, where the people had mockingly driven the papal legate away. But he made the mistake of being too arrogant and speaking in terms which his listeners could not understand. His words had no effect whatsoever. The Cistercians who continued the struggle after him went right inside the *castels*, the strongholds of heresy; but they too made little impression. A completely different approach was needed. It came from the orders of canons, who were better trained in preaching and chose to go to the heretical communities as disciples of Jesus – alone, barefoot and totally destitute. The pattern was set by a team of Castilians introduced into the region by the bishop of Osma, and they were followed by the cathedral chapter at Elne. Poor but educated, these new preachers gradually won over the Waldensians. In a great assembly in the palace of the count of Foix at Pamiers they were 'entirely convinced and confounded, together with most of the town's population, especially the poorest. Even the man who had instigated the debate and had himself been favourably disposed towards the Waldensians renounced heresy and put himself and all his goods at the disposal of the bishop of Osma: from that day forward he fought most courageously against heresy.' In the heart of a community of 'poor Catholics', Durand of Osca did likewise, and became the Cathars' most ardent opponent. This return to the offensive was to prove decisive. With the founding of the Dominican order, it heralded a complete renewal of the faith through popular preaching, the renunciation of worldly goods and the rationalization of dogma. The defeat of Catharism followed soon afterwards.

The Church also adopted repressive practices in the fight against heresy. The heretics were breaking the public peace – that is, the peace of God. Consequently, matters of faith (*negocium fidei*) and matters of peace (*negocium pacis*) became confused. The bishops were expected to employ the same sanctions against heretics as they invoked against pillagers – the anathema and the support of armed militias. Traditional peace-keeping methods were re-enforced by the principles of Roman law, in which the late-twelfth-century Popes were exceptionally well versed. They had studied at Bologna, and they applied the law in all its rigour. Those who broke the laws of the Church were deemed guilty of lèse-majesté, punishable by death and confiscation of lands and goods. Innocent III justified these measures, asserting that, 'just as civil law punishes criminals guilty of lèse-majesté by death and dispossession, so the Church cuts off from Christ all those who, straying from the true faith, attack God or his Son, to the great detriment of his divine majesty.'

There were three stages in the development of repressive measures. In 1163 a Church council at Tours defined its field of action against heresy as the southern provinces of the Kingdom. Fourteen years later, Count Raymond V of Toulouse raised the alarm. In a letter to the abbot of Cîteaux, he described how heretical beliefs and practices were rife throughout his lands. He explained lucidly that 'those who accepted heresy believed they were rendering true homage to God', and that it was easy for heresy to gain a foothold in families, where it quickly set women against husband or father. It had some support among the clergy, he went on; the churches were deserted, and 'all the sacraments of the Church count for nothing.' He referred also to the spread of Cathar dualism, which was a bigger problem. He accepted that it was his responsibility, as 'avenger and minister of the wrath of God' to crush the enemies of the true faith. But he confessed he was unequal to the task alone, and requested assistance from his feudal lord, the king of France. A mission led by the abbot of Clairvaux verified the facts. It reported to the Lateran Council of 1179, which had been called by the Church to decide on action against both heresy and brigandage. The pronouncement of a solemn anathema had no effect at all; there was no alternative to the force of the secular arm. On the advice of the bishops, nobles and knights took up arms. During their campaign, they were to enjoy crusading status, with all its immunities. Complete remission of sins was granted to those who fell in battle, as to knights on crusade. The rest would all win two years' indulgence. They were entitled to the confiscated goods of heretics and could reduce them to servitude. Anyone who refused to fight would be excommunicated. Although never given the name 'crusade', this was to all intents and purposes what it was, organized diocese by diocese within the traditional framework of actions for the peace of God.

But in Montpellier it soon became apparent that the knights of the area could not always be relied upon. The lords there were intent on fighting their neighbours, the Trencavel, and had come to terms with the heretics. As in Italy, the Papacy attempted to enlist the support of municipal institutions, binding the town consuls on oath to fight heretical doctrine. But the bishops were reluctant, and the consuls too dependent to free themselves from episcopal control. Then the new Pope, Innocent III, decided to remove from office the suspect prelates at Béziers, Narbonne and Toulouse. He excommunicated the 'pestilential' Raymond VI, who – with the support of his troops – refused to bring his private wars to an end and negotiate the peace that was an indispensable prerequisite for any common action. Innocent III accused him of misusing his God-given reason, employing it instead against God and (which amounted to the same thing) the 'universal Church', since any reasonable man would have the unity of the Church as his prime objective. For the Pope, the fate of the entire Church hung on events in southern France, and all Christendom was affected by them. In 1204, and then again in 1205 and 1207, the Pope pressed armed intervention upon Philip Augustus. He offered the king the same inducement as the Lateran Council had offered local lords: the addition of lands confiscated from the heretical nobles to his own. The turning-point came in January 1208, when the legate Peter of Castelnau was assassinated at St Gilles. The Pope had no doubt that Count Raymond was behind this murder; he and his accomplices were therefore to be 'deprived of their lands so that Catholic inhabitants might replace the banished heretics'. His solution was radical: nothing less than the extermination of heretics by fire and the sword, and the repopulation of the devastated land (forfeited as booty) by true believers.

These true believers were, of course, inhabitants of the kingdom of France. The king refused to play any part in the redirection of the crusading ideal against provinces held from the French crown. Now, for the first time, soldiers of Christ were employed with full crusading status to combat heresy in the very heart of the Christian community. In his reply, Philip Augustus also started to complain about Raymond VI, brother-in-law of King John of England: 'We have received no help from him or his men, although he holds one of the largest baronies of the kingdom.' But his reply to that great legal expert, the Pope, was couched in juridical terms to defend his feudal rights:

As to your intention to offer the count's lands to men who would welcome the opportunity to seize it, the opinion of both clerics and men of practical experience here is that you have no right to take such measures, since you have not condemned the count as a heretic [Raymond VI had in fact been excommunicated as an accomplice of the Cathars, not as a Cathar himself]. If he is a heretic, you should inform us and instruct us to dispose of his land, for it is held from us alone. You have not done this.

Preparations were made for the crusade without the king. Nevertheless, the prelates who journeyed down the Rhône in June 1209 and the lay lords who went with them (the duke of Burgundy and the counts of Nevers, St Pol and Bar) were all French or Burgundian, and the whole question of the faith lay once more in the hands of the Cistercians and a small group of knights from the Ile-de-France obsessed by the crusading ideal. A few years earlier, these men had gone to deliver Jerusalem; but in 1202 the expedition of which they were part had been diverted in Venetian interests, and told to conquer not Palestine, but Zadar (a Christian town in Dalmatia). They alone had adhered to their original goal of delivering the tomb of Christ. When no one followed them, they became disillusioned and bitter. This tough and implacable band of men was led by Simon, lord of Montfort-l'Amaury, vassal of the king of France and 'the most chaste of all those in the service of God, persevering to the very end', together with his kinsmen and household and his Cistercian friends from the abbey of Vaux-de-Cernay, whose lands abutted his own. They immersed themselves totally in this new enterprise, with no thought of pillage or conquest. They considered themselves bound to make reparation for the deflection of the Fourth Crusade by their own steadfast devotion to the cause of God.

Raymond of Toulouse gave satisfaction as they approached. He appeared naked before the abbey church of St Gilles to receive a penitential beating. Absolved, he made haste to join the French army. Now only the Trencavel lordship was available for plunder and this was quickly seized. Béziers fell before Carcassonne on 22 July. The indiscriminate massacre of heretics and orthodox (especially of women and children burnt to death in the cathedral, after the crusaders had challenged God to acknowledge his own) is remembered to this day. The atrocities were blamed on 'vagrants and barefoot ruffians, scantily clad and armed with clubs', the brigands and their unruly bands, whose services the crusaders had seen fit to employ. The *vicomte* of Narbonne died in prison on 10 November. He was buried with ceremony, for it was important that everybody should know that the lord of the conquered cities was dead. Both the duke of Burgundy and the count of Nevers were offered his lands, but they declined since, now that their vow was fulfilled, they were in a hurry to return. A commission of two bishops, four knights and the papal legate handed these lands over to Simon of Montfort, who remained with only thirty knights, a group of the most faithful friends, dedicated to the overthrow of heresy.

All around they saw heretics defying them from the high walls of the *castels*. The crusaders decided on a policy of systematic destruction –

reducing Minerve, Termes, Lavaur one after the other – and purging them of heresy, 'setting the cross of Christ at the top of the tower' as a sign of victory (above Simon of Montfort's banner, since it was Christ who had overcome the wicked in their fastnesses) and cheerfully burning *perfecti* a dozen or a hundred at a time. They also burnt the local lords, for the crusaders did not doubt for a moment that they were also guilty of heresy. It was arduous work. But the knights of Christ employed good Brabançon mercenaries and powerful siege-engines. A money-lender from Montpellier was responsible for raising the necessary funds. From the summer of 1210 onwards, re-enforcements arrived, some motivated by a pure desire to serve God, others by the promise of indulgences. Preaching throughout France, Gascony and Aquitaine mobilized the support of bishops, knights and barons. It was also particularly effective in the Rhineland and around Liège: fanatics from these areas arrived on foot, bringing with them a criminal element whose motives were altogether more suspect. The idea was gaining ground that henceforth it would be the poor who put an end to this evil 'by divine decree' – and this at a time when, in the kingdom of France, the 'children' (casualties of agricultural expansion) were forming into bands and wandering they knew not where, at a word from a rag-clad visionary, towards the perfect land of a millenarian Utopia.

In 1210 there was another attack on Raymond VI. His lands and regalian power were seized. Simon of Montfort took them, and his brother Guy those of the count of Foix, who had also been excommunicated. The papal legate, abbot of Cîteaux, was appointed archbishop of Narbonne, while the abbot of Vaux-de-Cernay became bishop of Carcassonne. A *parlement* (similar to the councils held to establish the peace of God) held at Pamiers in the winter of 1212 was attended by large numbers of clerics, knights and townspeople. They assembled 'so that good customs could be instilled, the filth of heresy swept away and sound practices established, in order that the orthodox form of Christian worship should be established, together with peace and security in the temporal sphere'. They promulgated statutes that had been prepared in great detail by twelve lawyers, two bishops, a Templar and a Hospitaller, four knights from the kingdom of France and four knights and two townspeople from the immediate region: 'Both French and native representatives had been elected to allay all suspicion.' The succession practices of northern France were introduced for both nobles and commoners; in particular, the stringent French customs relating to the holding of fiefs. For ten years, no heiress to a castle in the area was allowed to marry a local man without Montfort's authorization; but no restrictions affected marriage to knights from northern France. The French were therefore to replace through marriage the indigenous aristocracy of southern France in the way envisaged by the author of the

Geste des seigneurs d'Amboise (*History of the Lords of Amboise*) when he imagined the Merovingian past.

Then the political situation changed completely. The Pope was once more preoccupied with the Holy Land, and reconciliation became a primary goal. He turned to his vassal Peter II, king of Aragon, for support. Flushed with the glory of his victory over the Spanish Muslims, Peter came to Toulouse. The consuls of the city and the count did him homage, as well as the count's small son, who was betrothed to the king's daughter. The king took possession of the county of Toulouse and had charge of his young son-in-law; the boy had not been implicated in any charges of heresy and Peter promised Innocent III that he would instruct him in the true faith. This sudden change in papal policy and the new feudal relations in the south called into question the rights of the king of France. Philip Augustus gave his son permission to join the crusade, in order to defend these rights. But before Muret on 13 September 1213, God showed his favour to the warriors who fought for his cause, as he did at Bouvines the following year. Simon of Montfort and his knights, duly sanctified by confession, mass and the benediction of a fragment of the true cross, defeated the king of Aragon, the counts of Foix and Comminges and the townspeople of Toulouse in pitched battle. The defiled Peter II (who had spent the previous night with a woman) suffered a worse fate than the Emperor Otto, and was killed in the battle.

By the spring of 1215, Prince Louis had discharged his crusading obligation, and Montfort came to meet him. Together they made a formal entry into Montpellier, Narbonne and finally Toulouse. When the forty days of campaign (to which his crusade vows bound him) had elapsed, Louis listened to what the papal legate had to say and then departed. He had come as a pilgrim, like the rest, not as a conqueror. After the battle of Muret, Philip Augustus could count on Simon of Montfort to defend the interests of the French crown in the south. As for the Pope, he claimed that the lands belonging to heretics had been confiscated in the name of St Peter; a general council was to be held at the Lateran to decide their fate. Innocent III hoped that they would be restored to Raymond VI and held as a fief of the Holy See. The prelates refused to agree to this and the inheritance of the counts of Toulouse was divided. Those portions which lay within the Empire were to remain in the care of the Papacy, to be restored to Raymond VII when he was of age and 'if he showed himself worthy of pardon'. The rest, 'from the Rhône to the sea' (in other words, as far as the Pyrenees), were to be put in the hands of Simon of Montfort, so that he could receive lordships from those 'who had the right to yield them to him'. He lost no time in doing homage for these lands to the king of France.

Montfort believed that he would be able to hold Toulouse from the castle of Narbonne, where he had taken up residence. In the event, Toulouse proved untenable. This was not because of heresy, but because of the town's loyalty to its natural lord and its detestation of these strangers from the north, sentiments which were shared by the whole region. Toulouse drove out Simon of Montfort and opened its gates to the young Raymond. When Montfort was besieging the city in 1218, he was killed by a rock from a siege-engine. The following year Louis of France left for another forty days of crusading, massacring the inhabitants of Marmande on the way. He appeared before the walls of Toulouse and departed again: he had not come to win territories for himself or the French crown, any more than on his first expedition. Philip Augustus had refused to accept the rights that Simon's son, Amaury, proposed to cede to him. But in 1224, when Amaury himself arrived dispirited in Paris with his sixty remaining knights and renewed his offer, Philip's son – now King Louis VIII – accepted. At the same time, Louis took possession of the fiefs that the barons' court had sequestrated from John of England twenty-two years earlier. He seized La Rochelle, the Saintonge, the Limousin and Périgord without any difficulty. His knights even penetrated into Aquitaine as far as St Emilion without problems. Now that his hands were free (and motivated also by the desire to have his sovereign rights acknowledged in southern France), Louis VIII resolved to stamp out the Cathar heresy, which he knew was still being preached openly, and led a third crusade against the excommunicated Raymond VII. The Pope gave him permission to levy a tenth on the revenues of the French clergy, and promised to defend France against an English attack.

Like those of his father and grandfather in the Mâconnais, Louis' expedition to the south was not a strenuous campaign. The nobles of the Narbonnais rushed to pay homage, and the king did not hesitate to make his way along the left bank of the Rhône (in imperial territory), brandishing the French sword of justice. But his progress was unexpectedly checked at Avignon. The power of the great urban communities on the other side of the river had grown. Bargaining with the count of Toulouse for the price of their support, they had acquired new privileges and their Italian-style politics had made them tough little States. The knights and patricians who had recently supplanted the tradespeople in the magistrature made terms with Louis VIII: he could come inside the town walls with a small escort, while his army crossed the bridge. But when they saw the crusaders, the townspeople took fright, afraid of suffering the same fate as Béziers, and shut the gates. The king of France was bound on oath to chastise all rebel towns. Accordingly, he laid siege to Avignon for three months, under a leaden sky and plagued by hordes of mosquitoes. Finally he broke the town's strong defences; restraining his men from pillaging and satisfying himself with promises and 6,000 marks of silver, he was able to continue on his way without further difficulty. But on his return, he died of dysentery in the Auvergne, in November 1226. If William of Puylaurens is to be believed, Philip Augustus foretold that his delicate son would succumb to the malarial fevers of the south.

His place was taken by a valiant warrior, the lord of Beaujeu, who continued to fight for the faith. Raymond VII came to an agreement with Louis' widow, Blanche of Castile, now regent of France. On Good Friday 1229, the count and his supporters (who had also been found guilty of heresy) took part in a ceremony of atonement in the cathedral of Notre-Dame at Paris. Disinherited because of his involvement with Catharism, he acknowledged that he had lost all the rights enjoyed by his ancestors. But it was agreed that, since the count's penitence had cleansed him of all sin, the king of France (in his role as *patronus ecclesiae*, protector of the Church) would cede him lands in the dioceses of Toulouse, Agen, Rodez and Cahors by feudal grant, as long as he showed himself to be 'a good defender of the Church'. The king would keep the lordships of Trencavel in his own hands, together with all the other lands held by the counts of Toulouse on the west side of the Rhône, principally Beaucaire, Nîmes and St Gilles.

The lands were transferred with due ceremony, and the terms of this agreement are evidence of the inextricable intermingling of religion and what we today call politics. The fifteen-year-old king who received their homage was the hand of God on earth. God disposed, and it was his will that his enemies (increasingly arrogant because of their regional resistance to the invading crusaders) should be overcome. The Capetian king and his vassal Raymond VII agreed to make it their absolute priority to bring the fight of good against evil to a successful conclusion in each one of the lands in their control.

In our youth, at the outset of our reign [proclaimed Louis IX in an ordinance promulgated in the diocese of Nîmes] for the honour of God who had given us the highest honour upon earth, we ensured that his Church (which had been troubled for so long) should be honoured and led to the true faith . . . that those who had been excommunicated should be reconciled in accordance with the strict canon of the Church, and, if they were rebellious, at the end of a year they should be forcibly restored to the unity of the Church.

At Paris, the count of Toulouse had sworn to adopt a similar course of action. He would expel heretics and their sympathizers from his lands, sparing neither vassals, relatives or friends. He would instruct his officers (*bailes*) to unearth heretics everywhere, offering anyone who helped to discover a heretic the inducement of an annual rent of two marks for the first two years and after that one mark in perpetuity, 'and likewise for each heretic, if they took several'. The Church would recover her former power, collect tithes and first fruits in peace and, as a sign of her victory over heresy, build cathedrals like those in northern France, whose high towers and beautiful decoration celebrated the triumph of orthodoxy over pernicious doctrine. Raymond VII gave 4,000 marks for the foundation of a university at Toulouse (again, on the northern pattern); four masters of theology, two masters of canon law, six masters of the liberal arts and two rhetoricians would come from the Paris schools to provide a sound education for orthodox clergy. The system of repression had finally been perfected.

In 1184 the bishops were told to travel through their dioceses and judge notorious heretics on the spot. In 1199 and 1206 Innocent III had particularly instructed them not to rely upon public rumour, but to make their own investigations. In 1229 a provincial council held at Toulouse laid down how such an inquiry could most effectively be carried out.

In each parish a priest and three laymen are to be appointed to make diligent inquiries after heretics, to search houses and any suspicious cellars, one by one, and make a thorough investigation right up to the tiniest attic rooms and in all possible hiding-places. If they discover any heretics, or their supporters and protectors, they are to take every precaution to ensure that they cannot escape, and then denounce them with all speed before the archdeacon or the bishop, the local lord or his officer.

It was for the ecclesiastical authorities to judge them with due formality. Those who returned to the true faith of their own free will were to wear two prominent crosses, one on the right side and one on the left, in a different colour from their clothing; in addition, they had to have a deed of reconciliation from the bishop. As for the recalcitrant, 'their penance was imprisonment'. All believers, from youths over fourteen and girls over twelve, were to swear 'loyally to denounce heretics' and confess and receive communion three times a year in order to avoid suspicion. 'The laity were not to possess any book of Scripture, with the exception of the Psalter and the divine office, and these were not to be in the vernacular.' In 1233 the new orders of mendicant friars (followers of St Dominic and St Francis) were entrusted with 'the inquisition into heretical depravity'. The mendicant orders had emerged from the turmoil unleashed by the challenge of heresy, and the Pope could place virtually absolute trust in them. The inquisitors did their work very satisfactorily. In Toulouse between May and July 1246, they sentenced 134 individuals to wear crosses and 28 to life imprisonment. For a generation, they battled with the law of silence and the loyalties of family and neighbourhood, made all the stronger by humiliation and defeat. They also had to contend with the strong sense of regional identity which had forced the Parisian masters sent to the new University of Toulouse to pack their bags and leave. For a long while, force of arms gave the *castels* the upper hand. The last armed resistance occurred in 1242, when four inquisitors were killed as they went through Avignonnet. The murderers took refuge in Montségur, which fell two years later. From then on, heresy was slowly driven out of the towns into the surrounding countryside, then pushed further and further back into the mountain valleys. We know it still had a hold in remote villages such as Montaillou on the eve of the fourteenth century.

The peace concluded at Paris in 1229 joined Carcassonne, Beaucaire and the neighbouring region to the French royal domain. The institutions of the Capetian State were stronger; and the communications system sufficiently improved, so that it no longer seemed fanciful to govern such distant regions from the Ile-de-France. The French kings did not come to the area any more than they had in the past. They delegated their powers to the seneschals established by Simon of Montfort, who governed everything from their court, which was the exact counterpart of the royal court in Paris and similarly endowed with legal and financial experts.

These lands had been appropriated by the French crown because the kings of France wanted to be personally involved in the eradication of heresy, and because it seemed essential to have a bastion of support against the possible treachery of Raymond VII. These possessions also secured access to the sea, and that was very important; for the royal household dreamt less of annexation than of another crusade for the deliverance of Jerusalem. In any case, no one would have had any intention of seizing the entire patrimony of the counts of Toulouse, which had passed, as the direct outcome of a successful holy war, into God's hands. As God's earthly representative, the king was free to act as he wished, but merely contented himself with splitting up the great principality and linking most of it more closely to the French crown, but without any thought of annexation. Of the four dioceses he held in fee, Raymond was to possess that of Toulouse for his lifetime only. After his death it would revert to his daughter, his only legitimate child, who was betrothed to one of Louis VIII's sons. Only the descendants of this projected union would hold these lands: Jeanne of Toulouse and her descendants would succeed to all the lands of her ancestors if her father were to die without a son. She was then eight years old, and was jealously guarded at the French court until she reached child-bearing age. In 1237 she married Alfonso, one of the king's brothers. No one could have foreseen that Raymond VII would not remarry, or that Jeanne would be barren. She and her husband both died in 1271; purely by chance the lineage of which she was the last representative 'was wiped off the face of the earth'; and the entire Languedoc reverted to the French crown. The monarchical State was now in a position to absorb these lands; forty years earlier it had not been. Who could have conceived in their wildest dreams of anything other than a conglomerate of autonomous principalities, each joined to the kingdom by feudal contract and the much stronger ties of blood? Who could have envisaged the royal domain as anything other than a restrained and compact institution that could be easily administered by the king's servants? No one could have foreseen the annexation of Toulouse, much less planned it in 'imperialistic' terms. In 1229 national institutions were not sufficiently developed to sustain such designs, although in 1226 the process had gone far enough for Louis VIII to appoint his wife regent of France unopposed, when his oldest son was only twelve years old.

In the eleventh and twelfth centuries women had been of immense political importance. They bore children; they brought their lineage and territorial claims into their husbands' houses; and, when they were widowed, their sons asked respectfully for their advice. Their role was a passive one, however, facilitating the alliances which determined the fate of lordships quite as much as wars. As a result of the improved position of women at the end of the twelfth century, it became common to see a woman performing homage in the absence of her husband or father. She also received homage in the name of any son not yet of age, and managed the day-to-day business of his lands under the supervision of the lord appointed the boy's guardian. The place of several absent barons was taken by their wives at the coronation of Louis IX. Nevertheless, the arrangement in favour of Blanche of Castile was less a reflection of the higher status of women than that of royalty.

Since she wore a crown, the queen of France was no mere pawn in the marriage game. Her image corresponded to that of the Virgin in the tympanum of cathedrals, holding on her lap the infant God incarnate. Moreover, her husband – at the top of the feudal pyramid – had only God as his lord. God alone, therefore, could be the guardian of her young son, delegating the responsibility to one of his highest servants. So while Philip Augustus was crusading in the Holy Land, the archbishop of Rheims and the queen mother were guardians of Prince Louis, whose own mother had died in 1190. In 1226 there was the Albigensian Crusade and it was the turn of the cardinal of Sant' Angelo, the papal legate, to take God's place beside Blanche of Castile. He was a great help to her in these early years. But still more vital support came from the knights and clerics of the royal household, a tightly knit group controlling the offices of the various functions of the court, where ecclesiastical office was transmitted from uncle to

nephew and secular office from father to son. They were all descendants of
Walter of Nemours and related to the families of Clément and Cornut who,
in the space of four generations, produced four archbishops, ten bishops,
ten canons of Notre-Dame or St Martin at Tours (the two most important cathedrals of the kingdom) and fourteen chamberlains or marshals.
Henceforth, this tightly knit group of men protected the royal family
and was strong enough to sustain it in periods of stress. This was what
happened during the minority of Louis IX. Taking advantage of the
situation, the nobility attempted to loosen the shackles with which the
monarchy had imperceptibly bound them. The knights of the royal domain
and the townspeople brought the young king to the safety of Paris, to keep
him out of rebel hands, and here the queen mother held sway, surrounded
by the households of her husband and father-in-law. Good servants were
the surest bastion of feminine fragility.

The dead king had settled the succession in 1225 to ensure the continued
peace of the realm. Her inexhaustible fecundity was Blanche of Castile's
only fault. No fewer than five of her sons had survived the perils of
childhood. The youngest, Philip Dagobert, was destined for the Church.
Following what was established practice in all the principalities of the
kingdom – and which only the accident of birth had prevented from being
applied to the Capetian inheritance since the reign of Philip I – Louis VIII
divided the kingdom into four parts. The oldest received the crown of
France, all the gold and silver in the tower of the Louvre and the lands of
his ancestors, the dukes of Francia, together with Normandy. The second
son, Robert, came into Artois, inherited from his grandmother, with the
proviso that if he died without male heirs the fief was to revert to the
crown. Then there were the recent acquisitions: Anjou and Maine went to
the third son (he died in the event, and it was Charles, the sixth and
posthumous son, who eventually received this portion); Poitou and the
Auvergne went to the fourth, Alfonso, the future husband of Jeanne of
Toulouse. One after another, as they reached the age of majority, the
brothers took possession of these legacies, the portions that later began to
be known as 'apanages' (appanages), 'dependent on the crown of France'.
These grants of land in no way weakened the position of the crown. The
territories that had been shared in this way were still bound to it by feudal
contract, and those who held them remained closely allied to the crown.
Henceforth they alone were entitled to bear the royal fleurs-de-lis on their
coats of arms, and the authority of the oldest was accepted without
question in this austere and solemn family. In an anecdote about the
foundation of the Cistercian abbey of Royaumont, which relates how Louis
IX made his brothers carry blocks of stone, they appear to have been
entirely co-operative. This anecdote accurately reflects the harmony of

a family governed according to the precepts of a patriarchal morality, which underpinned the growth of the monarchy throughout the thirteenth century.

Louis IX respected the same principles in government; he was guided less by the narrow precepts traditionally ascribed to his mother's influence than by the example of his grandfather, Philip Augustus, to whose memory he was devoted. It fell to him to perfect the ideology of kingship that had emerged after the battle of Bouvines. Most importantly, he enhanced the prestige of the sacred French monarchy by his own probity and personal sanctity, which were much less suspect than those with which contemporaries had sought to endow Philip Augustus. He also employed every possible symbolic means to enhance royal power. Himself a shining example of *prudhomie*, combining the virtues of piety, wisdom and valour, literate, and constantly reading the Bible in his chamber, Louis IX had the *Ordo* (the French coronation liturgy) altered. The ritual of dubbing to knighthood was inserted between the triple promise (when the future king swore to uphold the 'true peace' by 'impartial arbitration') and the anointing, as an expression of the indissoluble link between the crown and chivalry.

In 1240 Louis IX acquired another crown, the crown of thorns worn by Christ on the cross. He placed it for all eternity in the very heart of the Sainte-Chapelle in Paris, the most splendid of all reliquaries. The king spent colossal sums on the magnificent setting for this vital symbol of monarchical power in the new chapel in his palace on the Ile-de-la-Cité. At the same time, theorists of civil law were refining their theories of monarchical power. One of them, John of Blanot (a clerk of humble origins from the Mâconnais), stated positively that the king had the right to demand service from his sub-vassals regardless of the wishes of their immediate lord. He maintained that these men were summoned to serve 'the public good . . . in the name of their country (*patrie*)' – by which he did not mean their immediate region, but the kingdom. Moreover, for Blanot (a Burgundian who ended up as the *official* of Lyon, in charge of the bishop's court), this was not France, synonymous with the kingdom of the Franks, but with the 'kingdom of Gaul'.

The great encyclopedia of human knowledge that Louis IX commissioned from his Dominican librarian, Vincent of Beauvais, began as a world history; but it was also a history of a dynasty, because he was in no doubt that the Capetian kings stood at the centre of the world stage. In it, the author demonstrates how both the prophecy of St Valery and that of the return of the crown of France to the descendants of Charlemagne had been fulfilled. To demonstrate that the rights of Louis VIII's descendants were guaranteed in the sight of God, Louis IX decided to rearrange the royal tombs at St Denis. At the same time, Abbot Matthew of Vendôme was collating all the texts describing the great deeds of the kings of France in a single manuscript, which became known as the *Grandes Chroniques de France* (*Great Chronicles of France*). The abbey church had been completely rebuilt in the Gothic style, which filled the interior with light. Here Louis IX had four great, intricately carved tombs built. There was one for Dagobert, facing the grave of the martyred St Denis; one for Charles the Bald, in the middle of the choir (these were the Merovingian Dagobert and Carolingian Charles who had given their names to two of the king's brothers). Finally, there were the tombs of Philip Augustus and Louis VIII. In 1267 the tombs of all the Merovingian and Carolingian kings of France (including Charles Martel, who was never actually king) were placed on the north side of the choir, those of the Capetians on the south. Space was made in front of this double row for three tombs for the most recent descendants of this triple lineage: Louis VIII in the centre, with his father on one side and on the other a tomb which would ultimately be Louis IX's final resting-place. This arrangement was intended to make it dazzlingly clear to the whole world that there had been a dramatic change in the government of France under Philip Augustus, heralding the birth of the French State.

13

The Thirteenth Century

Long after his death, the subjects of the king of France dreamed of another age of 'Monseigneur Saint Louis' (My Lord St Louis): they saw the reign of Louis IX as the golden age of universal happiness. Memory deceived them, however. Throughout his reign there had been well-documented epidemics and chronic food shortages, which quickly weakened the steady growth responsible for the flourishing economy of the previous century. There had been a continual increase in the numbers of workers crushed by the rich in towns and cities, as well as rural areas. The impoverishment of the lower classes was the price of building the last of the French cathedrals. The confidence they expressed was entirely illusory. The great flood of liquid capital that washed into the towns on the last waves of economic progress was just as deceptive, although town governments could draw on it without too much difficulty for all their needs. Scaled down and fine-tuned, the machinery of government acquired its final form during this period of affluence. Architecture that had previously been spontaneous and innovative froze into cold and predictable patterns in the course of this reign, just as the hitherto flexible body of customary law became encased in a rigid logical structure. At the very time when the Dominican Albertus Magnus was teaching 'nature is reason' in Paris and the Franciscan Bonaventura that 'reason is the natural image of the Creator', Louis IX (according to Joinville's account of a discussion with the bishop of Auxerre) was urging reason in the face of the Papacy's unreasonable demands. Admittedly, he cited God as his primary authority, and the most important instruction he gave to his heir was to love God, since God would reveal the wise course of action and love of God saves man from mortal sin. And so the dual symbols of reason and the love of God overshadowed the reign of Louis IX.

The king's rule was based on love for his feudal lords. He relied on this to control the entire kingdom, and did not hesitate to reduce his own powers in order to strengthen the nobility, whom he wanted to be broadly and securely based. He did in fact increase their power. Because King Henry III of England (son of King John) had finally become his vassal and paid him homage in the garden of the royal palace at Paris in December 1259, Louis IX decided to restore to him a large part of the lands in south-western France which he and his father had conquered, to be held as a fief in return for 'appropriate service'. Many of his companions-in-arms disapproved of this step. Their views were ignored because of the king's passionate desire for peace and his belief in a system defined in the *Livre de justice et de plaids* (*Book of Justice and of Pleas*), where it was stated that 'The king should not hold land from any other lord'; 'Dukes, counts, *vicomtes* and lords may hold land from each other and become another's man, saving the dignity of the king, which overrides all other feudal ties.' 'Castellans, vavasours, citizens and villeins are all subordinate to the king's men, and all things are in the king's hands.'

It is no coincidence that these quotations are from a lawyer, because the extension of monarchical power was principally the work of jurists in the king's pay. They were charged in his name to 'hold his lands according to local custom'. However, these customs were 'for the most part poor and antiquated', as Peter of the Fontaines, *bailli* of the Vermandois, put it in the *Conseils* that he wrote at this period for Louis' heir, Philip. Judges consequently considered themselves authorized to make decisions accord-ing to their 'will and reason'. For reason, which (as Cicero puts it) lives in man like a spark of divine intelligence, allows him to recognize the law which reflects our true nature and to act for 'the common good'. The judges gradually forged French customary law by eliminating elements in the body of custom (preserved in common memory) which did not seem to them 'reasonable', as defined by canon and civil law texts. This reaffirmed the king's prerogatives over allods (naturally inherited freeholdings not subject to any fedual superior), as well as fedual tenures; and people began to believe that it was only from the crown that allods could be held as fiefs.

Roman law, taught at the University of Orléans, affirmed that the Capetian king was 'Emperor in his kingdom'. The coinage was one of the clearest manifestations of his full sovereignty. An ordinance drawn up in 1263 by a council of merchants from Paris, Orléans, Sens, Provins and Laon laid down that the king's coin was to be the only legal currency in his domain and in the lands of those nobles who had no hereditary right to strike coins, and it was to be acknowledged legal tender everywhere. Three years later, the royal mint issued the large silver coins (worth one *sol tournois*) demanded by high finance, besides some purely symbolic gold coins on the Byzantine model, proclaiming the French king's imperial power.

Royal sovereignty did not only dominate lordships: it also penetrated them. The king's agents sought to extend royal power as far as possible, since this enhanced their own prestige and influence. They encroached on ecclesiastical privilege, confident in this instance of noble support. In 1264 the barons could be heard to protest against the 'false humility' of these 'sons of serfs who, once in holy orders, judge free men and the fiefs of free men according to their own law'. They recalled that 'the country had not been conquered by clerical arrogance, but by the blood of warriors.' And when, in about 1255, the bishop of Lodève complained of the presence of 'the seneschal, *baile*, *viguiers*, judges and other officers of the court of the lord king issuing summonses, investigating crimes, levying illegal taxes by force and intimidation, claiming the right to free passage' through lands under ecclesiastical jurisdiction, the nobility congratulated themselves upon these extensions of lay power. But they were not slow to complain when they were similarly affected, for lay jurisdiction was subject to comparable encroachments. For all his devotion to Louis IX, the lord of Joinville declined to join the king on a second crusade, declaring that royal officers had exploited his earlier absence in the Holy Land and impoverished his people.

Louis IX was nevertheless motivated by 'a burning desire for justice', convinced that his coronation had been ordained by God so that, like a new Solomon, he could ensure the rule of equity throughout the kingdom. The picture of the king seated beneath an oak-tree at Vincennes and decreeing that even the humblest should come to him in search of justice is ingrained in the French national memory. This fictitious image perfectly illustrates the king's own concept of the function of kingship, which prompted the court to organize itself around the single most important element, the king's Parlement, scene of speeches and judicial debates. Relegated to the *chambre des comptes* (chamber of accounts), those members of the royal household responsible for finance were superseded by legal experts, the masters of the Parlement, the French royal court of appeal. For their part, the lawyers received robes and liveries from the king's own hand on the appointed day, as well as wages, and carried out their task with enthusiasm. They were all deeply convinced that judgement was a sacred task. They despatched knights and clerics to investigate the *baillis*, who now resided within their areas of authority. If it was found that sentences passed there were clearly 'contrary to the custom of the land', it was the duty of the king, 'whose responsibility it was to maintain and enforce these customs', to redress miscarriages of justice. As a result of these inquiries, people became used to appealing to the Paris Parlement, where the '*dits*' (rulings) had been carefully recorded in registers of parchment since 1254. Nevertheless, the king believed he had to do more than this to fulfil the obligations of his coronation oath. When he was preparing himself, body and soul, for an expedition to the Holy Land in 1254, the king ordered an inquisition. His concern was not with the search for heretics, which he knew to be in good hands. His aim was the total reform of government throughout the kingdom, to the furthermost borders of distant Languedoc, putting an end to the abuses of those who rendered justice in his name and dismissing corrupt officials from office. This investigation was not entrusted to his own household officials, but to men of God, Dominicans and Franciscans, who were the spiritual brothers of those responsible for flushing out the Cathars and restoring orthodox belief. For Louis IX, the purge of his judiciary was a 'matter of faith' just as much as the Albigensian Crusade.

He took the cross in 1244, at the age of thirty, after an illness and inspired by a vision which he had seen as he lay in a coma. It has been estimated that he spent 100,000 *livres* on the undertaking, about four times the annual revenue of the kingdom: a quarter came from the towns, and the Church provided almost all the rest. At St Denis on 12 June 1248, the king took up the pilgrim's staff and scrip, raised the *oriflamme* and went barefoot, first to Notre-Dame and then to St Antoine, before leaving for the coast. St Gilles was now silted up and could not be used as a port. Embarkation took place at Aigues-Mortes, at the very edge of the kingdom, which had been especially created for the purpose. What happened on the crusade – the great adventure of the Nile Delta, all the adversities they suffered, the massacre at Mansourah, the king's capture and the ransom they had to pay the Saracens – all these events are best read in Joinville's marvellous eyewitness account, *Vie de St Louis* (*The Life of St Louis*). When Louis returned from crusade six years later, he was unrecognizable. Defeat and the long journey through the Holy Land (where the sacred places were still in the hands of the infidel), the sermon on justice he heard soon after disembarkation preached by the Franciscan Hugh of Barjois ('the madman of God') had all effected a true conversion in the king and completely transformed him. He remained penitent for the rest of his life. The queen mother had been a great supporter of the Cistercians (building Maubuisson, Lys and Chaalis), and before his departure for the East, the king had patronized this order more than any other. On his return, this too changed.

A room looking onto the church was especially reserved for him at the abbey of Royaumont. From now on, he lived surrounded by mendicant friars, who guided his reading and directed his devotions. His devotional life was not in itself out of the ordinary. The king's devotions were simply on a grander scale: he collected (for example) a large number of reliquaries, which on feast-days he liked to carry on his shoulders, lingering at the services. All the kings of France before him had given hospitality to the poor, but Louis fed far more of them – 130 each day in the royal household, 13 in the hall and 3 at his own table. It was above all in his personal life that the king followed St Francis in his imitation of the suffering Christ. He never smiled and was poorly dressed, rejecting the personal adornment he had loved in his youth. Tending lepers with his own hands, he carried out his kingly duties with an unquenchable zeal.

It was almost as if he wanted to afflict his people with the same bodily mortifications that he applied to his own flesh, to strengthen them and better prepare them for the renewed struggle with Islam. The ordinances issued in the last years of the reign of Louis IX were instruments of penitence, designed to put an end to the evil which the king believed he had not previously fought with sufficient vigour, which explained why his crusade had not found favour with God and had failed. These measures were taken 'for the common profit', 'for the benefit of his subjects' or, above all, 'to destroy sin' and 'for the better reformation of the kingdom'. More reform, in other words. At the same time, certain theologians at the University of Paris were teaching that the world was entering a third and final stage – the age of the Spirit, after that of the Father and of the Son – which would bring all men to the pure state exemplified in the monastic life. They specified an exact date for this change; one which was not too far distant. The French king worked for this same goal, issuing bans similar to those of two and a half centuries before, when bishops and rulers gathered round shrines in anticipation of the end of the world in the year 1000.

Continual echoes of the movement for the peace of God have run like a counterpoint through our political narrative. They experienced a near-resurrection in the reign of Louis IX. Driven by divine zeal, the king wanted the kingdom to be cleansed from sin. In Louis IX's eyes, his kingdom bore a threefold taint – with bloodshed, money and worldly pleasure – and he attempted to introduce measures to control each of these areas. First of all, it was defiled by wanton bloodshed. The judicial duel was therefore banned in the kingdom of France (in the hope that this example would be followed elsewhere), to reduce the 'risk of losing life or limb' and to prevent bloodshed. 'He suppressed trial by battle, putting oral and written evidence in its place.' Louis IX still dreamt of achieving the impossible and abolishing private war (war between Christian princes and nobles) for ever. He called on his officers to ensure the suspension of hostilities for forty days, so that tempers could cool and, guided by the terms of the treaty, the protagonists could settle their differences by discussion. Louis IX was also keenly aware of the corruption caused by money and all those who handled it – Lombards, Jews and other money-lenders were to leave. The king ordained that they should be expelled, an equally unrealistic measure. Finally, he saw the kingdom stained with worldly frivolity, fornication and blasphemy. Games of chance were proscribed, loose women confined to a specific quarter in the towns, and severe (but quite unenforceable) punishments were ordained for those who 'dared to use bad language' and 'swore by God, Our Lady or the saints'.

Powerless to bring paradise to his own lands, Louis IX went to find it. To the amazement of his household, he took the cross a second time and died before Tunis, a martyr to the faith. As one of the witnesses in the canonization proceedings said, 'As king he not only watched over the safety of his subjects and things corporeal in the government of the kingdom, but he was quite extraordinarily concerned with the salvation of his subjects' souls... so that he exercised priesthood like a king and kingship like a priest.' St Louis was the very embodiment of '*rex et sacerdos*' (king and priest) of his coronation oath. All this was confirmed by the Pope: his verdict was that Louis IX had first achieved self-control, repressing sensual desires by the exercise of reason, and then founded the rule of his subjects on justice and equity. Louis IX had enhanced Capetian prestige as much as Philip Augustus, through his exercise of reason and fervent love of God. Since his relatives occupied all the most important political offices, the canonization of Louis IX raised the reputation of the entire French royal family, both blood-relations and descendants. Charles of Anjou, king of Sicily, underlined this point, when he pressed for similar recognition for their two other brothers, Robert of Artois and Alfonso of Poitiers, one of whom had died on crusade, the other from its effects. Louis' son, Robert of Clermont, changed his name: he had previously styled himself 'son of the king of France'; henceforth he was known as 'son of my Lord St Louis', whose personal sanctity permanently sanctified the French monarchy.

On the death of St Louis in 1270, the shift in perspective which was gradually to overturn the entire social order became apparent, reflected first in contemporary perceptions of the world. The people of western Christendom discovered that the world was not only much bigger, but also – and this was more important – much more varied and less securely founded than they had imagined. Venetian traders in search of rare luxury goods (such as the silks, furs and spices without which no aristocratic celebration was complete) and the mendicant friars sent by the king of France to bring Christianity to the lands beyond Islam moved along the silk routes as far as the coast of China, explorers in an entire new world. It is questionable whether the news of the discovery of America two and a half centuries later was any more disturbing than the accounts of these travellers. At the same time, scholars discovered previously untranslated texts of Aristotle (the *Metaphysics*) and Averroës' commentary; they were both disturbed and amazed by the grandeur of a conceptual framework whose perfectly adjusted components presented an irrefutable contradiction of the tenets of the Christian faith. And while the Mongol hordes (who could easily have been mistaken for the people of Gog and Magog, forerunners of the Antichrist) approached Cracow, in the affluent princely households, where recent developments in taxation and credit finance ensured an extremely affluent life-style, noble society learnt that on the edges of the world there were ordered civilizations with rulers of exceptional wisdom, despite their total ignorance of the gospel. The nobility pondered upon the setbacks encountered by the crusaders, believing with Joinville that the counsellors who had permitted Louis IX to take arms against the infidel a second time were guilty of mortal sin. Would it not be more efficacious to turn the infidels from their errors by persuasion and personal example, as St Francis had done? How could Christendom still believe itself at the centre of the universe with a mission to spread the gospel across the earth? Little by little, the instability of an order which had previously been seen as immutable became apparent; people started to question their own destiny, which had previously seemed inevitable.

As the backbone of the established order and guide to Christendom's destiny, the institutional Church was inevitably called into question. Disillusion was followed by doubt. Did passive attendance at divine office really guarantee salvation? With the introduction of the rood-screen between nave and chancel, there was now a physical barrier separating priest and people. The laity began to wonder if they could not come closer to God by their personal prayer and devotion and by individual acts of charity, of which the king was such a shining example with his care of the poor who swarmed at the gates of his palace. Since good works and mystical ecstasy assured the soul's salvation and nature herself was intrinsically good, why should they not – in the intervals between devotions – relax and enjoy physical pleasures, accepting the happiness life had to offer? The value system of the last three centuries, based upon learning and morality, began imperceptibly to crumble.

Just as imperceptibly, the currents of prosperity also changed direction. Hitherto, they had favoured the French and had spread the fame of their learning and universities, their architectural methods and the courtly language of their knights throughout Western Christendom, as far as Cyprus in the east and Moorish Spain in the south. As exchange rates, trade and currency came to dominate the European economy, France's long period of supremacy was at an end, and passed to the bankers and navigators of Italy. Already, Tuscan and Lombard bankers who for generations had gone through northern France to meet their counterparts in England, Flanders and the Rhineland were beginning to alter their route, as new roads were built over the central Alps and bigger ships sailed between the Mediterranean and the North Sea.

The whole strength of the French economy was concentrated in the towns, and at first they did not appear to suffer from this change in the merchants' routes. The growth of credit had increased their control over the rural hinterland, while – through their control of long-distance trade in primary materials and finished goods – the patriciate's own power over artisans and middlemen increased. In Lyon, for example, municipal power was concentrated in the hands of eighteen closely linked families. In Rheims some fifty *bourgeois* families, weavers of cloth and active moneylenders, towered over both major and minor guilds, who bore the brunt of almost all forms of taxation. The population of Rheims numbered about 20,000 at this period, Paris ten times that number. The royal city and capital of the kingdom was by far the largest in the Christian West, and its market the most vigorous, for it was here that the richest households with the highest expenditure were to be found. Lombards from both Asti and Piacenza had banks there. The extensive activity at the fairs of Champagne (which reached their peak at this date) makes it easy to overlook the equal importance of Paris as a financial centre. Isolated behind their walls, the towns sustained the illusion of fertility and content in the kingdom, acting as a magnet for the poor of the surrounding region.

Outside the town walls, the other side of this relationship was apparent: townspeople had invested primarily in vineyards, sheep-farming and woodlands. The price of pasture therefore increased and the value of woodland was continually growing; in some areas it was worth twice as much as arable land. The corollary of this trend was that land used for food production near cities was increasingly turned over to viticulture; while on the edges of clearings, landholders abandoned the battle against poor soils whose return had dwindled to nothing. The combination of a decrease in the land available for food production and an increase in population inevitably spelt famine. In rural Picardy, only one peasant in ten had enough to live from – and he was better off than the neighbouring landowner. One in ten had nothing at all, and was forced to beg for food. As for the rest, households cultivating areas of less than three hectares (in other words, below the subsistence level), could only survive by selling their labour, the men lodging in the big farms and the women spinning for urban capitalists. In 1270 the population had ceased to grow, and this was a direct result of rural poverty: malnutrition was responsible for higher

16a Rebuilding the temple: a scene reflecting contemporary building techniques. Roda Bible (1030–60): Paris, B.N. MS lat. 6(3), 89v. (Reproduced by kind permission of Bibiothèque Nationale, Paris)

16b The death of Holofernes; below, mounted and unmounted warriors are ambushed from behind the rocks. Roda Bible: Paris, B.N. MS lat 6(3), fol. 134. (Reproduced by kind permission of Bibliothèque Nationale, Paris)

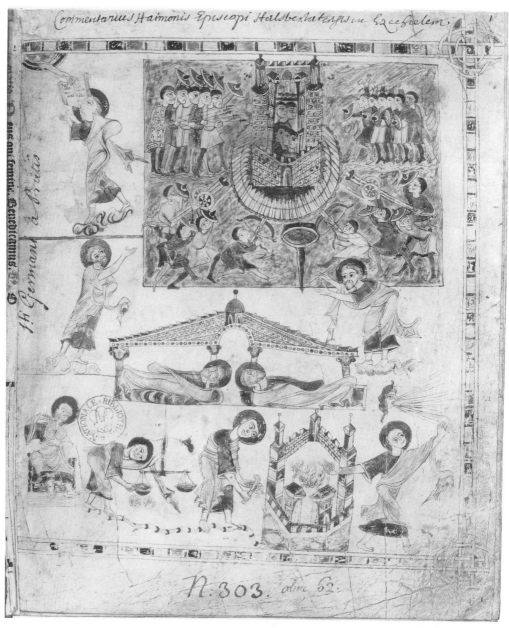

17 *Above:* the prophet Ezekiel points to a siege: note crossbows and battering rams. *Below:* the administration of justice and punishment of a contumacious town. Manuscript of a commentary on Ezekiel commissioned by Abbot Heldric of the important Cluniac monastery of St Germain-l'Auxerrois (*c.* 1000): Paris, B.N. MS lat. 12,302, fol. 1. (Reproduced by kind permission of Bibliothèque Nationale, Paris)

18 Cathedral of Notre-Dame, Paris: bas-relief above the southern portal showing the Virgin enthroned and Louis VII kneeling before her (second half of the 12th century). (Reproduced by kind permission of Alinari-Giraudon, Paris)

19 The victory of Largesse and Charity (portrayed as contemporary knights) over Avarice: carved capital from the choir of Notre-Dame du Port, Clermont-Ferrand: Musée des Monuments Français. (Reproduced by kind permission of Photographie Giraudon, Paris)

20 The angel clothed with a cloud gives his book to John (Book of Revelation, 10).
He has one foot on the sea (the mutable domain of paganism), the other on the firm
ground of true belief. Commentary on the Apocalypse from the abbey of St Sever (*c.*
1050–72): Paris, B.N. MS lat. 8878, fol. 150v. (Reproduced by kind permission of
Bibliothèque Nationale, Paris)

21 Carved capital showing the
fall of Simon Magus: nave of
Autun cathedral (1120–45).
(Reproduced by kind
permission of Photo
Zodiaque)

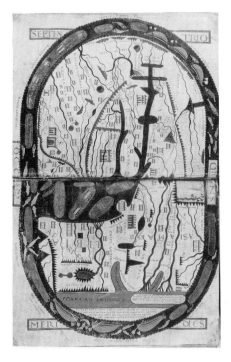

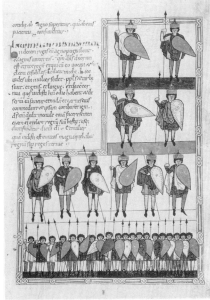

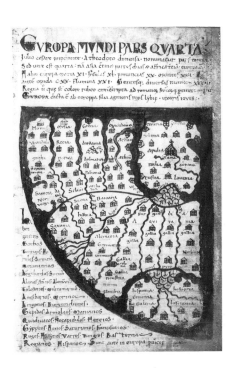

22a *Above left:* *Mappamundi* (or world map) from a commentary on the Apocalypse from the abbey of St Sever (*c.* 1050–72). Bisected by the Mediterranean, the known world focuses on Rome in the west and Jerusalem in the east. The Gascon abbey of St Sever is shown, topped with a cross, in the south: Paris, B.N. MS 8878, fols. 45bis v – 45ter r. (Reproduced by kind permission of Bibliothèque Nationale, Paris)

22b *Above right:* The ten kings defeated by the Lamb in the Book of Revelation, 17. Manuscript of a commentary on the Apocalypse from the abbey of St Sever (*c.* 1050–72): Paris, B.N. MS 8878, fol. 193. (Reproduced by kind permission of Bibliothèque Nationale, Paris)

23 *Below left:* Map of Europe from the *Liber Floridus* of Lambert of St Omer (1120). By contrast with the map in the St Sever manuscript (plate 22a), this shows the territories of the king of France ('Gallia') and of the Emperor ('Alemannia', 'Germania' etc): Ghent, University Library, MS 92, fol. 241r; Lambert of St Omer, Liber Floridus. (Reproduced by kind permission of Rijksuniversiteit Gent)

24 Stained glass showing scenes from the life of Charlemagne: Chartres cathedral, window in the north ambulatory (early 13th century). (© Sonia Halliday and Laura Lushington)

25 Twelfth-century marriage chest decorated with scenes of courtly life: Vannes, cathedral treasury. (Reproduced by kind permission of Caisse nationale des Monuments Historiques et des Sites © D.A.C.S./S.P.A.D.E.M. 1991)

26 The count of Toulouse kneels before the French king, surrounded by the twelve consuls of the town of Toulouse, who are determined to preserve its rights and privileges. Commentary on the *Customs of Toulouse* (1296): Paris, B.N. MS lat. 9187, p. 1. (Reproduced by kind permission of Bibliothèque Nationale, Paris)

27 *Above:* a lady gives her favour to a knight. Below: he rides off to a tournament with the favour fixed to his helm. *Le Roman de la poire*, northern French (*c.* 1275): Paris, B.N. MS fr. 2186, fol. 8v. (Reproduced by kind permission of Bibliothèque Nationale, Paris)

28 The author presents his manuscript to the king. Peter Salmon's *Replies to Charles VI and Lament to the King* (1409): Paris, B.N. MS fr. 23,279, fol. 53. (Reproduced by kind permission of Bibliothèque Nationale, Paris)

29 Coronation of Charles VI (surrounded by bishops and peers, with the common people below). Frontispiece of a manuscript of *Les Grandes Chroniques de France* (1375–9): Paris, B.N. MS fr. 2813, fol. 3v. *Margin*: illuminations showing (above) the battle of Bouvines, 1214; (below) the Dauphin Charles surrounded by members of the Estates General of 1356 from the same manuscript, fols. 253v, 399 bis. (Reproduced by kind permission of Bibliothèque Nationale, Paris)

30 Table to illustrate the length of the seasons; part of the intellectual equipment thought necessary for a southern French nobleman in Matfré Armengaud's *Breviary of Love* (early 14th century): Madrid, Escorial Library, S. Lorenzo, S.I.E. fol. 57r. (Patrimonio Nacional, Madrid)

mortality rates amongst children and a reduction in adult life expectancy; above all, the birth rate fell, because women were less fertile, and possibly also because economic conditions meant that people did not marry at such at an early age. And so, on the death of Louis IX, the complex development which had upheld all forms of progress in France since the early Middle Ages was arrested.

The zenith of Capetian power and prestige was reached with the flowering of the cult of St Louis during the reign of Philip IV the Fair. He was fair of face and king of a fair kingdom. The population was then larger than at any point before the reign of Louis XV in the eighteenth century. Short of money, the increasingly intrusive State was keen to record the number of taxable households, and consequently the historian can posit population figures with some confidence. Between 20,000,000 and 23,000,000 is a reasonable estimate for the whole of the area covered by present-day France. Moreover, the process by which France arrived at its current hexagonal shape was already under way. In the south, the king retreated and renounced his claims to Catalan lands south of the Pyrenees. The east saw expansion near Toul, Verdun and in the county of Bar, so that French supremacy stretched from Champagne to Lorraine. Both the dukes of Lorraine and the counts of Provence (a title now held by the descendants of Louis IX's brother, Charles of Anjou) distanced themselves from the Empire. The king of France had his men at Lyon, the duke of Burgundy lived in Paris and his daughter married one of Philip the Fair's sons; the court of France gave a money fief to the count of Savoy and the dauphin of the Viennois. The latter was soon to sell all his rights to the king, and his title was held henceforth by the French heir presumptive. Beyond the Alps, the riches of Italy spurred the ambitions of the princes of the blood; they sought adventure there without delay; Charles of Anjou became king of Naples, and dreamed of the reconquest of Sicily.

As ruler of the largest State in Europe, the king of France did not bother to assume the dignity of Emperor. He held imperial authority *de facto*. According to the civil lawyers, he was entitled to control the Church in his own realm, and it was his duty to guarantee its safety elsewhere. Control of the Papacy also passed imperceptibly into his patronage. It became accepted custom to hold great Church councils on the banks of the Rhône, rather than in Rome, because access was easier for prelates from all over Christendom. The curia was full of French cardinals. In 1261 Jacques Pantaléon, the son of an artisan from Troyes, who had graduated from the University of Paris and become chaplain to the Pope, was himself elected Pope Urban IV. It was not long before many of his former university companions were appointed cardinals. As a result, there was a strong element in the College of Cardinals which was extremely sensitive to

Capetian interests and did not feel at home south of the Alps. In 1305 they secured the election of a Gascon Pope, Clement V. He wanted to develop a good relationship with the Church council then meeting at Vienne. He therefore left Rome for the Comtat Venaissin, once the domain of the counts of Toulouse and ceded to the Holy See when they were dis-inherited. He established the Papal administration at Avignon and soon resided there himself. His successors followed suit. On the opposite bank of the river, Philip the Fair built a tower both defensive and assertive, a tangible expression of the incontestable supremacy of French royal power over papal authority.

At this period there was still no clear distinction between the king's household and the government of the State. Philip the Fair was first and foremost head of the royal family, continually surrounded by his closest relations. He prayed daily for his dead parents and for Louis IX, and he had decided to be buried beside his saintly grandfather. As he lay dying, Philip IV told his heir to follow the councils of his uncles above all. He was the head of an extended 'family', comprising several hundred individuals divided into the different specialized departments (*chambres*) of the household, who followed the king in his constant moves around the country. For Philip was always on the move, on campaign (when occasion required), making pilgrimages to Mont-Saint-Michel and Notre-Dame at Boulogne or retreats at Maubuisson and Poissy, as well as the endless hunting expeditions that he loved so much. As a result, the permanent administration became detached from the royal household and was estab-lished in the old palace on the Ile-de-la-Cîté. From this date, archives were very much better maintained and documentary sources give a much better picture of the functioning of central government and its officials than at any preceding period. Some financial officials were foreigners (known as 'Lombards'), such as Biche and Mouche from San Gimignano, whose bank was at Paris. But justice was still by far the most important department, entrusted to knights and clerks of the king's household. The former were known as '*chevaliers ès loi*' (knights-at-law) and employed two weapons, the sword they had received when they were knighted and the legal knowledge they had acquired at a university. Each of them was personally bound to the sovereign by homage and fealty, as well as by the special oath he had made to defend the person, honour and secrets of the king. Moreover, they were faithful: the king never had cause to dismiss one of them. They were his; they thought and worked for him alone, rewarded by his generosity.

Among them were a number of civil lawyers who had come from the areas of southern France that had only recently become part of the kingdom. William of Nogaret was probably the most famous. Their train-ing at Toulouse or Montpellier had instilled in them the precepts of Roman law. There, in the Rouergue or Quercy or the three *sénéchaussées* of the Languedoc, Roman law was the basis for all lawyers, judges, advocates or proctors, whether they were passing judgement or defending the interests of their clients. Now they exploited this knowledge for their royal master. However, it is easy to exaggerate the role of civil law in the process by which Capetian dominion was established within the kingdom. As far as his household was concerned, the king's power was grounded in feudal right and this was most important of all. The fief remained the essential mainstay of the army, since feudal tenure was the basis of training and equipping men-at-arms, and it was through the chain of vassalage that all the inhabitants of the kingdom were bound to 'serve and obey' the king.

This was clearly the view of Philip of Beaumanoir, a knight and legal official (*bailli*) in the Beauvaisis, who analysed the customs of the region in about 1280. We have already documented the emergence of the concept of lordship in the eleventh century, and it was this which Beaumanoir perceived as the fundamental basis of the temporal order, underpinning its entire fabric. All subjects, noble and non-noble alike, fell under the jurisdiction of a lord, whose responsibility it was to uphold the common good through (for example) the care of orphans, upkeep of roads and the enforcement of standard measures. But 'since all lay justice is held from the king, either as a fief or through subinfeudation', every lordship was an integral part of the kingdom. Every lord held his lordship by performing homage for it to his own superior lord, who was sometimes the king, but more probably an intermediate lord. The latter was responsible for the protection of churches, for modifying customs by legislation, and for assembling contingents to serve with the feudal host: he was in effect sovereign conjointly with the king, just as in the earliest period of feudalism the knights liable for castle guard duty had been co-possessors with the lord of their fortress. The cardinal point here is the permanence of this system. In a kingdom as large as France, shared lordship remained as imperative as it had been for the castellanies in the earlier period. In fact, the barons were all the king's men and his friends, just as the knights who performed castle guard had been friends of the castellan. The king was at the topmost rung of the feudal ladder. No baron could take a stand against the king, since only the king was authorized to set the entire kingdom on a war footing, 'in times of war, or if war is rumoured and in other times of necessity' – a clause which in particular justified the levy of subsidies by the king – and even in peacetime, if this was done 'reasonably' and 'after consideration in full council'.

'An entirely strong monarchy could have been founded on Beaumanoir alone' (J. Strayer). Civil law (that is, Roman law) merely re-enforced existing custom. There was no need to do more than apply custom strictly, with a little gentle pressure to influence the direction in which it was to evolve. This was the case with appanages: according to increasingly accepted custom, they were to revert to the crown, in order that the sons of the royal house should have adequate means of support. Outside the king's domain (which covered two-thirds of the kingdom), it was enough to allow free rein to the royal officials whose duty it was to ensure that custom was followed. The people continually denounced their rapacity. The administration certainly made increasing demands. But there was no corruption among the officials – seneschals, judges or *baillis*. Although humble origins were a frequent ground for complaint, this was seldom the case. However, since they had to pay themselves and give the serjeants who assisted them with criminals and debtors a salary, they used every opportunity to extend the field of their jurisdiction at the expense of both the Church and feudal lords. Eventually the fief-holders jibbed at this treatment and made leagues which renewed the old regional ties; after the death of Philip the Fair (1314), they succeeded in putting the clock back for a while.

Historians have long debated the role of the king in these developments. With Philip the Fair, we wonder for the first time what passed through the king's mind when he was not praying or hunting, what decisions he made and what role he really played. This is because the administrative machine had its own momentum and functioned independently now that every cog had its allotted task and the king was confident of its effective operation. An educated man, who had a French translation of Boethius read aloud to him, he kept at a distance from the action, except in war. Like the Aristotelian Peter Dubois, he believed that minor issues were beneath a ruler. The handsome king was rarely known to open his mouth. This is how one eyewitness (Bernard Saisset, bishop of Pamiers) described him: 'He could only stare at people, without speaking.' One thing is sure: throughout his life, he was devoted to the memory of St Louis and endeavoured to follow his grandfather's example. All his life, the king's dearest wish was to lead a crusade and perhaps die in the Holy Land. When he was old and widowed, he practised increasingly harsh mortifications of the flesh.

Louis IX had tightened his hold over the Gallican Church when he declared before the Pope at the council of Lyon in 1247 that his protection of the Church in France entitled him to unfettered control over it. The actions taken in Philip's name against Boniface VIII and the sequence of events right up to the outrage of Anagni (1303) are explained by the king's personal convictions. His overriding concern was for sanctity, not only in himself and his family, but in his subjects and the entire Church. Highly aware of his position as the vicar of Christ on earth, he was, moreover, acutely conscious both that he held power directly from God and that it was his duty (as the Dominican John of Paris explicitly told him) to excommunicate the Pope and personally depose him, if he brought shame to the Church. The king of France was convinced of the intrinsic unworthiness of the Pope for his exalted position. The evidence of their confessions likewise persuaded him of the Templars' guilt. He did not have them burned for the sake of the order's great wealth, but was prompted by the example of his 'ancestors, more concerned than any other ruler to eliminate heresy and all other errors', and aware that it fell to him to purge this scandal from the Church. These attitudes also explain why witch-hunts started in his courts. God lays a cruel burden on those he arms with the sword of justice.

The humbling of the proud in his own kingdom was another divinely appointed royal mission. During the thirty years of his reign, Philip the Fair constantly employed his army at the kingdom's farthest boundaries against two enemies, England and Flanders, allied as they had been on the eve of the battle of Bouvines. In the south-west he had to check the arrogance of his most powerful vassal, the king of England, who rendered desultory service and, above all, resisted the insidious encroachments by French royal officials upon the rights he held from the crown in Gascony, Saintonge and the Agenais. This obduracy was judged a felony and the fiefs were seized by the French king, to be returned visibly reduced after diplomatic negotiations.[1] The violence of the rebellion in the north was of an intensity that surprised Philip's counsellors. They had thought it would be a simple matter to raise money and taxes in the great Flemish towns, as they did in other cities in the royal domain, leaving the patriciate to levy it upon the common people. They reckoned without the count of Flanders or his kinsmen, who continued the struggle after the county was confiscated and then occupied. Above all, they failed to take account of the tenacity of the huge groups of savage Flemish weavers, tired of their subordination to urban capitalists and aflame in the defence of their nation. The Flemish artisans suddenly discovered their power. Before Courtrai on 11 July 1302, armed with knives like mercenaries, the weavers of Bruges had the temerity to challenge the gilt-spurred knights, who had arrogantly imagined that a few charges would crush these impudent yokels. They cut the throats of 'all the chivalry of France', as they lay unhorsed in the muddy ditches. There were more than 200 fatalities, amongst them Robert of Artois and the count of St Pol. Two years later, Philip the Fair avenged this disgrace, but only with great difficulty, for (like Philip Augustus before him) he was thrown beneath his horse, and it was only by dealing great blows with his battle axe that he was finally able to emerge victorious.

[1] Following the Anglo-French war of 1294–8 – tr.

He was still powerless to bring the rebels to heel, however, or curb a land whose language and customs made French culture completely foreign, even after the count had been forced to negotiate terms and to cede Lille, Douai and Béthune to the French crown.

Mounted troops, no matter whether they were heavily or lightly armed, were exceptionally expensive to maintain, because they required a constant supply of new mounts. Additionally, the king, 'poorly advised [according to Peter Dubois], had adopted the practice of paying wages to the counts, barons, knights and esquires who, under the terms by which they held their lands, were in fact bound to do military service at their own expense'. The State was obliged to use every possible means to raise the necessary capital, justifying this action with reference to sovereign right; expediency thus stimulated the rapid withdrawal of the monarchy from the feudal structure.

Although they were a continual and increasing burden on the State, these were still nominally 'occasional' expenses, and to meet these demands, royal officials now drew regularly upon the immense wealth of the Church in France. The French clergy still clung obstinately to the idea of a crusade, and the tenths which they paid the crown were theoretically set aside to prepare for it. But royal officials put a much more liberal interpretation upon the matter, and ignored papal claims to authorize such levies. Their main aim was to extract as much as possible from the king's 'subjects', and not only by playing the feudal game. Established practice in such areas was in fact created by royal ordinance overriding custom, ostensibly 'in time of war' or 'for the common good'. It was in this somewhat amateurish way that regular taxation was established. The administration experimented with various ways of raising money, none of which was a great success because of the difficulties of assessing taxable resources. Despite the prosperity of the country, there was surprisingly little coin in circulation. However, measures were also taken to ensure that it did not leave the kingdom, and the entirely new phenomenon of customs posts appeared along the border with Italy, home of the great banking houses.

There remained the coinage, a royal prerogative. It was the king's right to decide the type and value of each coin. He was entitled to change these types, decree one coin no longer valid and issue a new one, making a profit through debasement. But this policy upset the fragile equilibrium of the system, with gold coin now twice the value of silver and the exchange rates fluctuating constantly. The State became embroiled in the impossible task of controlling the coinage to meet its own requirements. In contemporary eyes, it was criminally irresponsible to destroy monetary stability in this haphazard way. The State was forced to justify its actions and reply to public recrimination. It had to distance itself from feudalism, rise above it and look for support from outside the old network of vassalage, to secure the loyalty of all its subjects. The State had to win the confidence of the nation, if it was to solve the problems that were a product of its own development. What is more, it had to explain policies, give undertakings itself, and establish a dialogue with the nation. At the beginning of the fourteenth century, the agents of the monarchy began to harangue assemblies composed of representatives of the three different 'estates' in the presence of their silent king. (By this date the social categories of the 'three estates' applied to urban as well as aristocratic society.) This marked the beginning of political debate in France. The bitter confrontation between the king of France and the Papacy was the occasion of the first of these dialogues between State and nation. There was a public discussion of the papal bull (*Ausculta fili*) asserting papal supremacy at the cathedral of Notre-Dame in Paris during April 1302. Clerics comprised most of the thousand-strong audience, but members of the royal family and representatives of both towns and nobility were also present. The Pope claimed that he was instigating reform of both the French kingdom and the Gallican Church. The king gave assurances that he would oversee such reform himself, and appropriate ordinances were issued, claiming to return 'to the time of my lord St Louis'. The king had to help himself if he was to secure the indispensable support of the people.

A series of debates were also held concerning the grant of subsidies, currency mutation and the imposition of new taxes, and the king gave similar undertakings on these issues. The opinion of the townspeople was crucial in these matters. It was vital to win their support through the local assemblies held in each town or region on a model borrowed from the Languedoc, where they had been an effective means of communication between town and State since the twelfth century. The State was forced into some hard bargaining, yielding on one point in order to secure agreement on another; sacrificing royal agents if need be, when their evident prosperity suggested excessive pilfering of State resources. For the townsmen were prepared to open their coffers for the defence of the realm, but not for the enrichment of royal officials or to prop up a bureaucracy they considered cumbersome and useless. Enguerrand of Marigny, the king's chamberlain, had risen to high office too fast, and was too closely associated with the treasury. He was the first of a series of scapegoats offered by the crown for public trial and sentence in an attempt to appease popular resentment of the ever-increasing burden of public taxation.

We should not underestimate the importance of the immorality which, in the last few years of the reign, crept into the very heart of the royal household, close to the person of the ascetic Philip the Fair himself. A final scandal broke, this time within the royal palace. The wives of the king's three sons had taken part in a courtly charade, but things grew out of hand, and two of them, according to the third, had committed adultery. In 1314, the year of the king's death, the adultery was revealed, and the court had to be purged as shockingly as possible of this appalling stain. The men were castrated and burnt alive, the guilty princesses imprisoned in Château-Gaillard. One died of cold the first winter, the other mouldered there for many years and ended her days in a convent. This was by no means a trivial episode, for it reveals the intense love of pleasure that had characterized the French nobility since the death of Louis IX. Frivolity now possessed the French court, where strict morality had previously held sway, setting it apart from other courts, closer to the heavenly kingdom. The lineage of the fleurs-de-lis had been desecrated in its turn. This sequence of events engendered a great aversion to women in Philip the Fair; for example, he dreaded the prospect of the appanage of Poitou falling into female hands. He therefore decreed that, in default of heirs male it should revert to the crown. The precedent of female exclusion from inheritance had been set.

Admittedly, women were already excluded from the royal succession, for excellent reasons. As the Franciscan Francis of Meyronnes wrote in his commentary on St Augustine's *The City of God*, royalty was not an inheritance, but a dignity, like that of the great priests of Israel who, as the biblical Book of Kings clearly reveals, were all male. No one doubted that the king of France was both king and priest, and the priesthood was closed to women. Neither Louis X's daughter nor any of the daughters of his two brothers were qualified to succeed to the throne. When the direct Capetian line died out as, one after the other, Philip the Fair's three sons died without male heirs, many of their contemporaries saw this as divine punishment for the sins of their wives many years before. Immorality had corrupted the entire dynasty. We should not be too confident that there was no connection between the licentious princesses at the French court and the problems that were to beset the crown of France for the next hundred years.

14

The Fourteenth Century

The year 1348 is undoubtedly the single most important date of the entire fourteenth century. This was the year the Black Death reached France, and afterwards nothing was ever the same again. This, above all, was the cardinal event which marked the end of the medieval period.

Bubonic plague (spread by the fleas of rats) and pneumonic plague (transmitted in saliva) both struck that year, with a frighteningly high mortality rate. The population level had been declining for some while and now it plummeted dramatically everywhere, although there were pronounced regional variations. Less accessible areas were probably not so badly affected, but this is little more than conjecture, because the documentary evidence is so scanty and difficult to interpret. What we do know is that the toll was appalling in densely populated areas, monasteries, armies and most towns. After its first brutal appearance in the summer of 1348, the plague never completely disappeared, but severe outbreaks recurred periodically, notably in 1353–5, 1357, 1377–8 and 1385–6. The scourge then retreated for a while, only to reappear in 1403 and 1419. Extensive research suggests that in 1390 the population level in Normandy was only 43 per cent of what it had been at the beginning of the century. A fall in population of 50 per cent is a reasonable estimate for the country as a whole.[1]

It is almost impossible for us to imagine the impact of the Black Death: in the Paris region alone, four or five million individuals took ill in a single summer; within a few hours, they had died from a totally incurable disease. Total confusion reigned. First of all, there had to be practical decisions about the disposal of gruesome mounds of corpses. Then other issues could be tackled. People inevitably looked for a specific cause of

---

[1] Other authorities suggest a figure of about 33 per cent – tr.

such a terrible affliction, and wondered what collective fault could possibly have brought this punishment upon them. What penance might protect them from further onslaughts of the plague? Man's conception of the universe and his relationship to the supernatural were both shaken to the core. People turned to God and his representatives on earth for a solution, unable to accept that Church and king were equally helpless. Were the sins of the leaders being visited on the people? They were forced to seek other mediators between God and man. Quite suddenly rulers were openly denounced, extraordinary forms of devotion sprang up and witchcraft gained ground. Doubt and the unorthodox moved suddenly out of the shadows and into the limelight.

Death was no stranger to these people, but its victims were usually predictable, mostly children and the poor. But plague struck at random, and neither wealth nor adulthood were proof against its ravages. It destroyed the existing social equilibrium and upset the balance of the labour market, where the previous superfluity of labour was succeeded by an acute shortage. The surviving workers could demand higher wages. Repeated royal ordinances failed to prevent price rises; the wages of a Paris mason increased threefold in the decade after the Black Death. The problems associated with the excessively high population levels of the first half of the fourteenth century of course disappeared completely: many villages and hamlets were deserted in the years following the Black Death, but this was because peasants moved from plots with poor soils and low yields to more fertile areas, which offered them a better quality of life. The population was reduced by half, and production certainly fell, but theoretically there should have been twice the capital for each survivor. There was an immediate improvement in the standard of living at every level of society. Only a tiny proportion of the artefacts of everyday peasant life from before the Black Death has survived. The great majority of furniture, tools, clothes and houses are of a later date. This is simply because their new-found affluence enabled people to build houses in stone instead of wattle and daub, to wear wool and linen instead of pelts, and to use something more than the most rudimentary forms of dishes and drinking vessels. Moreover, sections of peasant society which had previously subsisted on bread and water could now afford wine and meat.[2] There were only half as many peasants after the Black Death; but they were better fed, and consequently better able to sustain the money rents and labour services demanded by their lords. The nobility had consolidated their position, for plague had also decimated their ranks.

[2] For another view of peasant conditions, see R. Fossier, *Peasant Life in the Medieval West*, tr. J. Vale (Oxford, 1988) – tr.

Their position at the end of the fourteenth century was more secure than ever. At the same time, people were readier to accept the role of public authority. The evidence certainly suggests that taxation – one of the mainstays of the modern State – would not have been imposed with such relative ease, without the incursions of the Black Death.

Taxation increased because the warfare endemic since the reign of Philip the Fair now became permanent. This was the war known as the 'Hundred Years War', but which in reality lasted much longer. By 'war' I mean public war, waged by the king who summoned the *arrière-ban* (or feudal levy), in ever-increasing numbers. In the summer of 1340 there were nearly 50,000 knights and squires in the field, a total of some 80,000 combatants if their retinues are included.[3] The king had no difficulties recruiting them. With the return of fine weather each year, he offered all his fighting men the opportunity to indulge in their favourite activity. What is more, he paid in gold coin. For warfare was now a wage-based operation, and the State was consequently forced to draw more and more upon the country's resources. Collecting every possible *sou* from his subjects, the king redistributed this money amongst his nobles, the warrior class upon whom the country relied for its defence. The nobles still exercised lordship, but now the crown provided their principal means of support. For their part, the nobles were eager to serve their sovereign, fighting in small, close-knit groups of kinsmen, friends and neighbours. Things were not so very different during a truce, for then they ravaged the land. For on the fringes of public war, it was inevitable that private war – in practice little more than brigandage – should flourish.

France was the richest country in Europe, and foreign and internal conflict for such a magnificent prize was probably unavoidable. The essential change in the fourteenth century was that fighting was no longer confined to the frontiers of the kingdom, as it had been in the reign of Philip the Fair, but affected every part of it. France was trampled underfoot once more, just as in the early days of feudalism 300 years before, when it had been the prey of warring nobles. In fact, some aspects of what is known as the feudal system grew stronger. The practices which English historians have sometimes called 'bastard feudalism' (when nobles recruited large retinues by money contract rather than feudal obligation) developed at this period. Although the form was new, its roots went back to the very origins of feudalism. In the first place, it was highly compartmentalized: public and private war impeded communications and, once again, it became difficult to govern from a distance. As a result, attack and

[3] For a recent analysis of the composition of armies at this period, see P. Contamine, *War in the Middle Ages*, tr. M. Jones (Oxford, 1984), pp. 126–37 – tr.

defence were essentially localized operations, and old regional sentiments and alliances began to reassert themselves. The process was encouraged by the king himself, who was involved in detailed plans for the defence of France in the face of invasion, just as Charles the Bald had been before him. In 1358 and again in 1367 he gave orders for an inventory of all fortified places to be drawn up, so that they might be made more defensible. It was this period, rather than the eleventh century, which saw the castle-building which has left such a striking imprint on the French landscape today. New fortified towers appeared on parish churches, bridges and monasteries, as well as on manor-houses; they were no longer mere symbols of judicial authority, but had an essentially military function.

This period also saw a resurgence of the chivalric ethos. It was encouraged partly by the protracted state of war, which afforded ample opportunity for the individual knight to develop his skills, but – much more importantly – because it was in the interest of every ruler (including the king of France) to foster chivalric values. A tightly knit group of brave and loyal friends bound together in an order of chivalry was the surest defence against treason and disloyalty. Chivalry was now associated more closely with the power of the State than it had ever been before. Like the Templars and Hospitallers before them, the members of these exclusive secular orders were united by observance of shared liturgies and a common moral code. Now, however, their primary allegiance was to the person of the ruler, rather than the Church of Christ. At every level of the body politic, groups of clients started to gather round a patron, and this change was to have a greater long-term impact than the more conspicuous displays of chivalry. In this way, noble society became much more disparate. It tended to fragment into a number of small groups held together by oaths of loyalty, by written contracts promising the ruler specific services, and by all sorts of associations governed by mutual interest. There was fierce competition for booty among military companies and for patronage between the various factions at court. As the war was prolonged indefinitely, it affected the entire population. While the nobility saw profit as one of the incidental benefits of war, a whole host of adventurers whose only motive was material gain followed in their wake. Any man who was bold enough could – to use Froissart's habitual phrase – 'better himself in the profession of arms', or, in plain English, make a fortune from pillage.

With each of these changes, towns became more important. This was the great difference between fourteenth-century feudalism and that of 300 years earlier. Walled and heavily defended, towns were of prime strategic importance for military commanders, as well as the principal place of refuge for those whose lives were devastated by the movement of armies. The towns were continually depopulated by plague, then repopulated by a new influx of peasants seeking refuge from the excesses of soldiery. Refugees made up no less than a quarter of the population of Rheims at this period. By no means all of them were poverty-stricken wretches; they included many nobles and more affluent peasants. Similarly, in the south, a number of landowners whose lordships were inadequately protected by their local *bastide*, chose to administer their lands at a distance, from the safety of a fortified city, such as Aix. Above all, the towns were an essential source of financial support for the hard-pressed State, for – unlike many other sections of the community – they were at least in a position to pay.

Taxation erupted into this changed world. The crown's ordinary revenues were clearly inadequate for the conduct of war, and it was the 'necessity' of war that provided the king with the justification for demanding a subsidy from his subjects. The fiscal expedients to which the State had continual recourse disrupted every facet of economic life. Debasement of the coinage produced only relatively small profits, but precipitated the withdrawal of precious metals and disrupted the exchange rates. The full force of the subsidies granted by the clergy and nobility fell on the peasantry. Their impact was less in isolated regions, such as the Auvergne. But in Normandy – closer to the machinery of central government – the zeal with which the French crown flushed out what cash remained in the rural economy had a catastrophic effect upon peasant budgets. The impact on small peasant households (which were the mainstay of agricultural production) was devastating. Nevertheless, there was such widespread insecurity that villages were prepared to accept the burden of taxation: it paid for stronger fortifications, as well as the wages of the king's soldiers, whom they hoped would protect them from pillagers. In the mid-fourteenth century the common people became accustomed to the idea of paying regular taxes for the public good.

Ultimately, three sections of society benefitted from continual warfare. First of all, the persistent celebration of chivalric ideals raised the status of the nobility from the relatively uninfluential position into which it had been almost imperceptibly shouldered by the king's lawyers and by his financial advisers and administrators. Then there were the urban oligarchies, for whom the town's new military and – above all – political responsibilities more than compensated for the recession in long-distance trade. Since they were responsible for the defence of towns, the powers of municipal governments were extended and their right to levy taxes confirmed. Continual warfare resulted in decentralization, and this in turn prompted the proliferation of numerous provincial capitals. It is unlikely, for example, that Poitiers would have had anything like as much influence if the war had not given it a position of primary importance. The position was similar in Tours (head of an appanage, the newly created duchy of

Touraine), where the administration has been described as the town's single most important source of employment. Finally, while the Church lost ground as a result of the tribulations of war, there was a shift in power and influence towards the secular State (By which I mean the ruler and all his servants – that is, all those who acted in his name and were financially dependent upon him.) Securely founded upon its loyal towns (*bonnes villes*) and sustained by the grant of subsidies and by the personal bravery of its military leaders, who dreamt of surpassing the deeds of Lancelot and other heroes of romance, the State was the net beneficiary from the prolonged disorder of the Hundred Years War.

Yet at one point the stability of the State had been threatened. The initial uncertainty had been provoked by the decision of the nobles and clergy over the royal succession in 1328, when Philip the Fair's youngest son had died childless, like his brothers before him. The crown passed to one of his cousins, Philip of Valois. At his accession, it did not seem likely that this reign would see many changes. The Flemish appeared to have been finally brought to heel by the new king's victory over them at Cassel, and Philip VI began preparations for a new crusade. Nevertheless, there were inevitably changes with the accession of a man whose chances of becoming king had always been remote in the extreme and who had not been brought up as the future lieutenant of God on earth. Like his father before him, Philip VI spent much of his resources on entertainment and finery with gay abandon; this inevitably increased the pace of change at the French royal court, where the secular atmosphere of princely households now definitely prevailed. The money provided by taxation was no longer used only for the maintenance of God's order on earth and to celebrate divine glory, but also for court entertainments. The fourteenth-century kings of France – notably John II and Charles V – were nevertheless all extremely pious like their forebears, they spent long hours in devotion and many days in penitential retreat. Charles V and his contemporaries were not passionate devotees of hunting and fighting to the exclusion of every other occupation; cultured, with very decided tastes, this generation enjoyed refined pleasures in the luxury of enclosed gardens and comfortable apartments, surrounded by beautiful *objets d'art*. Like Henry II of England and Eleanor of Aquitaine, they patronized poets, painters and musicians, and commissioned translations of works by classical authors, as well as contemporary Italian humanists. France did not witness splendours quite like those of Trecento Italy or its outpost in the cardinals' households and the papal court at Avignon; nevertheless, this renaissance did not pass it by. If the direct line of descent from Louis IX had not died out, breaking the iron yoke of abstinence and rigorous piety which had enclosed the Capetian kings, these developments would never have taken place.

They reached their peak at Paris in 1400, when there was a respite from both war and plague.

However, the break in the dynastic succession was to have other consequences. No one expected a woman to wear the crown; but the decision of 1328 was based on the stark premise that women could not transmit a claim to the crown to their male descendants. This was contrary to all contemporary succession practices amongst the nobility; it was therefore easy for the two male heirs who had been excluded by this decision to contest it. They were Charles, king of Navarre (son of Jeanne), Philip the Fair's oldest grandchild, and Edward III of England, who was a grandson of Philip the Fair through his mother, Queen Isabella. Neither of them had the slightest intention of challenging Philip VI: once he had been anointed with holy oil at Rheims, the king's person was sacred and inviolable.[4] But it was possible that their claims might be renewed when the king died. Philip VI himself was aware of this, and died in a state of anxiety in 1350, whereupon John II had himself crowned without delay. Two years later, he thought it advisable to surround himself with the additional protection afforded by the Order of the Knights of the Star. The order's admission ceremonies deliberately presented a gradual ascent towards the blue and gold of the royal arms, symbolic of the sovereign's role at the heart of the chivalric ethos: the aspirant wore dark robes at first, progressing to scarlet during the vigil, and blue and gold when he was admitted as a full member of the order. This was the period which witnessed the full flowering of the chivalric ideal. Nevertheless, John the Good continued to feel insecure, and was convinced that he was surrounded by traitors – a neurosis which was responsible for violent outbursts of temper.

Charles of Navarre and Edward III were both determined to exploit the situation in the 1330s to the utmost, and the English king lost no time in invading France. While Philip VI was busy preparing a crusading fleet in Marseilles, Edward was plotting in Flanders, determined to win the support of the cloth-producing towns. When his duchy of Guyenne was once again confiscated – for harbouring the traitor Robert of Artois – Edward declared his rightful claim to the French throne, and in 1340 he also adopted the French royal arms. The young Edward III was little more than a frustrated adventurer with an enthusiastic following among the English nobility; he provided a focus for discontent in Normandy and Artois, as well as the Flemish towns. His intention was merely to make a brief but lucrative raid on France and return home laden with booty. In 1346 he was returning from Normandy with his spoils and heading for the ports around Boulogne as quickly as possible, with the French king in hot

[4] For an opposing view, see J. Le Patourel, *Feudal Empires*, ch. 12 – tr.

pursuit. Philip VI hoped to capture Edward and make an example of his audacity. Then the unexpected intervened: Welsh archers with longbows proved more effective than the Genoese crossbowmen in Philip VI's army, and the French knights were routed as ignominiously as Otto IV had been from the field of Bouvines thirty-four years before. In contemporary eyes, the hand of God showed itself at Crécy, validating Edward's claims to the French throne. Meanwhile Edward was content to capture Calais and garrison the town, thus providing himself with a bridgehead for future expeditions into the French kingdom.

Charles of Navarre (nicknamed 'the Bad') dared not risk such open defiance, as his marriage and upbringing linked him closely with the French royal house: not only was he the brother of Philip VI's second wife, but in 1352 he had married the sister of the new king, John the Good. Accordingly, he made no overt claims to the throne. He concentrated instead on enlarging his share of the Capetian inheritance, establishing rights in Champagne which he held through his mother and extending the Norman lands which he had inherited from his father, Louis of Evreux, brother of Philip the Fair. Because he was at the very centre of power, Charles had many influential friends – at the University of Paris, amongst the higher clergy and nobility, and in the household of his royal brother-in-law. When in 1356 John II (still obsessed with the idea of treason) seized Charles of Navarre in a fit of anger and had him imprisoned, his supporters took up arms on his behalf. This marked the beginning of a crisis which shook the French State to its very foundations.

A combination of truces and plague halted English invasions until 1356, when they began again in earnest. Edward III's oldest son, Edward the Black Prince, made a series of savage raids into the Languedoc from his base in Guyenne. The duchy of Guyenne remained unswervingly loyal to England right up to the mid-fifteenth century. This is partly explained by the extraordinary volume of the wine trade – no fewer than 102,000 tuns were exported to England in the year 1308–9. The level of public money required to defend the population against these attacks was even higher than usual. An assembly of the three estates of the kingdom (later known as the Estates General) was held in Paris for northern French representatives, with Etienne Marcel as spokesman for the 'third estate'.

The royal court saw Paris as a palace annexe and its businessmen as their household servants. Marcel was the city's provost, presiding over the powerful Parisian merchants, whose influence had grown continually ever since their mariners' guild had won the right to navigate the Seine from that of Rouen. In the king's eyes, Marcel was no more than a sort of grand domestic, midway between the members of his household and the subordinates whose job it was to provision it. In this respect the king gravely underestimated the power of the Parisian merchant class. Their power lay in accumulated reserves of cash, a distinctive culture and their ascendancy over the middle classes: in the city and the surrounding towns and countryside, they protected tradespeople and substantial peasants – indeed all individuals of substance – from the harassment of the king's financial officers. Of course this power was puny compared with that of the sovereign. The fortunes of even the most successful merchants were dependent on the State, and it was in their interests to have a strong and stable government. No thought of subversion ever crossed the mind of Etienne Marcel. A member of one of the dynasties which had dominated city affairs for generations, descended on his mother's side from a line of royal household officials and on his father's from a family of court suppliers, Marcel was very conscious of his connections with the royal household. He wanted a just order of things and to ensure that money was not squandered by dishonest officials. However, he also harboured a grudge against some royal officers over an inheritance dispute. In December 1355 the Estates granted the subsidy demanded by the crown, in return for the promulgation of a reforming ordinance. This was almost routine. Like the ordinance of 1303 which it confirmed, this document aimed for a return to the situation that pertained in the 'good old days' of Louis IX, to a form of government free from abuses and above all a sound and stable coinage. To achieve these goals, the Estates referred to a plan devised at the University of Paris, proposing a logical distinction between the king's personal income and public funds. Public finance was entrusted to elected representatives (*élus*) of the different orders of society. This innovation was an inevitable consequence of the growth of government administration.

And so John II received the funds to put an army in the field. Then the unthinkable happened a second time, when the French army was overwhelmingly defeated near Poitiers on 19 September 1356. Contemporaries saw this second English victory as further divine confirmation of English claims. Hard on the heels of the Black Prince, King John had been taken prisoner himself, when the English stood their ground and gave battle. No one doubted the personal courage of the French king, who fought like a lion – like Louis IX at Mansourah, he had merely been unlucky. His subjects did not blame John II, but pitied him and readily accepted the financial sacrifice needed for his ransom and speedy release. Their rage vented itself instead against the nobility who, for all their show, had been unable to prevent this ignominious defeat and whose ineffectual posturing is so vividly described by Froissart. As far as the rest of the population was concerned, if the nobility were unable to defend the king and protect his people, their hauteur and privileges – to say nothing of their judicial

authority – were quite unendurable. The consensus which had been
the basis of 300 years of seigneurial jurisdiction was abruptly broken,
unleashing hitherto unsuspected levels of violence. In the aftermath of
defeat, soldiers dispersed to all parts of the kingdom, and the peasantry
were left to defend themselves single-handed against these bands, who
were kept at bay only by walled towns, and roamed the countryside in
Normandy, Berry, Touraine, Poitou, the Auvergne and the Ile-de-France.
The peasants were only armed with makeshift weapons – axes, pitchforks
and cudgels – but they were so enraged that they did not hesitate to attack
the occasional manor-house or castle belonging to the despised nobility.

Administrative reform had never been so pressing, and in Paris its
supporters had a free hand: the king was away, his place taken by the
sickly and inexperienced Dauphin Charles, who was only eighteen and –
like the rest of the king's subjects – stood in great awe of his father. In the
months that followed the defeat at Poitiers, the Estates of northern France
first decided to release Charles the Bad from imprisonment; they then co-
opted twenty-eight members to take the place of the 'wicked counsellors'
whose advice had been responsible for catastrophe. The year 1357 was
spent in confrontation: on the one side, the royal household (bastion of the
king's personal, unaccountable power) attempted to strengthen its position
with the support of the very distant Estates of southern France and, nearer
home, that of the Emperor Charles IV, the Dauphin's uncle and his formal
guardian; on the other were representatives of public power, the delegates
of the clergy, nobility and the towns of the old Frankish kingdom. In the
second camp, the keenest proponents of reform were not to be found –
as one might have anticipated – amongst the townspeople, but among
members of the nobility closely related to the king and concerned for the
common good. Most of this group supported Charles of Navarre, who
realized that this was the moment to fulfil his ambitions. He entered
into negotiations with the English, with a view to seizing the whole of
Normandy and Champagne.

Nevertheless, the uncertain conditions prevailing throughout the
kingdom forced autonomy on every region, and were sufficient to ensure
the failure of a centralized, representative government operating from the
capital. The nobility gradually left Paris for the provinces, to ensure that
their interests were effectively represented there. The Estates which met
in Paris in 1358 were no longer a truly representative body, but were
composed largely of clergy and businessmen. Etienne Marcel's influence
grew disproportionately as Paris became increasingly isolated. As time
passed, he realized that the Dauphin was passing beyond his sphere of
influence and he made a grave error of judgement. In an attempt at
intimidation, he committed the treasonable crime of lèse-majesté and went

armed into the young prince's chamber, ordering all those whom he believed responsible for misleading the Dauphin to be massacred before his very eyes. Charles was utterly terrified and fled; he received immediate support from the regional nobility outside the capital. In Paris, people began to be apprehensive about the possible future resentment of a king who had been humiliated in this way. With a sudden *volte-face*, the city ruthlessly disposed of Marcel. He had overplayed his hand and failed to keep the peace. It was well known that he planned to open the gates of the city, exposing it to the depredations of the Navarrese free companies and all manner of lawlessness. He had already made tentative overtures to the '*Jacques*' (rebellious peasantry). Their revolt (the Jacquerie) was neither directed against the king, nor inspired by poverty. Rather, the rage and resentment of the better-off peasantry in the Beauvaisis against the soldiery had finally boiled over. One fine day at St Leu-d'Esserent, they went so far as to attack them – as indeed peasants were attacking brigands everywhere. Inspired by their own audacity, they set about firing castles, killing the nobility and raping their wives and daughters. In contemporary eyes these men were no more than beasts, fit only to be crushed underfoot – a task gladly undertaken by the nobility, including Charles the Bad.

It was certainly not premature to delegate the king's public powers to the representatives of the three Estates in 1355. Fifty years of dialogue between king and nation had prepared the way for this step, made more pressing by war. But the initiative was soured by the French defeat at Poitiers and the turmoil that followed unleashed all kinds of excesses. For ever afterwards, the king mistrusted the people of Paris: one of Charles V's first acts as king was the building of the Bastille as a symbol of the authority he intended to exert. The overall result of rural revolt was only to tighten seigneurial control. Peasant violence discredited all plans for reform. Finally, both crown and nobility emerged stronger from this crisis, and on this dual foundation the monarchical State continued to grow apace.

King Edward III of England was not slow to exploit France's internal problems, and invaded the country again in 1360. His aim was to have himself crowned king of France in Rheims; but the city gates remained closed against him, and he had to be content with a peace treaty instead. In return for renouncing his claim to the French crown, the terms of the treaty of Brétigny granted Edward III full sovereignty over a greatly expanded Aquitaine (as held by Eleanor in the twelfth century) and a vast sum in gold coin as ransom for the French king. Glorying in his liberty, and with the Dauphin fully under his control once more, John II made a triumphant progress round the towns of his kingdom. Henceforth he was sure of his rights and feared neither the usurpations of Charles the Bad,

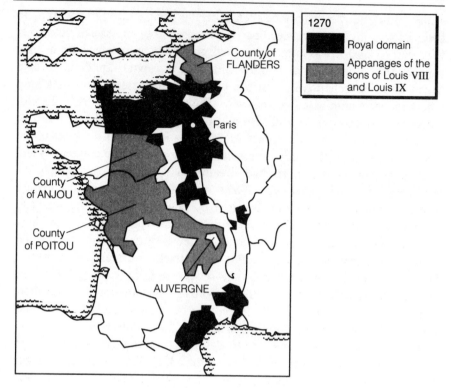

Figure 7   France in 1270

nor the fragmentation of his remaining lands. To the people, the king represented peace in the face of the free companies who had been pursuing their own quarrels after the end of public war. He was the symbol of a kingdom standing firm against the pillaging captains, who were ravaging their land and whom it was imperative to expel at the earliest possible opportunity. Even after all these disasters, the French king could contemplate the prospect of a new crusade. Just as no public consent had been required for the taxes levied for his ransom, so now John II raised the finance for his expedition to Jerusalem without any formal grant. He raised the money as and where he pleased, exempting only the privileged nobility.

This period witnessed the desacralization of power, coinciding with a movement away from the liturgy of the institutional Church towards private and individual devotion. But it is important to be careful in any discussion of the sacred: it is easy to think that it has vanished, when there

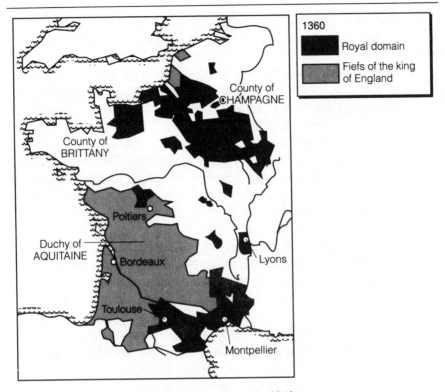

Figure 8   France in 1360

has merely been a shift of emphasis. Public enthusiasm for the 'divine' did not wane in the second half of the fourteenth century; indeed, it has been justifiably described as 'immense'. What was new was that it was now to be found outside the institutional Church. With all its courts, finances and hordes of busy officials, the Church was also a State, on an equal footing with the secular State. Charles V's refusal to allow the papal curia to return to Rome, insisting that it stay within his reach at Avignon, was largely responsible for the Great Western Schism (1378–1417), which itself accentuated the Church's secular characteristics. After the rift was healed in 1417, the Pope was forced to negotiate with secular rulers in order to restore his authority over the universal Church and, in particular, to acknowledge the liberties of the Church in France. There was a general desire for ecclesiastical reform and for the Church to confine itself to its own specific tasks. Priests were thought to be as necessary as ever; but they were expected to stick to their appointed tasks of administering the sacraments and preaching the gospel, without meddling in other affairs. The laity realized that Church reform was impossible, however. Preaching, drama, songs, the collective devotions of confraternities – all these things had made them better educated and they developed their own essentially private religion, which spoke to the heart of the individual. It was a blend of charitable works, secret mortifications of the flesh and silent prayer before the retable of a private chapel, or before the most primitive and inexpensive images of Christ or his saints which they had in their homes or carried about with them. There were two important associated developments: the greater availability of paper and the invention of printing were both to facilitate mass production of images of this kind. There was consequently a discrepancy between the form and substance of the institutional Church. Spiritual life and thought took different forms amongst the educated and uneducated, with the result that the two groups eventually ceased to understand each other.

A comparable change occurred in the monarchical State. Academics busied themselves with perfecting its theoretical basis, and there were any number of treatises on the nature of power, which undoubtedly reveal an increasingly secular bias. Political writers no longer referred only to the gospels, the Old Testament Books of Kings and St Augustine, but also liked to mention philosophical works such as Aristotle's *Politics*. They drew a parallel between kingdom and magistracy: the individual who ruled by inheritance was undoubtedly still seen as appointed by God, but to exercise his office well and defend the State (*res publica*), he had also to take account of reason and natural law. It goes without saying that such ideas were only current in very limited academic circles. The king and his officers had to take much more account of the political concepts that had gradually trickled down to the very lowest strata of society. Popular images of power – concrete and mystical – were also highly significant. It had become impossible for the king to rule unless he conformed to the people's image of kingship. Public opinion was appalled, for example, whenever the king appeared to be unduly lenient and granted a formal pardon to criminals guilty of crimes that were unforgivable in the black-and-white mind of the populace. It was impossible for the State to ignore either its propaganda role or the value of direct communication with the people. It communicated directly with them through speeches, but made increasing use of the written word, especially in political tracts, which found an ever-increasing audience. Most important of all in projecting the public image of the State were lavish pageants and theatrical displays.

There was a proliferation of these expressions of public authority in the second half of the fourteenth century. The majesty of power was revealed in royal palaces, and the most creative work in sculpture, painting and architecture now tended to be found in secular buildings, rather than great cathedrals. Statues of the merciful ruler were displayed there in contrived attitudes of wisdom, together with the friends who gave him advice in the privacy of his council. Whenever the king appeared in person – at formal sessions of the Paris Parlement, for instance, where royal judgements were pronounced with a great display of the king's sovereign power – he was set in the middle of a sumptuous decorative scheme. When he travelled through the regions of France, the king was greeted outside the gate of each town by its dignitaries and formally presented with its keys, which he returned, after promising to govern the town justly. Each time, this was in some sense a reiteration of the coronation ceremony, renewing the contract made then between sovereign and people. Afterwards the king made his formal entry into the town, with a rich canopy above him all the time, similar to that used to cover the sacrament in Corpus Christi processions. Scaffold stages were set up all along his route. In front of each one a platform decorated with emblems of royal power represented some aspect of government. At each of these stages, the king had to stop and watch an allegory about good government. Here the decorative scheme was provided by the people themselves for the ruler's pleasure, revealing to him the concepts of kingship which found their approval. They reminded him that there were some things which a king could not brook, recalling the contract which bound government and society together.

Undoubtedly many of the attitudes and conduct that had once been reserved for God were now directed towards the king, the incarnation of immutability clothed in human form. Similarly, the very rich now devoted more of their wealth to worldly pleasures. The divine was less central to society. In reality, a dichotomy similar to that in the institutional Church also operated in the secular State: there was, on the one hand, an increasingly complex, objective and finely tuned administrative machine and, on the other, the common people's uncritical adulation of their king. They continued to see the king as a quasi-divine healer whose hands, by virtue of the unction of his coronation, could miraculously conquer disease, so long as he led a pure life. This distortion was revealed only too clearly in the unhappy course of events in the war with England.

The least robust government departments (the domestic offices closest to the king) did not survive this period, while the executive arm became stronger and less rigid. The University of Paris fell under ecclesiastical jurisdiction; but although it lay outside the royal administration, it lived in the shadow of the crown, and its real independence was very much less than it imagined. Study in the faculty of arts was an essential prerequisite for a career in either secular or ecclesiastical administration, for this was the background of almost all the middle- and high-ranking bureaucrats. The masters of arts (eminent scholars, some of humble origin, who had followed a further lengthy course of study) were cleverer than anyone else in debate, and had been invited to solve the serious issues of papal and conciliar authority which were responsible for the continued schism within the Western Church. As a result, they came close to believing themselves some of the most important people in the entire world. Whenever crisis shook the capital, they acted as self-appointed advisers, heard respectfully by the royal court. The opposing factions there sought to win them over – not in itself a difficult task – with small favours and outward marks of respect. These susceptible individuals inevitably supported the *status quo*. Their prime endeavour was to provide the theoretical basis for an ideal political structure which they hoped would one day be a logical and coherent whole.

The Paris Parlement, supreme court of appeal, was the pillar of this political structure. In the uncertainties of the mid-fourteenth century, the king had decided that it should be strengthened. Until then, a varying number of secular and ecclesiastical lawyers had been appointed annually to pass judgement in his name. But after 1345 these were permanent appointments, with just over eighty masters sharing out the business of the various courts between them. The majority were of good birth, and those of humble origin lost no time in securing letters of ennoblement. The Parlement became increasingly autonomous in the uncertain conditions that prevailed for the rest of the century. Its presidents, counsellors and advocates all gained the right to appoint their successors. The new appointees were inevitably nephews, cousins or sons of the previous office-holders. Some of the clerics were mere time-servers, waiting until a bishopric came their way, but all the rest were like a great clan, jealous of their interests and increasingly powerful. More co-option followed, as office-holders in the Parlement were granted the right to delegate their responsibilities as they chose. These officials were exempt from taxation, and the Parlement provided a blueprint for a new kind of nobility, conferred purely through office-holding, the so-called *noblesse de robe*.

While the executive arm of the State thus became increasingly secure, the royal household (or rather households, for one was attached to each member of the royal family) showed signs of growing instability and confusion. At the turn of the fifteenth century, court life was in fact far from the royal palace, and this was another reflection of its essential dichotomy. The court flourished in the new district built on the recently drained marshland on the right bank of the river Seine. There the courtiers led an idyllic existence in enchanting walled gardens set in meadowland outside the city, in the intervals between their devotions, hunting expeditions and spectacular processions. The revels continued by torchlight far into the night. But these courtly entertainments took place behind high walls, and only the merest echo reached the ears of the common people.

They guessed at the dissolute nature of these entertainments, and suspected that money they had paid in taxes, like the *aide* (tax for the costs of war) or the *gabelle* (salt tax), was squandered here instead of being directed to the maintenance of law and order for the common good. But their confidence in the king never wavered. He had only to unfurl the *oriflamme* (as he did against the Flemings at Roosebeke in 1383) for all hint of criticism instantly to disappear, as the glory of the royal house shone victorious in all its splendour. But they intensely disliked all the useless young nobles – as they saw them – who gathered round the king, and were suspicious of their influence upon him. The people would have liked to cut their throats – and, indeed, on occasion did just that. At its most brilliant, the court was not merely sinful, but positively scandalous, with the rumoured liaison between Queen Isabella of Bavaria and her brother-in-law Louis, duke of Orléans.

The people had a wise king in Charles V, who stayed in his apartments full of beautiful manuscripts and treasures, directing the administrators and military commanders who acted on his behalf. By the end of his reign, the English had been driven back; on his deathbed Charles V decreed that the *fouage* (hearth tax) was to be abolished, overcome with remorse at the amount he had wrung from the poor by this means. In Charles VI, however, they had a mad king whose lucid intermissions were sufficiently frequent to make it impossible to think of deposing him – and which also roused great pity for his suffering throughout France. What was significant about this situation was that there was once more a dichotomy between political power and the royal domain because they were shared among the various branches of the royal family. Like Louis VIII and Louis IX, John II had many sons. Each of them had to be provided with his own patrimony and as a result, Berry, Anjou and Burgundy became appanages of the French crown. They were in effect satellite States, each with its own capital, administration and lawcourts; these were soon followed by universities, to train the requisite officials. The duke was allowed to retain a proportion of the crown revenues levied in his lands for his own use. Just as in the reign of Louis IX, this division of the kingdom seemed necessary and desirable. Charles V would have been unable to overcome the difficulties that faced him without the support of his brothers. As Dauphin, Charles had already shared lieutenancy of the country during his father's captivity with the eldest of his brothers: while he defended the north, his younger brother had been dispatched to the south, with orders to hold the free companies in check, fight the English, and negotiate with representatives of the Estates. The spirit of brotherly co-operation under the aegis of the oldest son generally worked well until the end of the reign. But it was quite a different matter when the princes close to the throne were the king's uncles, rather than his brothers, and still more so when their sovereign nephew went mad, and another tried to usurp the throne. For there was no ultimate check on Charles VI's three uncles, nor upon his brother. Great quantities of royal funds were diverted for their own ends: for the famous patron John, duke of Berry, to build up his glorious collection of beautiful manuscripts, curios and *objets d'art* of all kinds, and for Anjou, Burgundy and the young Orléans (the other dukes) to pursue their political ambitions in Italy and the Low Countries. Self-interest was their guiding principle, and each jealously resented any criticism of the way in which he appropriated very considerable sums from the *impôt* for his own use. In such a climate it was inevitable that Charles V's abolition of the tax from his deathbed was completely ignored.

This rivalry developed into bitter hatred between the two cousins, Louis, duke of Orléans (brother of Charles VI), and John the Fearless, duke of Burgundy. Each had his own following. Louis of Orléans' supporters numbered Queen Isabella and the king himself (who was very fond of him), virtually all the royal family and his Armagnac relatives. John of Burgundy – who was fond of citing the common good – was influential in Paris, popular with the citizens and in the university. Both of them relied on hand-picked men, prepared to do anything their master asked. This reveals clearly the true nature of public power at the highest level of society. Nothing had really changed: power remained intimately linked with the sacral; supported by the new feudalism, it remained essentially a matter of family and patronage. This nexus explains why rifts in the royal family tore the State apart. The Burgundy–Orléans feud effectively undermined the morale of the French royal family, which had always placed a greater premium on ties of blood than any other. John the Fearless had Louis of Orléans assassinated, precipitating a private war in which Paris paid the highest price. Blinded by hatred, overtures were made to Henry V of England, who lost no time in exploiting France's disarray.

The battle of Agincourt followed in 1415, the third French defeat, where almost the entire nobility was lost upon the field. Four years later, John the Fearless was murdered in his turn, in revenge for the death of Louis: this act finally broke all ties between Burgundy and France. In 1420 the court party came to terms with the English, giving Henry V custody of the mad king, Charles VI, and arranging a marriage between Henry and Charles's daughter Catherine, so that he might 'drive from the French lands which he still holds Charles, the self-styled Dauphin of Vienne, guilty of the most appalling crimes'. But only two years later (in 1422), the regent of France, John, duke of Bedford, had an announcement made in a setting redolent of French monarchical power, among the royal tombs at St

Denis, re-enforced by emblems brought from churches all over France. Heralds proclaimed the baby Henry VI king of England and France; his father, Henry V, and his grandfather, Charles VI, had both died in the interim.

15

The Maid of Orléans

Joan of Arc appeared when all seemed irrevocably lost and hope was at its lowest ebb; with her the supernatural came to the forefront of the political arena. There was nothing intrinsically surprising about this, since magic was an integral part of the later medieval mind – something that should be remembered if we are to understand these remarkable events. Documentary evidence is of prime importance in placing them in an accurate context, and the records of Joan's trial, judgement and rehabilitation offer invaluable insights into the workings of the contemporary mind.

Joan was in the tradition of groups of peasants in the recent past – often no more than children – who had left their flocks and homes and taken to the roads, convinced that it was their divinely appointed mission to restore justice in the absence of effective formal government by their superiors. They went under a variety of names ('*pauvres*', '*enfants*' and '*pastoureaux*' were just some of them) and came especially to the fore during the captivity of John II in England. Joan's home village of Domrémy was in the castellany of Vaucouleurs, on the French side. The Burgundians on the other side were periodically challenged by boys from the village. Apart from Tournai, Mont-Saint-Michel and Orléans, Vaucouleurs was the only remaining stronghold north of the Loire in the hands of the Armagnac party, who supported the so-called king of Bourges, the Dauphin Charles.

Joan was a shepherd girl, but her background was not one of abject poverty. Her family was affluent and was influential in village affairs – the sort of background, in fact, that had produced supporters of the Jacquerie in the previous century. She owed her intense religious convictions to her mother and their village priest; but she had also been greatly influenced by the preaching of itinerant friars, who were such a familiar sight in the countryside. At the same time, like any other country girl, she joined in the timeless rituals of the countryside, going with her friends to hang crowns from the sacred tree. Like everyone else at this period, she had an implicit belief in the supernatural. Her piety was clearly exceptional, and her contemporaries referred to her as a '*béguine*', a term used to describe an exceptionally devout woman. She had an especial devotion to the Blessed Virgin, the holy name of Jesus, the angels and the popular saints of the time – especially Michael (the weigher of souls and victor over Satan, whose shrine at Mont-Saint-Michel in Normandy had stood firm against every English onslaught) and Catherine and Margaret, virgin saints of particular relevance for a young girl. St Margaret was said to have fled from her father's house disguised as a man in order to escape marriage. In the middle of all the physical problems of puberty (which we know never really left her) at the age of thirteen, Joan heard voices. It happened at midday, as she guarded her flocks in the fields alone. The voices came from her right, so she knew they were good, rather than evil. At their command, she made a vow of virginity; she became aware of the hand of God directing her life. Henceforth she obeyed only God, and resisted the laws of men. This was how she braved her parents' anger and found the courage to refuse the husband they had chosen for her, breaking the marriage contract.

Soon there was a rumour that the kingdom of France, which had been lost by one wicked woman (Isabella of Bavaria, wife of Charles VI), was to be saved by a girl from the marches of Lorraine. Soon the voices of her 'brothers in paradise' spelt out the nature of her divine mission. They told her that out of his great pity for the people of France, God had decreed that she should make her way to the banks of the Loire, where French resistance was concentrated. Joan took everyone entirely by surprise and overcame all opposition. Despite the protests of her father, one of her uncles took her to Robert of Baudricourt, captain of the castle of Vaucouleurs. She demanded safe conduct and an escort to the Dauphin. Exasperated, Baudricourt finally agreed to her requests. She set out on horseback, dressed in a man's clothes for greater safety, and accompanied by two squires from her region, who had total faith in the authenticity of her mission. Her business was with the Dauphin, legitimate king of France. Addressing him as '*gentil*' (nobly born), she explained that, although his birth made him the rightful heir to the crown and he had called himself king ever since his father's death, he was not truly king until he had been crowned.

At Chinon, on 6 March 1429, the Dauphin Charles listened to this girl in armour with hair cropped short like a boy, who claimed she had been commanded by God to lead him to Rheims, so that he could be anointed as the true king of France. Surrounded by his courtiers, he heard the unfamiliar speech of the common people. Through Joan, the popular view that kingship was above all no earthly matter was communicated, as well as the conviction that the crown could not be disposed of at will. God alone could bestow it through his angels on the individual whose birth made him the rightful heir. Joan's prime goal was to 'reassert the supremacy of the French royal dynasty' and defend it, redressing the wrongs that had been perpetrated against it. Charles VI, she argued, had possessed no right as an individual to disinherit his oldest son, contrary to all laws, natural and divine. Finally, she expressed the view that the rightful place of the English was back across the Channel, where God had first set them, and that was where they should now return. Through her, God proclaimed his intention of constraining them to do so.

'Given the desperate straits in which he found himself,' Charles's courtiers advised him to make use of the Maid from Lorraine, but also insisted that she should first be subjected to a thorough examination, for visionaries of this kind had sometimes proved mad, or merely eccentric, in the past. It was essential that she was tested 'by human wisdom' as well as 'through devout prayer, in order to discover some positive indication of divine approval'. She was therefore sent to Poitiers, where some of the Paris theologians were to be found. They examined her 'life and habits' closely, and 'discovered that she was a good Christian, lived according to the orthodox Catholic faith, and was never to be found idle'. She was put in the care of a group of women for further assessment, who gave an account of her manners and behaviour to the council, and confirmed that Joan was indeed a virgin. And so the Dauphin Charles 'kept her with him for six weeks, so that everyone might see her'. She talked with many, 'in public and in private'. If anyone expressed surprise at her belief that she could miraculously drive back the enemy by her mere presence alone, she would reply: 'Give me a company of soldiers; they will do their part and God, in his turn, will provide the victory.' Now came the second trial, for no one suggested that she should lead the king's soldiers without a 'sign' to justify such faith in her. 'In God's name,' she replied, 'I did not come to Poitiers to give you signs; take me to Orléans and there I will give you incontrovertible proof that I have been sent by God.'

That spring (1429) the Anglo-Burgundians were besieging Orléans and the surrender of the exhausted garrison was expected daily. The town had enormous symbolic value, for it had been the very heart of the first Capetian kingdom, as well as the centre of the appanage of the murdered Duke Louis, leader of the Armagnac faction. If Orléans fell, it would be the beginning of the end. 'Placing his hope in God – for to doubt the Maid, or to desert her without any evidence of evil, would be to reject the Holy Spirit and render himself unworthy of divine aid', Charles was content that Joan should be styled his principal commander. On 22 March she gave her

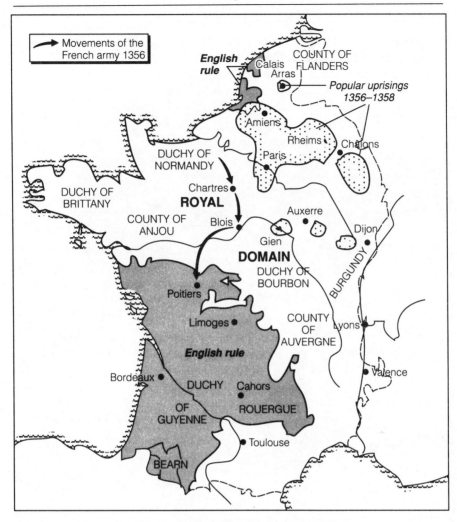

Figure 9   War and insurrection, 1356–1358

name to a letter of defiance addressed to the English king and his regent in France. It demanded that they 'should obey the king of heaven' and hand over 'the keys of all the French towns they had captured and violated'; peace terms were offered if they brought the reply to Orléans and raised the siege. With only a small invading force, Joan succeeded in gaining entry to the town and – contrary to all expectation – the Anglo-Burgundian force retreated. The unhoped-for deliverance of Orléans on 8 May 1429 was a dazzlingly clear sign of divine approbation. The dauphinist cause had previously seemed hopeless; now all things were possible.

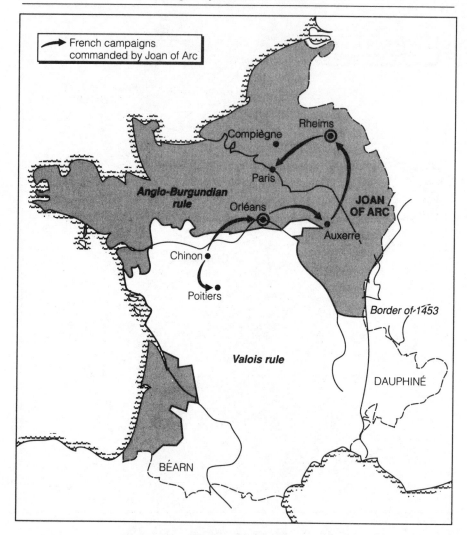

Figure 10   Fifteenth-century France (c.1429)

The news spread rapidly to all parts of the kingdom, and crowds flocked to see Joan. Her powers were apparently boundless, even to the extent of bringing stillborn infants to life. The Dauphin's forces took heart and turned from the defensive to the offensive, fighting bravely under her banner. They were inspired by the beautiful girl whom they had seen half-naked when she was wounded, but whose body miraculously stirred no desire in their own. The Maid had achieved the impossible, and on 17 July Charles VII was anointed king in Rheims cathedral. This act put an end to uncertainty, for the coronation annulled the treaty of Troyes, and gave

France the rightful king her people had lacked for the past seven years.

This complete reversal seemed literally miraculous to contemporaries, with the English and Burgundian forces appearing to flee from Joan as if she were the devil incarnate. Convinced 'that there was something fateful about her', they decided she must be a witch. All those for whom this turn of events was a disaster justifiably asked themselves whether this was not really the work of Satan, rather than God. They could only wait and see, as Joan's mission continued. Her work was not yet complete, for she had still to rid France of the English and, it was rumoured, to recapture Paris. Paris was quite a different proposition from Orléans. There was a strong Burgundian faction there, who had everything to lose if the city fell. They held out against the dauphinist forces, who were equally unsuccessful at La Charité-sur-Loire. Finally, they attacked Compiègne, and here Joan was taken prisoner by the Burgundians.

This new turn of events seemed to reveal divine disapproval; it spread uncertainty in the circles close to Charles VII and hope amongst his enemies. In Paris she was gleefully denounced by the Dominicans as 'a woman of exceptional cruelty', who displayed herself scandalously before soldiers dressed in men's clothing. They also accused her of violence, saying that she had beaten senseless those who were reluctant to join her cause. Finally, she had boasted of going straight to heaven, when in fact she was sullied 'with blood and fire, and the murder of innocent Christians'. Two days after her capture, the University of Paris announced that she was to be tried 'for crimes relating to heresy'. The English could not wait to get their hands on Joan of Arc; a large sum was paid to the Burgundians for her transfer into their hands, and they imprisoned her without delay in their most secure dungeon, in the castle at Rouen. It was their intention to put her to death, but they wanted first to prove that she was possessed by the devil, and that Satan, in the guise of St Michael, St Catherine and St Margaret, had dictated all her actions. By this means they planned to demonstrate that Charles VII had been a mere puppet of diabolical forces – that, in other words, he had been bewitched.

On 3 January 1431 Henry VI, 'by the grace of God king of England and France', commanded Peter Cauchon, bishop of Beauvais (in whose diocese she had been captured) to institute proceedings against the Maid, 'according to divine and canonical law'. The bishop was an uncompromising supporter of the Burgundians exiled in Rouen; he could be relied upon to take the right line. The presence of the supernatural effectively transformed a clear political issue into one of faith, and Joan was to be tried before a tribunal of the Inquisition. We should not denigrate the judges; for neither Cauchon nor his assessors derived any personal advantage from the outcome of her trial. They were very frightened – of the English

commander at Rouen (Richard Beauchamp, earl of Warwick), but much
more of the devil, whom they saw active in every sphere of life. To understand their attitude, we have to realize that later medieval Christianity had
been profoundly affected by the success of popular devotional movements.
The humble beliefs and naïve, uncontrolled outpourings of ordinary people
had crept into the logical framework created by scholars in the thirteenth
century. By the 1420s, they had permeated the beliefs of even the most
sophisticated theologians. These academics, who were so proud of their
logical skills, had an unshakeable faith – possibly stronger than Joan's own
– in manifestations of the supernatural in the form of voices or spirits.
Their task was to disentangle good from evil in the dense jungle of
supernatural phenomena. They did their best, using methods developed by
their predecessors in the Inquisition against the Cathars, in an attempt to
break down the suspect's resistance and force a confession, although in this
instance they avoided physical torture. For Joan was no simple country
girl. She had mixed with the highest levels of society and won their active
support, as well as their confidence. The people had fervently acclaimed
her their champion. She was well aware of these considerations, and so
were her judges, who consequently stood in awe of her. They were afraid
of what evil powers she might employ against them if she were truly a
witch; if she were not (as many of them clearly believed – certainly the
Augustinian Isembart of La Pierre and the Dominican Martin L'Advenu),
then they were afraid that her captors would force them to condemn her,
despite her innocence.

In fact, 'idolatry' and 'converse with the devil' were not the only
charges. She was also accused of 'schism', a term pregnant with meaning at
the time. Western Christendom had only just emerged, with difficulty,
from the Great Schism, and the term 'schism' was synonymous with
rebellion. There could be no doubt whatsoever that Joan was guilty on
this count. For all her piety, she obdurately refused to submit to the
authority of the Church, acknowledging instead the supremacy of the
Church celestial and calling directly upon God without the mediation of
the institutional Church. Her voices returned again during her harsh
imprisonment, giving her fresh courage. Unusually, in trials of this kind,
Joan stood her ground and only weakened when she was totally exhausted
and demoralized by the continual withholding of the Eucharist. But she
recanted almost instantly, once more refusing to comply with the institutional Church. The tribunal's doubts were allayed after this relapse: Joan
was excommunicated, cut off from the Christian community 'like a rotten
limb' and handed over to the officers of secular justice. The *bailli* of Rouen
had been anticipating this development. Without further formality, he had
Joan 'piteously' burnt at the stake in front of the people at Rouen on 30

May 1431. For some, her death put an end to the witchcraft exploited by the wicked Charles VII; for others, the Maid died a martyr's death, sacrificed for the rightful king of France.

Setting an example of personal sanctity, Joan expressed the people's view of kingship and government, which could only be exercised under strict divine control. Joan had expressed this view so clearly that her brief appearance on the political scene had extraordinary repercussions. Although she had died, with her intervention the tide had suddenly and miraculously turned. Despair was banished, and even her death could not check the movement that she had initiated. It was to lead to the liberation of France from English occupation twenty years later. As the Languedoc (which had been spared the worst ravages of occupation) also remained loyal during the expulsion of the English, Charles VII was securely established on the French throne. He was the embodiment of peace and order, with prudence as his watchword. Moreover, he was wise enough not to interfere with the regional diversity which had emerged in the previous decades; indeed, this was the foundation on which the reconstruction of the State depended. Regional customs, assemblies, capitals and individual institutions were all preserved. Within this framework, the crown was able to organize the judicious distribution of fiscal privileges amongst the *bonnes villes*, trade guilds and all those in royal service.

In 1449 Charles VII formally entered Rouen – which had fallen into French hands – and gave orders for a full inquiry into the trial of Joan of Arc. It was crucial for him that no one should believe that he owed his crown to witchcraft. The Pope was not enthusiastic, for he did not want to draw attention to the fate of a rebel who had stood out against the institutional Church. He thought it would be better not to involve the University of Paris, the principal actor in the proceedings, realizing that the investigation would inevitably compromise it. However, the Norman Cardinal Estouteville, whose family had been at the forefront of resistance to the English, held his ground, and forced the hand of the vacillating royal court. Finally, a new tribunal was appointed to investigate the affair in 1455.

Inquiries had been made in Lorraine and Orléans (where the anniversary of the town's liberation was celebrated and for which Estouteville had granted indulgences), then at Rouen and Paris. Twenty-five years after the trial, a number of key witnesses were no longer to be found, and no one wanted to rake up uncomfortable memories. Witnesses who appeared before the court were only asked to state that Joan could not be suspected of heresy or schism. They were careful not to raise the issue of the Maid's voices or the ultimate source of her 'counsel'. There was no reference to the deposition made in 1450 by the theologian John Beaupère, one of the few surviving judges. He had stated that, in his view, 'the apparitions had their origins in human aspirations, and their cause was natural rather than supernatural.' His dignified conclusion denied nothing, but referred to 'the subtleties that are the preserve of women' (possibly a reference to witchcraft); he also had to admit that he had 'no evidence whatsoever that she had any carnal knowledge'. The decision was left to the lawyers, who made strenuous efforts to find procedural objections to the original verdict. It was then a short step to declare the trial of 1431 null and void, condemn those who had been a party to it and had since conveniently died and, finally, rehabilitate the Maid of Orléans. Prudence dictated that they should not go so far as to glorify Joan's memory, bearing in mind her attitude to the institutional Church. Nevertheless, she was the true foundation of the recuperating French State. Now that the war was over, the wheels of the administration began to turn again much as they had before.

Joan's memory remained deeply embedded in the consciousness of the people, but their perception of her varied across the centuries. For a long while it was little more than a dim recollection, weakened still further by the Enlightenment. In his *Abrégé chronologique de l'histoire de France* (*Chronological Summary of the History of France*), published in The Hague in 1733, the count of Boulainvilliers referred to her appearance only in passing as 'this strange occurrence'. He reported the trial verdict briefly in a few dispassionate words, mentioning the accusation of witchcraft, but not her subsequent rehabilitation. Instead, he focused on another supposed 'soldier girl', who was said to have 'appeared soon afterwards in Lorraine claiming to be the Maid; she subsequently married in Metz, and her descendants are still to be found'. His account is fairly representative of attitudes to Joan of Arc at this period. It was the Age of Reason, and Voltaire was not alone in scoffing at the ideal of virginity. Joan's memory was still green at Orléans, however, where there was a procession every year on 8 May and a statue had been erected in her memory. The monument was destroyed as a superstitious relic by extremists during the French Revolution, but it was soon replaced during the Consulate (1799–1804).

In the aftermath of the French Revolution and the turbulent period of developing nationalism that followed, there was a great upsurge of interest in Joan, sustained by the Catholic revival and the interest of the Romantics in history, especially that of the Middle Ages. This was backed up by scholarly discussion and Jules Quicherat's publication of the trial documents. The political right acclaimed her piety and her role as the divine instrument which secured the restoration of the rightful king, symbolized by the presence of her standard next to the fleurs-de-lis at the coronation –

witness Ingres' famous painting of 1854, now in the Louvre. The left hailed her as a daughter of the people standing up to the wiles of the clergy, a woman with mysteriously redemptive powers – the characterization to be found in Michelet's *Histoire de France* (*History of France*). National sentiment fanned the flame of memory on all sides. The image of a heroine emerging from the suffering land, who did not hesitate to sacrifice herself in order to free France from the yoke of subjugation, was held up to generations of French schoolchildren. The Church saw her story as an example of devout Catholicism, which could be used to good effect against the liberal anticlerical sentiment of the late nineteenth century; and this element was added to the popular conception of the Maid. The Vatican decided to beatify Joan, then – as late as 1920, in the aftermath of the Great War – to canonize her. It would be interesting to know (from the documentation of the Vatican's canonization process) what criteria were used to justify elevating to the company of the saints a woman who had defied the authority of the institutional Church until the moment of her death. At the end of the First World War, much of France lay in ruins. I can only think that when the Papacy responded to patriotic expectation and gave this patron saint to France – victorious, but totally exhausted – it must have seemed politically astute to revive the concept of sacrality at the very heart of the essentially republican and secular French State.

Epilogue

Modern French historical writing has placed the birth of the modern State between 1280 and 1360. In my opinion, this development took place earlier, at the begining of the thirteenth century. I would argue that the various elements that constituted the political system in France until the end of the ancien régime were all in place at the death of Philip Augustus. Significantly, the revolutionaries of 1789 summed up all that they wanted to destroy in the French State in the one contentious word 'feudalism'. It is certainly true that power remained rooted in household government and consecrated authority. The household was still the centre of power, the place where the head of the family had his seat and, with the advice of his council, administered his lordship. This was a community in which recollection of the dead was an important element; it was based on conviviality and friendship, as well as the exchange of service between men bound by blood, marriage or the ties of homage. They believed God was the source of all power, and that it was the duty of his delegates on earth to work for the establishment of Christ's kingdom there; it was therefore their solemn duty to take the cross, as well as to support the Inquisition. Nevertheless, the ideas that would eventually break these traditional structures were already developing within them.

In the period following the death of Philip Augustus, there was a feeling of euphoria because there was progress in so many different fields; and at this time the ideas that nature was essentially good gained ground. This concept was undoubtedly responsible for the retreat of Catharism, which was ultimately discarded because of its denial of the flesh. It was also after the death of the Philip Augustus that scholars who were already familiar with Aristotle's logic discovered his philosophical writings. They then appropriated the distinction between divine and human law that had been employed by ecclesiastical reformers two centuries before to demonstrate the superiority of the spiritual over the temporal. Now, however, the distinction between nature and divine grace was used to assert that the State was ultimately dependent on natural law, rather than the institutional Church. After lengthy discussion and reflection, scholars concluded that it was the quintessential nature of grace to operate outside the confines of logic and to lie beyond formal analysis; it could only be understood through the positive response of the heart to the simple words of the gospel. Reason, on the other hand, was man's crowning glory and could be freely applied to every aspect of the natural world. These theories gradually found expression in the second half of the thirteenth century and later. They were current only in very limited circles at first; but the lay population was already favourably disposed towards them, from the king, who resented the claims of the Roman curia to authority over any aspect of his rule, to the peasants, who no longer wanted to pay their tithes. There was support from every section of the laity for the view that the Church must be made to abandon its pretensions to earthly power. They had no doubt that this power should be vested wholly in the State – that is, the monarchy. Admittedly, this was still a hereditary and quasi-priestly institution; but it delegated responsibility for public administration to offiials who were increasingly detached from the sovereign's private life and household. All the distinctive features of the subsequent history of government were already in place at the end of the reign of Philip Augustus.

Chronology

983	Otto III, king of Germany.
985	Conversion of Stephen of Hungary.
987	Hugh Capet, king of the Franks.
989	Beginning of the movement for the peace of God.
990	Rebuilding of porch and cloister of St Germain-des-Prés, Paris.
996	Otto III, Emperor.
	Robert II, 'the Pious', king of France (associate since 987).
997	Stephen, king of Hungary.
999	Gerbert of Aurillac, Pope Sylvester II.
1000	Creation of the archbishopric of Gniezno.
1002	Henry II, king of Germany.
1002–5	Conquest of Burgundy by Robert the Pious.
1006	Start of building work at St Philibert of Tournus.
1009	Holy Sepulchre at Jerusalem destroyed by Al Hakim.
	Christians capture Cordova (Spain).
1014	Henry II, Emperor.
1022	Heretical uprising at Orléans.
1023	Meeting between Robert the Pious and Henry II.
1024	Conrad II, king of Germany.
c.1025	*Carmen* of Adalbero of Laon.
1025	Grant of papal bull of exemption to the monastery of Cluny.
1026	Start of building work at Fleury-sur-Loire.
1027	Conrad II, Emperor.
1031	Henry I, king of the Franks.
	Council of Limoges.
c.1033	*Life of Robert the Pious* of Helgaud.
1034	Council of Lisieux.
1038	Revolt of the archbishop of Bourges.

1039	Henry III, king of Germany.
1044	Touraine held by the count of Anjou.
c.1040–6	*Historia* of Ralph Glaber.
1046	Imperial coronation of Henry III and Agnes (daughter of William V of Aquitaine). Norman conquests in Italy recognized by Henry III.
1049	Leo IX, Pope; Church reform. Council of Rheims. Hugh I, abbot of Cluny (d. 1109).
1052	Acknowledgement of the authenticity of the relics at St Denis.
1053	Council of Embrun.
1054	Peace council at Narbonne. Split between Rome and Constantinople.
1055	Annexation of the *comté* of Sens by Henry I.
1056	Henry IV, king of Germany.
1060	Philip I, king of the Franks.
1061	Alexander II, Pope.
1063	Seizure of Maine by William of Normandy.
1064	Capture of Barbastro by the duke of Aquitaine. Ferdinand I of Castile advances to Coïmbra.
1066	Conquest of England by William of Normandy.
1067	Homage of the count of Anjou to the Pope.
1068	Acquisition of the Gâtinais by Philip I.
1069	Revolt at Le Mans.
1071	Usurpation of Flanders by Robert of Frisia.
1073	Gregory VII, Pope.
1076	Seljuks at Jerusalem. Deposition of Gregory VII at the Synod of Worms; retaliatory excommunication of Henry IV.
1077	Submission of Henry IV at Canossa. Philip I inherits the Vexin.
1078	Spanish expedition of Hugh, duke of Burgundy.
1081	The count of Provence does homage to the Pope, becomes a papal vassal.
1085	The count of Mauguio becomes a papal vassal.
1086	Christian defeat in Spain by the *Almoravides* at Sagrajas (Zalaca).
1088	Urban II, Pope. Work starts on the third abbey church at Cluny. Yvo of Chartres consecrated bishop of Rheims in Rome.
1089	French crusade in Spain preached by Urban II.
1092	Marriage of Philip I and Bertrada of Montfort (Anjou).
1094	Council of Rheims summoned by Philip I. Excommunication of Philip I by Hugh of Die at the Council of Autun.

	Capture of Valencia by El Cid. Consecration of St Mark's, Venice.
1095	Council of Clermont: First Crusade in the East preached by Urban II.
1096	Urban II in Anjou.
1096–9	First Crusade.
1097	War of Prince Louis with William Rufus of England.
1098	Foundation of the abbey of Cîteaux. Capture of Antioch by the crusaders.
1099	Capture of Jerusalem. Pascal II, Pope.
c. 1100	*Chanson de Roland (Song of Roland).*
1100	Henry I, king of England.
1101	*Vicomté* of Bourges acquired by Philip I.
1102	War of Prince Louis and the count of Roucy.
1103	Treaty of Dover between Henry I of England and the count of Flanders.
1105	Penance of Philip I.
1107	Meeting of Pascal II with Philip I and Louis.
1108	Louis VI, 'the Fat', king of the Franks.
1108–13	Foundation of St Victor at Paris.
1109	Communes at Beauvais and Noyon. Capture of Tripoli and Beirut by the crusaders. War between Louis VI and Henry I of England.
1111	Henry V, Emperor. Sack of Paris by the count of Meulan.
1111–12	Campaigns of Louis VI against Henry I, Theobald of Champagne and the lord of Le Puiset.
1112	Commune of Laon.
1115	Louis VI attacks Thomas of Marle. *Mémoires* of Guibert of Nogent. Foundation of Clairvaux by St Bernard.
1116–17	Commune of Amiens.
1118	Capture of Saragossa by French and Spanish crusaders. Foundation of the Order of the Temple. Baldwin II, king of Jerusalem.
1119	Defeat of Louis VI at Brémule by Henry I. Council of Rheims. Charles the Good, count of Flanders.
1121	Condemnation of Abélard at the Council of Soissons.
1122	Peter the Venerable, abbot of Cluny. Suger, abbot of St Denis.
1124	War between Emperor Henry V and Louis VI. Famine in Flanders.

1125–50	*Pèlerinage de Charlemagne* (*Pilgrimage of Charlemagne*).
1126	Commune at Soissons.
Before 1127	*Histoire de la croisade à Jérusalem* (*History of the Crusade*) of Foucher of Chartres.
1127	Assassination of Charles the Good, count of Flanders. Communes at Bruges, Lille and St Omer.
1128	Commune at Laon.
1130	Innocent II, Pope. Roger II, first king of Sicily.
fl. 1130–48	Provençal troubadour Macabru.
1131	Coronation of Louis VII. Fulk of Anjou, king of Jerusalem.
1132	Building works at abbey of Vézelay completed.
1132–44	Building of abbey church of St Denis.
1133	Lothar III, Emperor.
1135	Stephen of Blois, king of England.
c.1135–60	Building of the cathedral of Sens.
1136	War waged by Louis VI on Thomas of Marle. Barons' revolt in England.
1137	Marriage of Louis VII and Eleanor of Aquitaine. King of France acknowledged as feudal superior by the count of Forez. Conrad III, Emperor.
1139	Second Lateran Council.
1140	Condemnation of Abélard at Sens. Gratian's *Decretum* published.
1141–4	Conquest of Normandy by Geoffrey Plantagenet.
1142	War between Louis VII and Theobald of Champagne. Appearance of heretics in the Rhine valley.
c.1145	Royal portal at Chartres.
1145	Election of Eugenius III (a Cistercian) as Pope.
1146	Second Crusade preached by St Bernard.
1147	Departure of Louis VII on crusade. German crusade against the Slavs.
1148	Failure of Louis VII and Conrad III to capture Damascus.
1152	Marriage of Eleanor of Aquitaine to Henry Plantagenet. Frederick Barbarossa, king of Germany.
1153	Vigilance against heresy urged by Eugenius III. Death of St Bernard.
1154	Henry II Plantagenet, king of England. Adrian IV, Pope (English).
c.1155	*Sentences* of Peter Lombard. Customs of Lorris.
1156	Frederick Barbarossa, Emperor.

1157	Rift between Pope and Emperor.
1159	Alexander III, Pope. Schism: Frederick Barbarossa secures election of an anti-Pope.
*c.*1160	Beroul's *Tristan*.
1162	Alfonso II, king of Aragon: the count of Barcelona leaves the allegiance of the king of France.
1163	Council of Tours. Papal curia established at Sens because of the schism. Conflict between Henry II and Thomas Becket in England. Work starts on the cathedral of Notre-Dame, Paris.
1165	Canonization of Charlemagne by the anti-Pope Paschal III.
1166	Seizure of Brittany by Henry II.
1169	Heretical assembly in the Lauragais (southern France).
1170	Murder of Thomas Becket. Completion of the façade of St Gilles.
*c.*1170	Conversion of Pierre Valdes, merchant of Lyons and founder of the Waldensian sect.
1174–82	Monreale (Sicily) built.
*c.*1175	*Histoire des ducs de Normandie* (*History of the dukes of Normandy*) of Benedict of St Maure; *Lais* (*Lays*) of Marie of France.
1176	Victory of the Lombard League over Frederick I.
1177	Meeting between Pope and Emperor at Venice.
1178	Papal mission to the Albigensians.
1179	Attempt to end schism by the Third Lateran Council. Raid of Saladin on Tyre.
1180	Philip II, 'Augustus', king of France. Seizure of French Jews. Philip II's campaign in the Mâconnais. Consecration of the high altar of Notre-Dame, Paris.
1181	*Perceval* of Chrétien of Troyes.
1182	Slaughter of crusaders at Constantinople.
1183	Peace of Constance: liberties of the Lombard towns recognized by Frederick I.
1184	Surrender of Montargis to the French king.
1185	Acquisition of Arras and the Vermandois by Philip II.
1186	*Treatise on Courtly Love* of Andreas Cappellanus.
1187	Capture of Jerusalem by Saladin.
1187–8	Seizure of Berry by Philip II.
1189	Richard I, 'the Lionheart', king of England. Henry VI, king of Germany.
1190	Departure of Philip II from Vézelay on the Third Crusade. Work started on Paris city walls. Portal of Sens cathedral.
1190–1	Philip II on crusade.

1191	Henry VI, Emperor.
1192	Seizure of Artois by Philip II on return from crusade.
1193	Repudiation of his wife, Ingeborg, by Philip II.
	Capture of Richard I in Austria.
	Seizure of Plantagenet lands in France by Philip II.
1194	Recovery of French lands by Richard I; defeat of Philip II at Fréteval.
	First 'prisée des sergents'.
	Synod of Compiègne: French bishops annul marriage of Philip II and Ingeborg.
	Work starts on new cathedral of Notre-Dame at Chartres.
1195–1200	*Commentary on the Apocalypse* of Joachim de Fiore.
*c.*1196	*Histoire des rois de France (History of the kings of France)* of Andrew of Marchiennes.
1196	Building of Château-Gaillard.
	Decision of the Synod of Compiègne annulled by Celestine III.
1198	Innocent III, Pope.
	French routed before Gisors by Richard I.
	Fourth Crusade preached by Fulk of Neuilly.
1199	Transfer of Gien to Philip II.
	John 'Lackland', king of England.
	First recension of the *Très Ancien Coutumier de Normandie (Most ancient Custumal of Normandy)*.
*c.*1200	Foundation of the University of Paris.
	France placed under interdict by Innocent III.
	Philip II acknowledges Ingeborg his lawful wife.
	County of Evreux becomes part of the royal domain.
1201	Philip Hurepel legitimized by Innocent III.
	Champagne under royal jurisdiction.
1202	Confiscation of King John's French lands by the court of Philip II.
1202–4	Fourth Crusade.
1203	Capture of Constantinople by the crusaders.
1204	Occupation of Normandy, Anjou and Poitou by Philip II.
	Foundation of Christian Empire in the East.
	Baldwin IX, count of Flanders, elected Emperor in Constantinople.
	King Peter of Aragon becomes a papal vassal.
	Campaigns of Genghis Khan begin.
1206	Henry of Flanders, Emperor of Constantinople.
	Principality of Morea founded in Greece.
	Work started on west front of Chartres cathedral.
1207	Preaching of St Dominic in Languedoc.
	Conversion of Francis of Assisi.
1209	Ordinance of Villeneuve-sur-Yonne on homage.
1209–13	Albigensian Crusade.
	Statutes of Pamiers, imposing customs of Paris on the areas around Toulouse and Albi.

1210	Excommunication of Otto IV by Innocent III.
1211	Frederick II, king of Germany. Rebuilding started on Rheims cathedral.
1211–18	Building of Mont-Saint-Michel.
1212	Children's Crusade.
1213	Battle of Muret. Vermandois, Valois and the Auvergne absorbed into the royal domain.
1214	John of England invades France. French victory at Bouvines. Establishment of a new port at Paris by Philip II.
1215	Fourth Lateran Council. Statutes of Robert of Courçon for the University of Paris. *Magna Carta* sealed in England, condemned by Innocent III. Royal authority imposed by Frederick II in Germany.
1216	Formal papal approval of the Dominican Order. Prince Louis wages war in England. Fifth Crusade preached by Pope Honorius III. Henry III, king of England.
1217	Peter of Courtenay, Emperor of Constantinople.
1218	Death of Simon of Montfort before Toulouse.
1219	Capture of Damietta by crusading forces. Prince Louis' expedition in the Languedoc. Franciscan house at Paris.
1220	Frederick II, Emperor. First statutes of Montpellier University. Building work starts on the cathedral of Bourges.
1222	Will of Philip II.
1223	Louis VIII, king of France.
1224	Areas round Albi and Carcassonne surrendered by Amaury of Montfort to Louis VIII. Conquest of the Saintonge and Poitou complete.
1225–6	Louis VIII's campaign in the Languedoc.
1225–30	Aristotle's *Metaphysics* translated into Latin.
1226	Death of Francis of Assisi. Regency of Blanche of Castile, mother of Louis IX.
1227	Gregory IX, Pope.
1228	Papal ban on teaching of Aristotle at the University of Paris.
1229	Treaty of Paris between Louis IX and Raymond of Toulouse; Carcassonne, Béziers, Nîmes and Beaucaire become part of the royal domain. Council of Toulouse: organization of the Inquisition and foundation of the University of Toulouse.
c.1230	*Roman de la Rose* (*Romance of the Rose*) of William of Lorris.
1233	Inquisition entrusted to the friars.
1234	Marriage of Louis IX and Margaret of Provence.

1236	Capture of Cordova by Ferdinand III of Castile.
1237	Marriage of Jeanne of Toulouse and Alfonso of Poitiers.
1239	Defeat of Sixth Crusade at Gaza.
	Frederick II excommunicated.
1240	Crown of Thorns purchased by Louis IX.
1241–2	Mongol invasion of Poland and Hungary.
1243	Innocent IV, Pope.
1243–8	Building of the Sainte-Chapelle.
1244	Capture of Cathar castle of Montségur.
1245	Papal embassy of John of Plano Carpine to the Mongols.
	Louis IX's great inquiry into the kingdom.
1245–6	The Dominican, Albertus Magnus, teaches at Paris.
1246	Heretical trials at Toulouse.
1247	Council of Lyons.
1248	Commentaries of the Franciscan, St Bonaventura, at Paris on the *Sentences* of Peter Lombard.
1248–54	Seventh Crusade: Louis IX in the East.
1249	Capture of Damietta.
	Alfonso of Poitiers, count of Toulouse.
1250	Retreat of Louis IX from Mansourah.
	First reference to the Paris Parlement.
1250–1318	Building of Strasbourg cathedral.
1252–7	Dispute between the friars and the University of Paris.
1252–9	Thomas Aquinas first teaches at Paris.
1254	Alexander IV, Pope.
*c.*1255	Reforming ordinances of Louis IX.
1257	Foundation of a college (later known as the Sorbonne) by Robert of Sorbon.
1258–63	*Summa 'contre les Gentils'* of Thomas Aquinas.
1259	Treaty of Paris between Louis IX and Henry III.
	Composition of *Livre de justice et de plet (Book of Justice and of Pleas)*.
1260	Judicial duel banned.
1261	Urban IV, Pope (French).
1262	Capture of Cadiz.
1263–6	French monetary policy includes imposition of a single currency for the entire kingdom and creation of the '*gros tournois*'.
1264	Baronial uprisings in France.
1265	Clement IV, Pope (French).
1266	Marco Polo at Peking.
1267	Rearrangement of royal tombs at St Denis.
1267–73	*Summa theologica* of Thomas Aquinas.
1268	Defeat of last descendant of Frederick II by Charles of Anjou.
	Antioch falls to the Saracens.
1269–72	Thomas Aquinas's second period of teaching at Paris.

*c.*1270	New ceremony for the coronation of the French king.
1270	Eighth Crusade; death of Louis IX at Tunis.
	Philip III, king of France.
1271	Gregory X, Pope.
	County of Toulouse annexed to the French crown by inheritance.
1272	Edward I, king of England.
1273	Rudolph of Habsburg, Emperor.
1273–4	Canonization process of Louis IX inaugurated.
1274	First translation of the *Grandes Chroniques de France* (*Chronicles of St Denis*) into French.
	Council of Lyons.
	Gift of the comtat Venaissin to the Pope.
1276	Hugh III, king of Jerusalem, abandons Syria.
	Second part of *Romance of the Rose* of John of Meung.
1277	Failure of Charles of Anjou's claim to the kingdom of Jerusalem.
	Some doctrines of Thomas Aquinas condemned by the bishop of Paris.
1281	Martin IV, Pope (French).
1282	Second process of canonization for Louis IX.
	Le Jeu de Robin et de Marion (*The Play of Robin and Marion*) of Adam of La Halle.
1283	*Coutumes du Beauvaisis* (*Customs of the Beauvaisis*) of Philip of Beaumanoir.
1284	Acquisition by Prince Philip through marriage of the administration of Champagne and Navarre.
	Collapse of the nave of Beauvais cathedral.
1285	Philip IV, 'the Fair', king of France.
1286	Treaty of Paris between England and France resolving the problem of the Quercy and the Saintonge.
1287	Agreement on Naples and Sicily between Philip the Fair and Alfonso III of Aragon through the arbitration of Edward I.
1290	Confirmation of clerical privileges by Philip IV.
1291	Fall of Acre and the crusading States in Syria.
1292	Lyons taken under royal protection.
1294	Confiscation of Plantagenet Aquitaine by Philip IV.
	Boniface VIII, Pope.
1295	First major French monetary crisis.
1297	Canonization of Louis IX (St Louis).
	Capture of Lille by Philip IV.
*c.*1300	Laws and customs of northern France collected in the *Etablissements de Saint Louis*.
1301	Boniface VIII calls on Charles of Valois to pacify Italy.
	Arpad dynasty replaced by the Angevins in Hungary.
1302	Papal bull *Ausculta Fili* against Philip IV; the Estates General support the French king against papal claims.

1303	Revolt in Flanders; defeat of the French at Courtrai. Proposed excommunication of Philip IV. French ambassdors attack the Pope at Anagni; death of Boniface VIII. Benedict XI, Pope.
1305	Clement V, Pope (Gascon).
1306	Expulsion of Jews from France.
1307	Arrest of the Templars.
1309	Papal curia established at Avignon by Clement V.
1311	*Vie de Saint Louis* (*Life of St Louis*) presented to Prince Louis by Joinville.
1312	Suppression of the Order of the Temple by the Pope. The treaty of Pontoise gives Lille, Douai and Béthune to the French crown.
1314	Alleged adultery in the French royal family. Louis X, king of France.
1316	John XXII, Pope (southern French). Five-day reign of John I, 'the Posthumous', baby son of Louis X; women excluded from the French royal succession. Philip V, 'the Tall', king of France. County of Burgundy becomes part of the French kingdom.
1320	Reform of French royal financial administration (creation of the *cour des comptes*).
1322	Charles IV, 'the Handsome', king of France.
1323–8	Revolt of maritime Flanders.
1325	University of Paris lifts ban on the doctrines of Thomas Aquinas.
1328	French bishops and nobility elect Philip VI of Valois king of France, in preference to Edward III of England, grandson of Philip the Fair. Secular imperial coronation of Lewis of Bavaria.
1329	Edward III does homage to Philip VI for Aquitaine. Treatises of William of Ockham criticizing the temporal power of the Papacy.
1332	University of Paris supported by the king in dispute with the Papacy. Condemnation of Robert III of Artois because of his claims to Artois.
1332–42	First papal palace built at Avignon.
1334	Benedict XII, Pope.
1337	Start of the Hundred Years War; claim of Edward III to the French crown; confiscation of Aquitaine by Philip VI. Ockham condemned by the University of Paris.
1338	Ottoman Turks reach the Bosphorus.
1340	English destroy French fleet at Sluys.
1344	Death of Simone Martini at Avignon.
1346	French defeated by the English at Crécy.
1347	English capture of Calais.
1348–50	Western Europe ravaged by the Black Death.

1349	Purchase of Montpellier by Philip VI; transfer of the Dauphiné to the crown; the king's grandson Charles takes the title of Dauphin.
1350	John II, 'the Good', king of France.
1352	College of cardinals attempts to win control of the Church.
1355	The Dauphin Charles becomes duke of Normandy.
1356	Victory of the Black Prince over the French at Poitiers; John II and his eldest son prisoners in England; the Dauphin summons the Estates General, as lieutenant-general of the kingdom.
1357–8	The Jacquerie. Revolt of Etienne Marcel in Paris against the Dauphin; the capital is handed over to the English ally Charles 'the Bad' of Navarre. Assassination of Etienne Marcel.
1360	Treaty of Brétigny ratified at Calais: Edward III abandons claims to the French throne in return for sovereignty over Aquitaine. Release of John II.
1364	Charles V, king of France. Royal control over finance and the army greatly tightened. Defeat of Charles the Bad at Cocherel. Monetary stabilization: creation of the gold franc.
1369–77	Recovery of Normandy and part of Aquitaine by the French.
1370	Louis I of Anjou, king of Hungary, inherits the Polish crown.
1371–3	Reconquest of Poitou, the Aunis and the Saintonge. First book of *Chroniques* (*Chronicles*) of Jean Froissart.
1375–81	Tapestry of the Apocalypse woven at Angers.
1377	Richard II, king of England. The Pope leaves Avignon: Papacy once more established at Rome.
1378	Confiscation of the lands of Charles the Bad in Normandy.
1378–1417	Great Western Schism. Loyalty of Charles V to Clement VII.
1382	Urban revolt in Paris, Rouen and the Languedoc.
1384	Philip 'the Bold', duke of Burgundy, inherits the county of Flanders.
1390	Work starts on the castle of Pierrefonds.
1392	Madness of Charles VI of France; co-regency of his uncles. Expedition of Louis of Orléans to Italy.
1394	Expulsion of French Jews.
1395	Jean Gerson, chancellor of the University of Paris.
1396	Struggle between the dukes of Burgundy and Orléans as a result of the king's madness.
1410–16	The *Très Riches Heures* illuminated for the duke of Berry.
1413	Protest of the Estates General against civil war. Revolt at Paris. Henry V, king of England.
1414–18	Council of Constance puts an end to the Great Schism.
1415	French defeat at Agincourt.

1416	John the Fearless, duke of Burgundy, recognizes Henry V as king of France.
1420	Treaty of Troyes.
1422	Accession of Henry VI, with his uncle John, duke of Bedford, as regent. Charles VII also claims the French throne.
1428	Attempted English advance southwards; siege of Orléans.
1429	Meeting of Joan of Arc and the Dauphin Charles at Chinon; capture of Orléans and coronation of Charles at Rheims.
1430	Joan fails to take Compiègne, and is captured by the English.
1431	Imprisonment, interrogation and burning at the stake of Joan of Arc. Coronation of Henry VI at Paris.
1431–49	Council of Basel.
1432	Ghent altarpiece painted by Jan and Hubert van Eyck.
1435	Charles VII wins the support of the duke of Burgundy. Franco-Burgundian agreement at Arras. Ile-de-France returns to French hands.
1436	Capture of Paris by Charles VII.
1450	Gutenberg sets up printing workshop at Mainz.
1452	Last papal coronation of Emperor (henceforth always a secular ceremony).
1453	End of the Hundred Years War; Charles VII regains the whole of Gascony. Constantinople taken by the Ottoman Turks.
1455–6	Rehabilitation of Joan of Arc.

Bibliography

The bibliography has been supplemented for the English edition by the translator, but is deliberately selective. For further information, the reader is referred to the comprehensive bibliographies in the works cited below by E. James, J. Dunbabin and B. Guenée, *States and Rulers*.

Adalbero of Laon, *Poème au roi Dagobert*, ed. and tr. C. Carozzi. Paris, 1979.

Baldwin, J. W., *The Government of Philip Augustus. Foundations of French Royal Power in the Middle Ages*. Berkeley/Los Angeles/London, 1986.

Bautier, R.-H., 'Paris au temps d'Abélard', in *Abélard en son temps. Actes du colloque international organisé à l'occasion du 9ᵉ centenaire de la naissance de Pierre Abélard (14–19 mai 1979)*, pp. 21–77. Paris, 1981.

Bisson, T. N., *Conservation of Coinage: Monetary Exploitation and its Restraint in France, Catalonia and Aragon*. Oxford, 1979.

Bonnassie, P., *La Catalogne, du milieu du Xᵉ à la fin du XIᵉ siècle. Croissance et mutations d'une société*. Toulouse, 1976.

Bournazel, E., *Le Gouvernement capétien au XIIᵉ siècle (1108–1180)*. Paris, 1975.

Contamine, P., *War in the Middle Ages*, tr. M. Jones. Oxford, 1984.

'Conventum inter Guillelmum Aquitanorum comes et Hugonem Chiliarchum', ed. J. Martindale, *English Historical Review*, 84 (1969), pp. 528–48.

Debord, A., *La Société laïque dans les pays de la Charente (Xᵉ–XIIᵉ s[iècle])*. Paris, 1984.

Dockès, P., *La Libération médiévale*. Paris, 1979.

Duby, G., *Hommes et structures du Moyen Age*. 2nd edn, Paris/The Hague, 1984. (1st edn partially tr. C. Postan as *The Chivalrous Society*. London, 1977.)

Duby, G., *The Knight, the Lady and the Priest*, tr. B. Bray. London, 1981.

Duby, G., *The Legend of Bouvines. War, Religion and Culture in the Middle Ages*, tr. C. Tihanyi. Cambridge, 1990.

Duby, G., *La Société aux XIᵉ et XIIᵉ siècles dans la région mâconnaise*. 3rd edn, Paris, 1982.

Dunbabin, J., *France in the Making 843–1180*. Oxford, 1985.

Favier, J., *Philippe le Bel*. Paris, 1978.

Fossier, R., *Peasant Life in the Medieval West*, tr. J. Vale. Oxford, 1988.

Fossier, R., *Enfance de l'Europe (X^e–XIIe siècles). Aspects économiques et sociaux.* Paris, 1982.

Gillingham, J., *The Angevin Empire.* London, 1984.

Guenée, B., *Histoire et culture historique dans l'Occident médiéval.* Paris, 1980.

Guenée, B., *States and Rulers in Later Medieval Europe,* tr. J. Vale. Oxford, 1985.

Hallam, E. H., *Capetian France 987–1328.* London/New York, 1980.

Iogna-Prat, D., *'Agni immaculati'. Recherches sur les sources hagiographiques relatives à saint Maïeul de Cluny (954–994).* Paris, 1987.

Jaeger, S., *The Origins of Courtliness, Civilizing Trends and the Formation of Courtly Ideals, 939–1210.* Philadelphia, 1983.

James, E., *The Origins of France. From Clovis to the Capetians, 500–1000.* Basingstoke/London, 1982.

Joinville, John of, *The Life of St Louis,* tr. R. Hague. London, 1955.

Keller, H., *Adelherrschaft und städtische Geschichte in Oberitalien: 9. bis 12. Jahrhundert.* Tübingen,1979.

Kidson, Peter, 'Panofsky, Suger and St Denis', *Journal of the Warburg and Courtauld Institutes,* 50 (1987), pp. 1–17.

Lemarignier, J.-F., *Le Gouvernement royal aux temps des premiers capétiens (987–1108).* Paris, 1963.

Le Patourel, J., *Feudal Empires: Norman and Plantagenet,* ed. M. Jones. London, 1984.

Lewis, A. W., *Royal Succession in Capetian France: Studies on Familial Order and the State.* Cambridge, Mass., 1981.

Magnou-Nortier, Elisabeth, *La Société laïque et l'Eglise dans la province ecclésiastique de Narbonne (zone cispyrénéenne), de la fin du VIIIe à la fin du XIe siècle.* Toulouse, 1974.

Moore, R. D. *The Origins of European Dissent,* 2nd edn Oxford, 1985.

Murray, A., *Reason and Society in the Middle Ages.* Oxford, 1978.

Richer, *Histoire de France,* ed. R. Latouche. 2 vols. Paris, 1937.

Rivet, A. L. F., *Gallia Narbonensis. Southern France in Roman Times.* London, 1988.

Rosenwein, Barbara, *To be the Neighbour of St Peter: The Social Meaning of Cluny's Property.* Ithaca, N.Y., 1989.

Spiegel, G. M., *The Chronicle Tradition of Saint-Denis.* Brookline, Mass., 1978.

Strayer, J., *Les Gens de justice du Languedoc sous Philippe le Bel.* Toulouse, 1970.

Strayer, J., *The Reign of Philip the Fair.* Princeton, 1980.

Toubert, Pierre, *Les Structures du Latium médiéval. Le Latium méridional et la Sabine du IXe à la fin du XIIe siècle.* Rome, 1973.

Vale, M. G. A., *The Angevin Legacy and the Hundred Years War.* Oxford, 1990.

Werner, K.-F., *Histoire de France,* ed. J. Favier. Vol. 1: *Les Origines.* Paris, 1984.

Index